W9-CST-776

LONE WOLF

子連れ狼

AND CUB

story
KAZUO KOIKE

art
GOSEKI KOJIMA

DARK HORSE COMICS

translation
DANA LEWIS

lettering & retouch
DIGITAL CHAMELEON

cover illustration
MATT WAGNER

publisher
MIKE RICHARDSON

editor
TIM ERVIN-GORE

assistant editor
JEREMY BARLOW

consulting editor
TOREN SMITH for **STUDIO PROTEUS**

book design
DARIN FABRICK

art director
MARK COX

Published by Dark Horse Comics, Inc., in association
with MegaHouse and Koike Shoin Publishing Company.

Dark Horse Comics, Inc.
10956 SE Main Street, Milwaukie, OR 97222
www.darkhorse.com

First edition: March 2002
ISBN: 1-56971-591-2

1 3 5 7 9 10 8 6 4 2

Printed in Canada

Lone Wolf and Cub Vol. 19: The Moon in Our Hearts

To find a comics shop in your area, call the
Comic Shop Locator Service toll-free at 1-888-266-4226.

THE MOON
IN OUR
HEARTS

By **KAZUO KOIKE**
& GOSEKI KOJIMA

VOLUME
19

A NOTE TO READERS

Lone Wolf and Cub is famous for its carefully researched re-creation of Edo-Period Japan. To preserve the flavor of the work, we have chosen to retain many Edo-Period terms that have no direct equivalents in English. Japanese is written in a mix of Chinese ideograms and a syllabic writing system, resulting in numerous synonyms. In the glossary, you may encounter words with multiple meanings. These are words written with Chinese ideograms that are pronounced the same but carry different meanings. A Japanese reader seeing the different ideograms would know instantly which meaning it is, but these synonyms can cause confusion when Japanese is spelled out in our alphabet. *O-yurushi o* (please forgive us)!

TABLE OF CONTENTS

Four Seasons of Death 9

Wives and Lovers 69

The Marksman 130

A Mother's Flavor 190

The Moon in Our Hearts 250

Glossary 311

Creator Profiles 313

the ninety-third

Four Seasons of Death

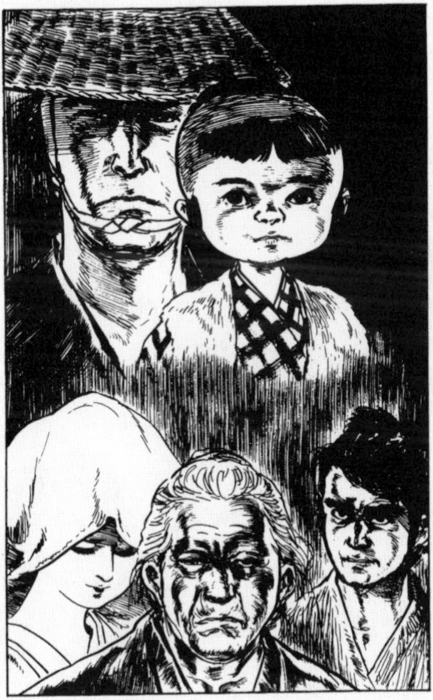

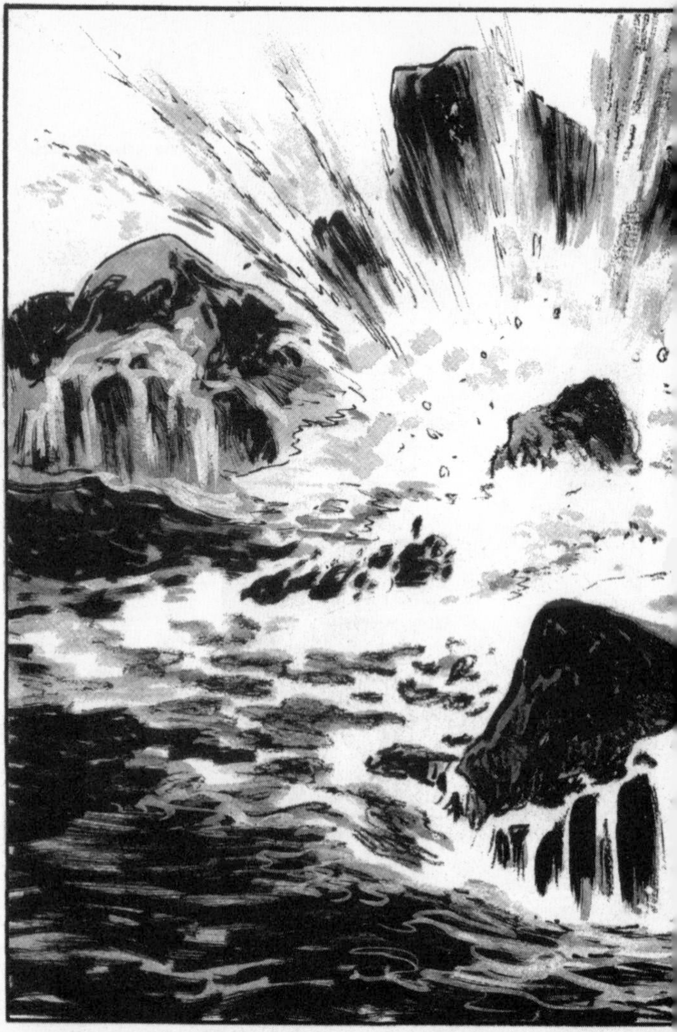

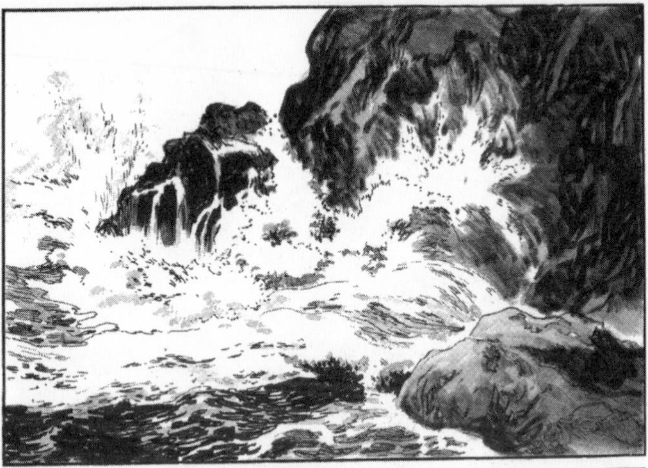
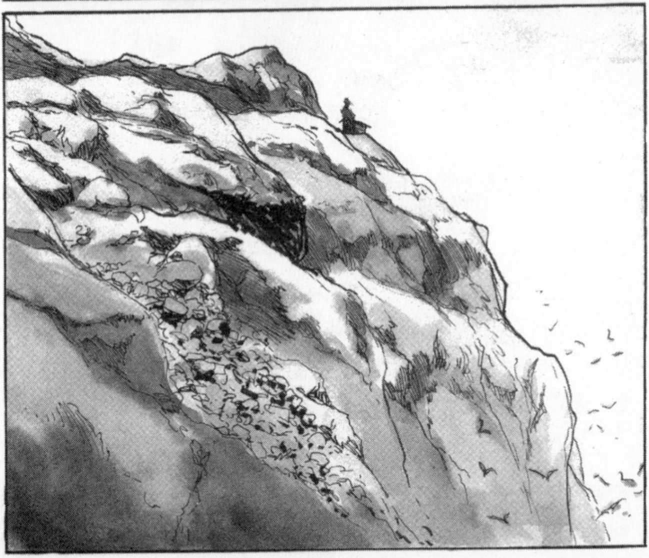

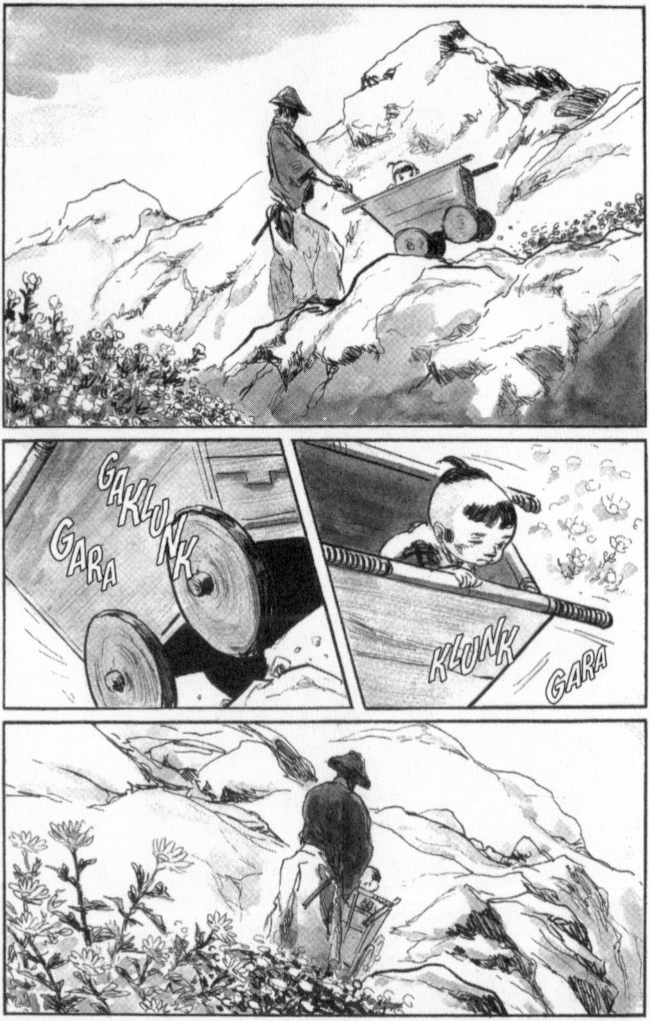
GAKLUNK
GARA
KLUNK
GARA

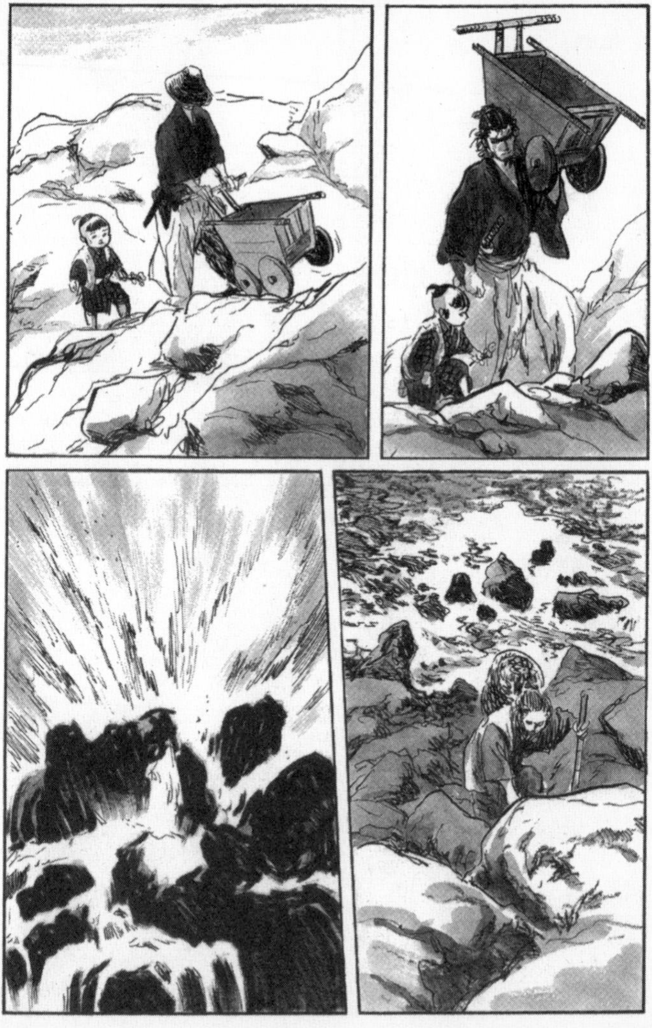

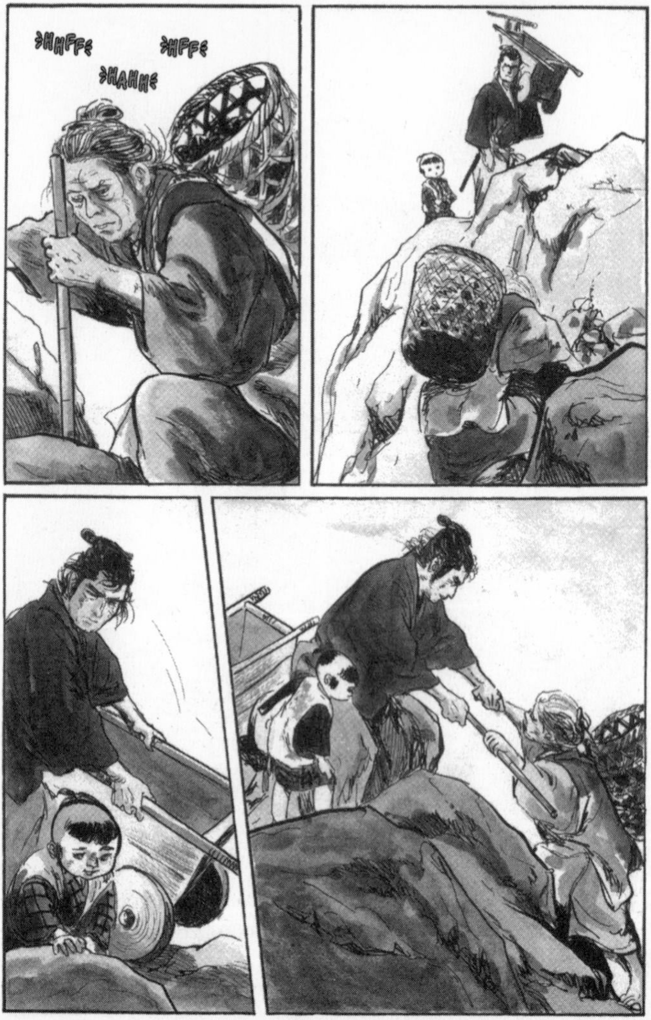
HHFF
HAHH
HFF

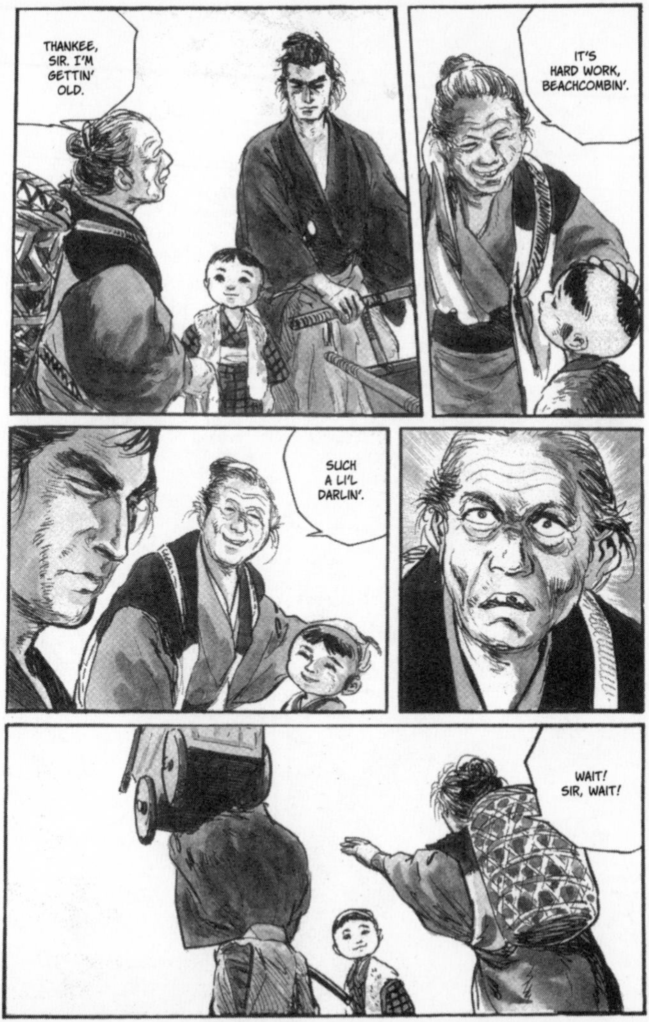
THANKEE, SIR. I'M GETTIN' OLD.
IT'S HARD WORK, BEACHCOMBIN'.
SUCH A LI'L DARLIN'.
WAIT! SIR, WAIT!

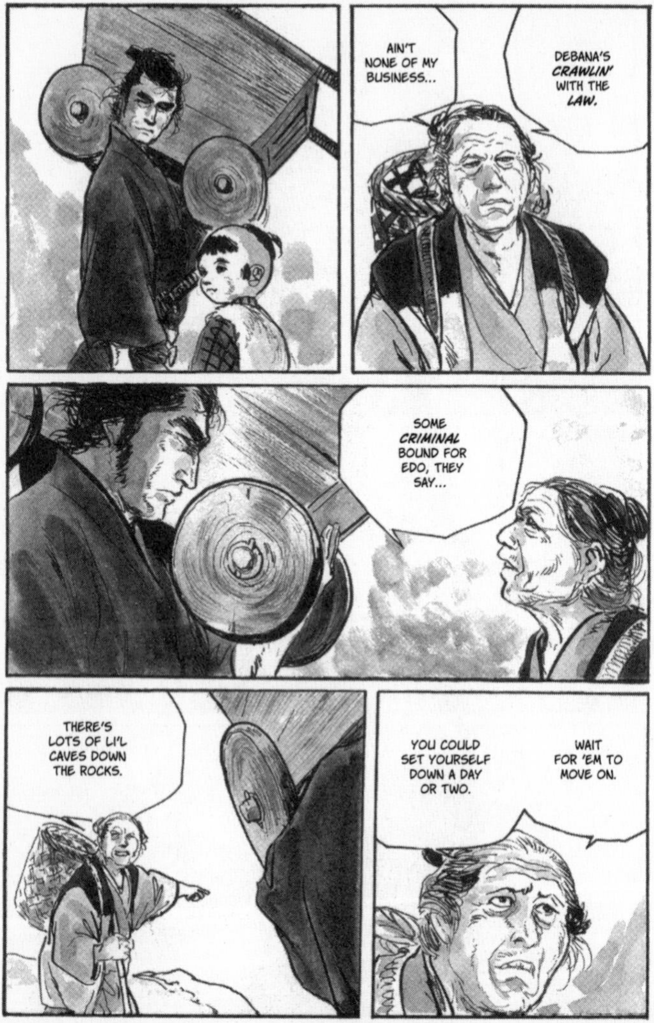
AIN'T NONE OF MY BUSINESS...
DEBANA'S *CRAWLIN'* WITH THE *LAW.*
SOME *CRIMINAL* BOUND FOR EDO, THEY SAY...
THERE'S LOTS OF LI'L CAVES DOWN THE ROCKS.
YOU COULD SET YOURSELF DOWN A DAY OR TWO.
WAIT FOR 'EM TO MOVE ON.

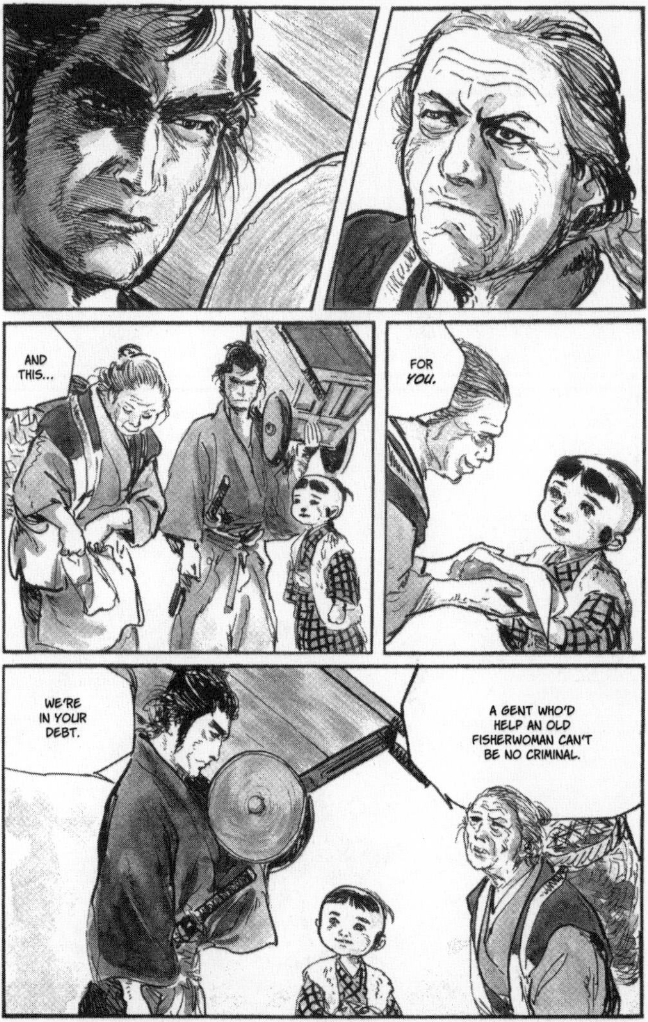
AND THIS...
FOR *YOU.*
WE'RE IN YOUR DEBT.
A GENT WHO'D HELP AN OLD FISHERWOMAN CAN'T BE NO CRIMINAL.

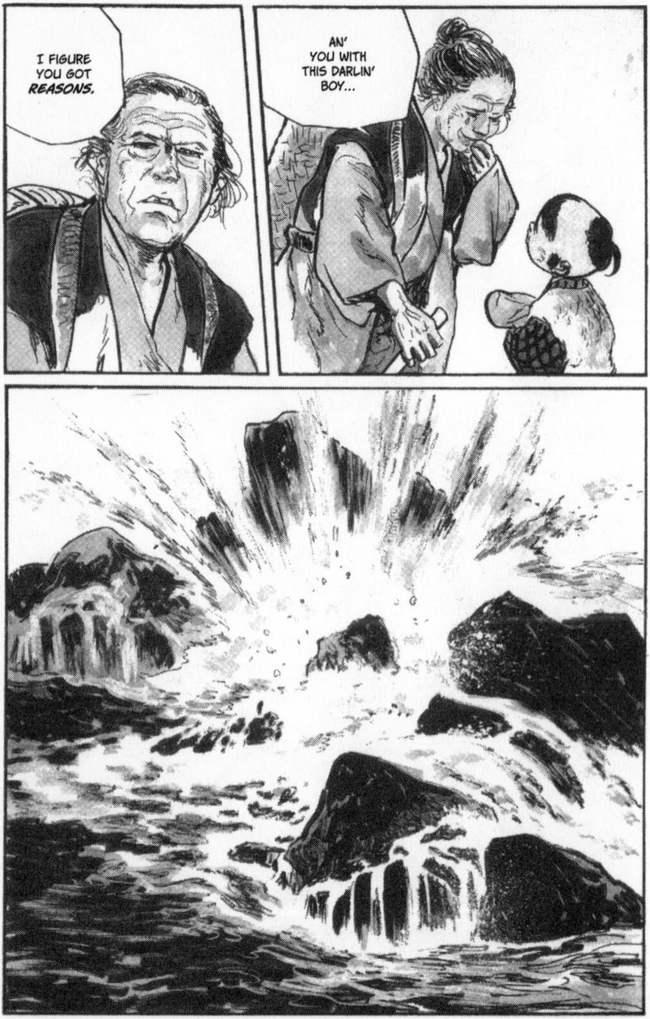
I FIGURE YOU GOT *REASONS.*
AN' YOU WITH THIS DARLIN' BOY...

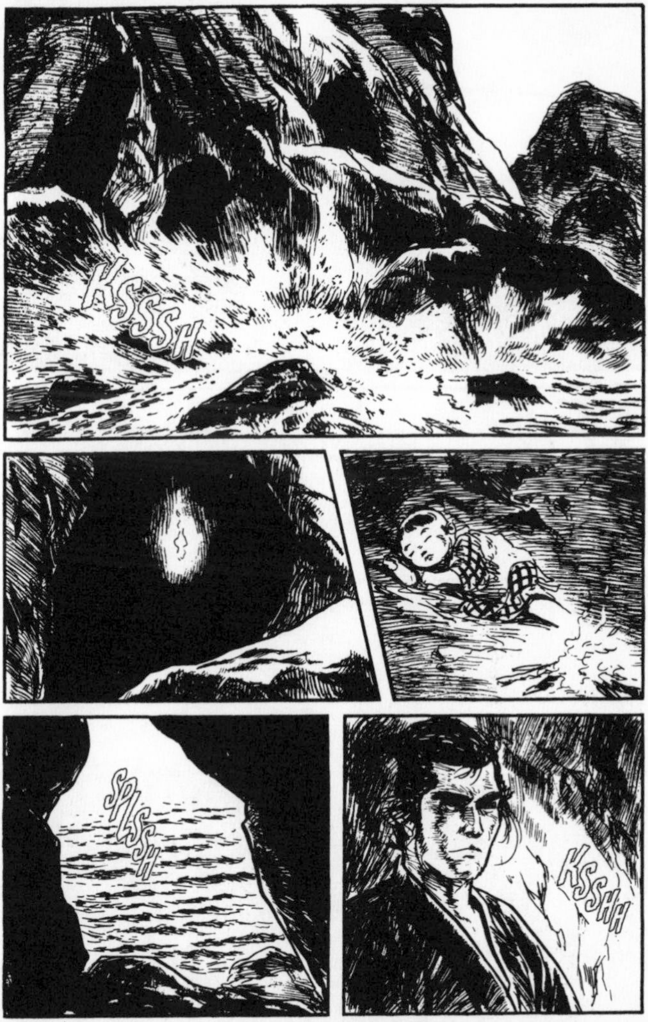
KSSSH
SPLSSH
KSSHH

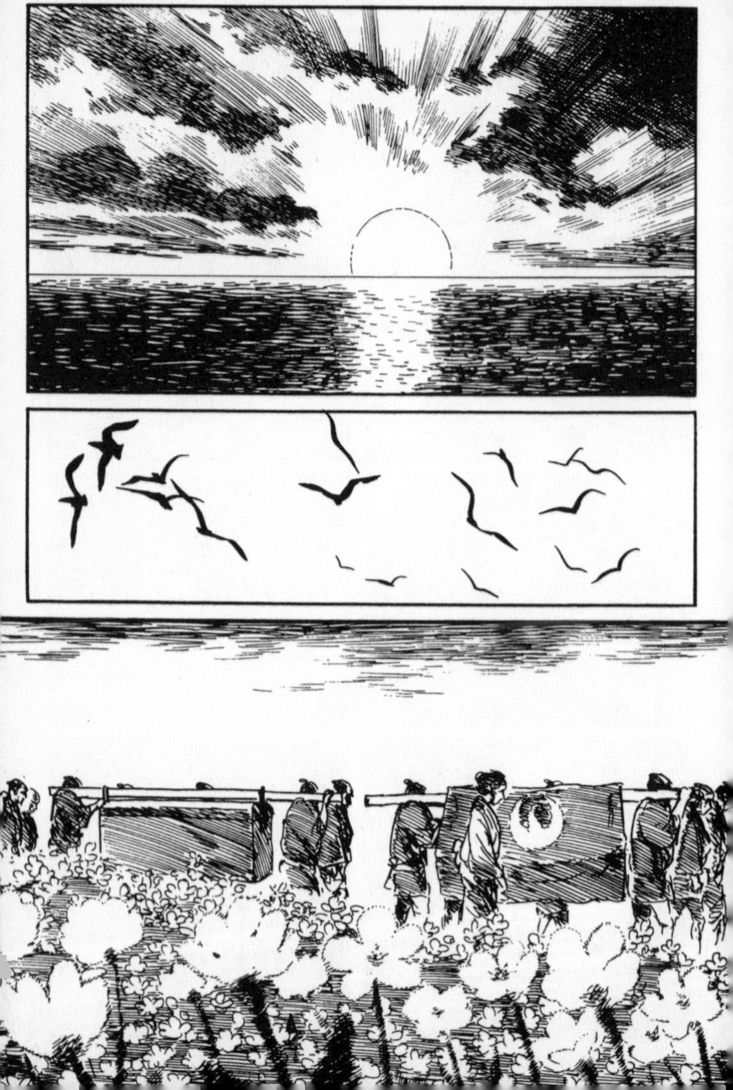

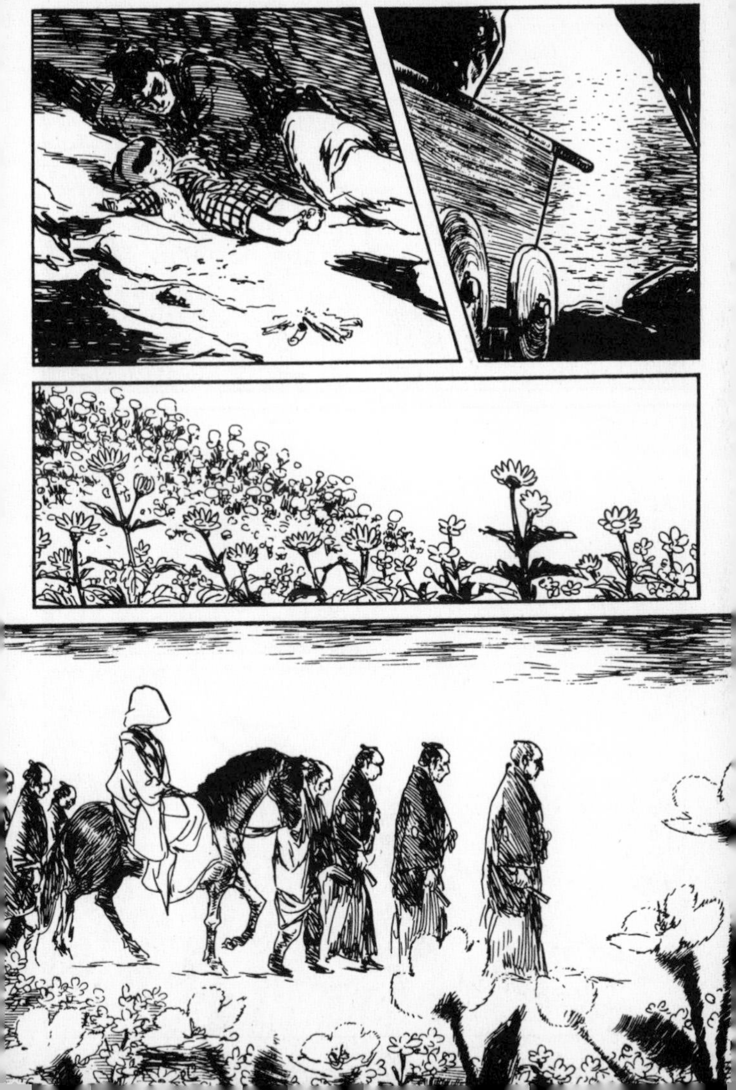

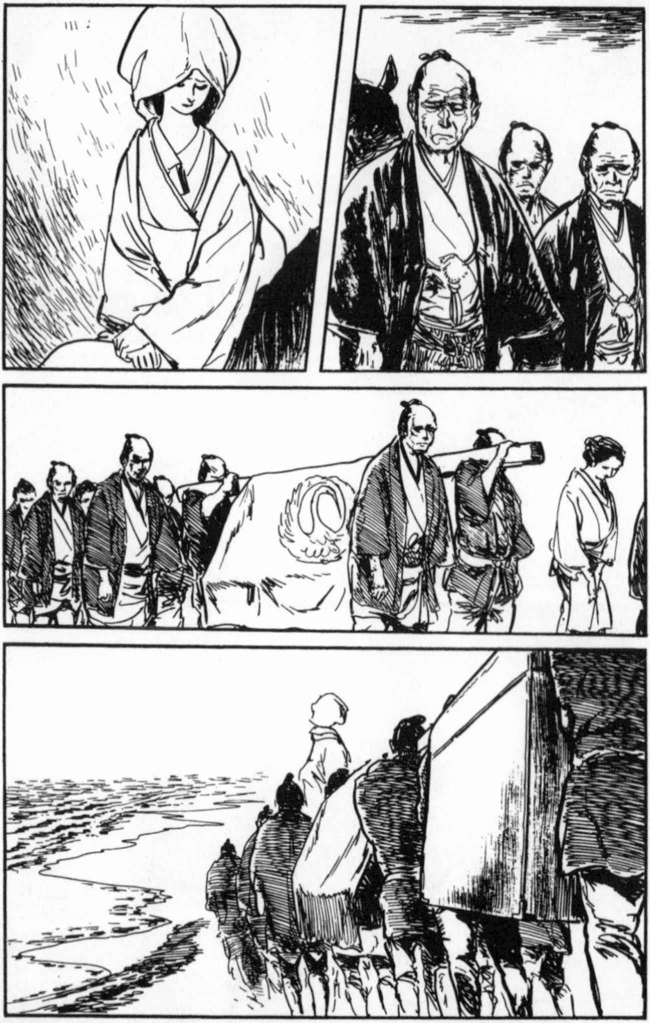

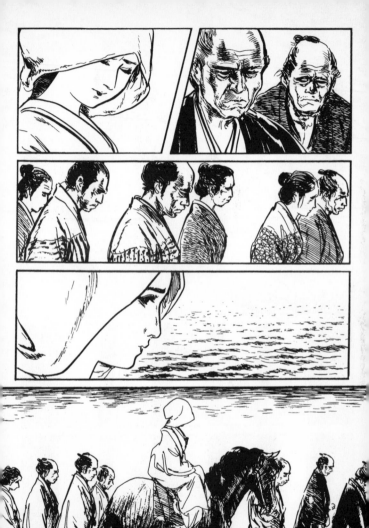

KLOP KLOP KLOP

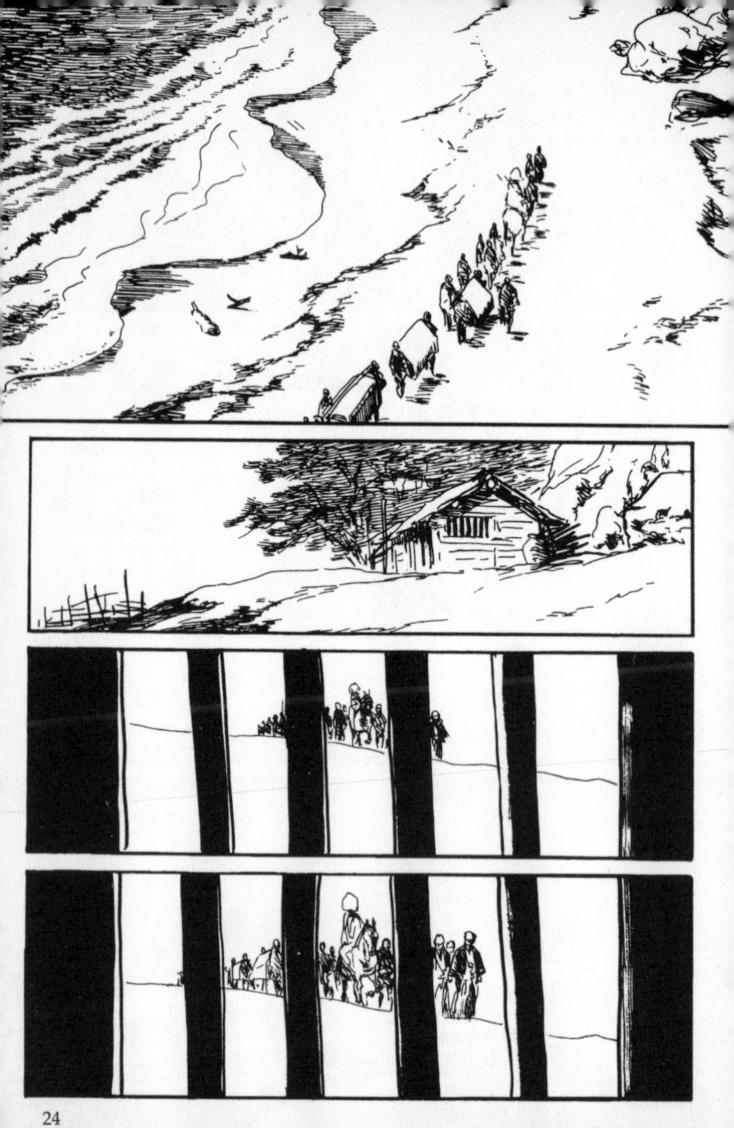

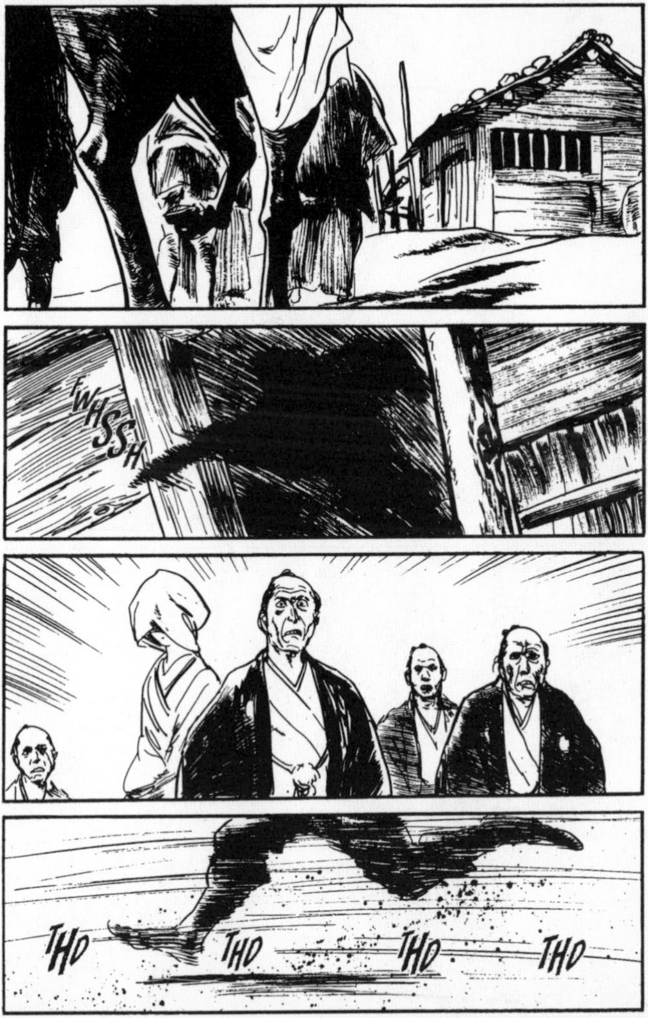
FWHSSSH
THD
THD
THD
THD

RYAHHHH!

DAIKICHI-SAN!

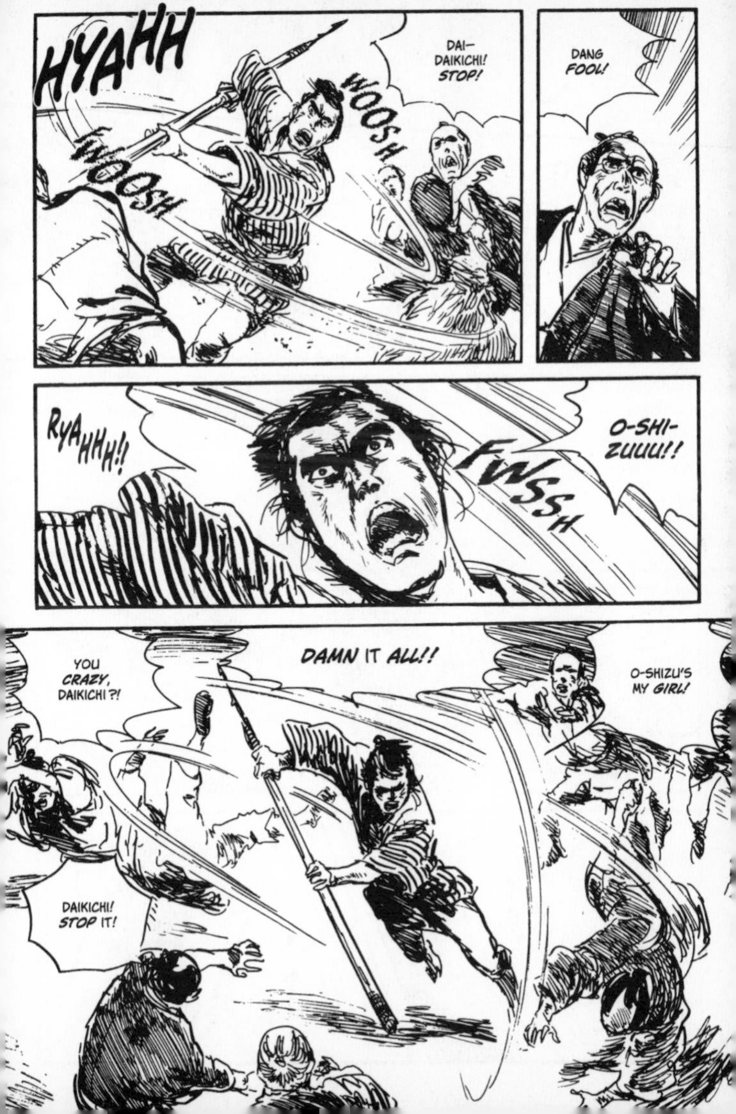
HYAHH
WOOSH
WOOSH
DAI—DAIKICHI! STOP!
DANG FOOL!
RYAHHH!!
FWSSH
O-SHI-ZUUU!!
YOU CRAZY, DAIKICHI?!
DAMN IT ALL!!
O-SHIZU'S MY GIRL!
DAIKICHI! STOP IT!

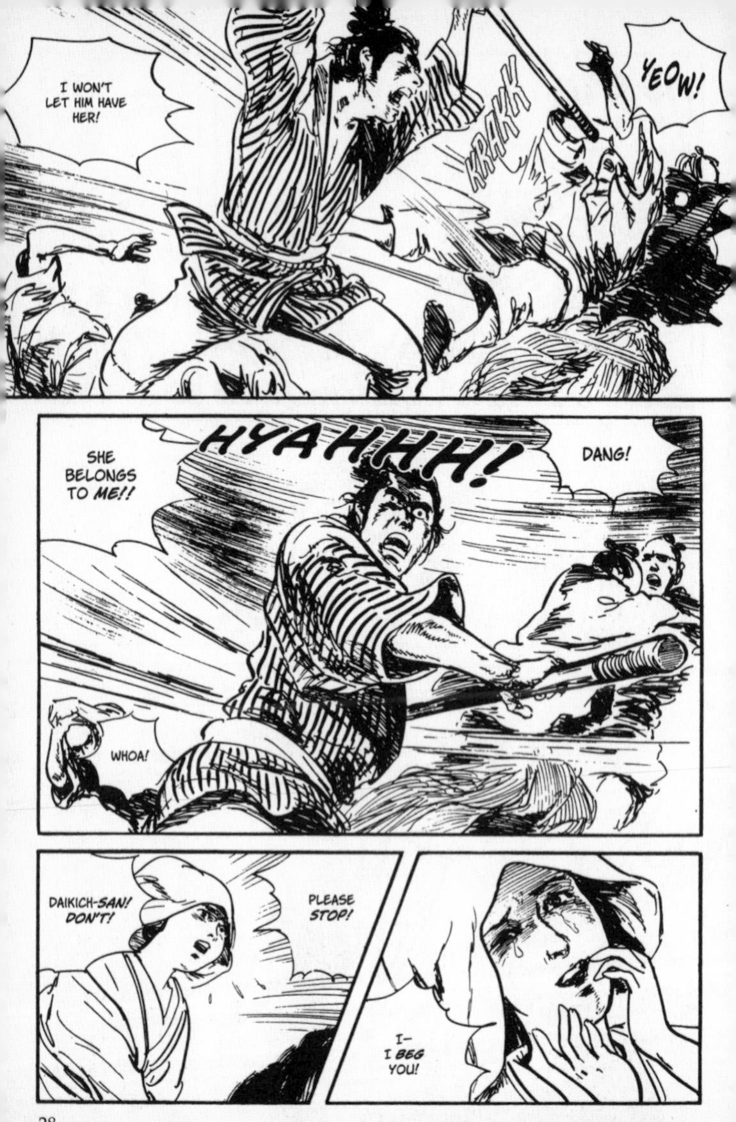
I WON'T LET HIM HAVE HER!
KRAKK
YEOW!
SHE BELONGS TO ME!!
HYAHHHH!
DANG!
WHOA!
DAIKICH-SAN! DON'T!
PLEASE STOP!
I— I BEG YOU!

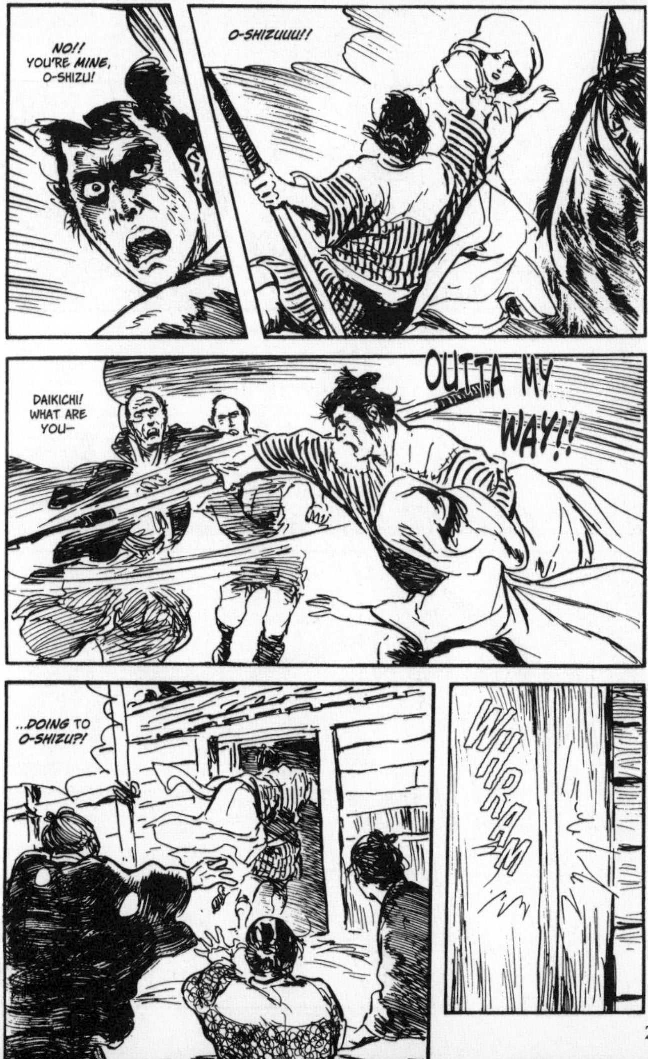
NO!! YOU'RE MINE, O-SHIZU!
O-SHIZUUU!!
DAIKICHI! WHAT ARE YOU—
OUTTA MY WAY!!
...DOING TO O-SHIZU?!
WHAM

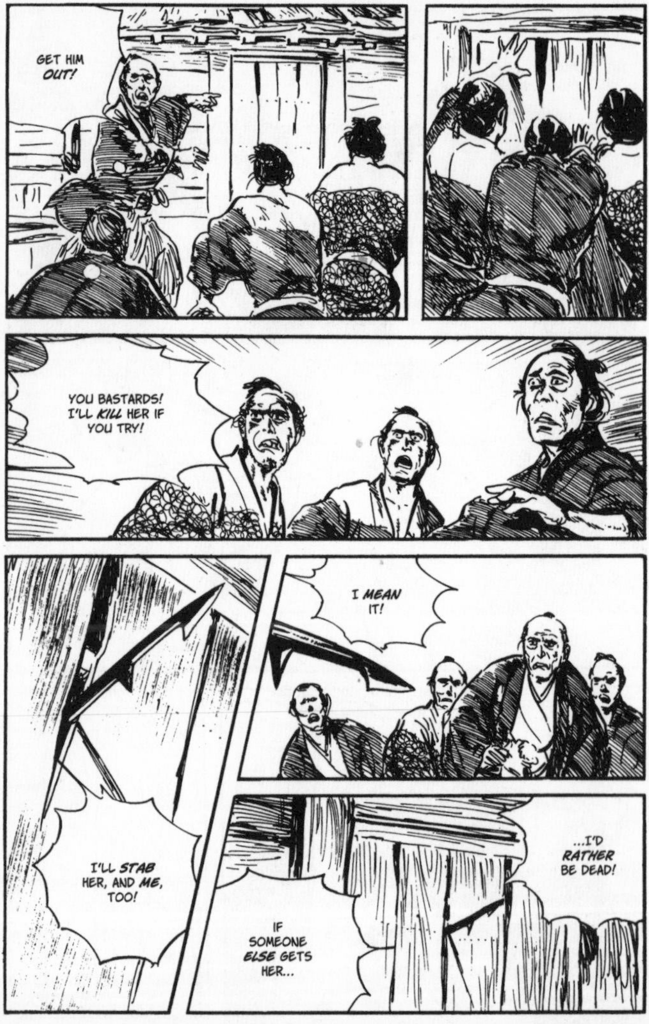
GET HIM *OUT!*
YOU BASTARDS! I'LL *KILL* HER IF YOU TRY!
I'LL *STAB* HER, AND *ME*, TOO!
I *MEAN* IT!
IF SOMEONE *ELSE* GETS HER...
...I'D *RATHER* BE DEAD!

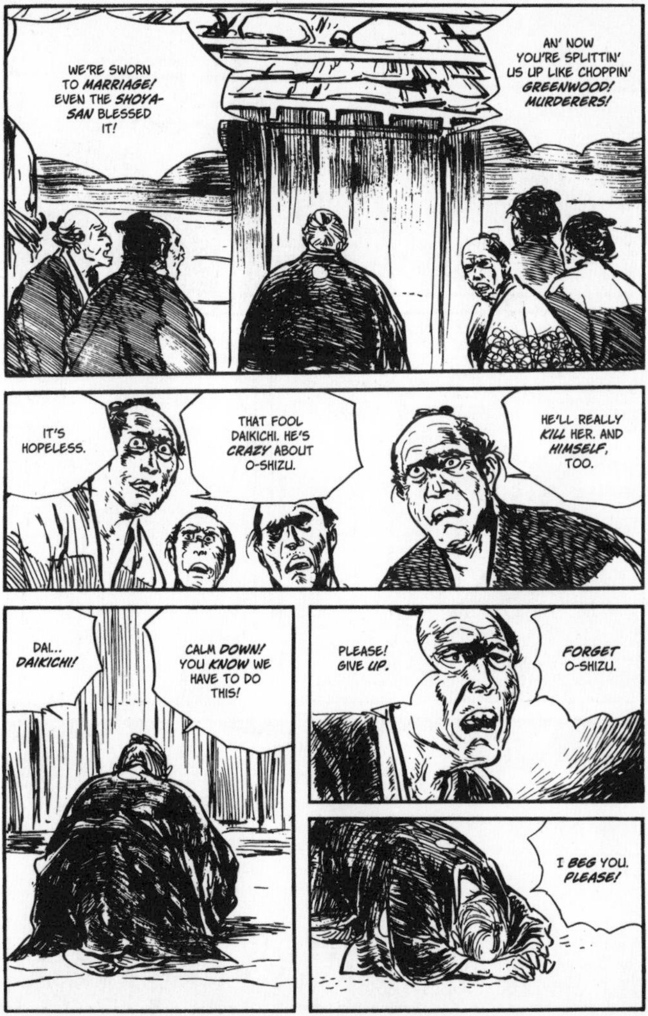
WE'RE SWORN TO MARRIAGE! EVEN THE SHOYA-SAN BLESSED IT!
AN' NOW YOU'RE SPLITTIN' US UP LIKE CHOPPIN' GREENWOOD! MURDERERS!
IT'S HOPELESS.
THAT FOOL DAIKICHI. HE'S CRAZY ABOUT O-SHIZU.
HE'LL REALLY KILL HER. AND HIMSELF, TOO.
DAI... DAIKICHI!
CALM DOWN! YOU KNOW WE HAVE TO DO THIS!
PLEASE! GIVE UP.
FORGET O-SHIZU.
I BEG YOU. PLEASE!

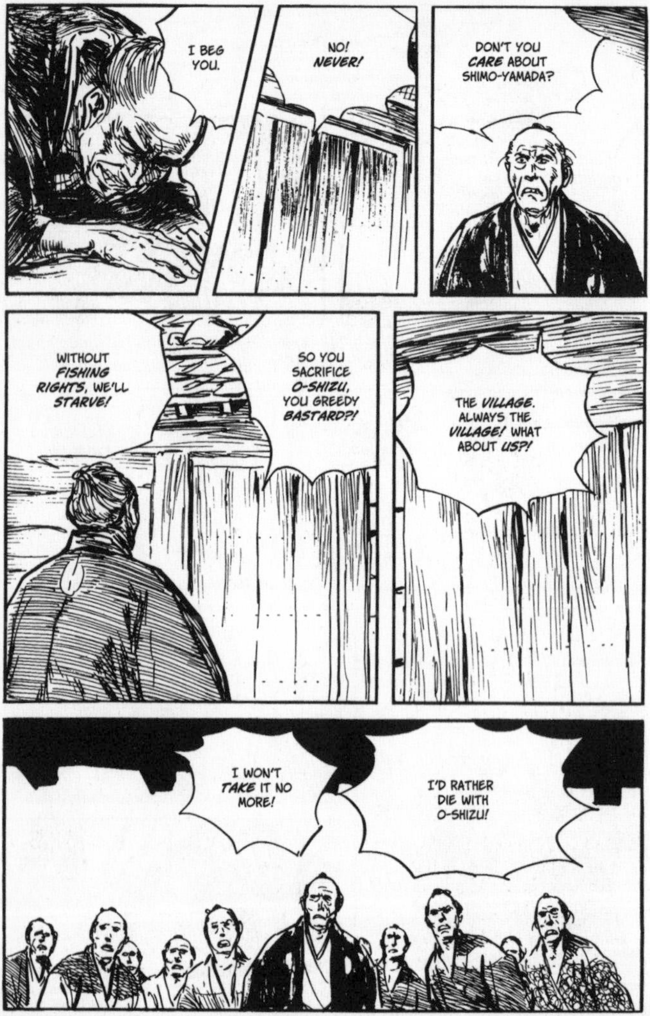
I BEG YOU.
NO! NEVER!
DON'T YOU CARE ABOUT SHIMO-YAMADA?
WITHOUT FISHING RIGHTS, WE'LL STARVE!
SO YOU SACRIFICE O-SHIZU, YOU GREEDY BASTARD?!
THE VILLAGE. ALWAYS THE VILLAGE! WHAT ABOUT US?!
I WON'T TAKE IT NO MORE!
I'D RATHER DIE WITH O-SHIZU!

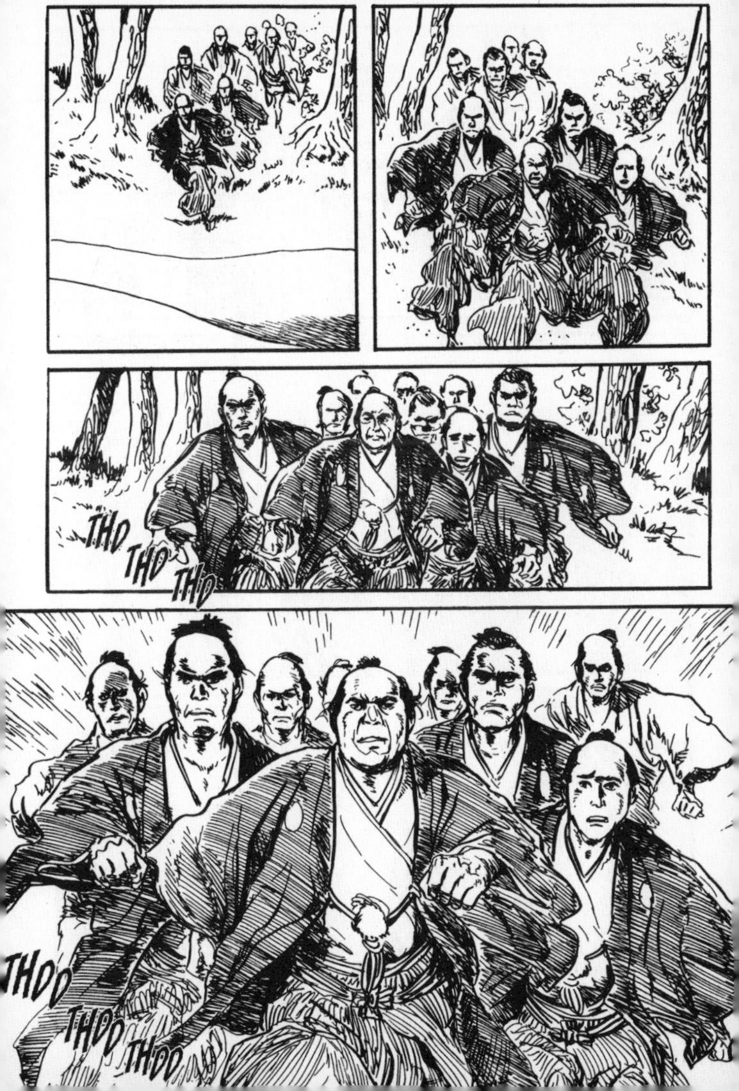
THD
THD
THD
THDD
THDD
THDD

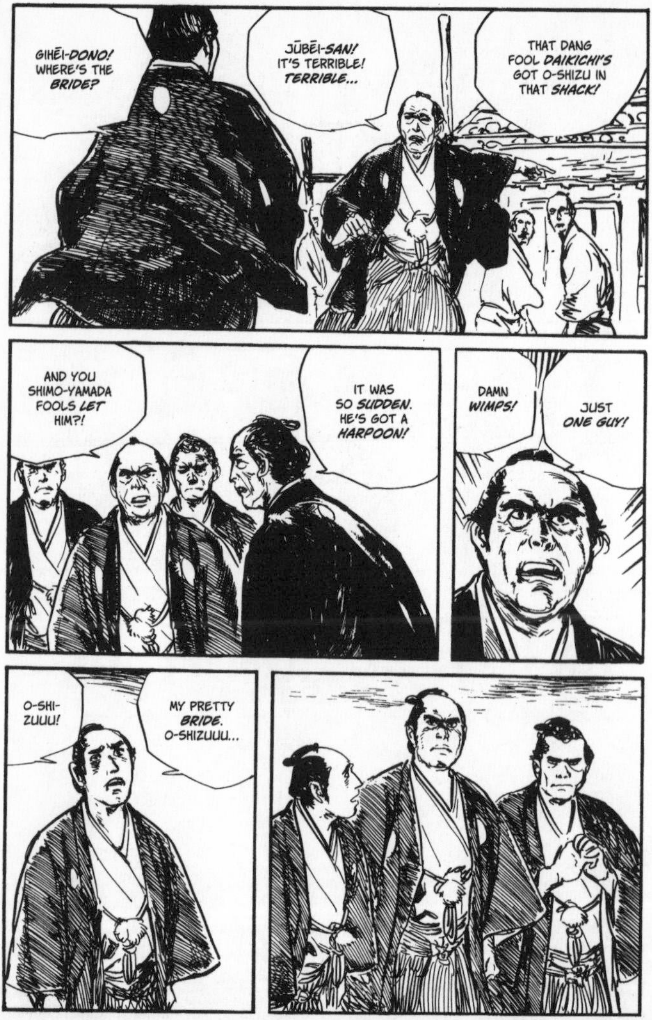
GIHĒI-DONO! WHERE'S THE BRIDE?
JŪBĒI-SAN! IT'S TERRIBLE! TERRIBLE...
THAT DANG FOOL DAIKICHI'S GOT O-SHIZU IN THAT SHACK!
AND YOU SHIMO-YAMADA FOOLS LET HIM?!
IT WAS SO SUDDEN. HE'S GOT A HARPOON!
DAMN WIMPS!
JUST ONE GUY!
O-SHI-ZUUU!
MY PRETTY BRIDE. O-SHIZUUU...

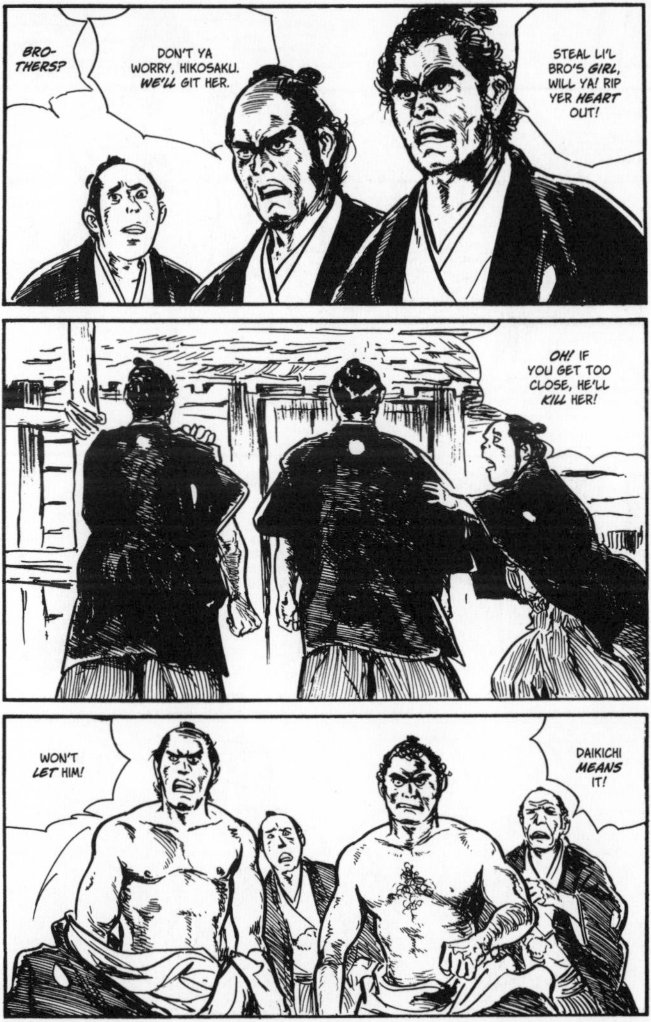
BRO-
THERS?
DON'T YA WORRY, HIKOSAKU. WE'LL GIT HER.
STEAL LI'L BRO'S GIRL, WILL YA! RIP YER HEART OUT!
OH! IF YOU GET TOO CLOSE, HE'LL KILL HER!
WON'T LET HIM!
DAIKICHI MEANS IT!

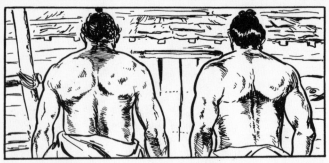

HEY! RED AND BLUE *DEMONS* OF *DEBANA!* ONE *STEP,* AND I *STAB* HER!

DAIKICHI!

YUH GONE TOO *FAR...*

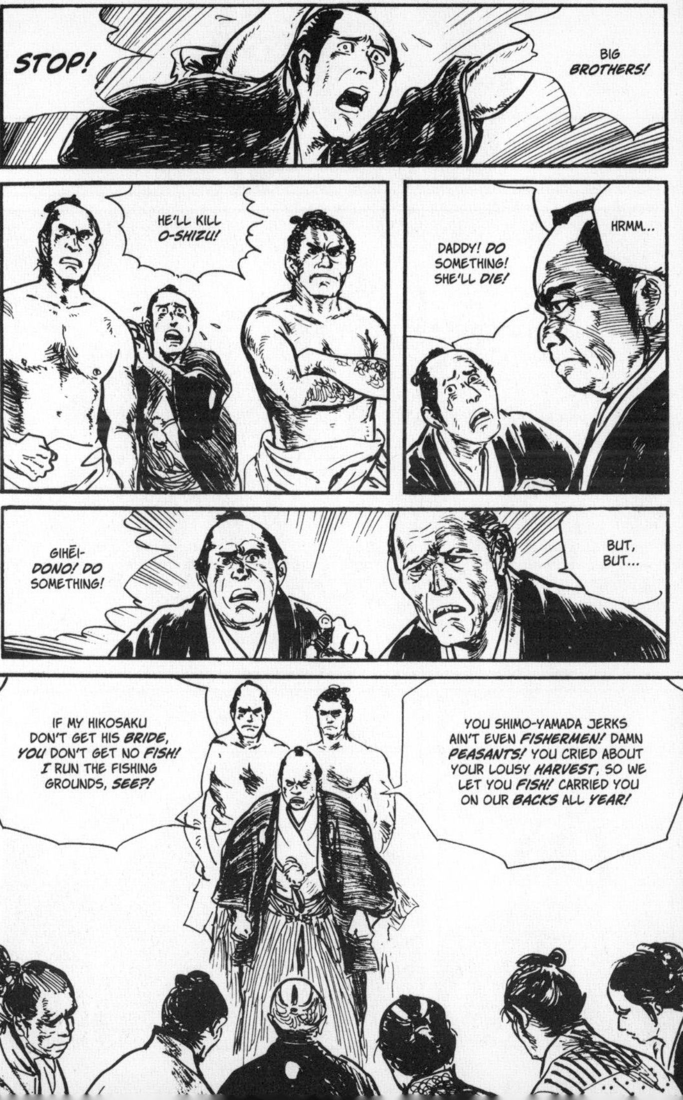
STOP!
BIG BROTHERS!
HE'LL KILL O-SHIZU!
DADDY! DO SOMETHING! SHE'LL DIE!
HRMM...
GIHĒI-DONO! DO SOMETHING!
BUT, BUT...
IF MY HIKOSAKU DON'T GET HIS BRIDE, YOU DON'T GET NO FISH! I RUN THE FISHING GROUNDS, SEE?!
YOU SHIMO-YAMADA JERKS AIN'T EVEN FISHERMEN! DAMN PEASANTS! YOU CRIED ABOUT YOUR LOUSY HARVEST, SO WE LET YOU FISH! CARRIED YOU ON OUR BACKS ALL YEAR!

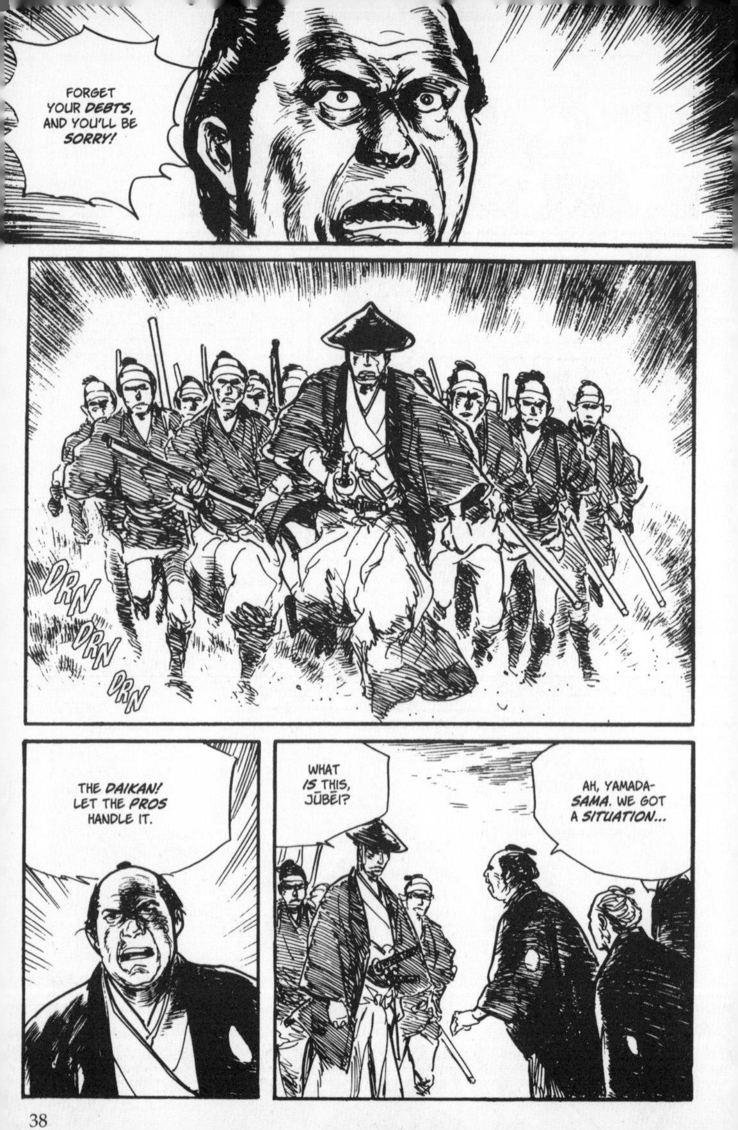

FORGET YOUR DEBTS, AND YOU'LL BE SORRY!
DRN DRN DRN
THE DAIKAN! LET THE PROS HANDLE IT.
WHAT IS THIS, JŪBEI?
AH, YAMADA-SAMA. WE GOT A SITUATION...

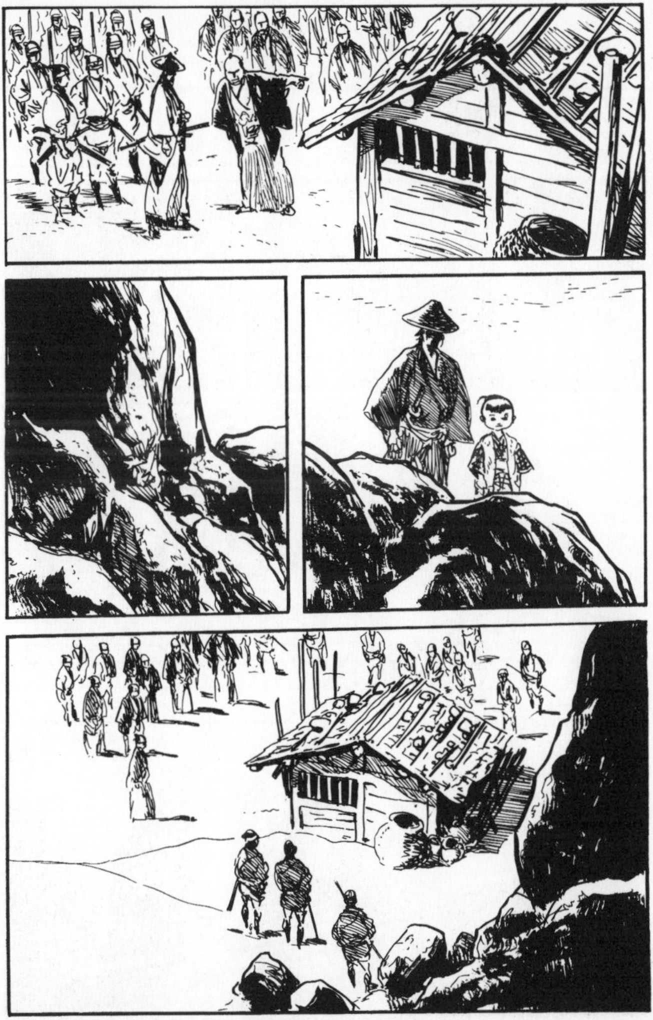

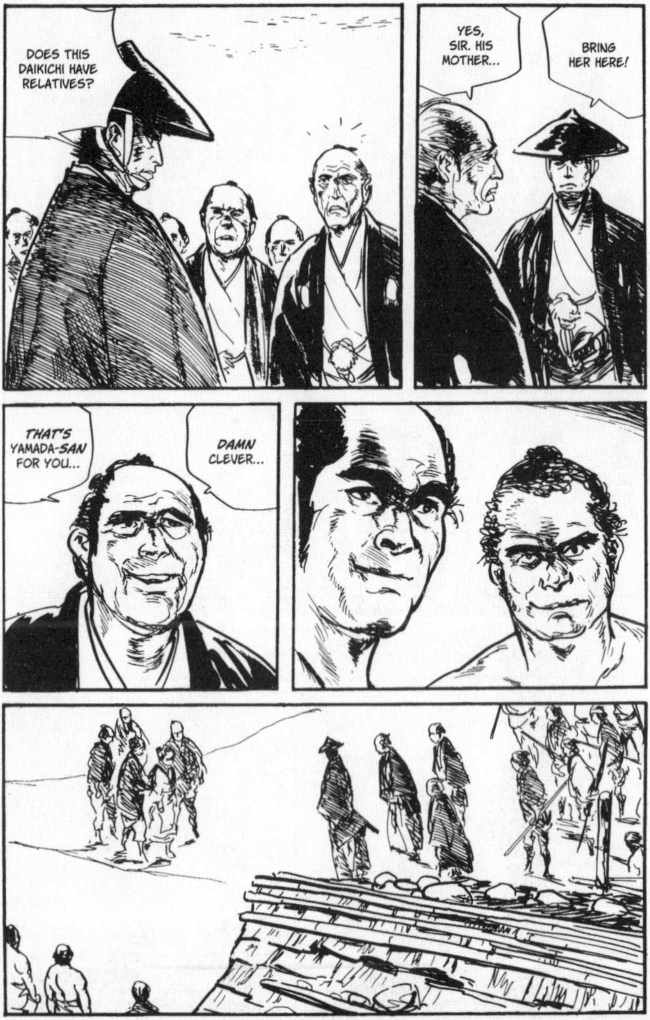
DOES THIS DAIKICHI HAVE RELATIVES?
YES, SIR. HIS MOTHER...
BRING HER HERE!
THAT'S YAMADA-SAN FOR YOU...
DAMN CLEVER...

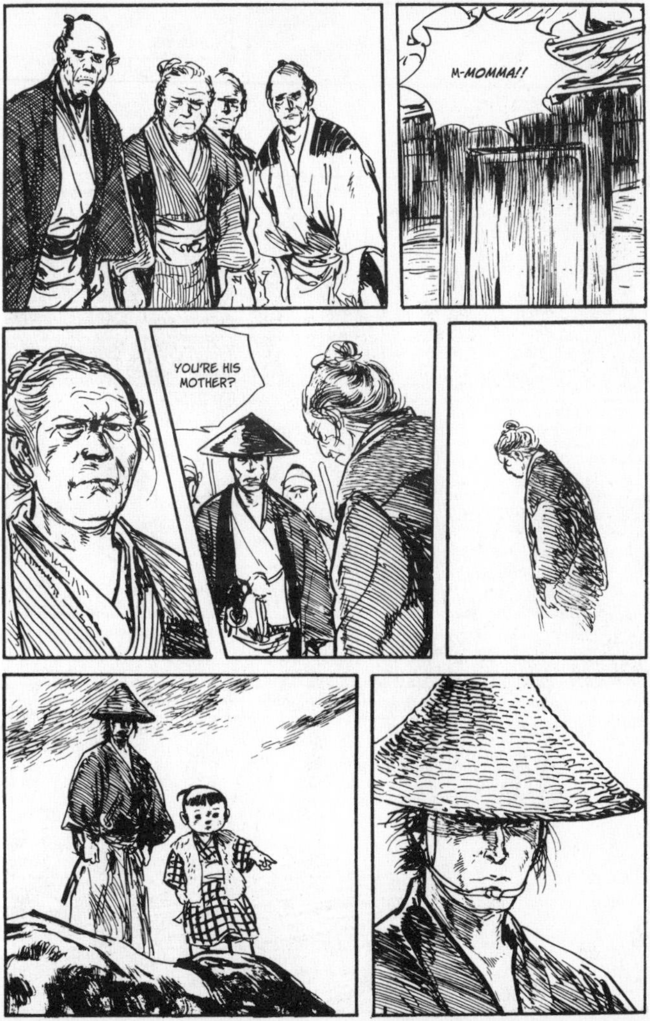
M-MOMMA!!
YOU'RE HIS MOTHER?

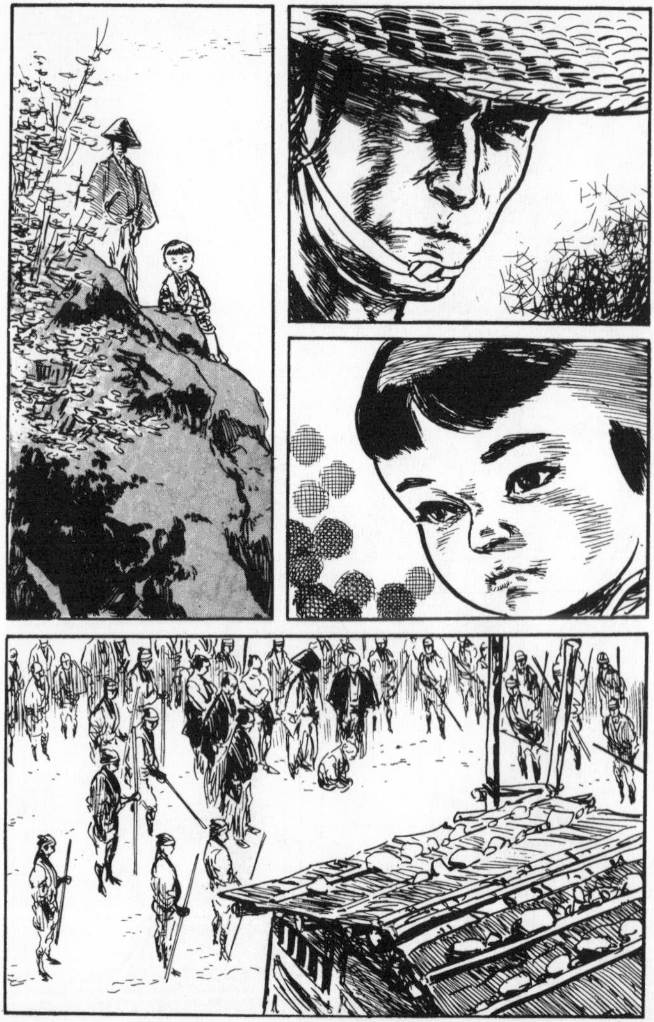

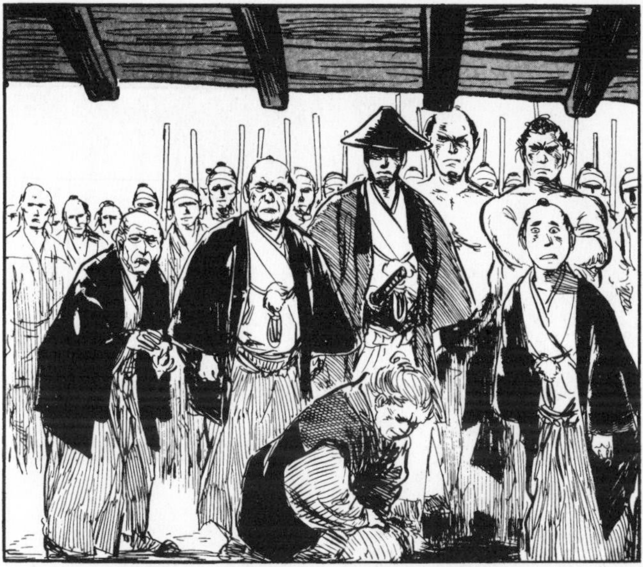

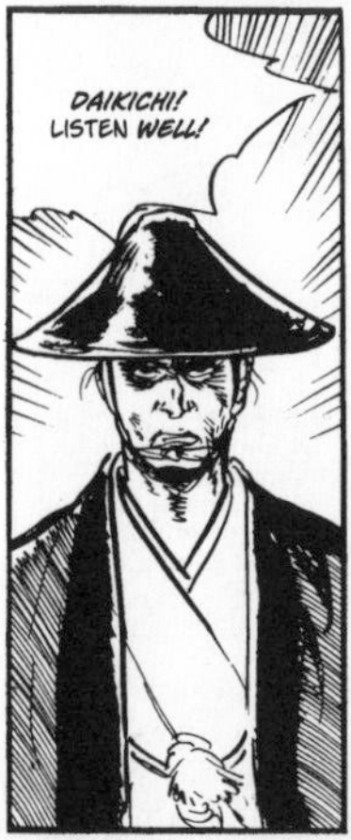
DAIKICHI! LISTEN WELL!

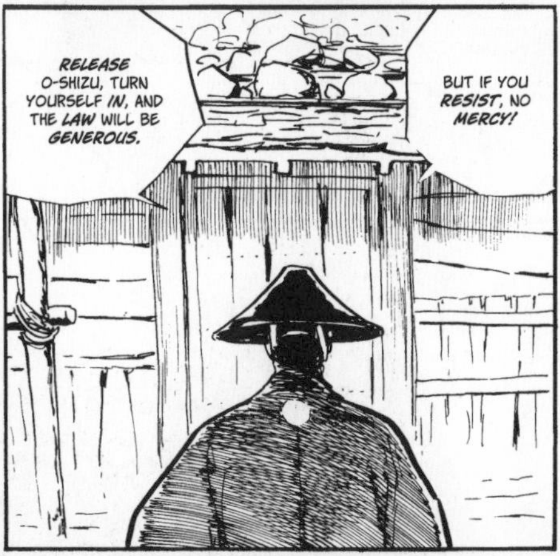
RELEASE O-SHIZU, TURN YOURSELF IN, AND THE LAW WILL BE GENEROUS.
BUT IF YOU RESIST, NO MERCY!

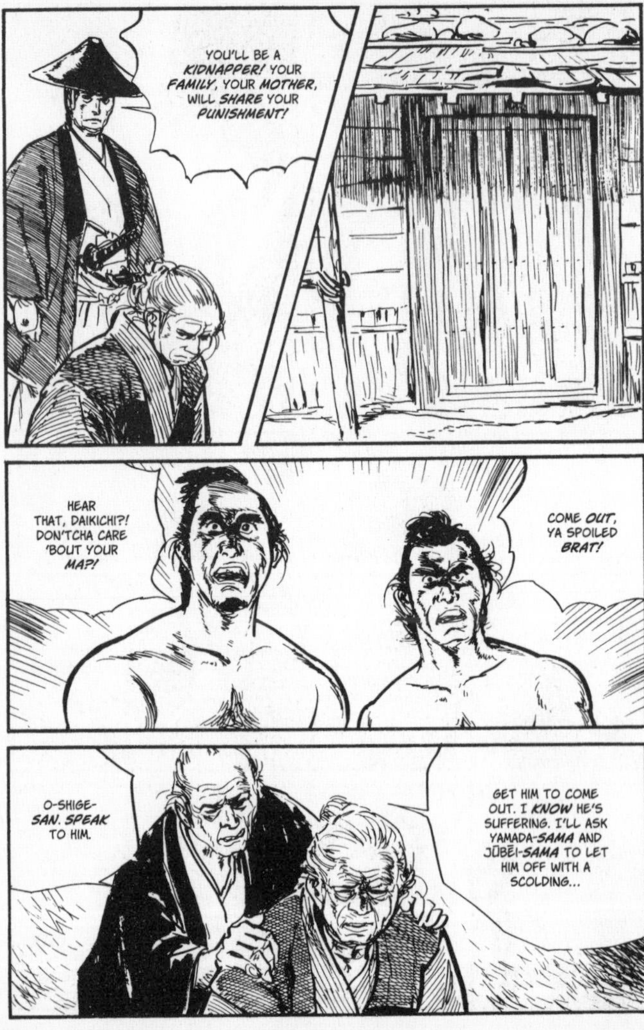
YOU'LL BE A KIDNAPPER! YOUR FAMILY, YOUR MOTHER, WILL SHARE YOUR PUNISHMENT!
HEAR THAT, DAIKICHI?! DON'TCHA CARE 'BOUT YOUR MA?!
COME OUT, YA SPOILED BRAT!
O-SHIGE-SAN. SPEAK TO HIM.
GET HIM TO COME OUT. I KNOW HE'S SUFFERING. I'LL ASK YAMADA-SAMA AND JŪBEI-SAMA TO LET HIM OFF WITH A SCOLDING...

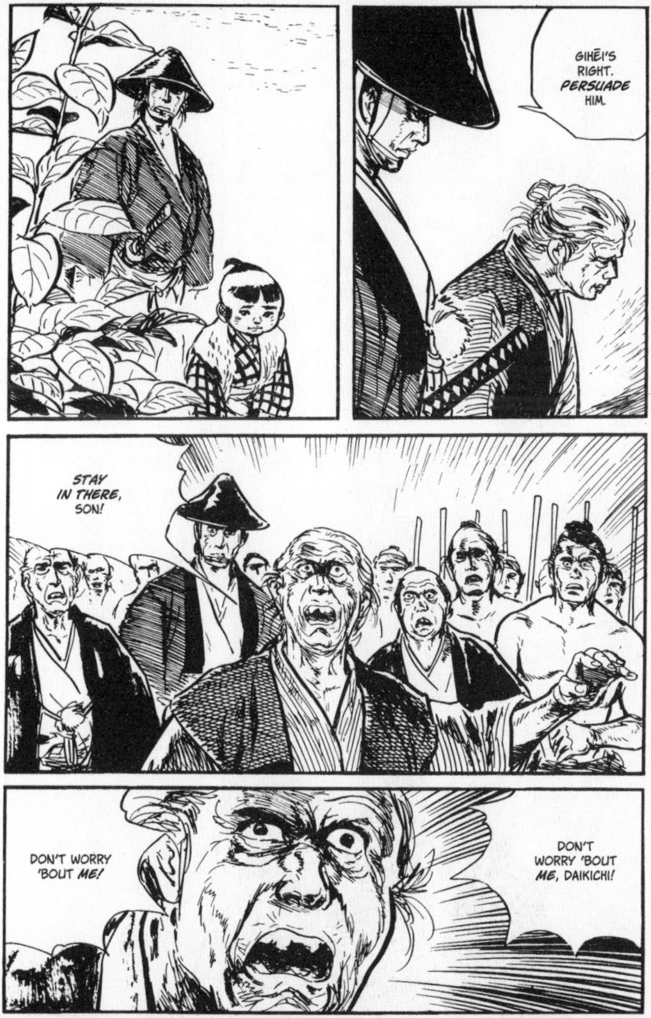
GIHĒI'S RIGHT. PERSUADE HIM.
STAY IN THERE, SON!
DON'T WORRY 'BOUT ME!
DON'T WORRY 'BOUT ME, DAIKICHI!

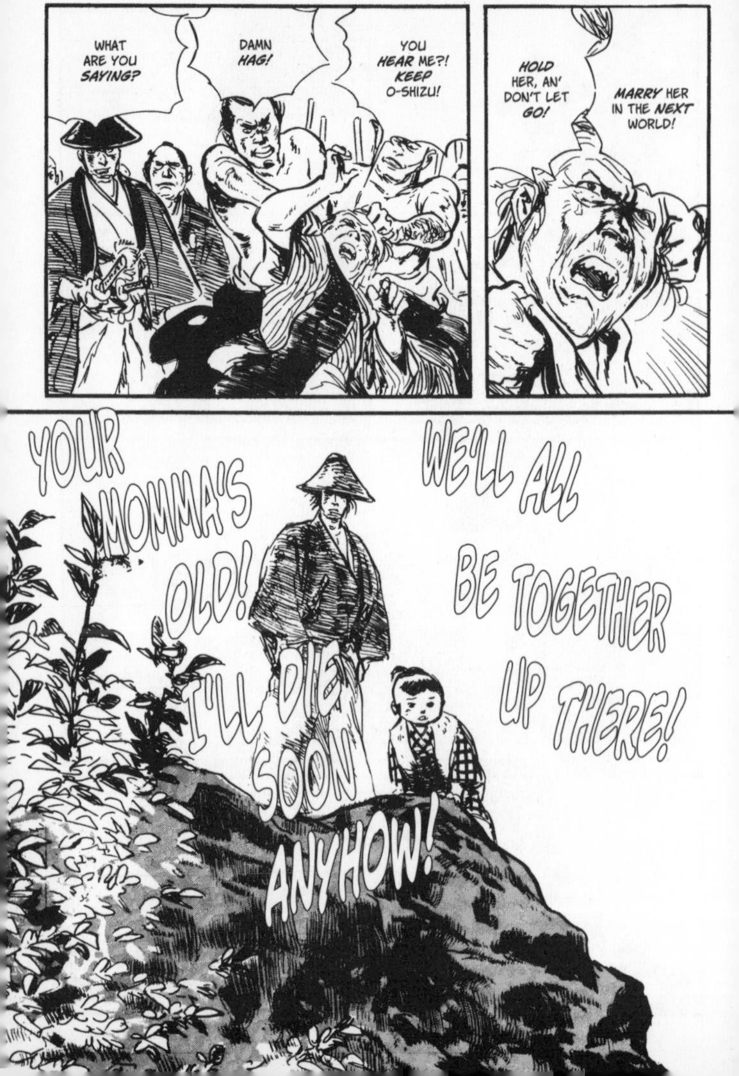

WHAT ARE YOU SAYING?
DAMN HAG!
YOU HEAR ME?! KEEP O-SHIZU!
HOLD HER, AN' DON'T LET GO!
MARRY HER IN THE NEXT WORLD!
YOUR MOMMA'S OLD!
I'LL DIE SOON ANYHOW!
WE'LL ALL BE TOGETHER UP THERE!

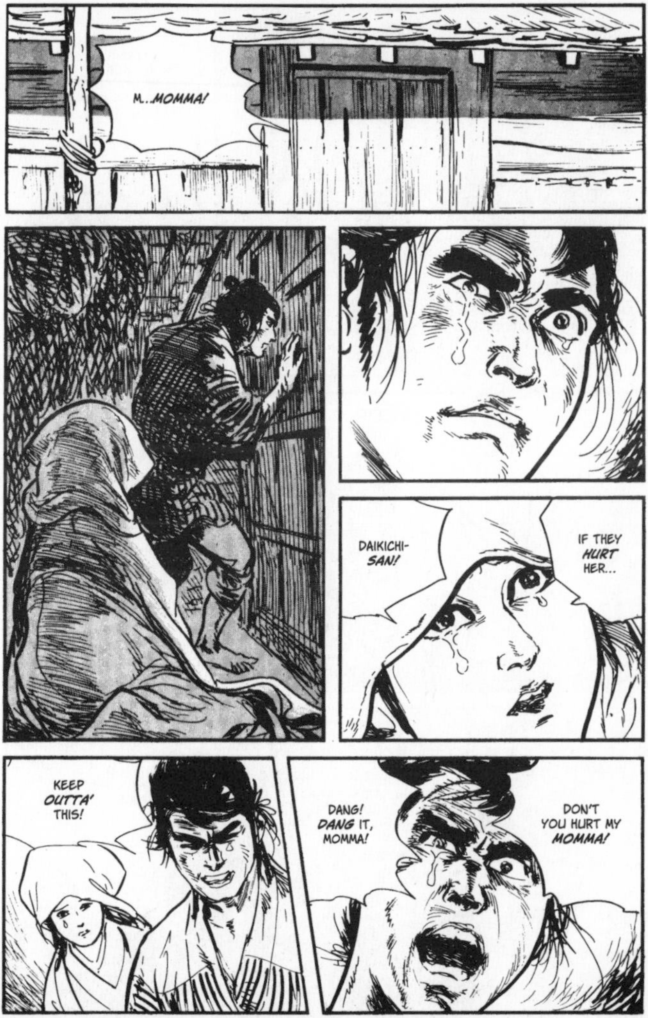
M...MOMMA!
DAIKICHI-SAN!
IF THEY HURT HER...
KEEP OUTTA' THIS!
DANG! DANG IT, MOMMA!
DON'T YOU HURT MY MOMMA!

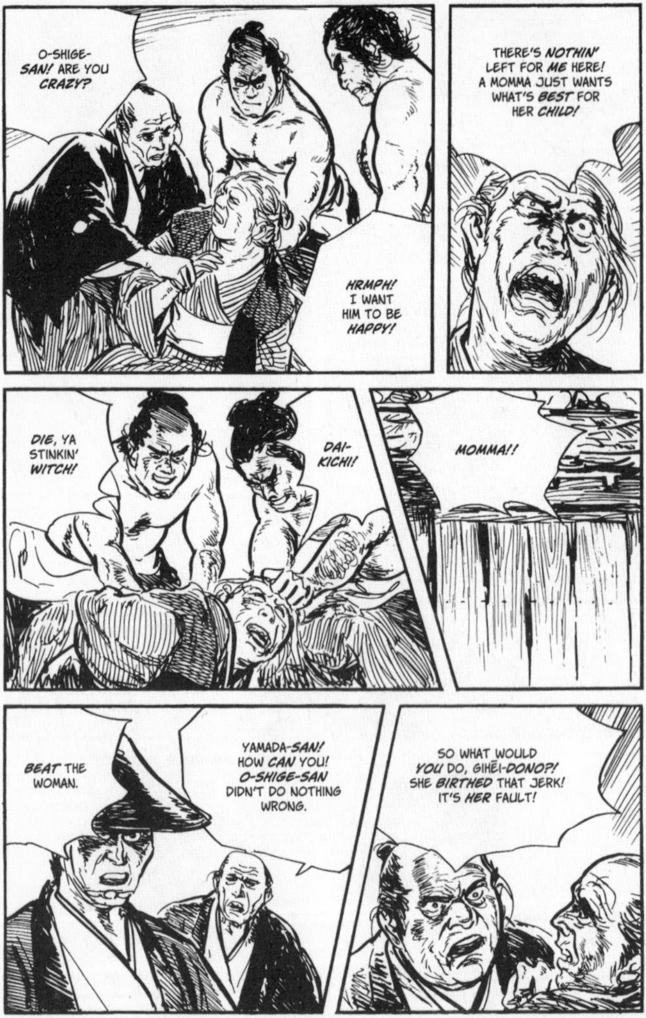
O-SHIGE-SAN! ARE YOU CRAZY?
HRMPH! I WANT HIM TO BE HAPPY!
THERE'S NOTHIN' LEFT FOR ME HERE! A MOMMA JUST WANTS WHAT'S BEST FOR HER CHILD!
DIE, YA STINKIN' WITCH!
DAI-KICHI!
MOMMA!!
BEAT THE WOMAN.
YAMADA-SAN! HOW CAN YOU! O-SHIGE-SAN DIDN'T DO NOTHING WRONG.
SO WHAT WOULD YOU DO, GIHĒI-DONO?! SHE BIRTHED THAT JERK! IT'S HER FAULT!

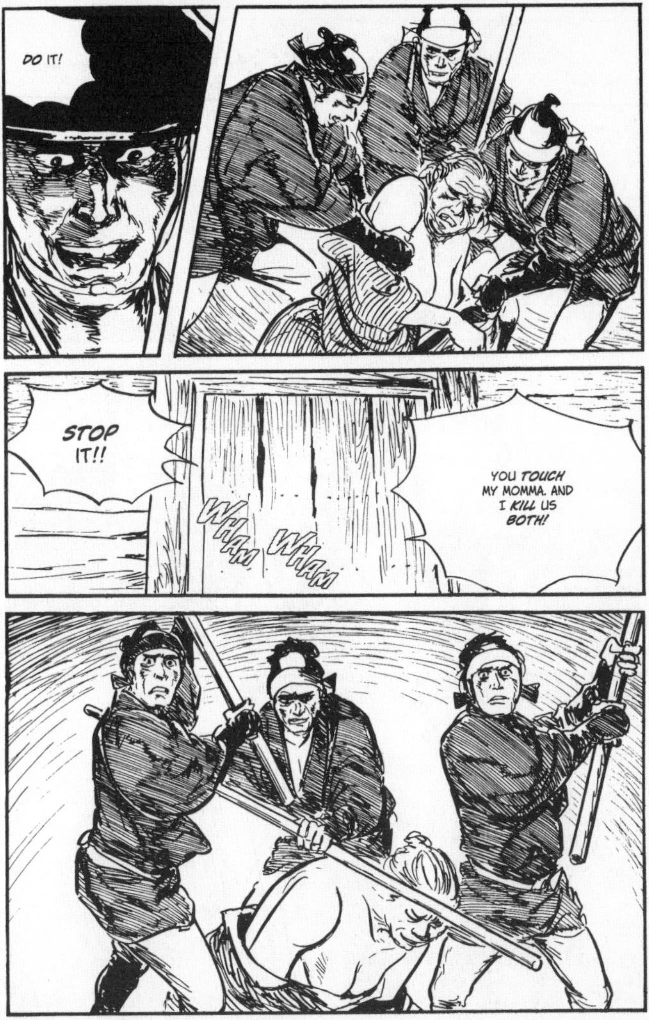
DO IT!
STOP IT!!
WHAM WHAM
YOU TOUCH MY MOMMA. AND I KILL US BOTH!

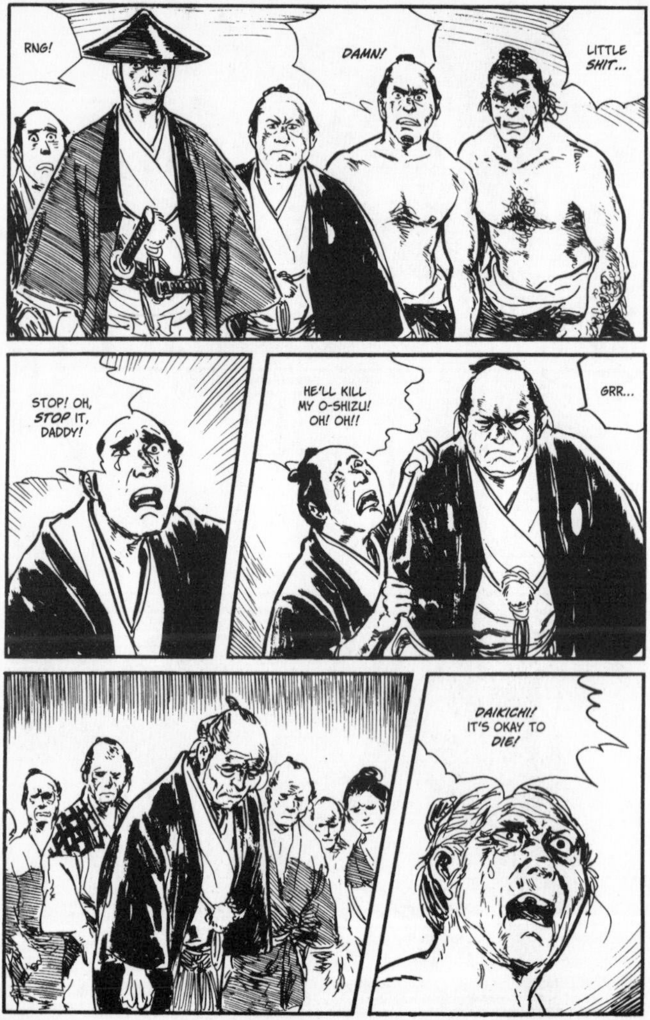
RNG!
DAMN!
LITTLE SHIT...
STOP! OH, STOP IT, DADDY!
HE'LL KILL MY O-SHIZU! OH! OH!!
GRR...
DAIKICHI! IT'S OKAY TO DIE!

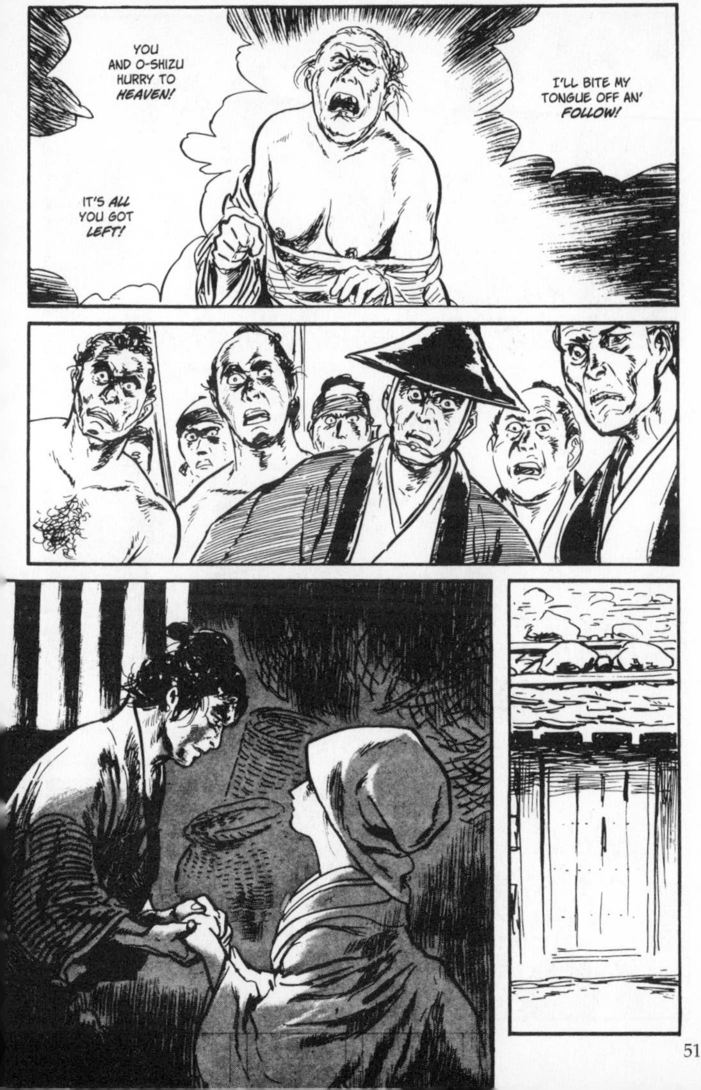
YOU AND O-SHIZU HURRY TO HEAVEN!
IT'S ALL YOU GOT LEFT!
I'LL BITE MY TONGUE OFF AN' FOLLOW!

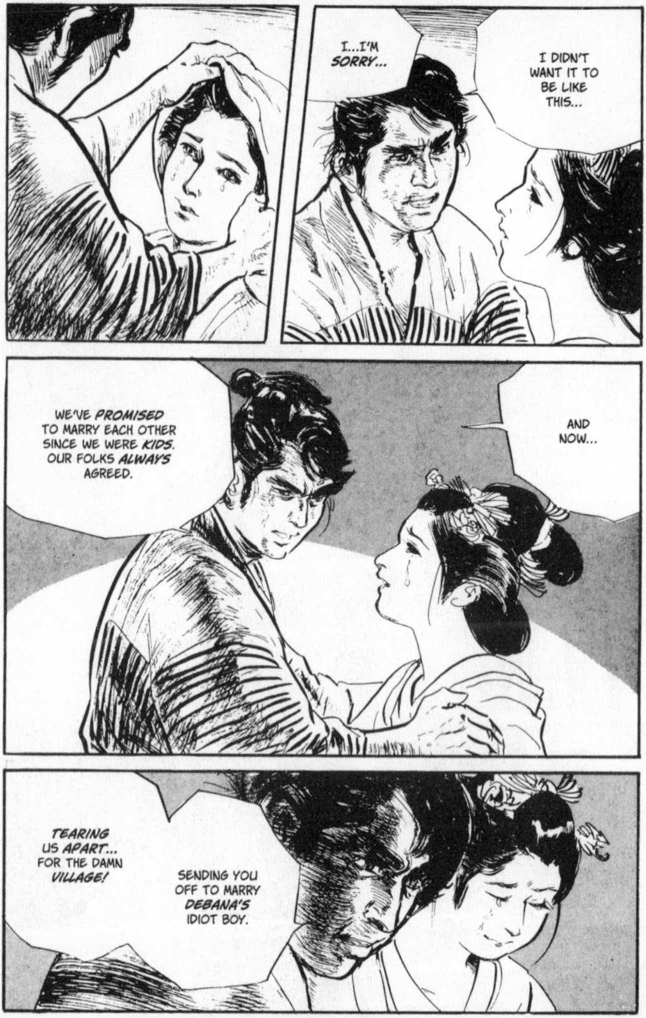
I...I'M SORRY...
I DIDN'T WANT IT TO BE LIKE THIS...
WE'VE PROMISED TO MARRY EACH OTHER SINCE WE WERE KIDS. OUR FOLKS ALWAYS AGREED.
AND NOW...
TEARING US APART... FOR THE DAMN VILLAGE!
SENDING YOU OFF TO MARRY DEBANA'S IDIOT BOY.

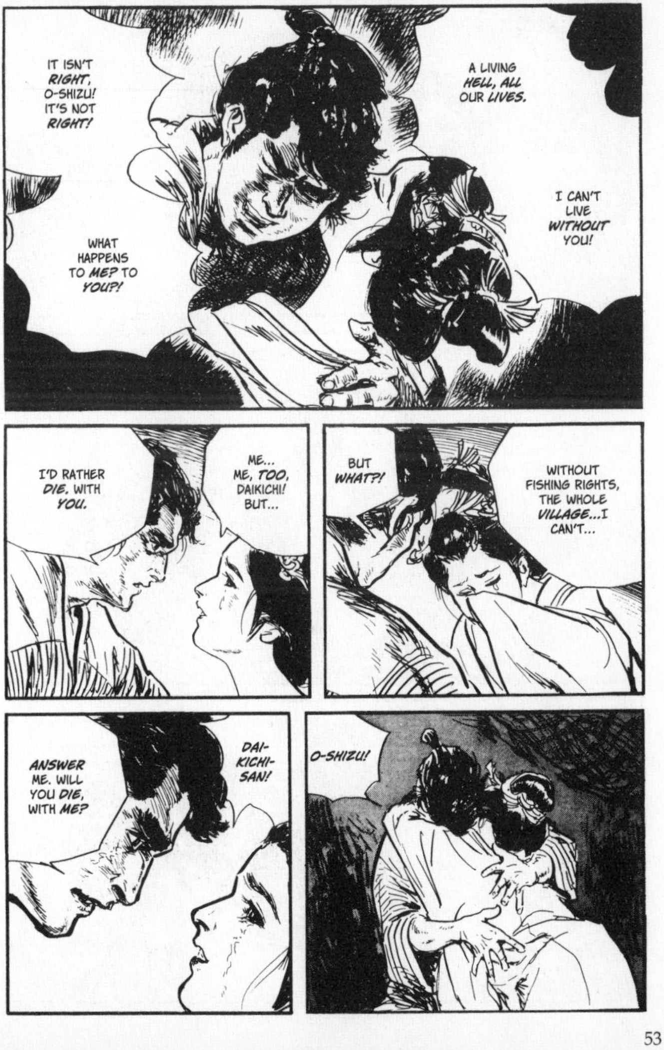
IT ISN'T *RIGHT*, O-SHIZU! IT'S NOT *RIGHT!*
WHAT HAPPENS TO *ME?* TO *YOU?!*
A LIVING *HELL, ALL* OUR *LIVES.*
I CAN'T LIVE *WITHOUT* YOU!
I'D RATHER *DIE*, WITH *YOU.*
ME... ME, *TOO*, DAIKICHI! BUT...
BUT *WHAT?!*
WITHOUT FISHING RIGHTS, THE WHOLE *VILLAGE*...I CAN'T...
ANSWER ME. WILL YOU *DIE*, WITH *ME?*
DAI-KICHI-SAN!
O-SHIZU!

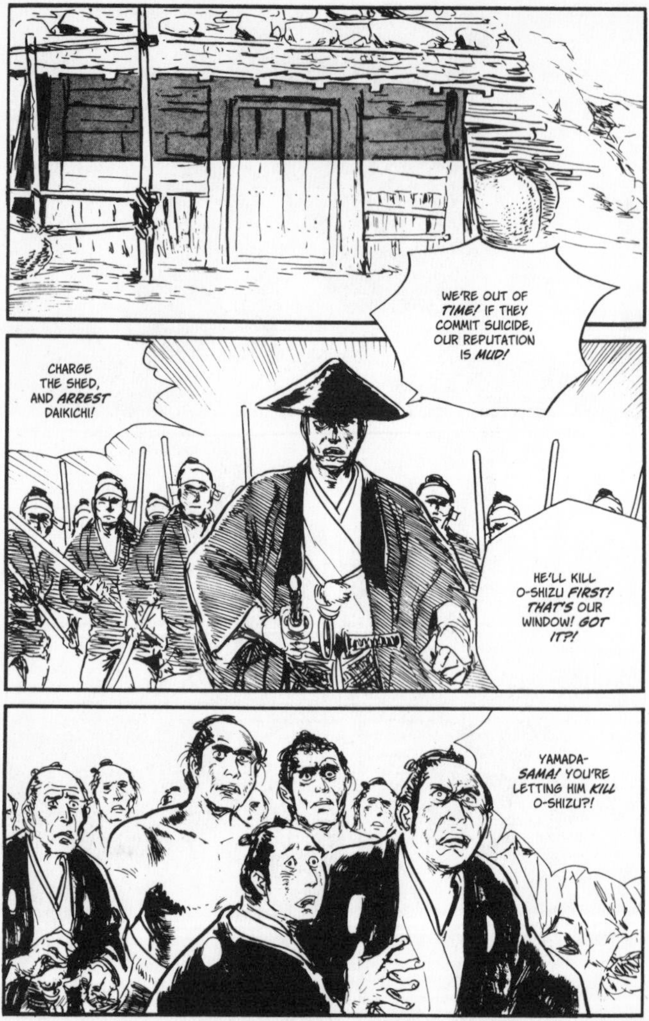
WE'RE OUT OF TIME! IF THEY COMMIT SUICIDE, OUR REPUTATION IS MUD!
CHARGE THE SHED, AND ARREST DAIKICHI!
HE'LL KILL O-SHIZU FIRST! THAT'S OUR WINDOW! GOT IT?!
YAMADA-SAMA! YOU'RE LETTING HIM KILL O-SHIZU?!

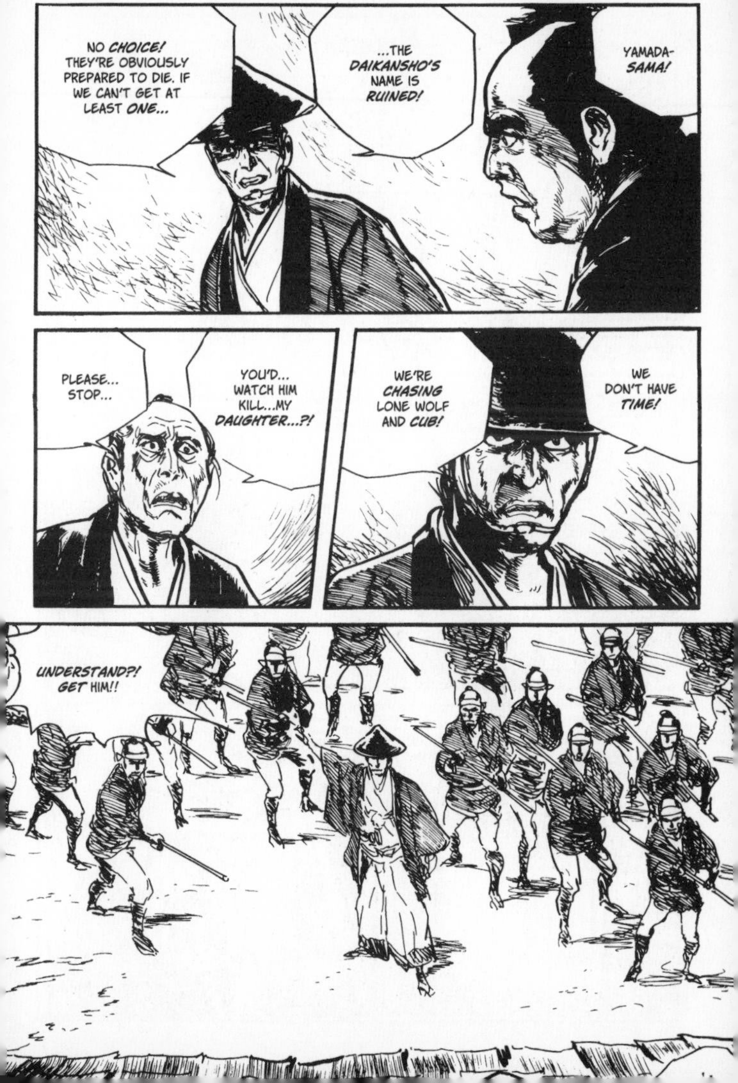
NO CHOICE! THEY'RE OBVIOUSLY PREPARED TO DIE. IF WE CAN'T GET AT LEAST ONE...
...THE DAIKANSHO'S NAME IS RUINED!
YAMADA-SAMA!
PLEASE... STOP...
YOU'D... WATCH HIM KILL...MY DAUGHTER...?!
WE'RE CHASING LONE WOLF AND CUB!
WE DON'T HAVE TIME!
UNDERSTAND?! GET HIM!!

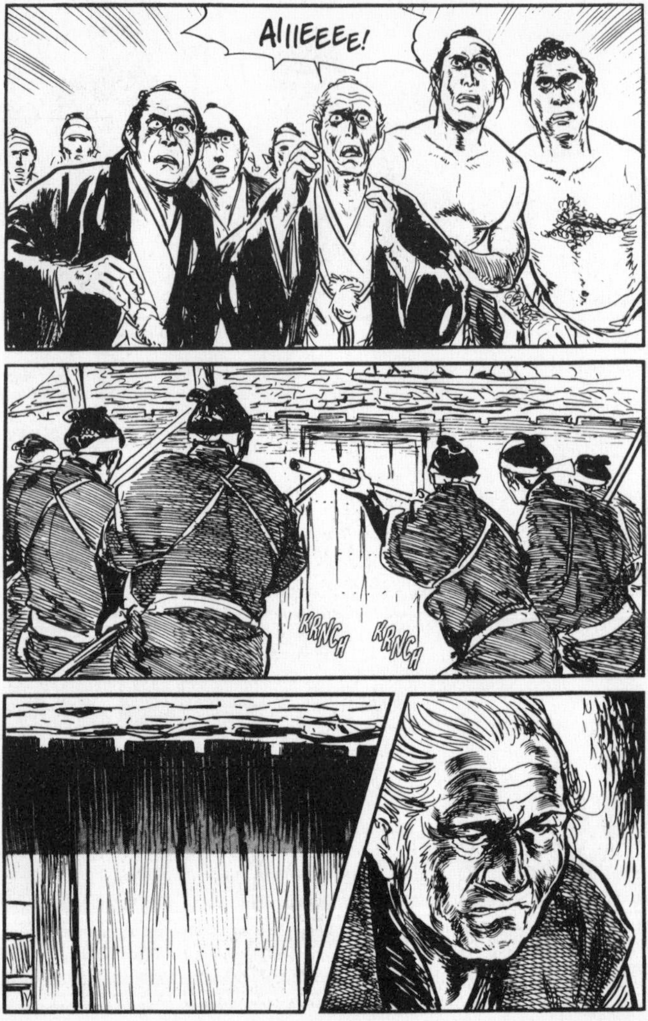
AIIIEEEE!
KRNCH
KRNCH

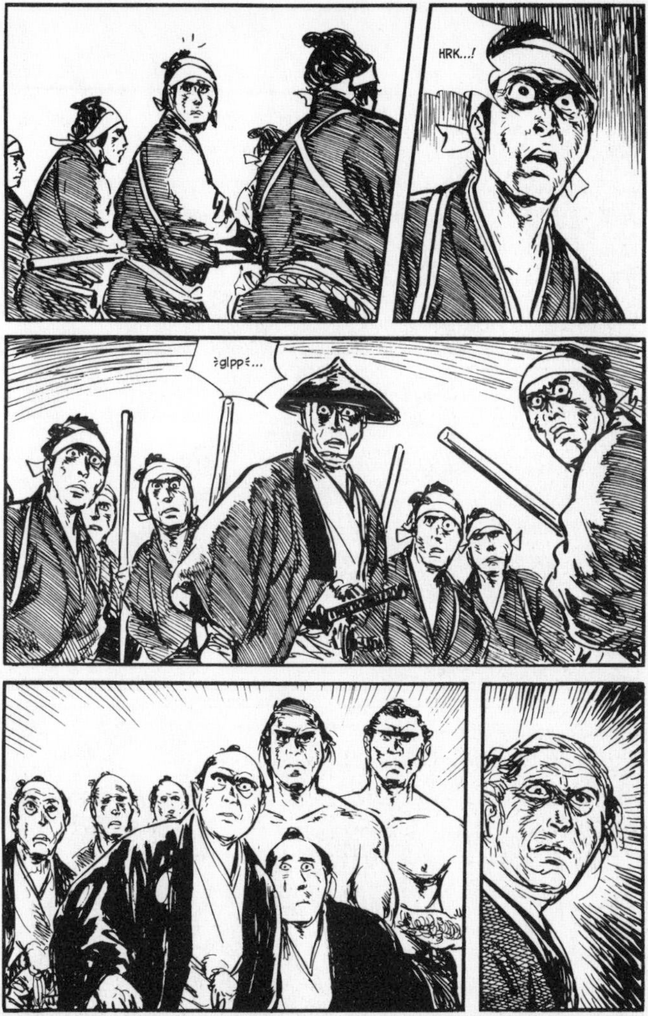
HRK...!
glpp...

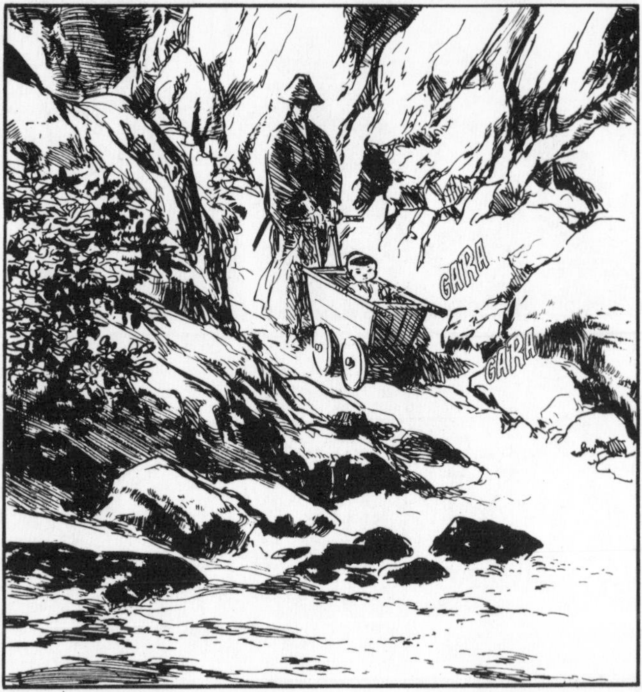
GARA
GARA
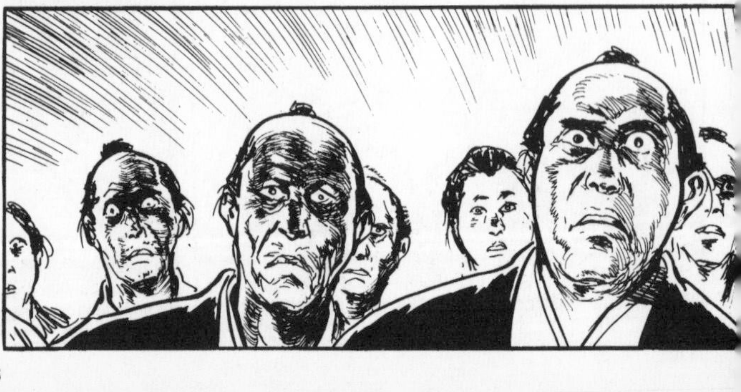

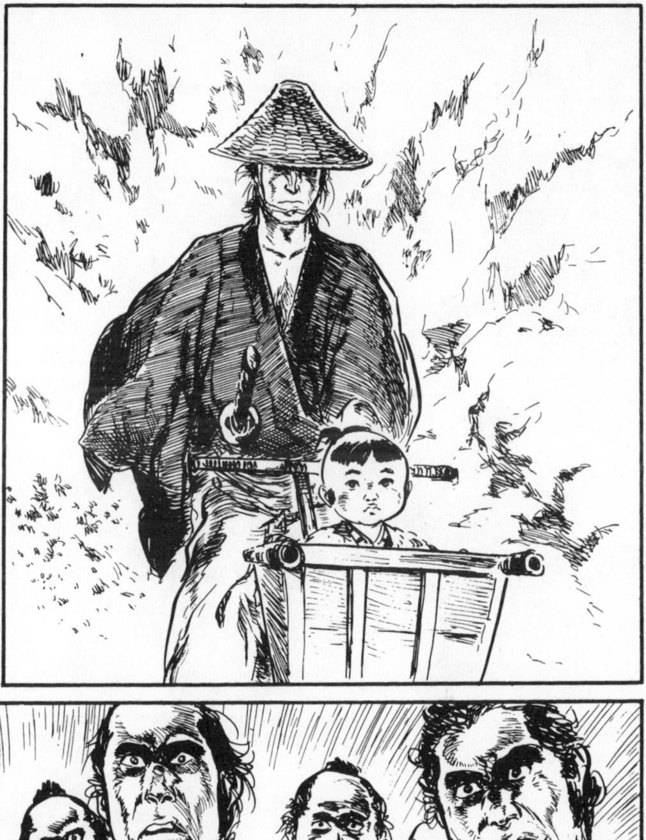

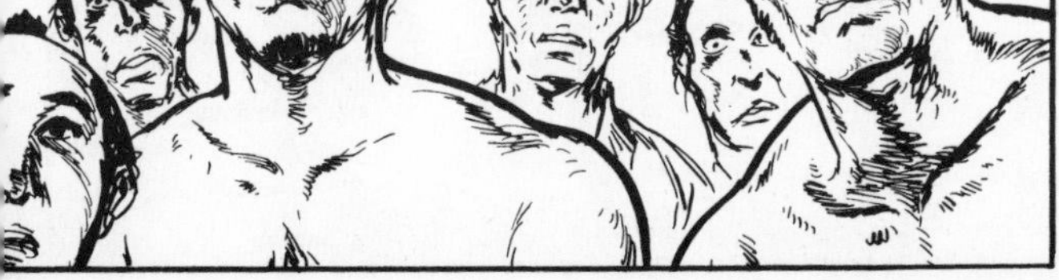

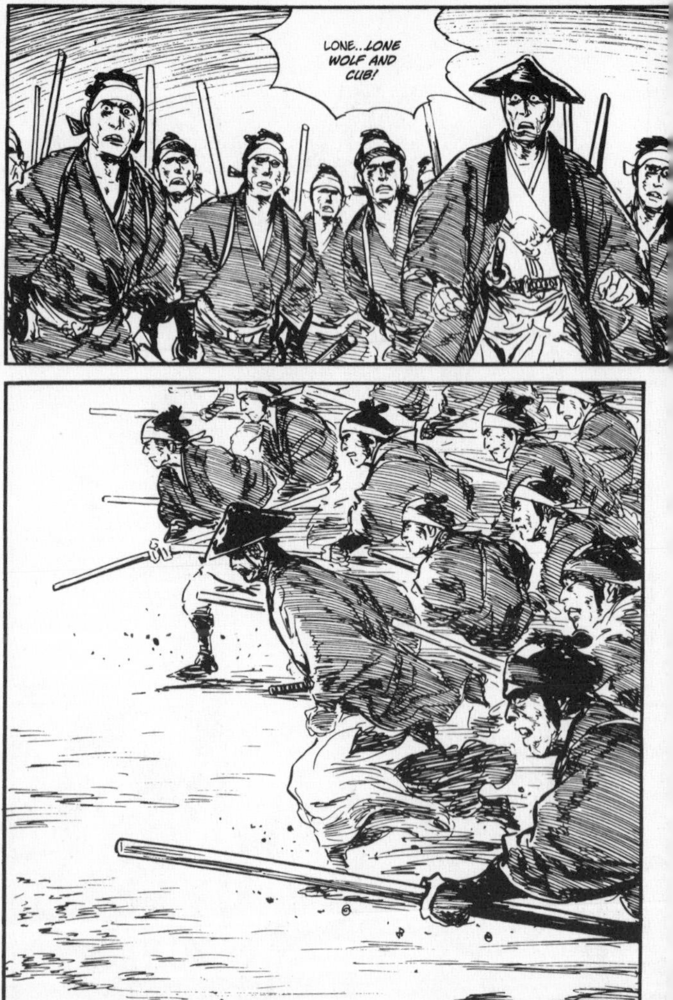
LONE...LONE WOLF AND CUB!

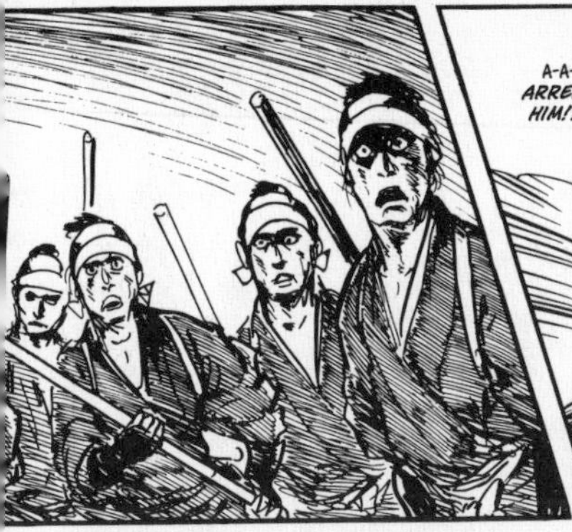

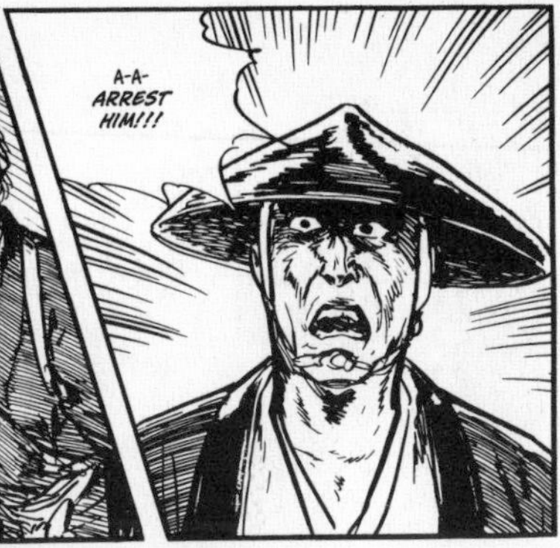
A-A-
ARREST
HIM!!!

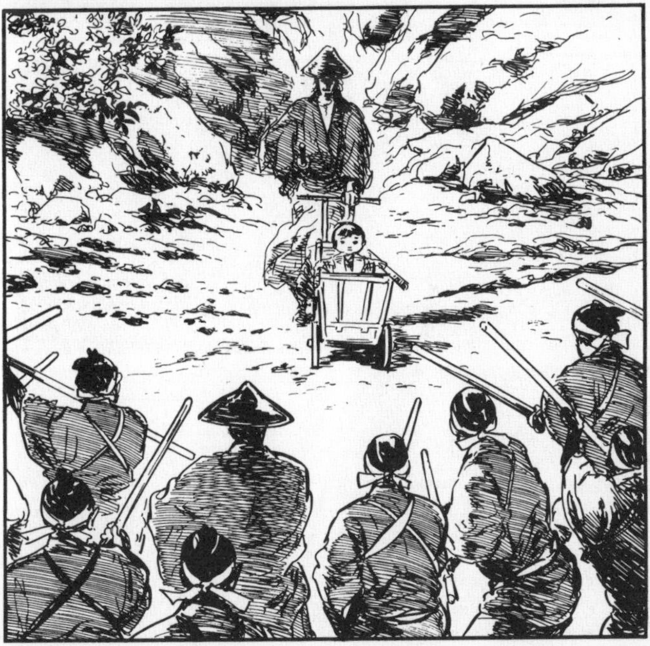

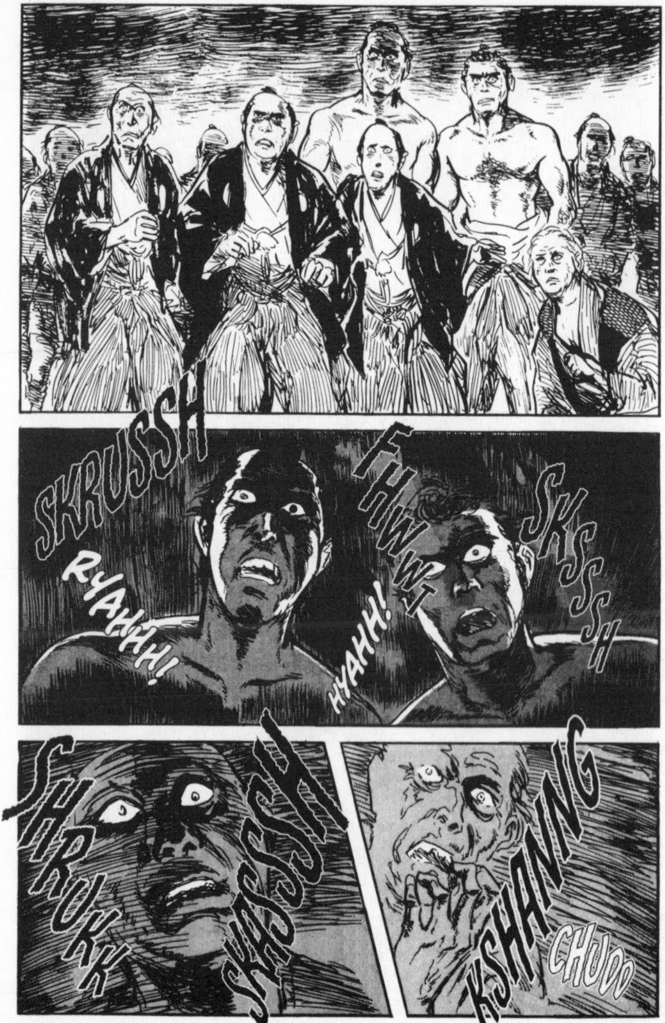
SKRUSSH
RYAHHH!
FHWWT
HYAHH!
SKSSSH
SHRUKK
SKSSSH
KSHANG
CHUOO

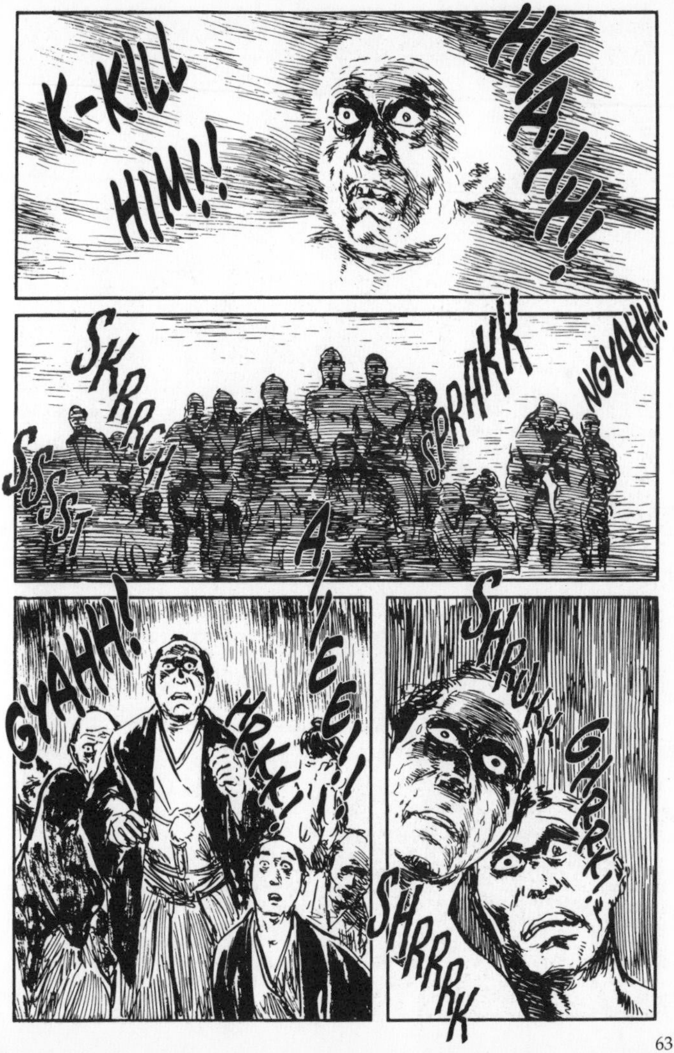
K-KILL HIM!!
HYAHHH!!
SKRRRCH
SSSSST
SPRAKK
NGYAHH!!
AIIEEE!!
GYAHH!
HRKK!
SHRUKKK
GHRRK!
SHRRRRK

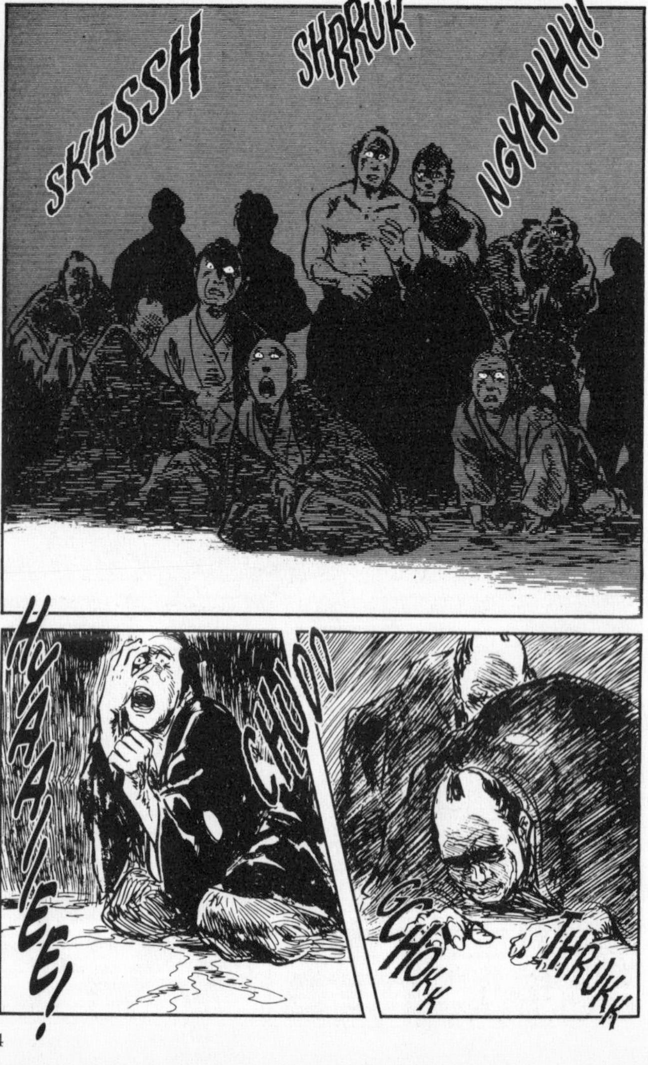
SKASSH
SHRRUK
NGYAHHH!
HYAAIIEEE!
CHUDD
GCHOKK
THRUKK

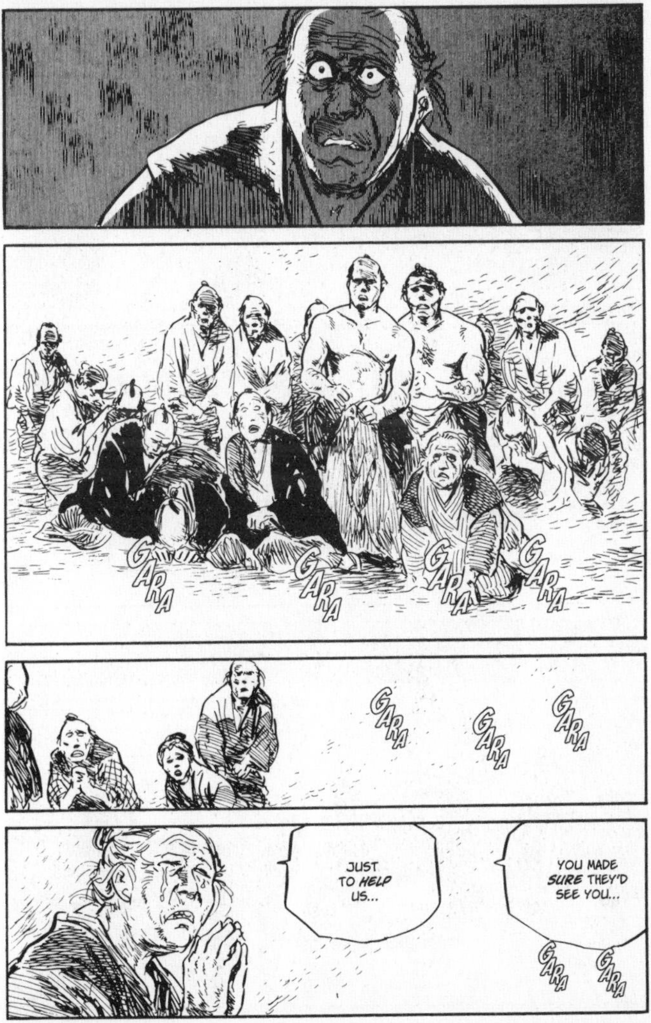
GARA
GARA
GARA
GARA
GARA
GARA
GARA
JUST TO HELP US...
YOU MADE SURE THEY'D SEE YOU...
GARA
GARA

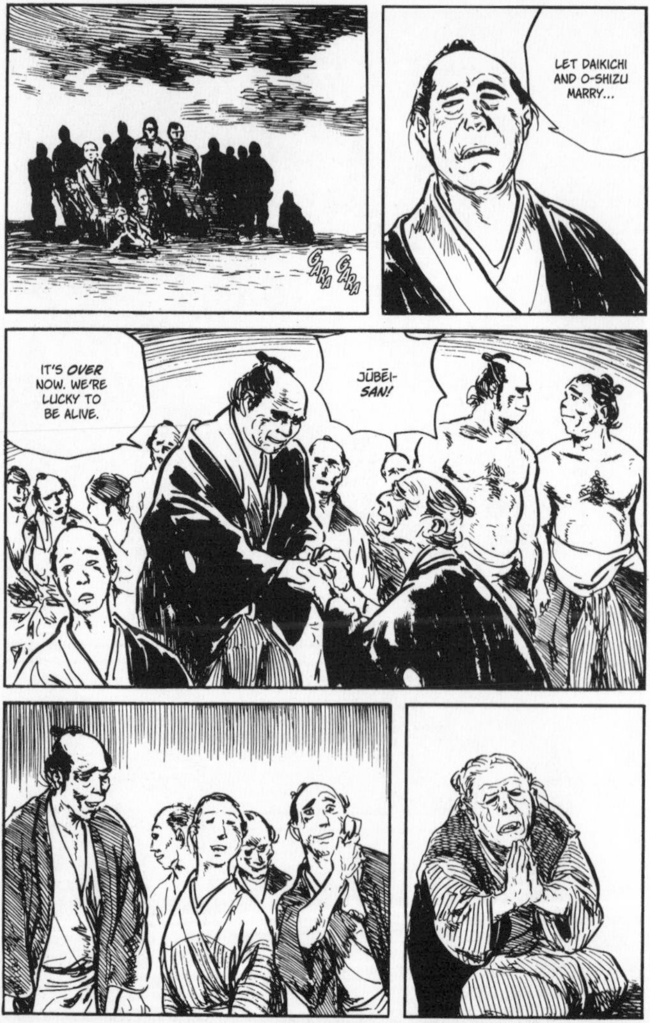
GARA GARA
LET DAIKICHI AND O-SHIZU MARRY...
IT'S OVER NOW. WE'RE LUCKY TO BE ALIVE.
JŪBEI-SAN!

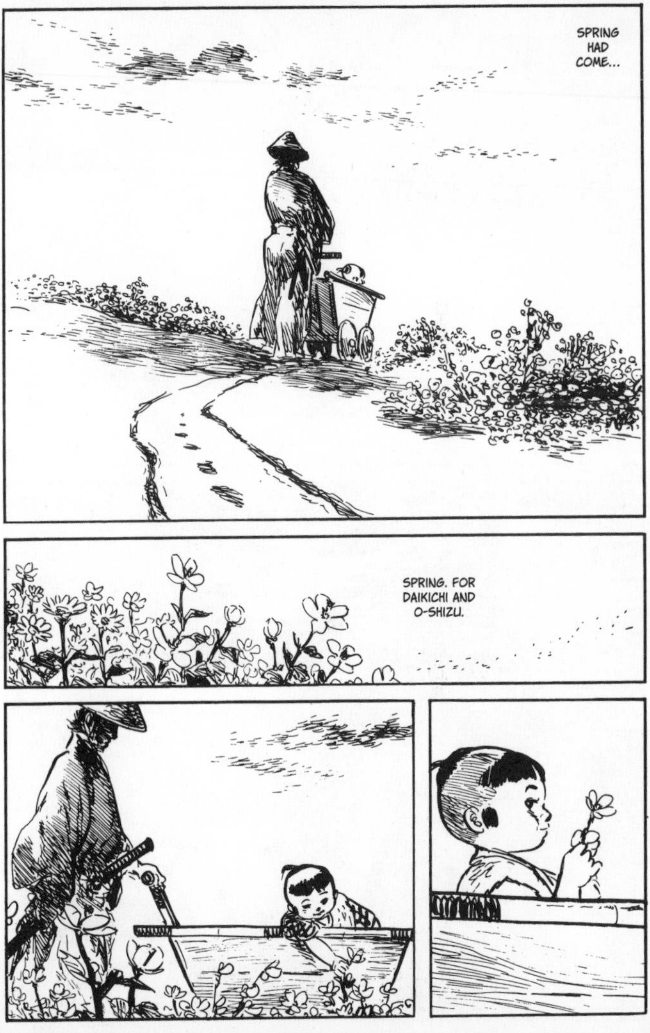
SPRING HAD COME...
SPRING. FOR DAIKICHI AND O-SHIZU.

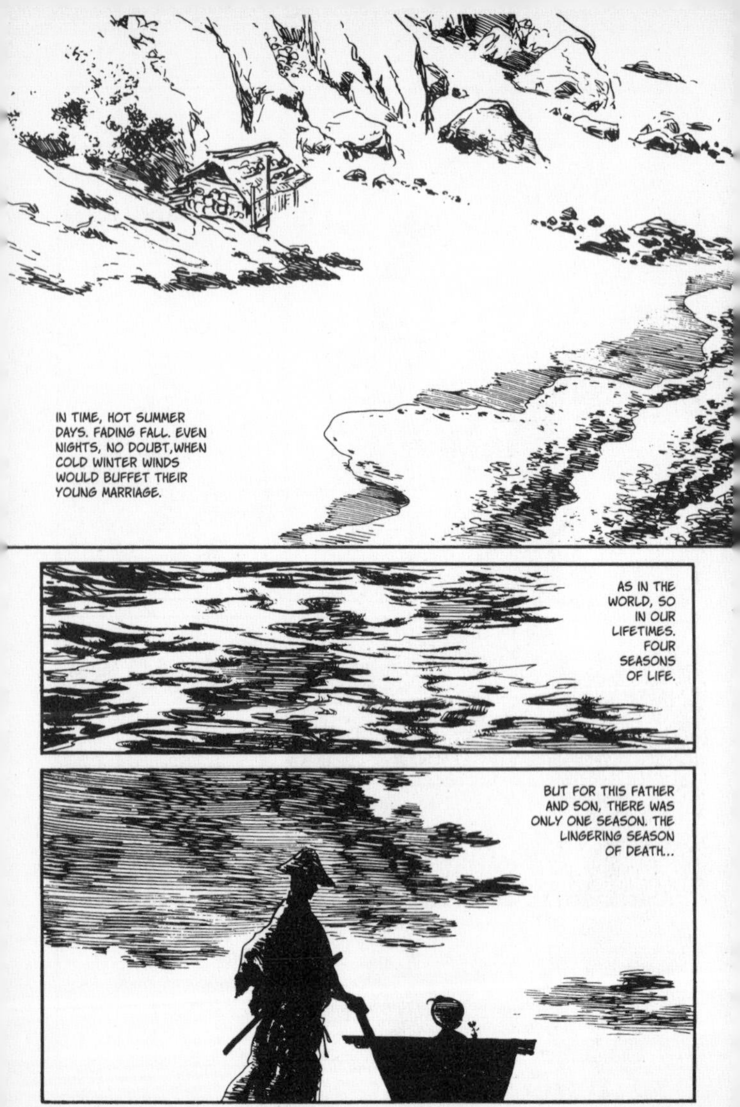
IN TIME, HOT SUMMER DAYS. FADING FALL. EVEN NIGHTS, NO DOUBT, WHEN COLD WINTER WINDS WOULD BUFFET THEIR YOUNG MARRIAGE.
AS IN THE WORLD, SO IN OUR LIFETIMES. FOUR SEASONS OF LIFE.
BUT FOR THIS FATHER AND SON, THERE WAS ONLY ONE SEASON. THE LINGERING SEASON OF DEATH...

the ninety-fourth

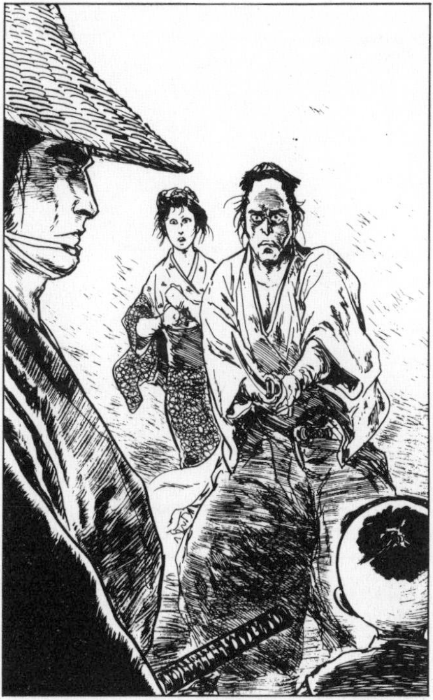

Wives and Lovers

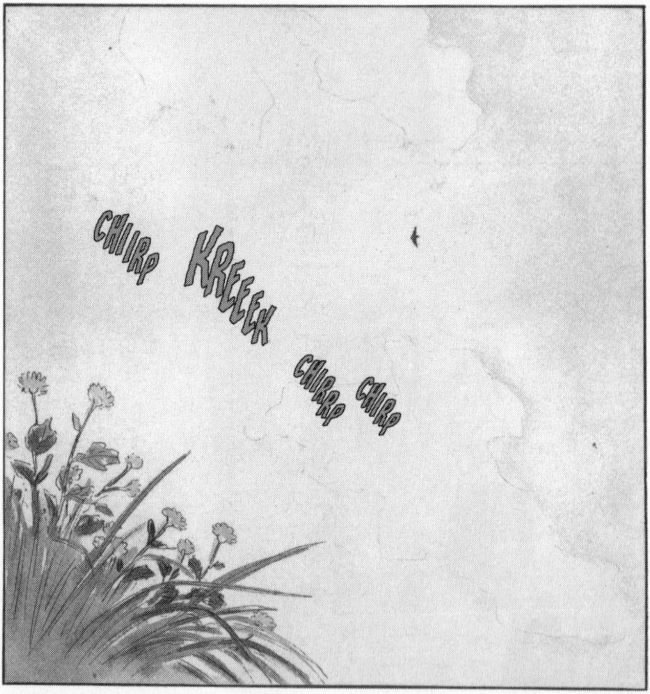
CHIRP
KREEEK
CHIRP
CHIRP
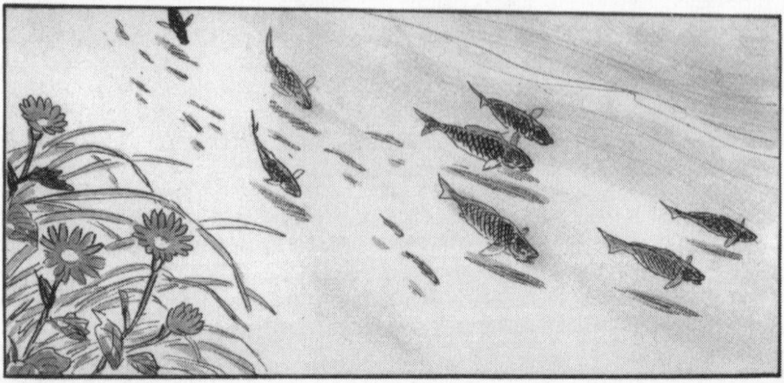

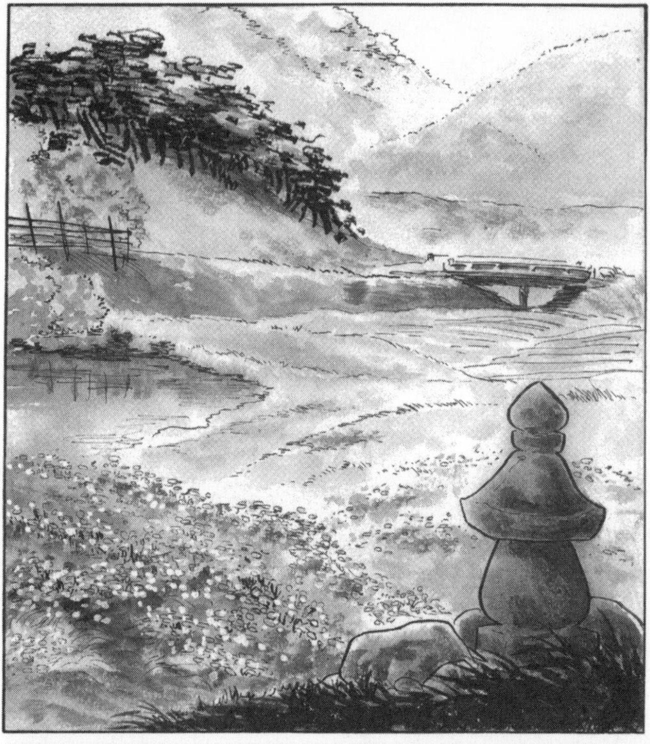
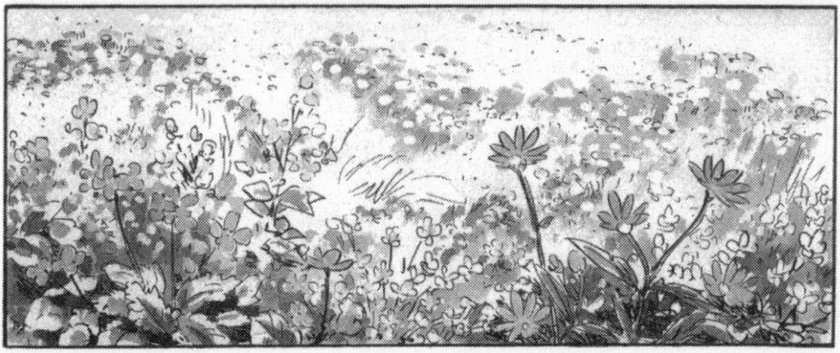

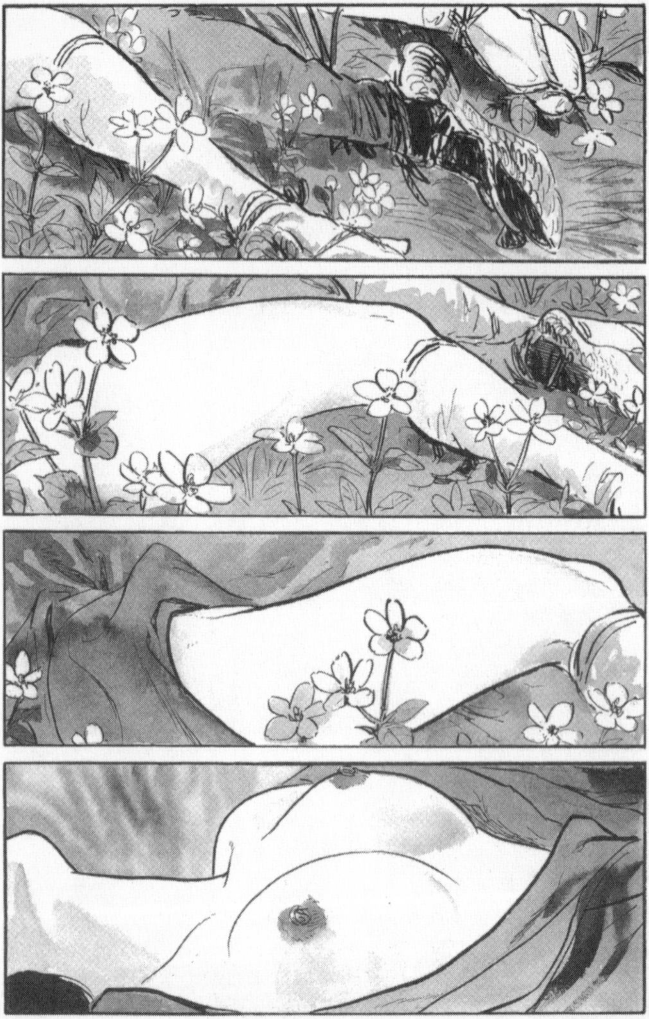

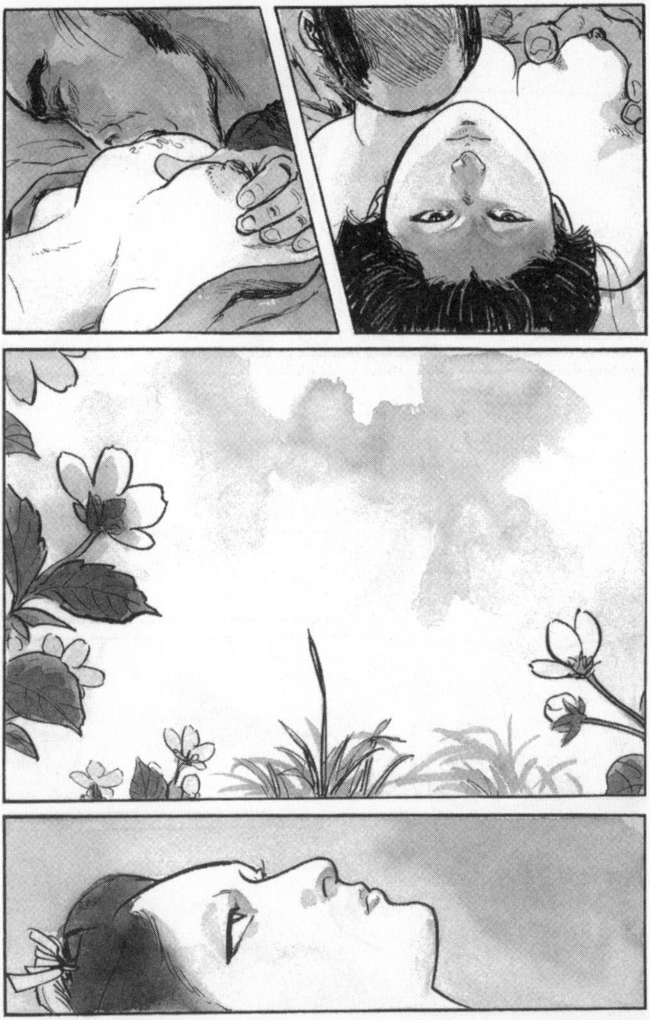

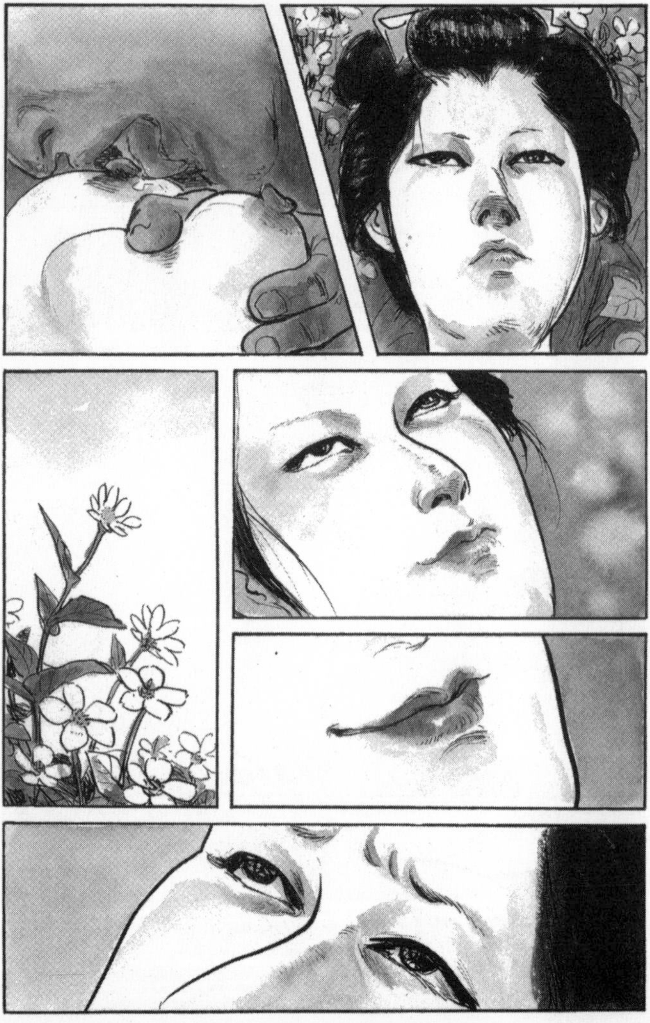

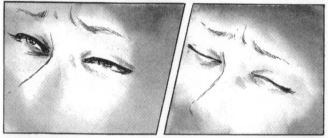

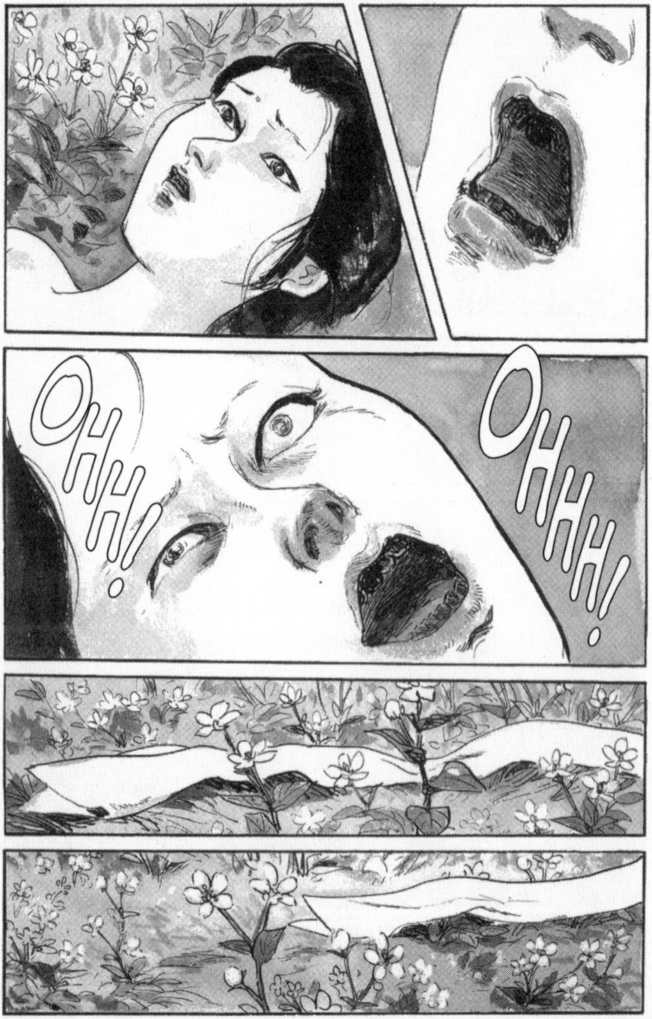
OHH!
OHHH!

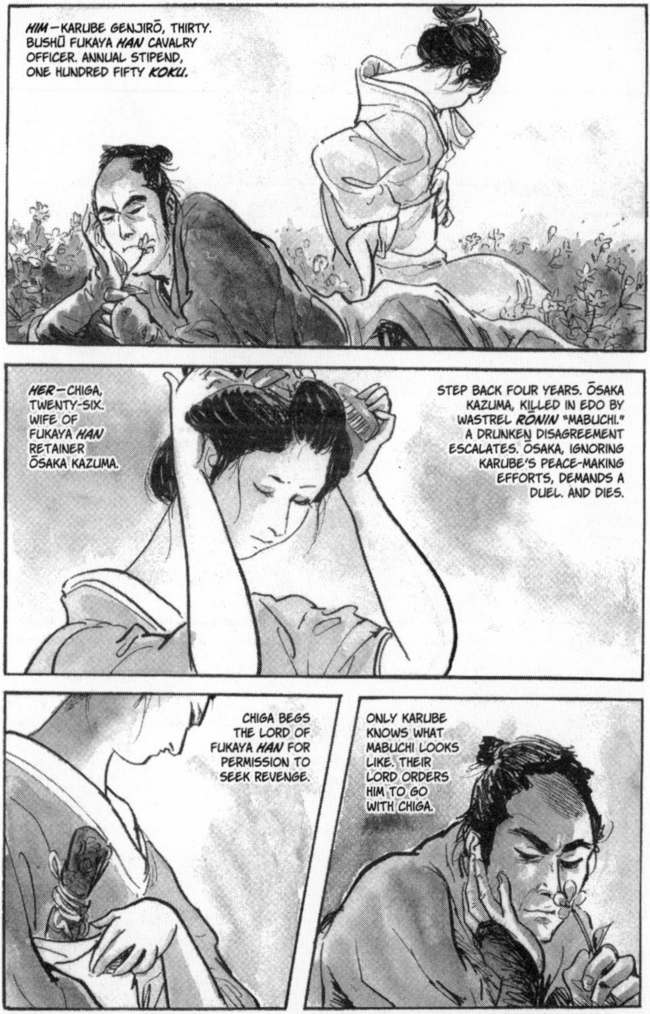

HIM—KARUBE GENJIRŌ, THIRTY. BUSHŪ FUKAYA HAN CAVALRY OFFICER. ANNUAL STIPEND, ONE HUNDRED FIFTY KOKU.
HER—CHIGA, TWENTY-SIX. WIFE OF FUKAYA HAN RETAINER ŌSAKA KAZUMA.
STEP BACK FOUR YEARS. ŌSAKA KAZUMA, KILLED IN EDO BY WASTREL RŌNIN "MABUCHI." A DRUNKEN DISAGREEMENT ESCALATES. ŌSAKA, IGNORING KARUBE'S PEACE-MAKING EFFORTS, DEMANDS A DUEL. AND DIES.
CHIGA BEGS THE LORD OF FUKAYA HAN FOR PERMISSION TO SEEK REVENGE.
ONLY KARUBE KNOWS WHAT MABUCHI LOOKS LIKE. THEIR LORD ORDERS HIM TO GO WITH CHIGA.

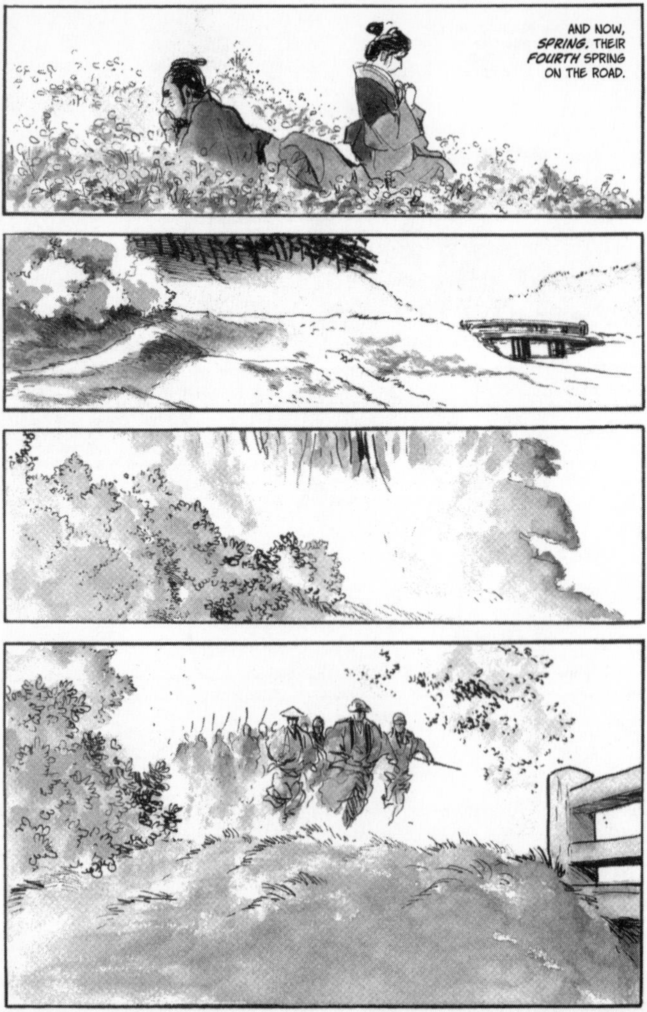
AND NOW, *SPRING.* THEIR *FOURTH* SPRING ON THE ROAD.

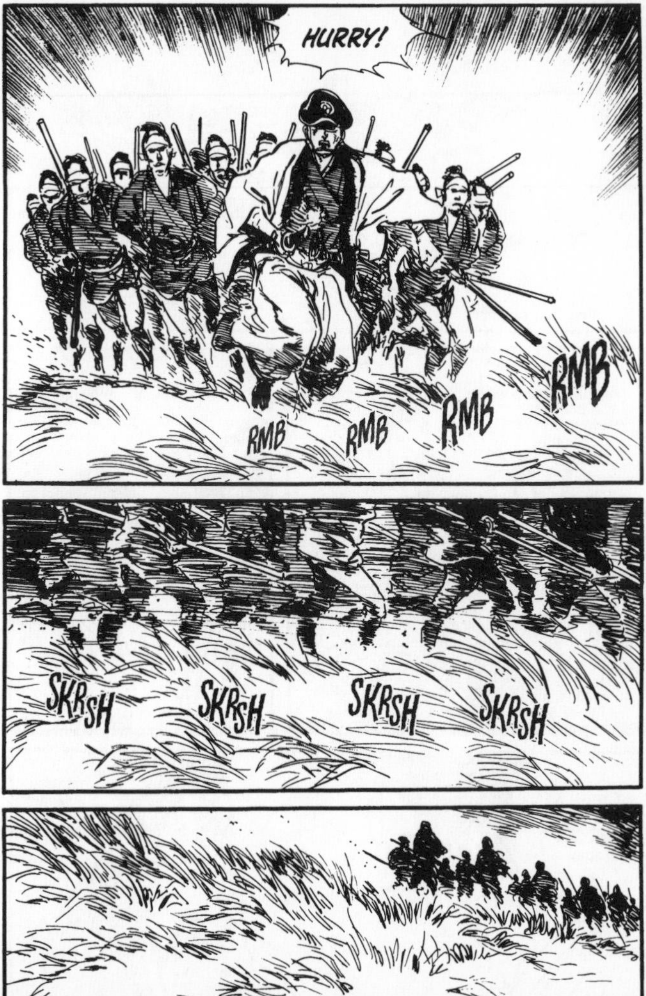
HURRY!
RMB
RMB
RMB
RMB
SKRSH
SKRSH
SKRSH
SKRSH

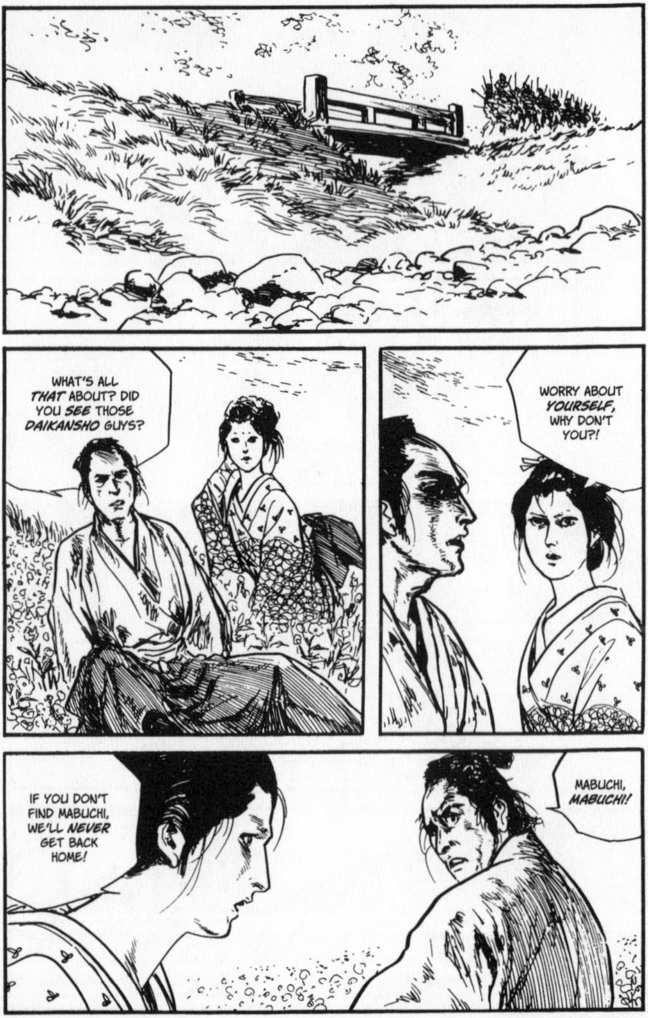
WHAT'S ALL *THAT* ABOUT? DID YOU *SEE* THOSE *DAIKANSHO* GUYS?
WORRY ABOUT *YOURSELF,* WHY DON'T YOU?!
IF YOU DON'T FIND MABUCHI, WE'LL *NEVER* GET BACK HOME!
MABUCHI, *MABUCHI!*

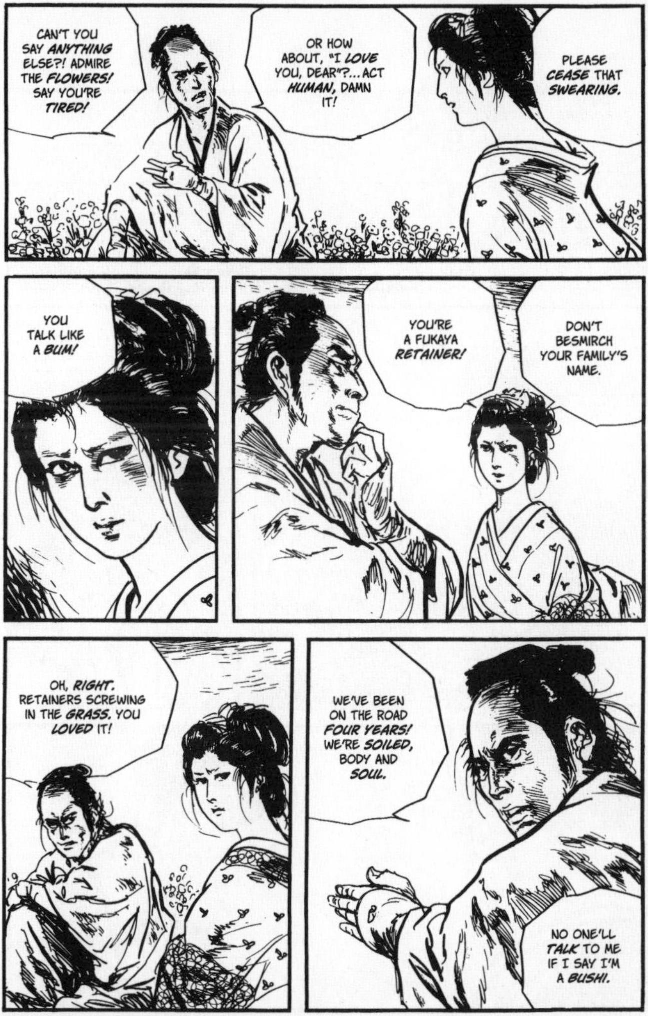
CAN'T YOU SAY ANYTHING ELSE?! ADMIRE THE FLOWERS! SAY YOU'RE TIRED!
OR HOW ABOUT, "I LOVE YOU, DEAR"?... ACT HUMAN, DAMN IT!
PLEASE CEASE THAT SWEARING.
YOU TALK LIKE A BUM!
YOU'RE A FUKAYA RETAINER!
DON'T BESMIRCH YOUR FAMILY'S NAME.
OH, RIGHT. RETAINERS SCREWING IN THE GRASS. YOU LOVED IT!
WE'VE BEEN ON THE ROAD FOUR YEARS! WE'RE SOILED, BODY AND SOUL.
NO ONE'LL TALK TO ME IF I SAY I'M A BUSHI.

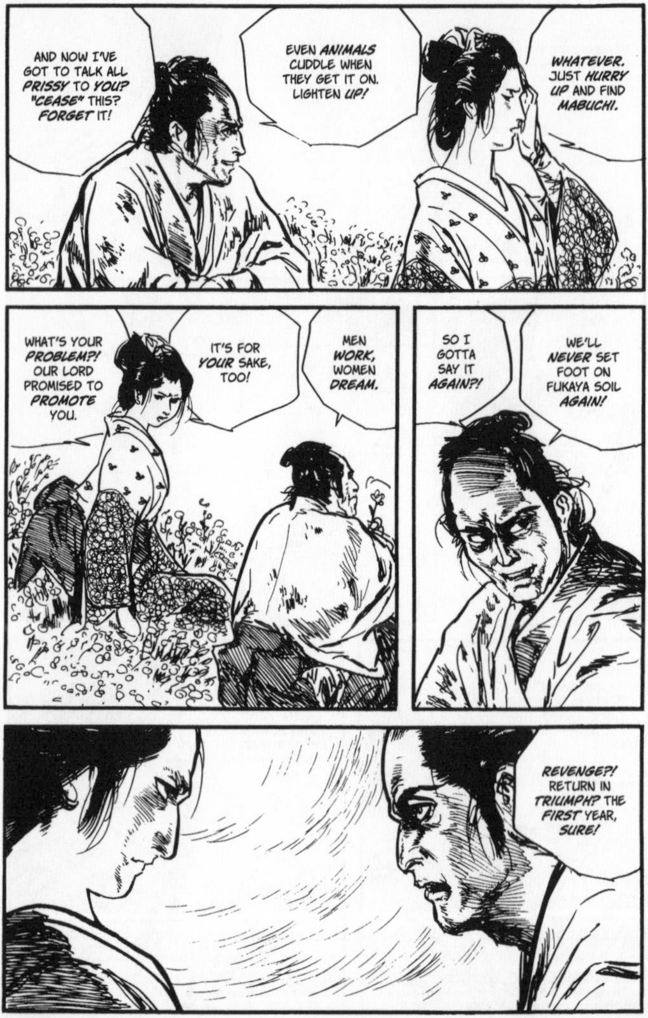
AND NOW I'VE GOT TO TALK ALL PRISSY TO YOU? "CEASE" THIS? FORGET IT!
EVEN ANIMALS CUDDLE WHEN THEY GET IT ON. LIGHTEN UP!
WHATEVER. JUST HURRY UP AND FIND MABUCHI.
WHAT'S YOUR PROBLEM?! OUR LORD PROMISED TO PROMOTE YOU.
IT'S FOR YOUR SAKE, TOO!
MEN WORK, WOMEN DREAM.
SO I GOTTA SAY IT AGAIN?!
WE'LL NEVER SET FOOT ON FUKAYA SOIL AGAIN!
REVENGE?! RETURN IN TRIUMPH? THE FIRST YEAR, SURE!

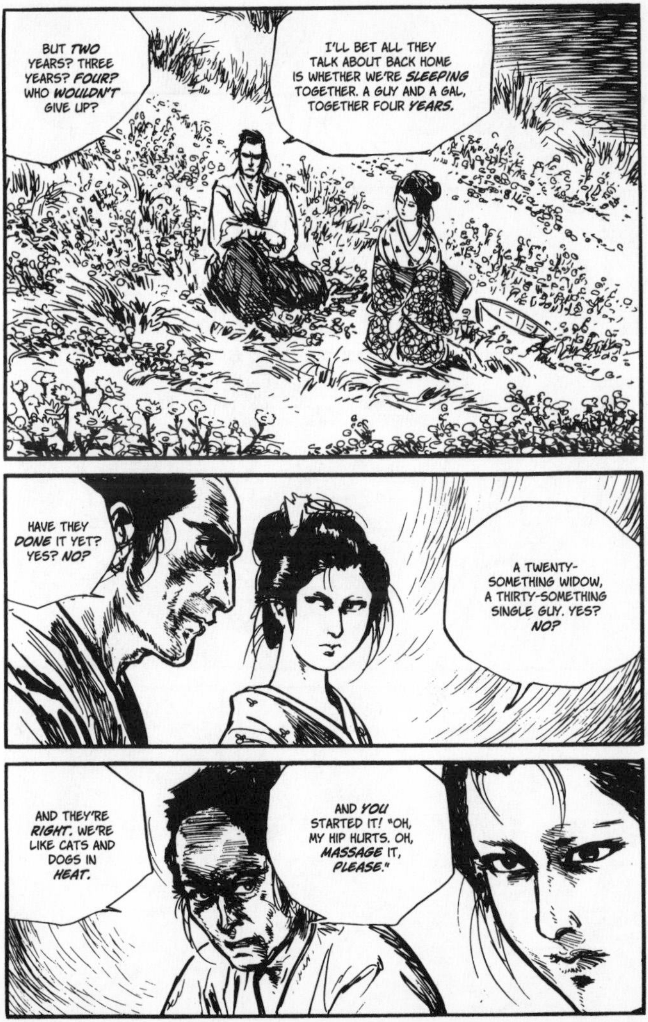
BUT TWO YEARS? THREE YEARS? FOUR? WHO WOULDN'T GIVE UP?
I'LL BET ALL THEY TALK ABOUT BACK HOME IS WHETHER WE'RE SLEEPING TOGETHER. A GUY AND A GAL, TOGETHER FOUR YEARS.
HAVE THEY DONE IT YET? YES? NO?
A TWENTY-SOMETHING WIDOW, A THIRTY-SOMETHING SINGLE GUY. YES? NO?
AND THEY'RE RIGHT. WE'RE LIKE CATS AND DOGS IN HEAT.
AND YOU STARTED IT! "OH, MY HIP HURTS. OH, MASSAGE IT, PLEASE."

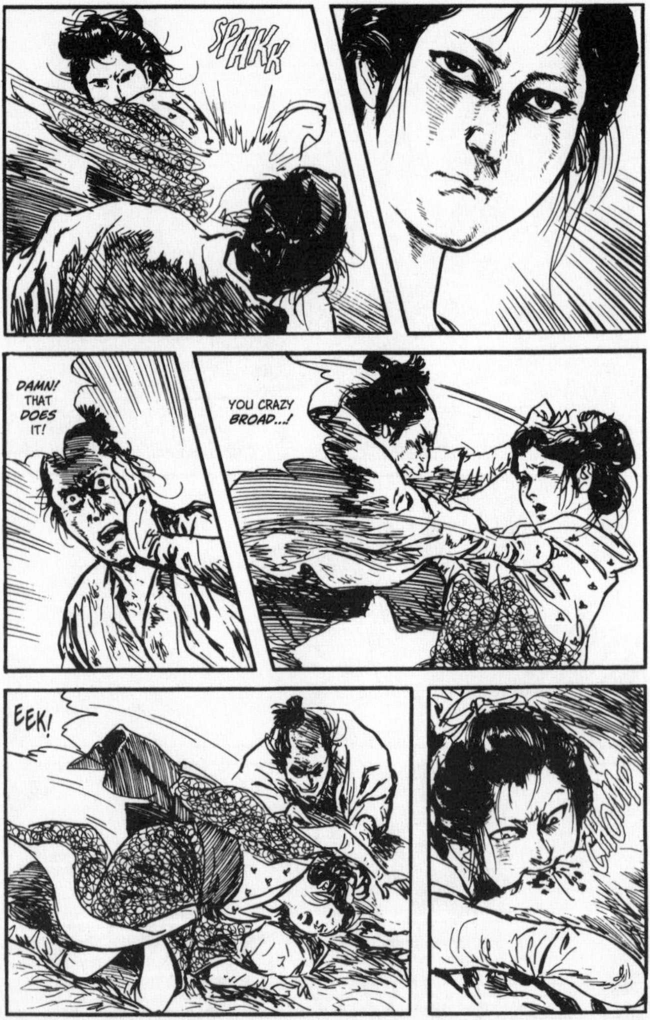
SPAKK
DAMN! THAT DOES IT!
YOU CRAZY BROAD...!
EEK!
CHOMP

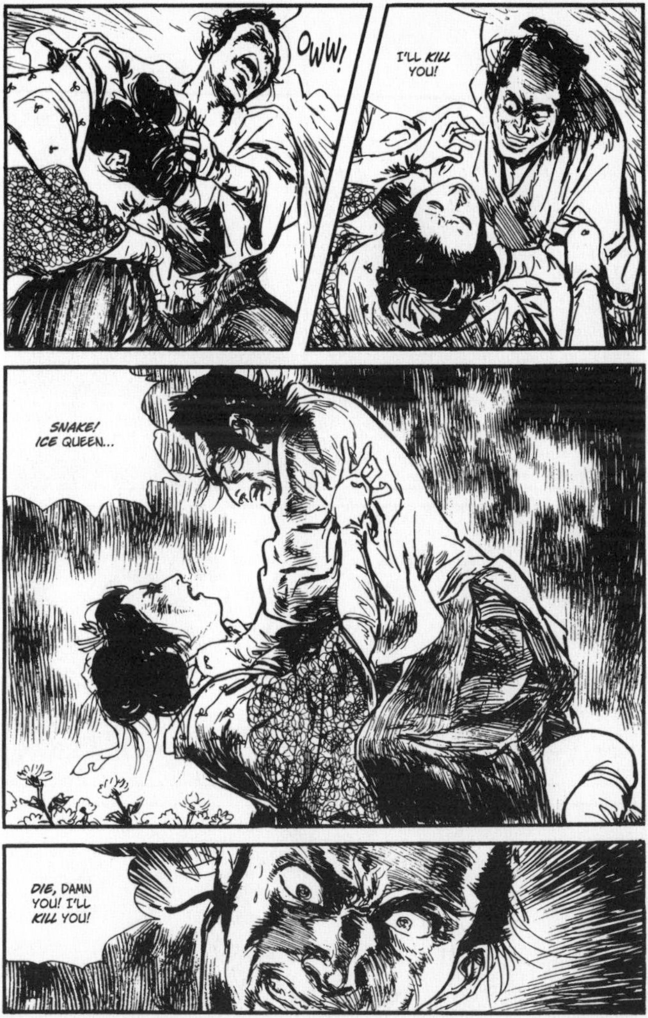
OWW!
I'LL KILL YOU!
SNAKE! ICE QUEEN...
DIE, DAMN YOU! I'LL KILL YOU!

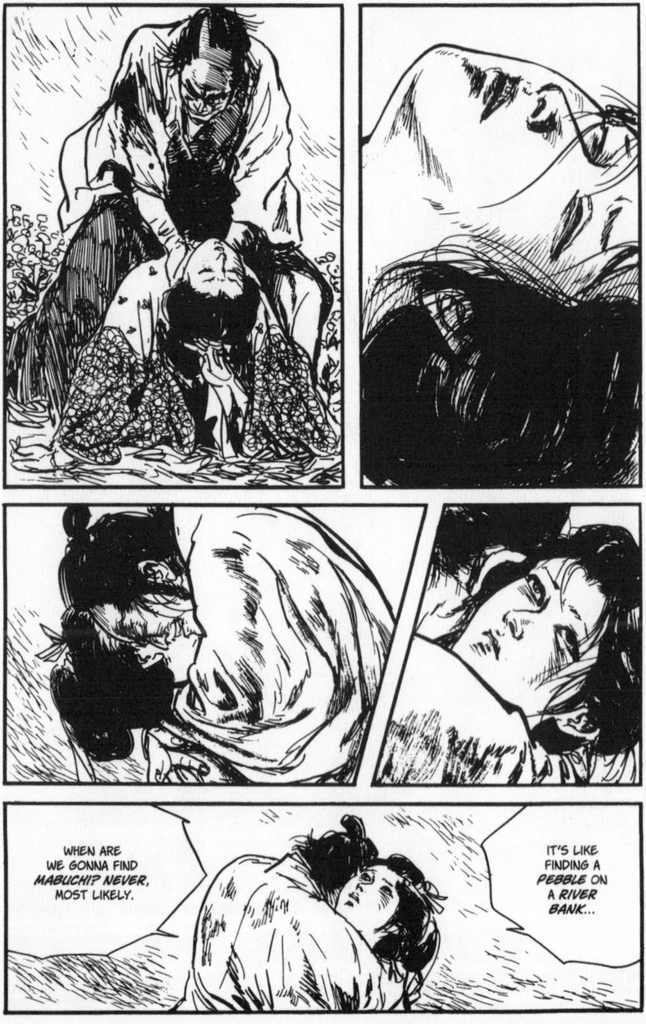
WHEN ARE WE GONNA FIND MABUCHI? NEVER, MOST LIKELY.
IT'S LIKE FINDING A PEBBLE ON A RIVER BANK...

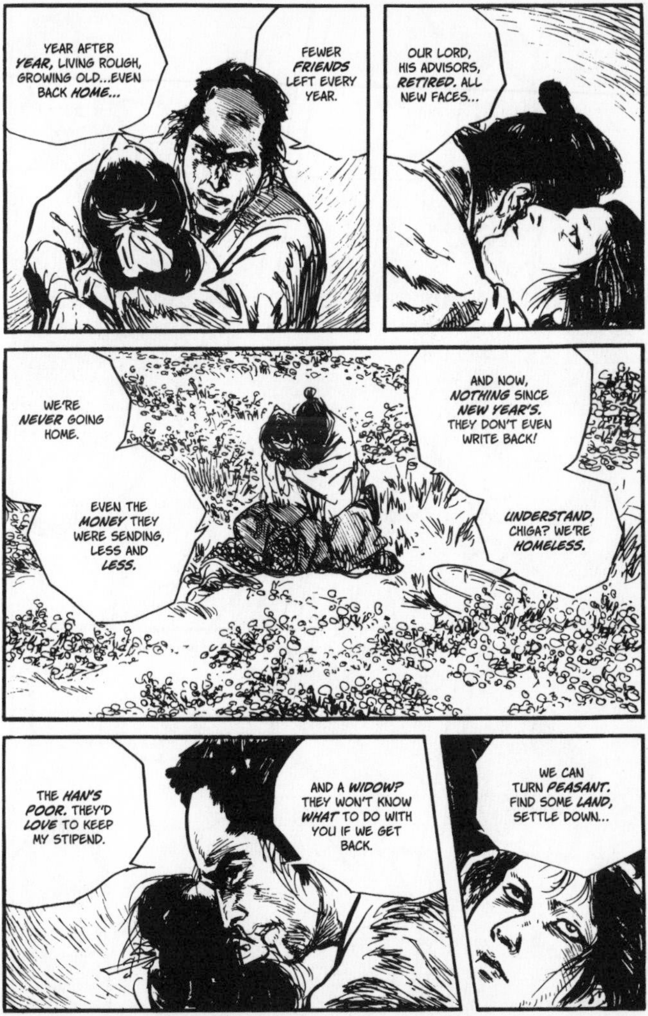
YEAR AFTER YEAR, LIVING ROUGH, GROWING OLD...EVEN BACK HOME...
FEWER FRIENDS LEFT EVERY YEAR.
OUR LORD, HIS ADVISORS, RETIRED. ALL NEW FACES...
WE'RE NEVER GOING HOME.
EVEN THE MONEY THEY WERE SENDING, LESS AND LESS.
AND NOW, NOTHING SINCE NEW YEAR'S. THEY DON'T EVEN WRITE BACK!
UNDERSTAND, CHIGA? WE'RE HOMELESS.
THE HAN'S POOR. THEY'D LOVE TO KEEP MY STIPEND.
AND A WIDOW? THEY WON'T KNOW WHAT TO DO WITH YOU IF WE GET BACK.
WE CAN TURN PEASANT. FIND SOME LAND, SETTLE DOWN...

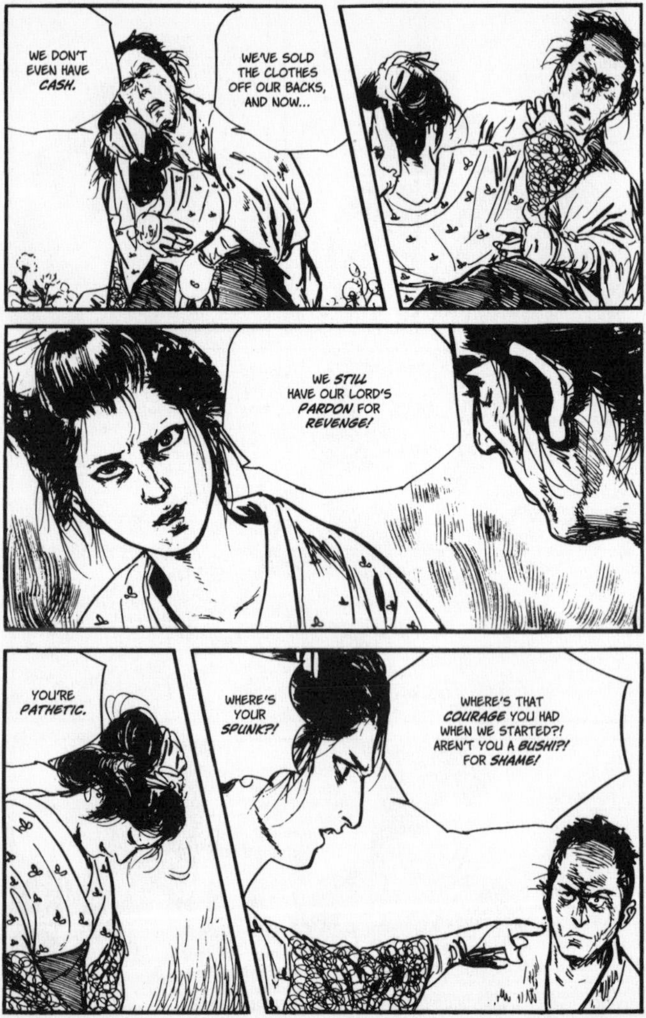
WE DON'T EVEN HAVE CASH.
WE'VE SOLD THE CLOTHES OFF OUR BACKS, AND NOW...
WE STILL HAVE OUR LORD'S PARDON FOR REVENGE!
YOU'RE PATHETIC.
WHERE'S YOUR SPUNK?!
WHERE'S THAT COURAGE YOU HAD WHEN WE STARTED?! AREN'T YOU A BUSHI?! FOR SHAME!

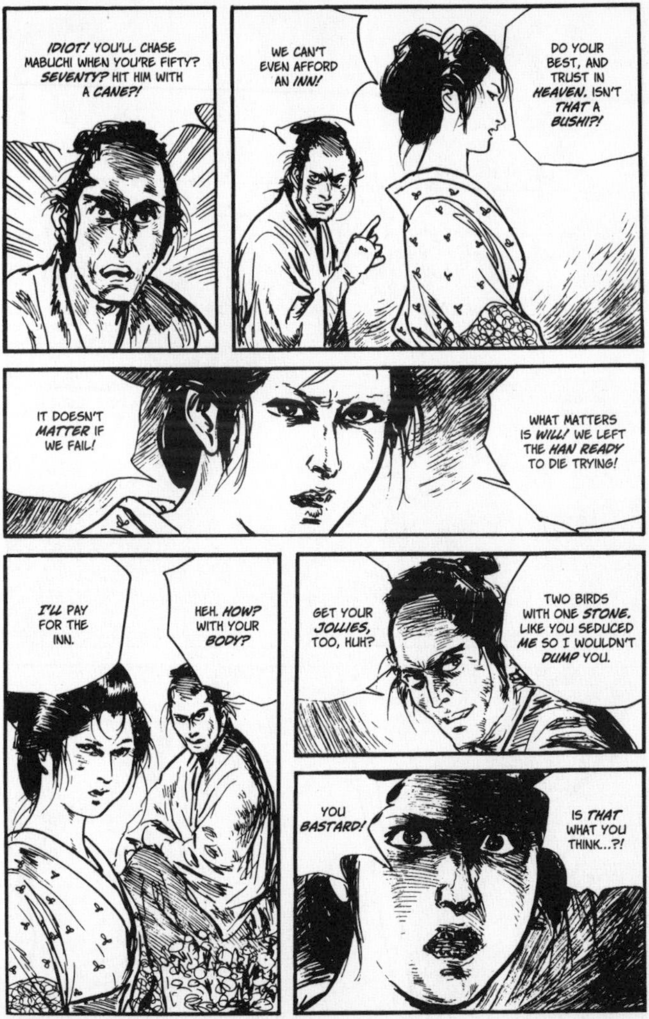
IDIOT! YOU'LL CHASE MABUCHI WHEN YOU'RE FIFTY? SEVENTY? HIT HIM WITH A CANE?!
WE CAN'T EVEN AFFORD AN INN!
DO YOUR BEST, AND TRUST IN HEAVEN. ISN'T THAT A BUSHI?!
IT DOESN'T MATTER IF WE FAIL!
WHAT MATTERS IS WILL! WE LEFT THE HAN READY TO DIE TRYING!
I'LL PAY FOR THE INN.
HEH. HOW? WITH YOUR BODY?
GET YOUR JOLLIES, TOO, HUH?
TWO BIRDS WITH ONE STONE. LIKE YOU SEDUCED ME SO I WOULDN'T DUMP YOU.
YOU BASTARD!
IS THAT WHAT YOU THINK...?!

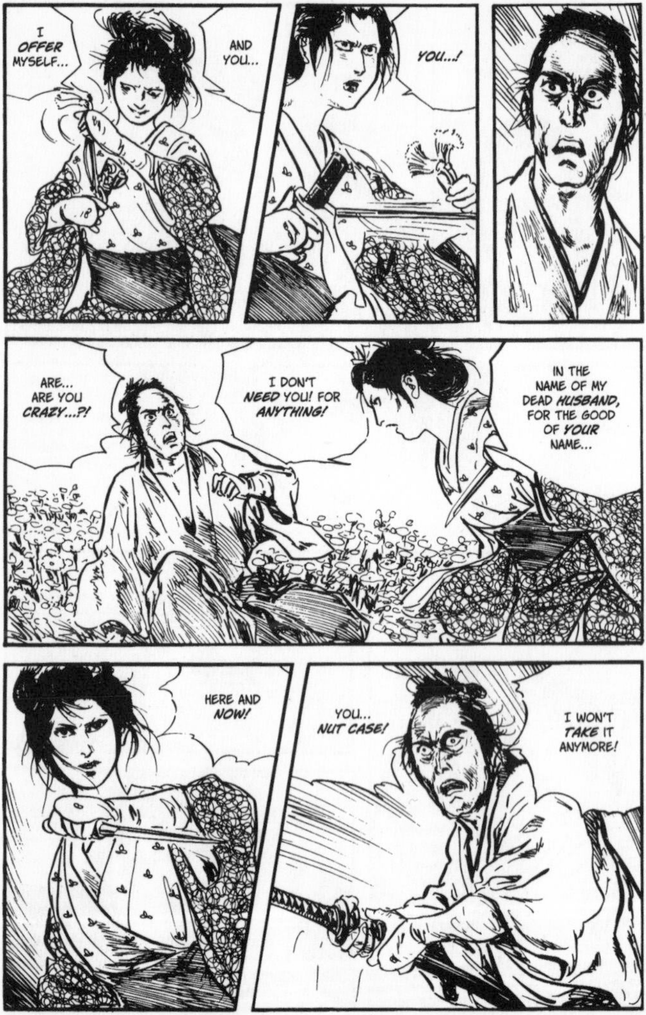
I OFFER MYSELF...
AND YOU...
YOU...!
ARE... ARE YOU CRAZY...?!
I DON'T NEED YOU! FOR ANYTHING!
IN THE NAME OF MY DEAD HUSBAND, FOR THE GOOD OF YOUR NAME...
HERE AND NOW!
YOU... NUT CASE!
I WON'T TAKE IT ANYMORE!

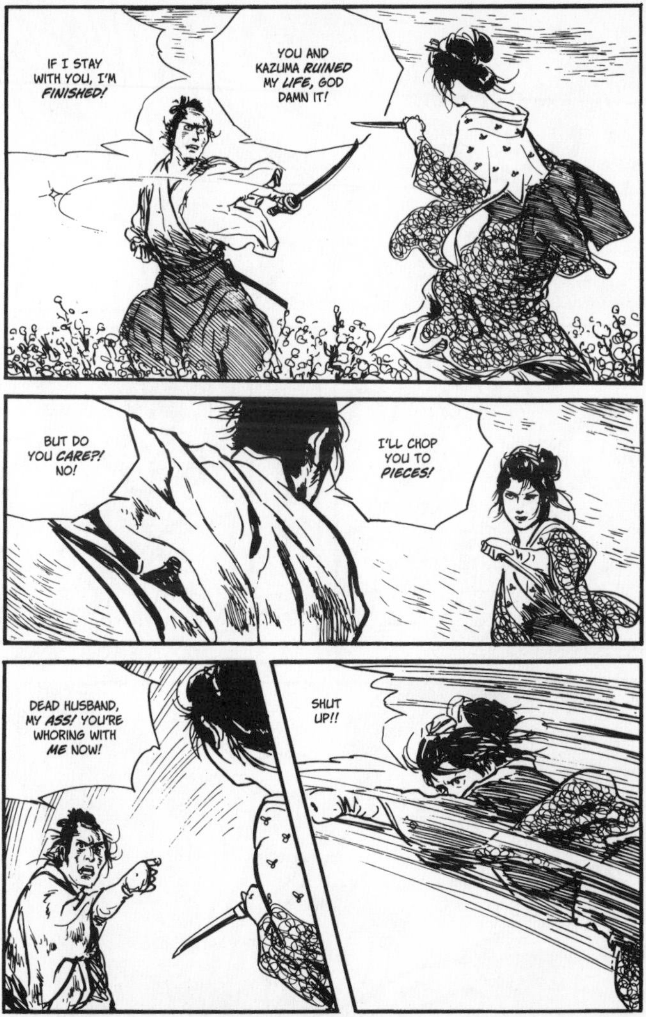
IF I STAY WITH YOU, I'M FINISHED!
YOU AND KAZUMA RUINED MY LIFE, GOD DAMN IT!
BUT DO YOU CARE?! NO!
I'LL CHOP YOU TO PIECES!
DEAD HUSBAND, MY ASS! YOU'RE WHORING WITH ME NOW!
SHUT UP!!

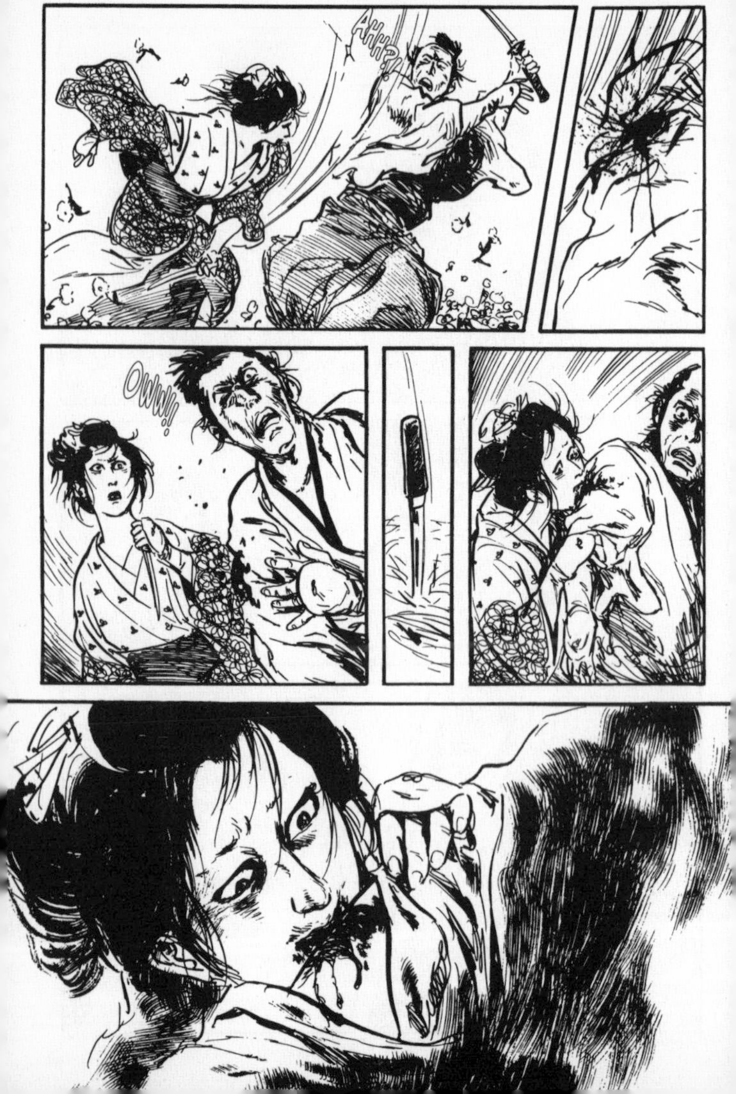
AHH?!
OWW!!

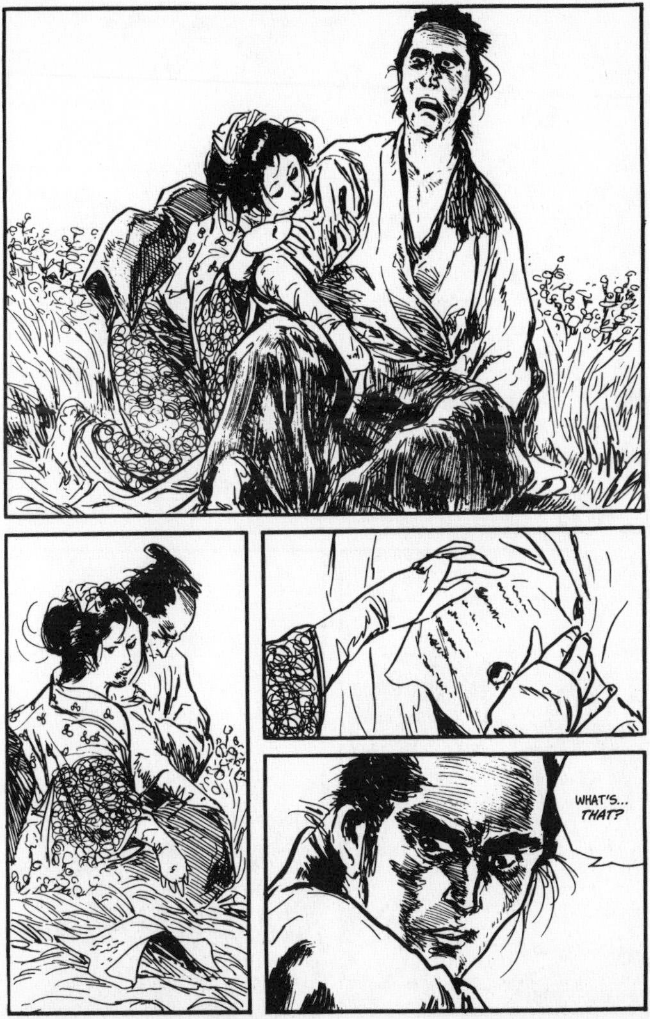
WHAT'S...
THAT?

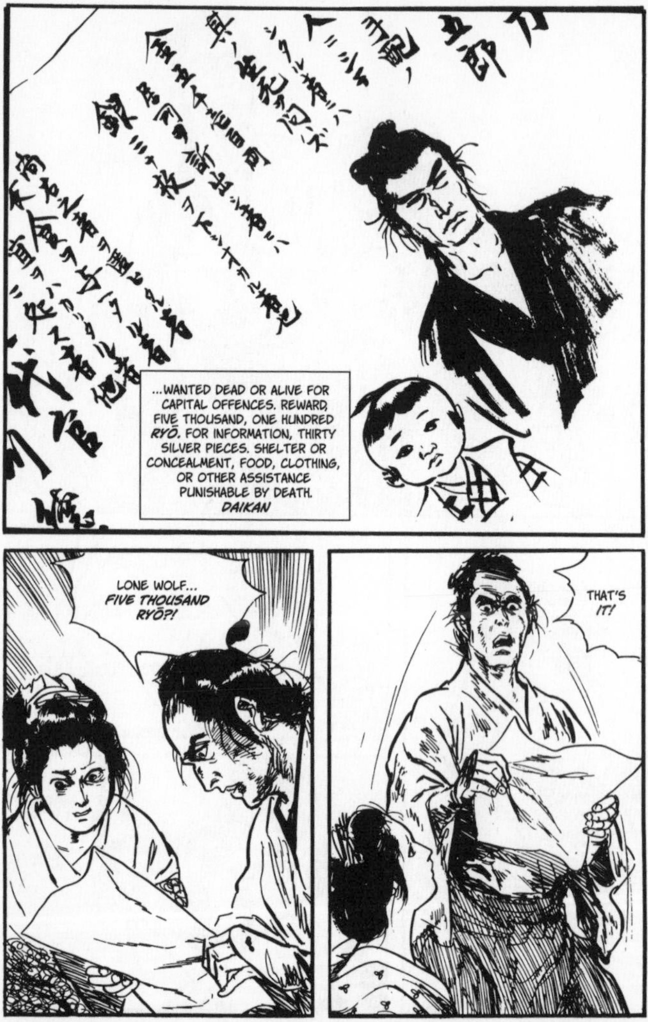
...WANTED DEAD OR ALIVE FOR CAPITAL OFFENCES. REWARD, FIVE THOUSAND, ONE HUNDRED *RYŌ*. FOR INFORMATION, THIRTY SILVER PIECES. SHELTER OR CONCEALMENT, FOOD, CLOTHING, OR OTHER ASSISTANCE PUNISHABLE BY DEATH. *DAIKAN*
LONE WOLF... *FIVE THOUSAND RYŌ?!*
THAT'S *IT!*

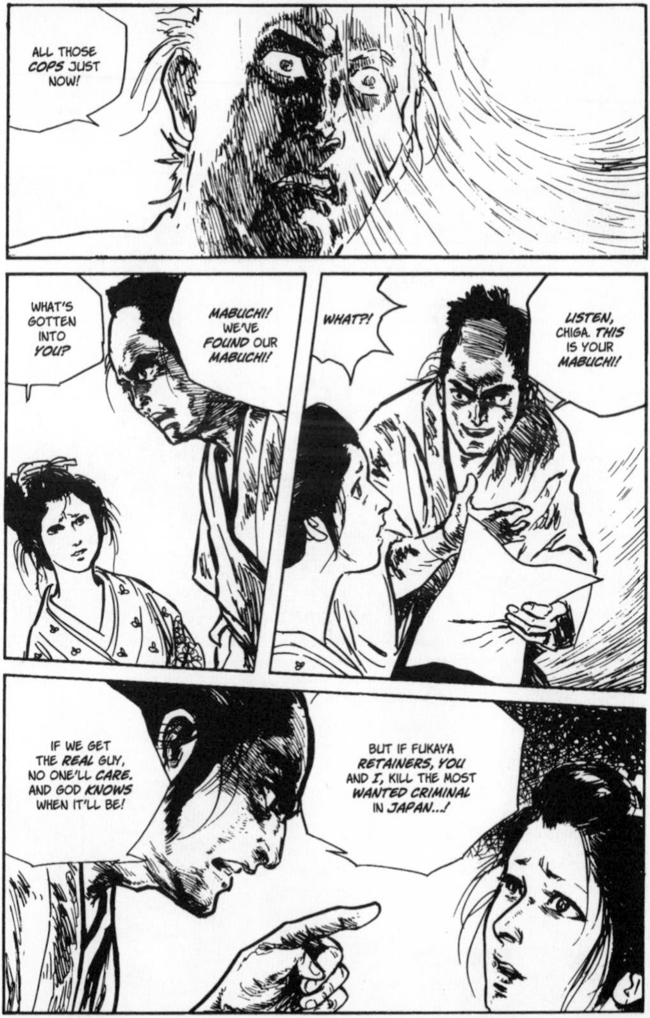
ALL THOSE COPS JUST NOW!
WHAT'S GOTTEN INTO YOU?
MABUCHI! WE'VE FOUND OUR MABUCHI!
WHAT?!
LISTEN, CHIGA. THIS IS YOUR MABUCHI!
IF WE GET THE REAL GUY, NO ONE'LL CARE. AND GOD KNOWS WHEN IT'LL BE!
BUT IF FUKAYA RETAINERS, YOU AND I, KILL THE MOST WANTED CRIMINAL IN JAPAN...!

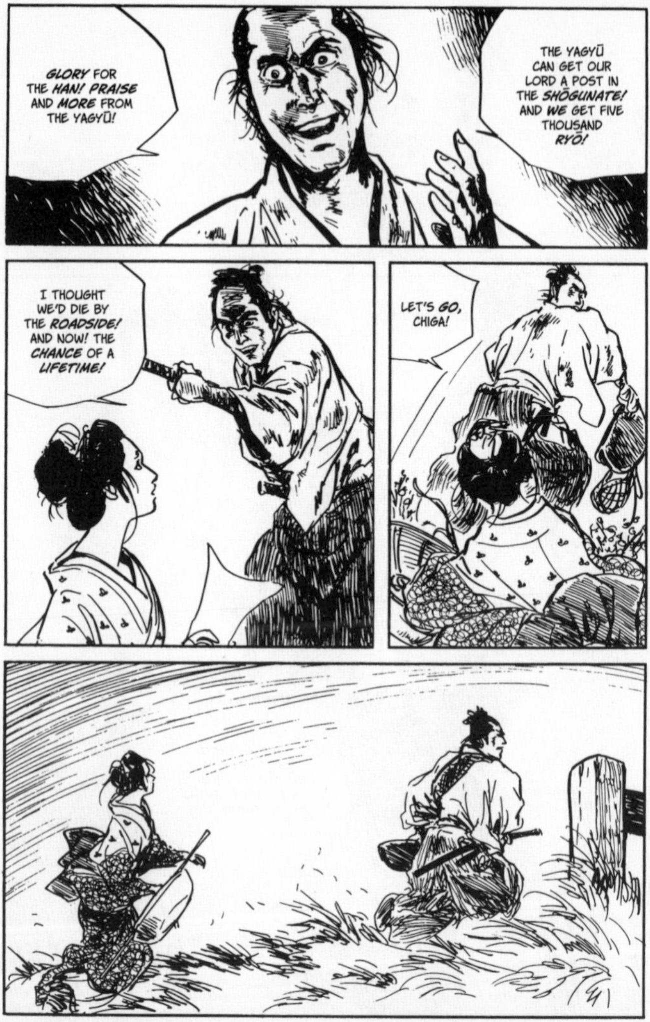
GLORY FOR THE HAN! PRAISE AND MORE FROM THE YAGYŪ!
THE YAGYŪ CAN GET OUR LORD A POST IN THE SHŌGUNATE! AND WE GET FIVE THOUSAND RYŌ!
I THOUGHT WE'D DIE BY THE ROADSIDE! AND NOW! THE CHANCE OF A LIFETIME!
LET'S GO, CHIGA!

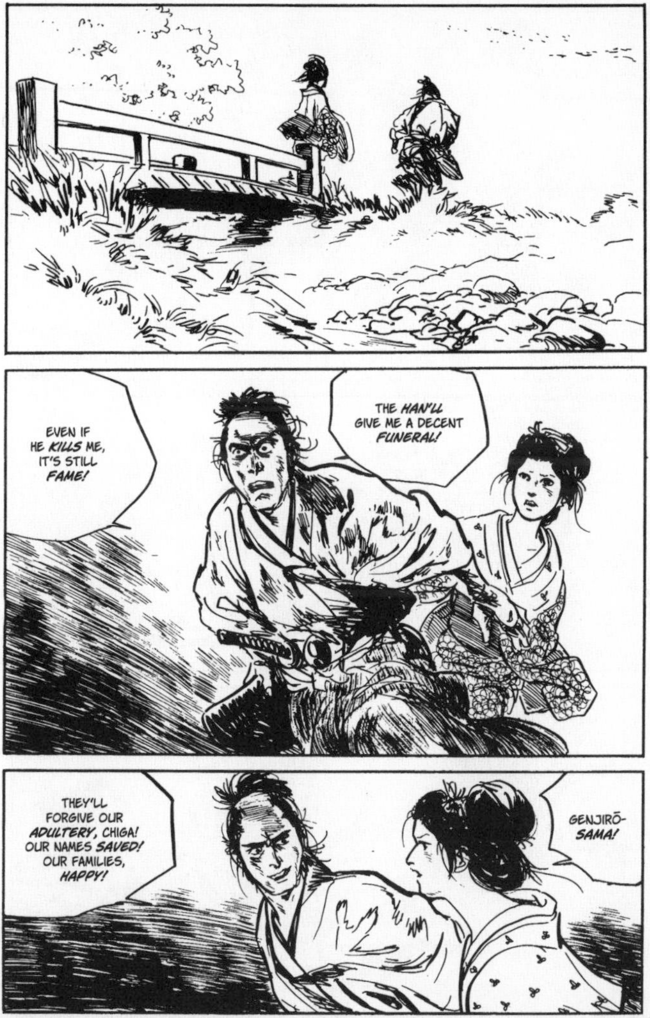
EVEN IF HE *KILLS* ME, IT'S STILL *FAME!*
THE *HAN'LL* GIVE ME A DECENT *FUNERAL!*
THEY'LL FORGIVE OUR *ADULTERY*, CHIGA! OUR NAMES *SAVED!* OUR FAMILIES, *HAPPY!*
GENJIRŌ-*SAMA!*

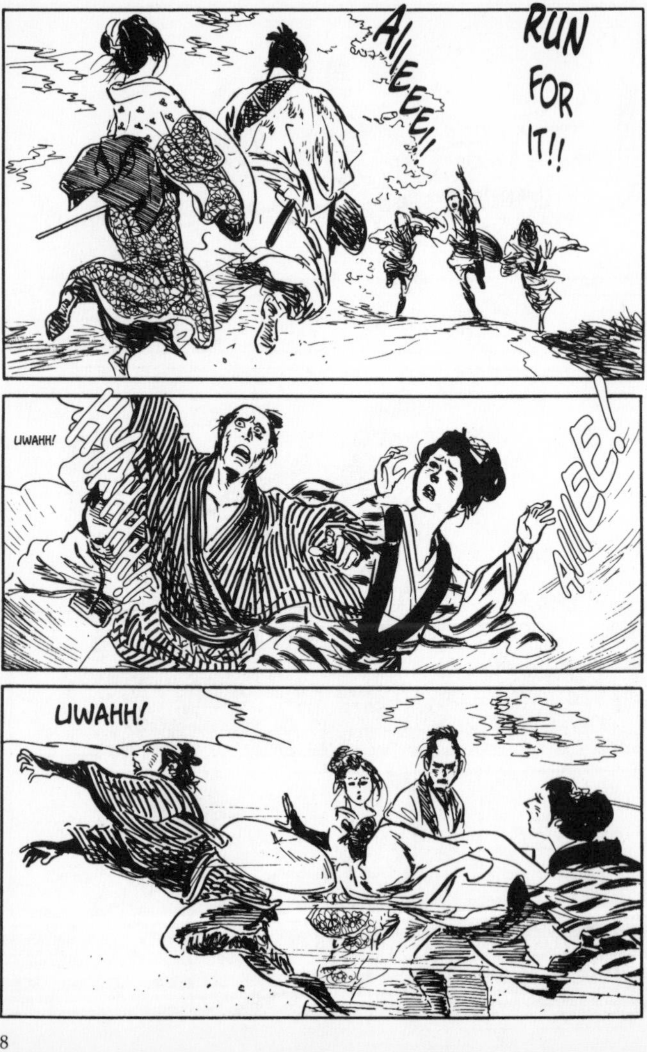
AIEEEE!!
RUN FOR IT!!
UWAHH!
HYAAHHH!!
AIIEEE!
UWAHH!

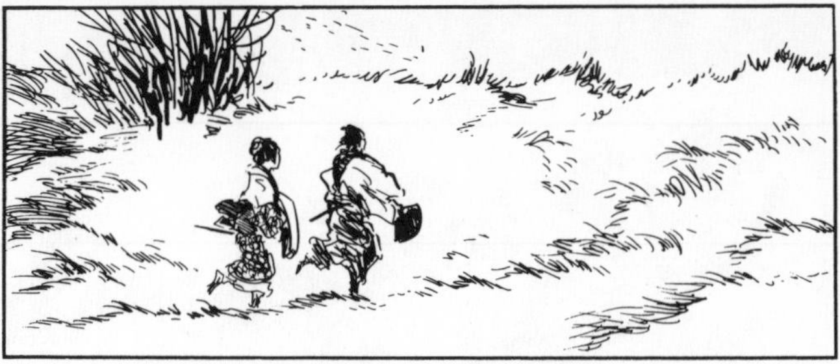
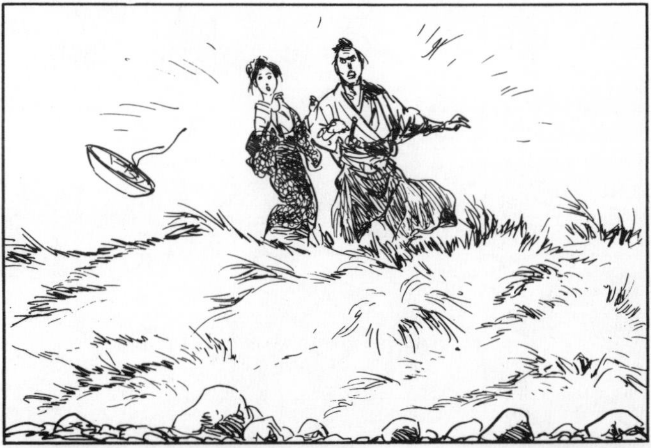
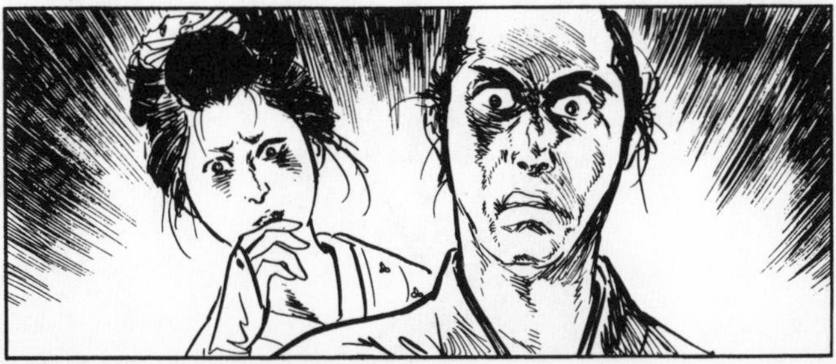

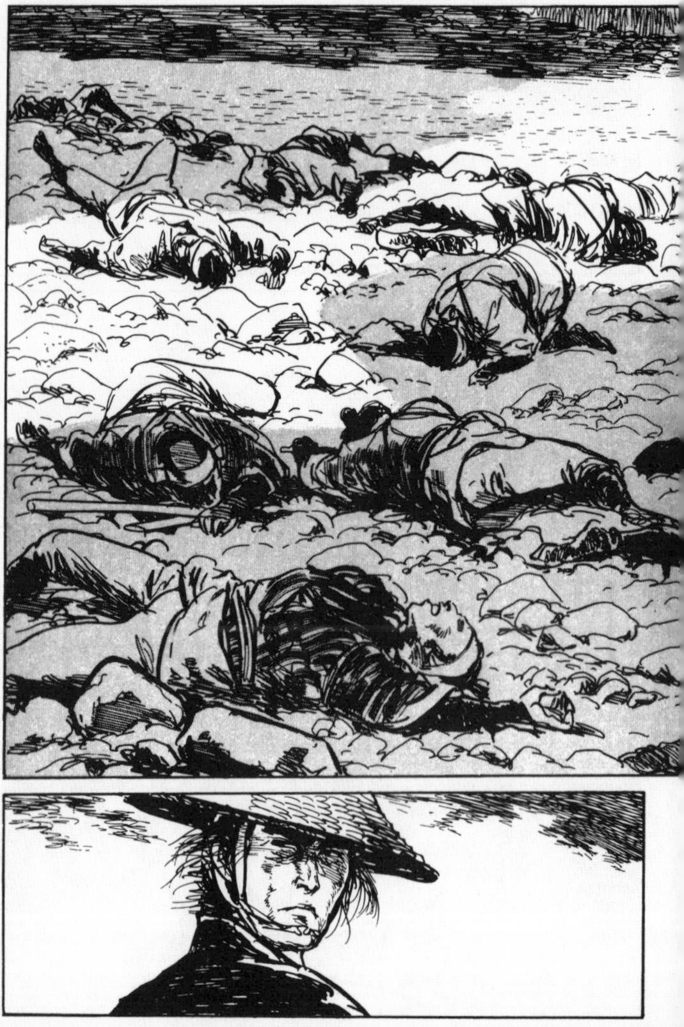

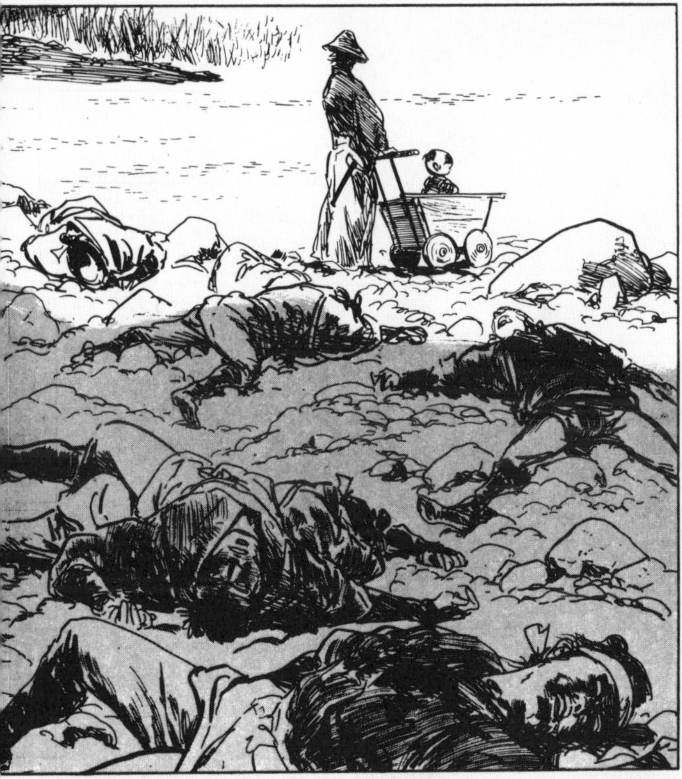

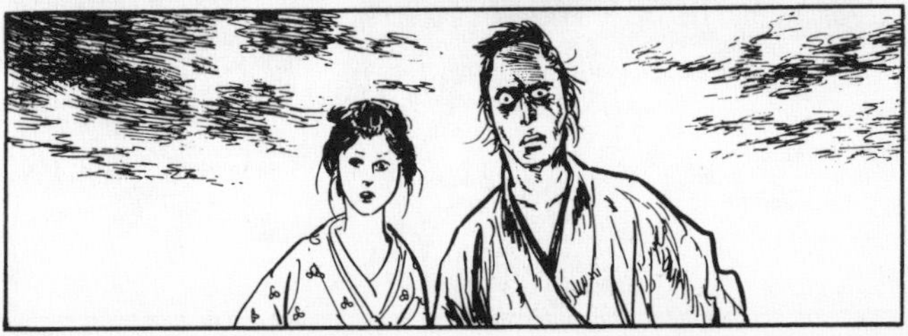

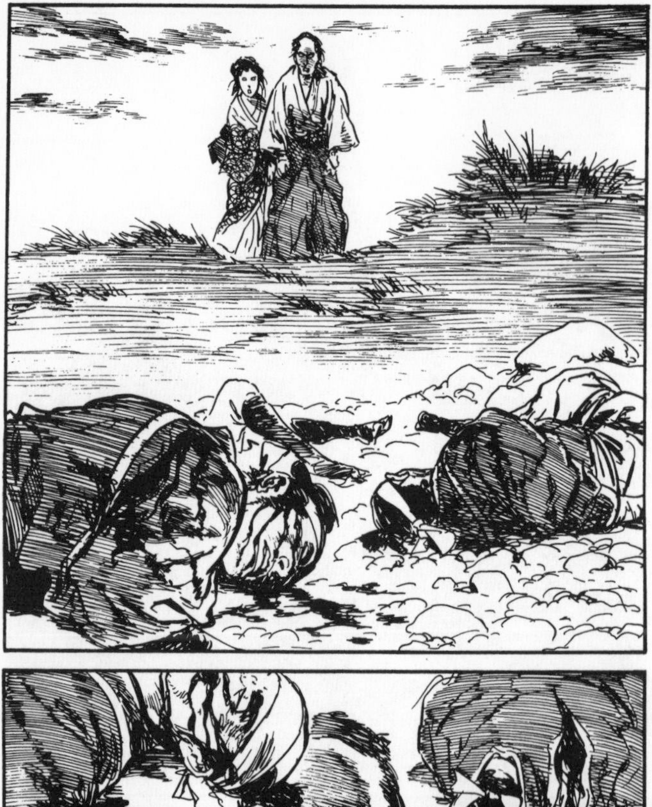

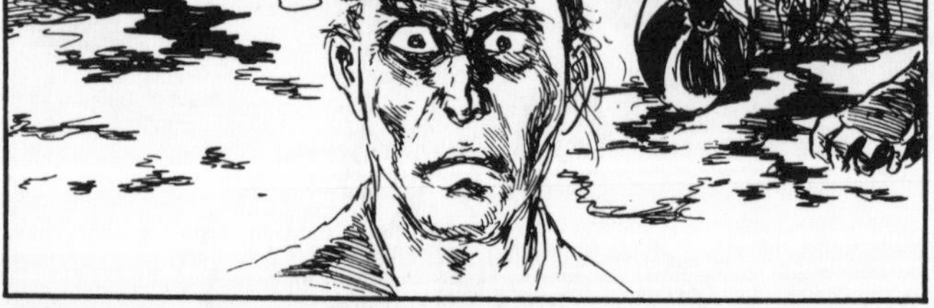

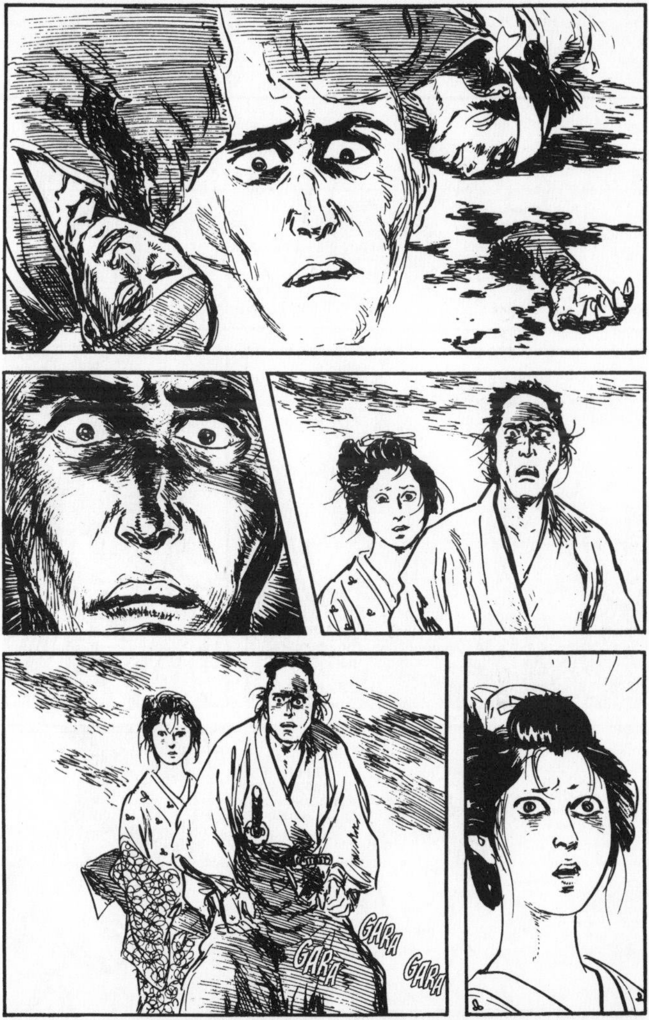
GARA
GARA
GARA

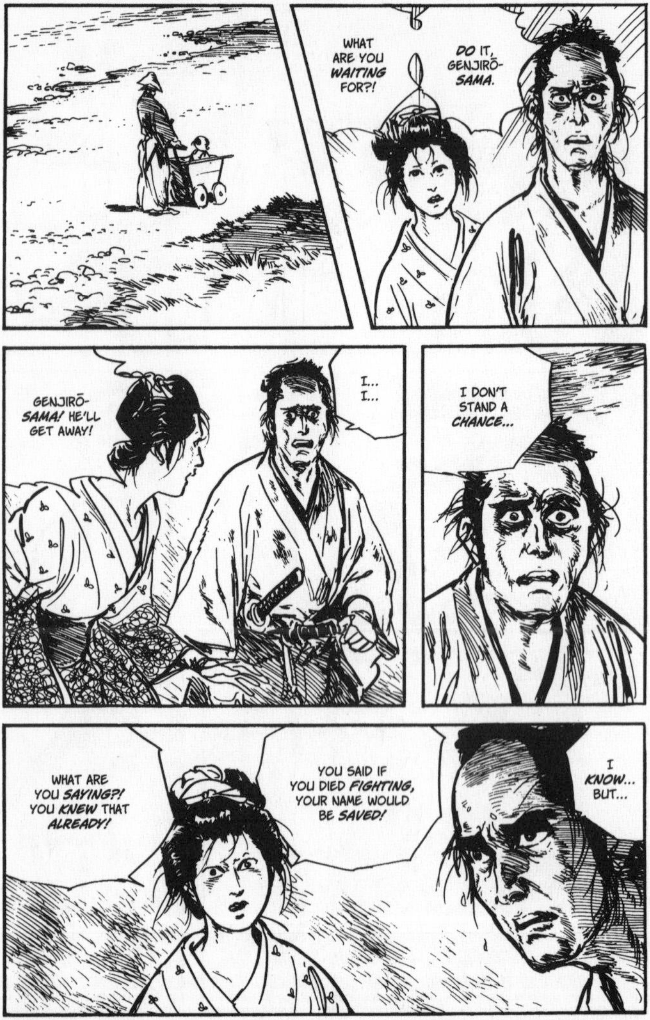
WHAT ARE YOU WAITING FOR?!
DO IT, GENJIRŌ-SAMA.
GENJIRŌ-SAMA! HE'LL GET AWAY!
I... I...
I DON'T STAND A CHANCE...
WHAT ARE YOU SAYING?! YOU KNEW THAT ALREADY!
YOU SAID IF YOU DIED FIGHTING, YOUR NAME WOULD BE SAVED!
I KNOW... BUT...

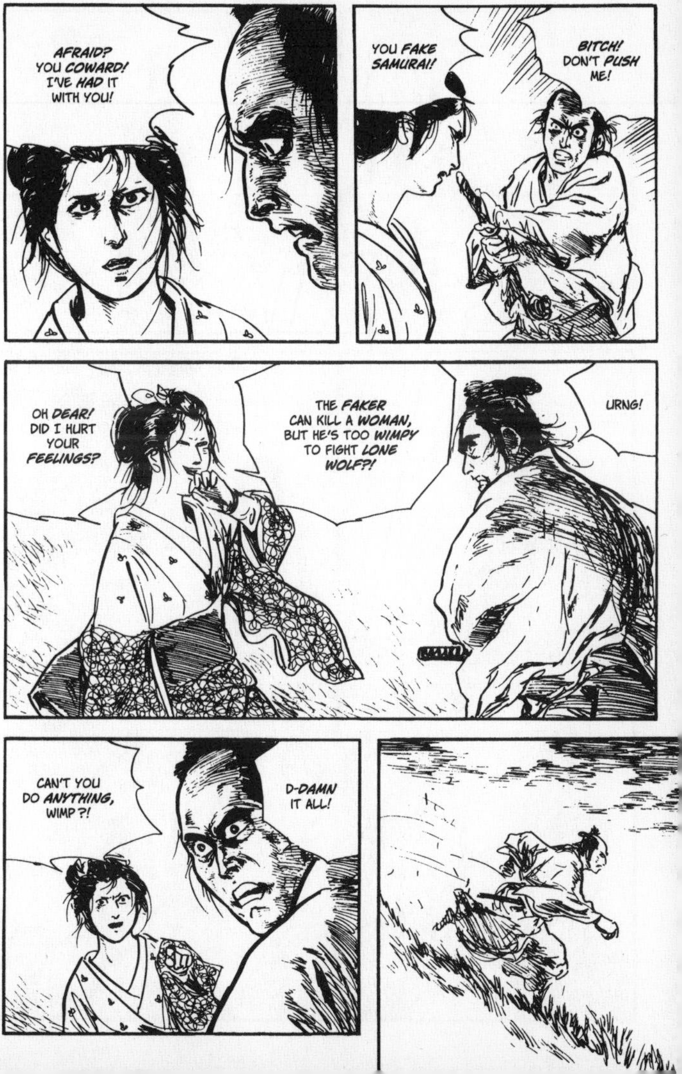
AFRAID? YOU COWARD! I'VE HAD IT WITH YOU!
YOU FAKE SAMURAI!
BITCH! DON'T PUSH ME!
OH DEAR! DID I HURT YOUR FEELINGS?
THE FAKER CAN KILL A WOMAN, BUT HE'S TOO WIMPY TO FIGHT LONE WOLF?!
URNG!
CAN'T YOU DO ANYTHING, WIMP?!
D-DAMN IT ALL!

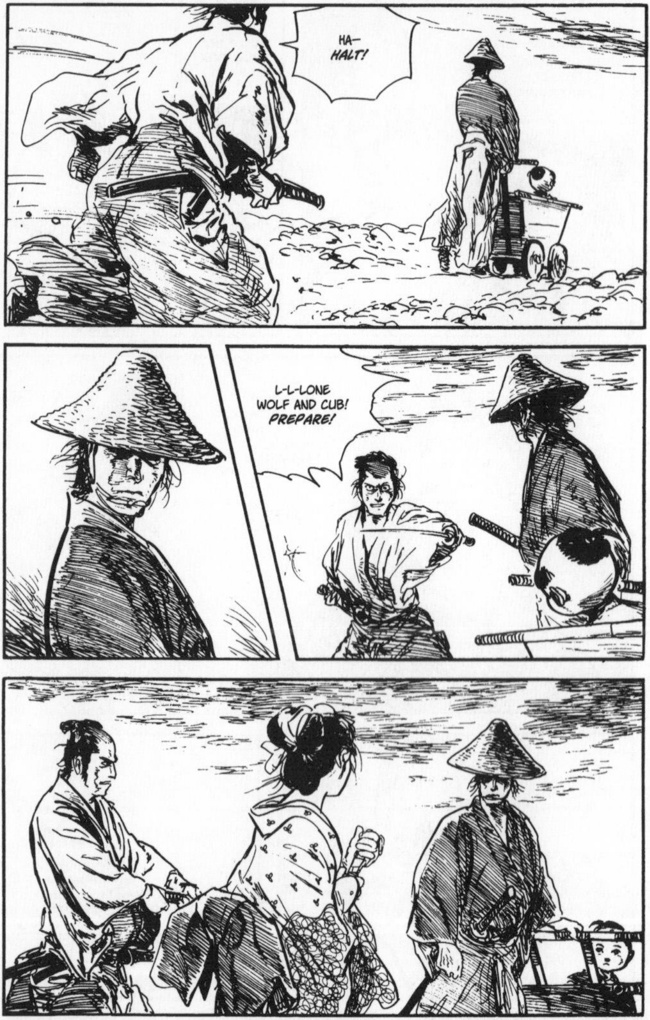
HA-
HALT!
L-L-LONE
WOLF AND CUB!
PREPARE!

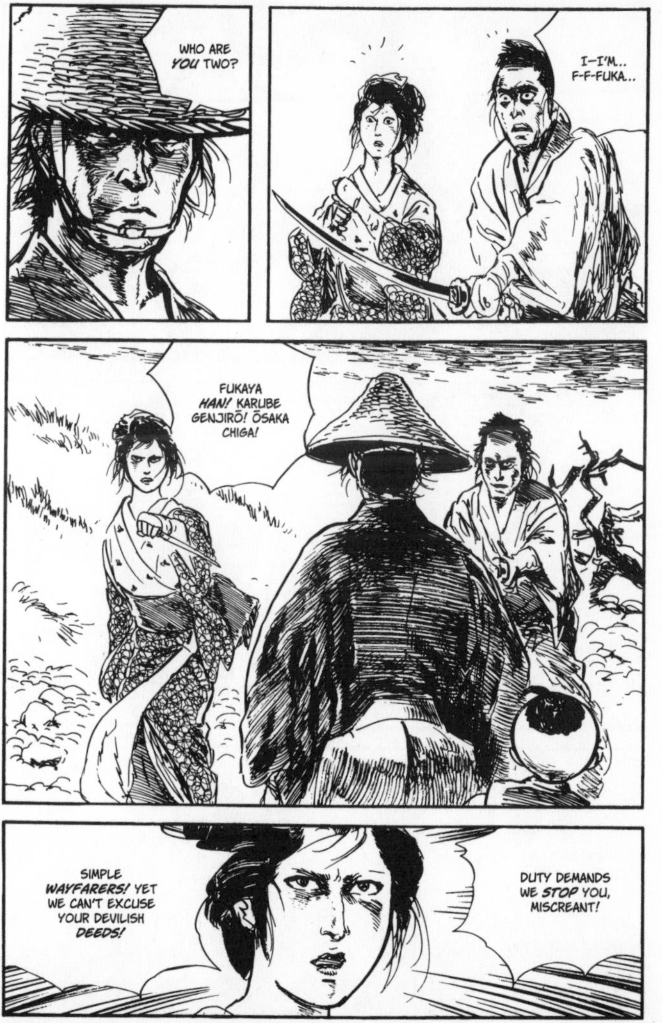
WHO ARE *YOU* TWO?
I—I'M.. F-F-FUKA...
FUKAYA *HAN!* KARUBE GENJIRŌ! ŌSAKA CHIGA!
SIMPLE *WAYFARERS!* YET WE CAN'T EXCUSE YOUR DEVILISH *DEEDS!*
DUTY DEMANDS WE *STOP* YOU, MISCREANT!

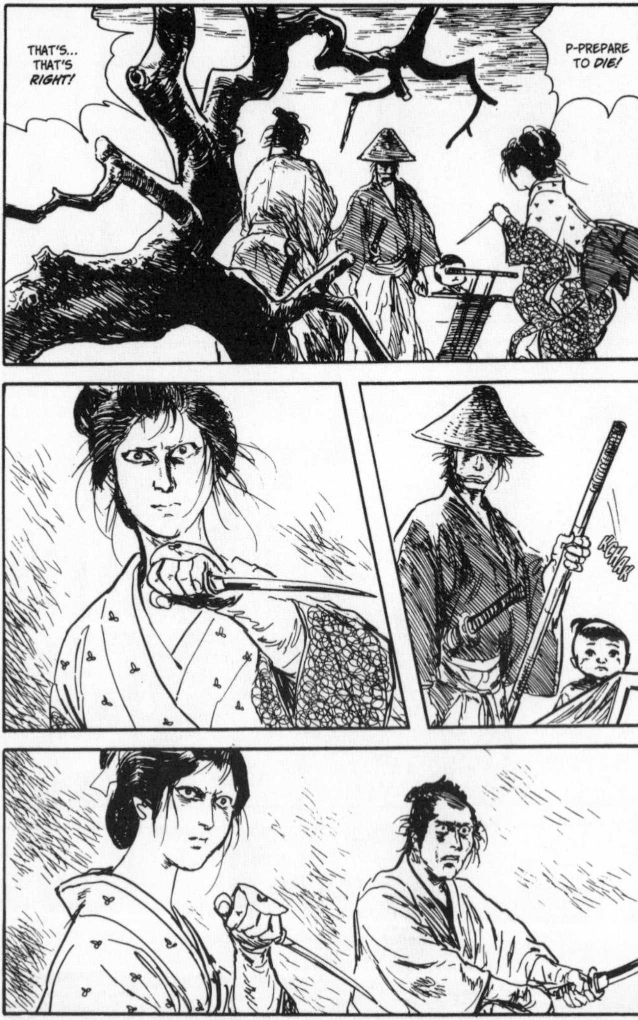
THAT'S... THAT'S *RIGHT!*
P-PREPARE TO *DIE!*
KCHAK

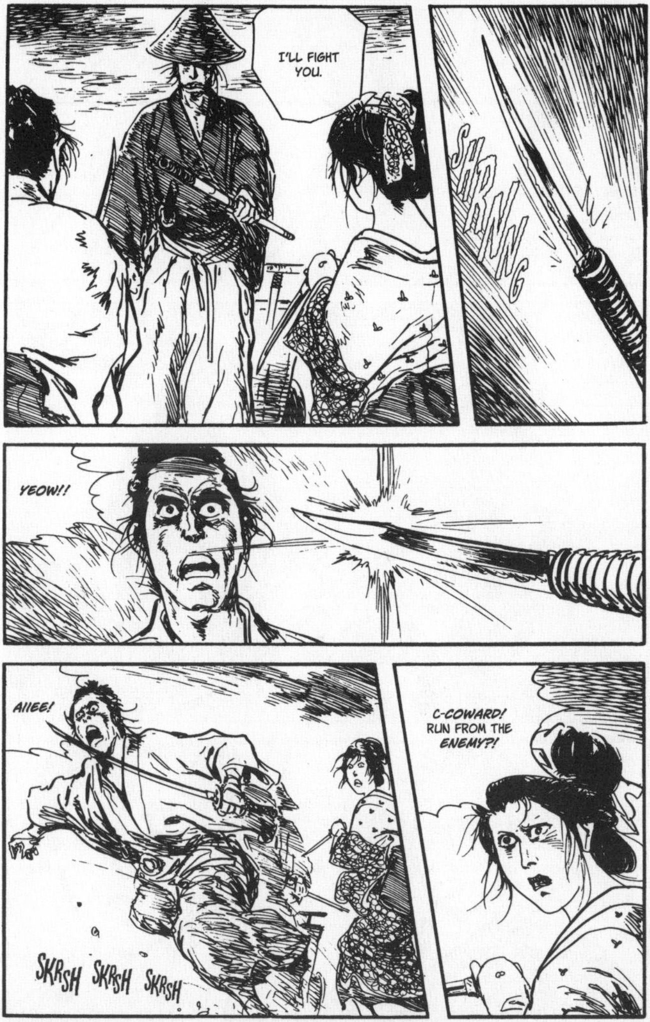
I'LL FIGHT YOU.
SHRING
YEOW!!
AIIEE!
SKRSH SKRSH SKRSH
C-COWARD! RUN FROM THE ENEMY?!

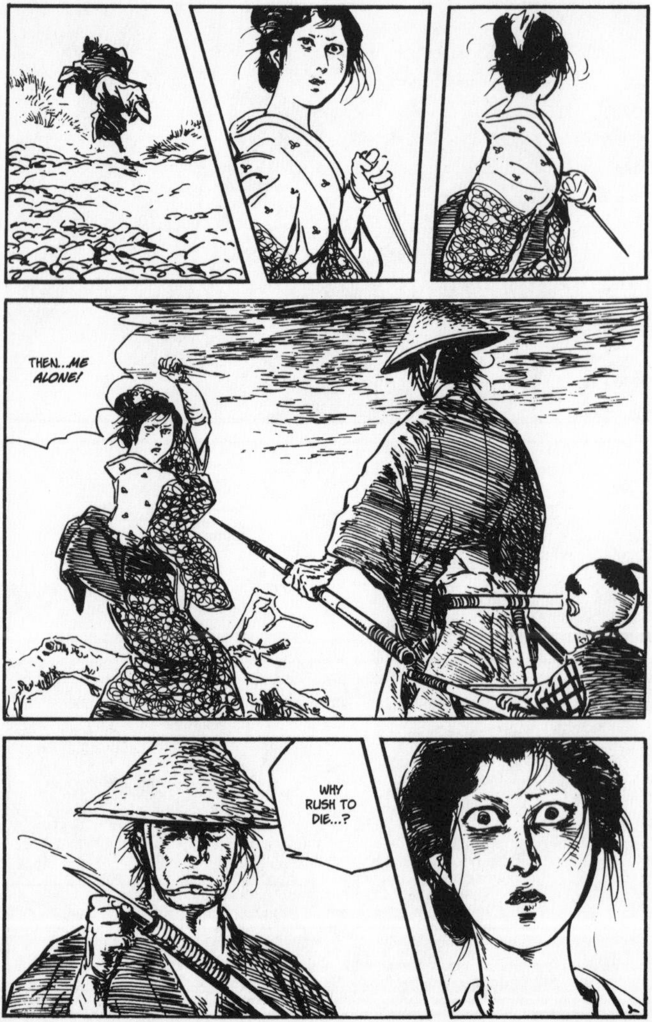
THEN... ME ALONE!
WHY RUSH TO DIE...?

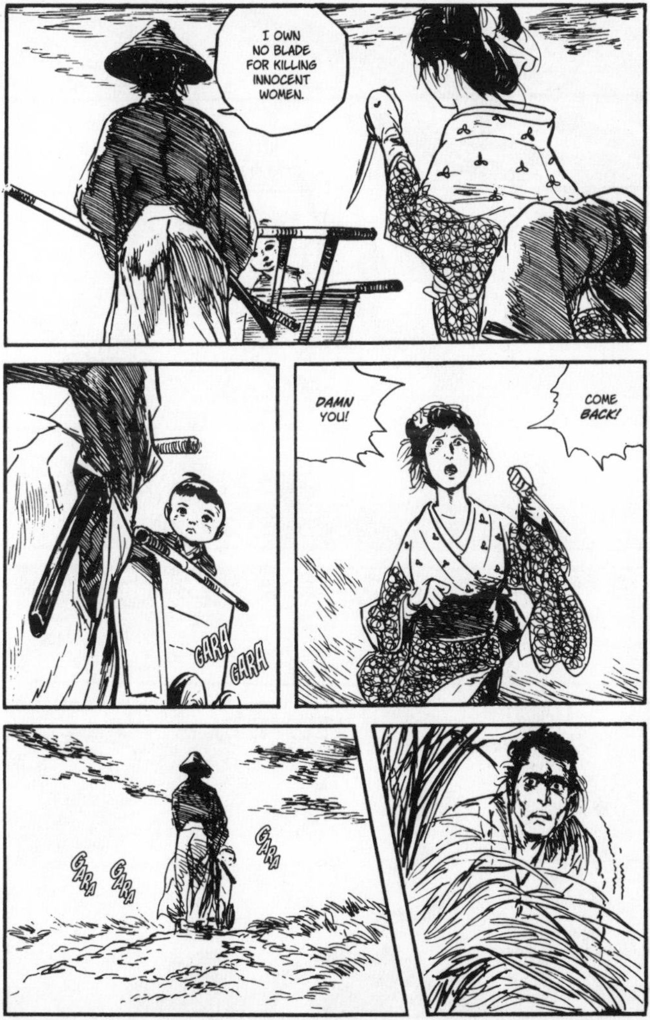
I OWN NO BLADE FOR KILLING INNOCENT WOMEN.
GARA
GARA
DAMN YOU!
COME BACK!
GARA
GARA
GARA

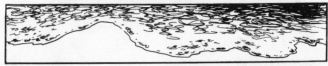

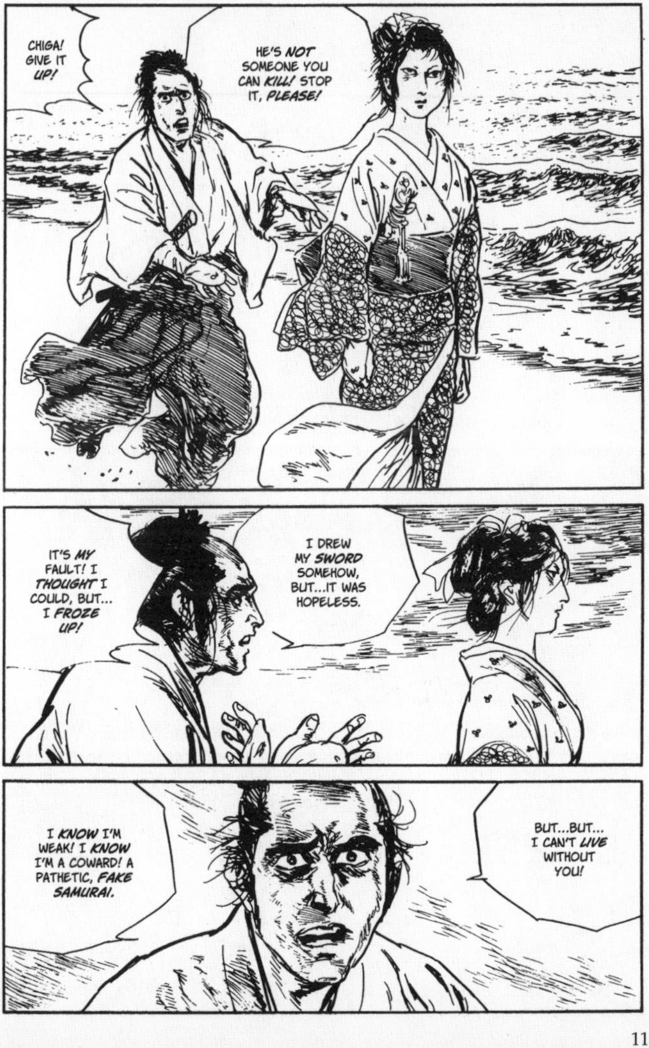

CHIGA! GIVE IT *UP!*
HE'S *NOT* SOMEONE YOU CAN *KILL!* STOP IT, *PLEASE!*
IT'S *MY* FAULT! I *THOUGHT* I COULD, BUT... I *FROZE UP!*
I DREW MY *SWORD* SOMEHOW, BUT...IT WAS HOPELESS.
I *KNOW* I'M WEAK! I *KNOW* I'M A COWARD! A PATHETIC, *FAKE SAMURAI.*
BUT...BUT... I CAN'T *LIVE* WITHOUT YOU!

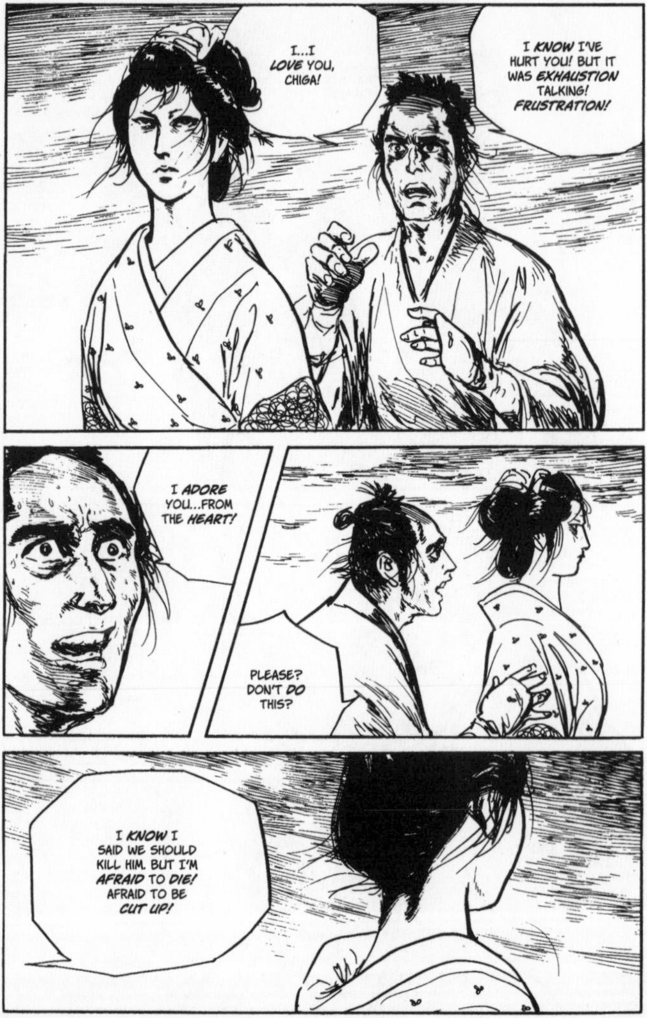
I...I LOVE YOU, CHIGA!
I KNOW I'VE HURT YOU! BUT IT WAS EXHAUSTION TALKING! FRUSTRATION!
I ADORE YOU...FROM THE HEART!
PLEASE? DON'T DO THIS?
I KNOW I SAID WE SHOULD KILL HIM. BUT I'M AFRAID TO DIE! AFRAID TO BE CUT UP!

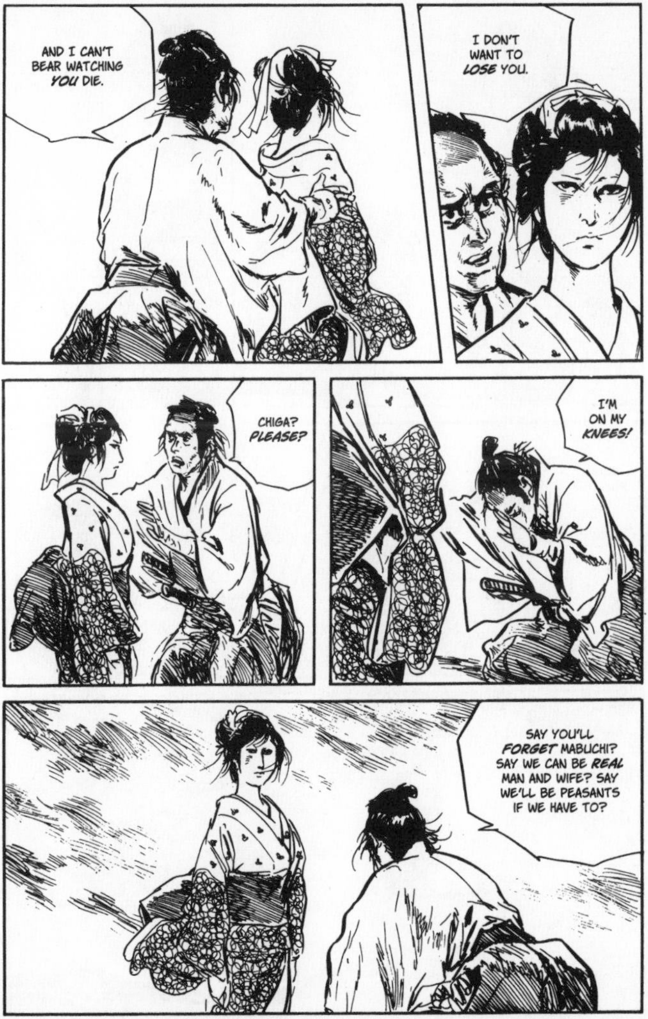
AND I CAN'T BEAR WATCHING *YOU* DIE.
I DON'T WANT TO *LOSE* YOU.
CHIGA? *PLEASE?*
I'M ON MY *KNEES!*
SAY YOU'LL *FORGET* MABUCHI? SAY WE CAN BE *REAL* MAN AND WIFE? SAY WE'LL BE PEASANTS IF WE HAVE TO?

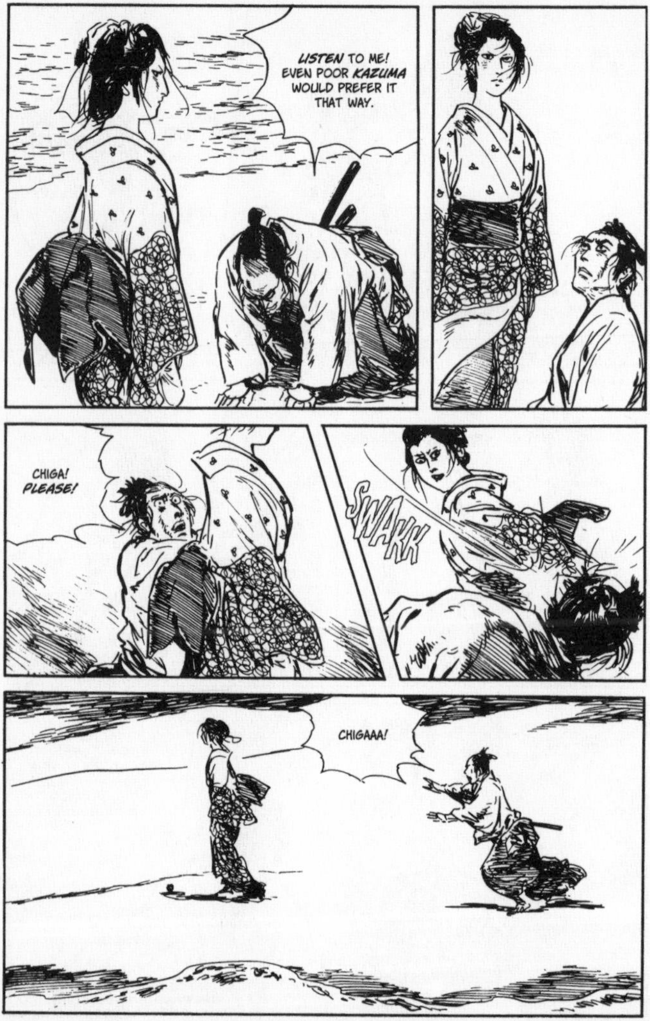
LISTEN TO ME! EVEN POOR KAZUMA WOULD PREFER IT THAT WAY.
CHIGA! PLEASE!
SWAKK
CHIGAAA!

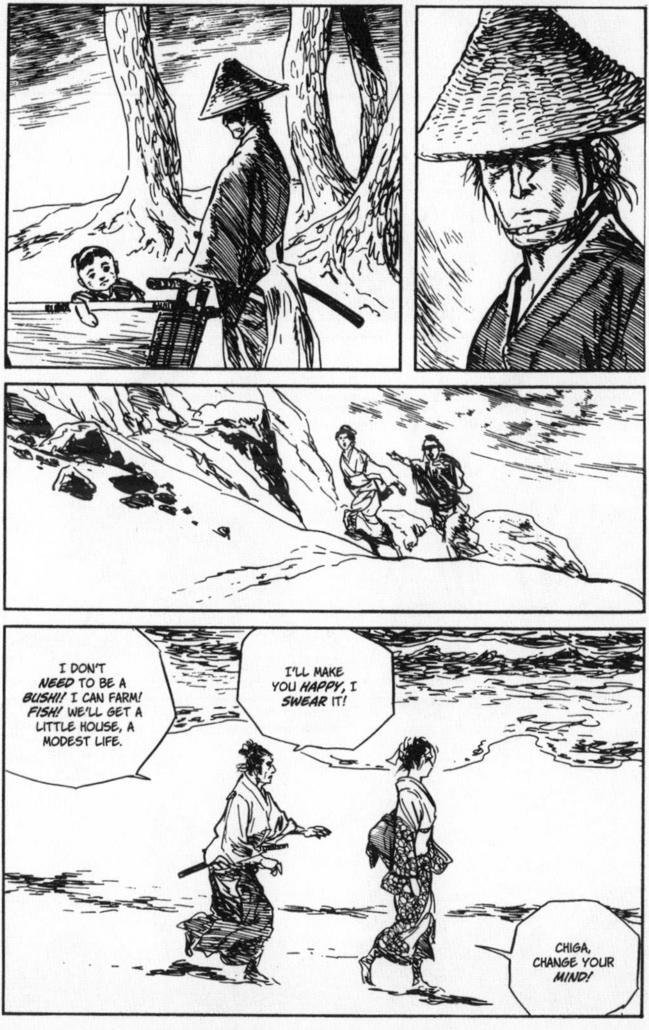
I DON'T NEED TO BE A BUSHI! I CAN FARM! FISH! WE'LL GET A LITTLE HOUSE, A MODEST LIFE.
I'LL MAKE YOU HAPPY, I SWEAR IT!
CHIGA, CHANGE YOUR MIND!

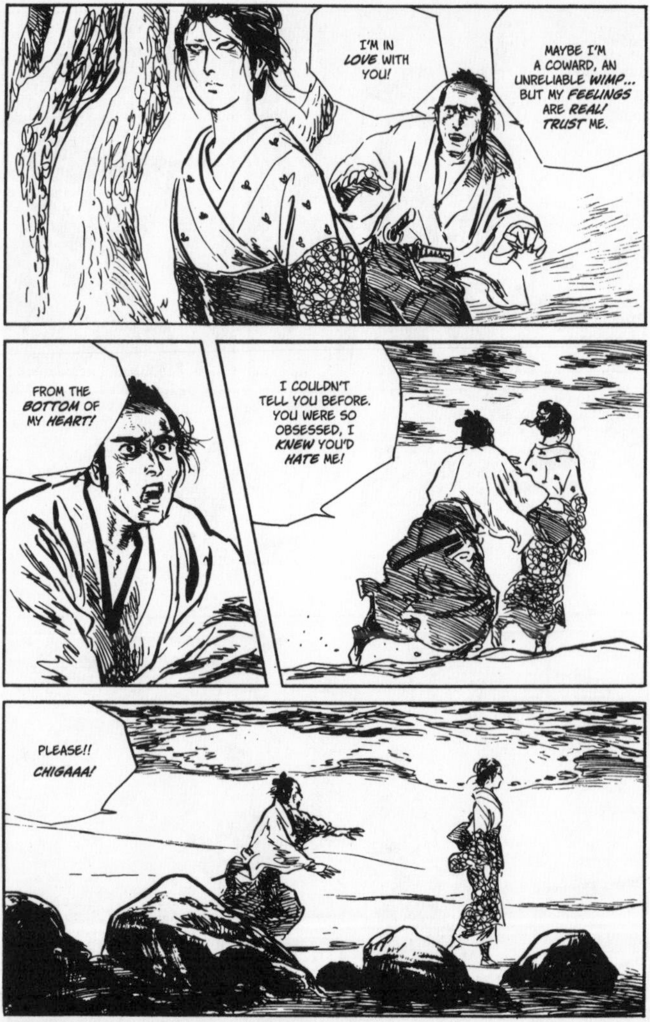
I'M IN LOVE WITH YOU!
MAYBE I'M A COWARD, AN UNRELIABLE WIMP... BUT MY FEELINGS ARE REAL! TRUST ME.
FROM THE BOTTOM OF MY HEART!
I COULDN'T TELL YOU BEFORE. YOU WERE SO OBSESSED, I KNEW YOU'D HATE ME!
PLEASE!! CHIGAAA!

119

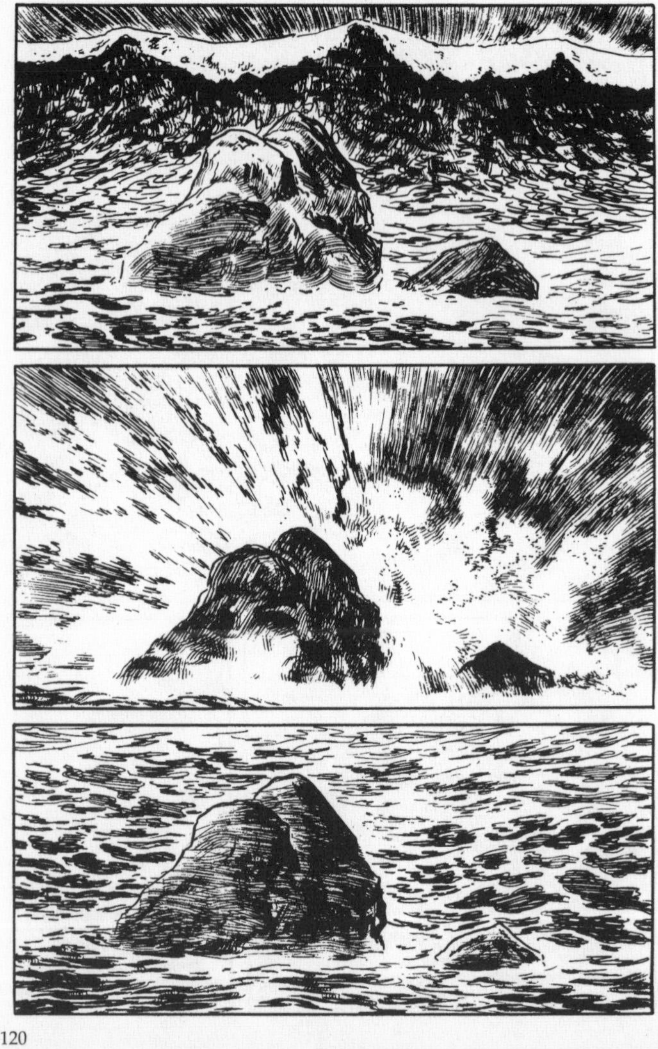

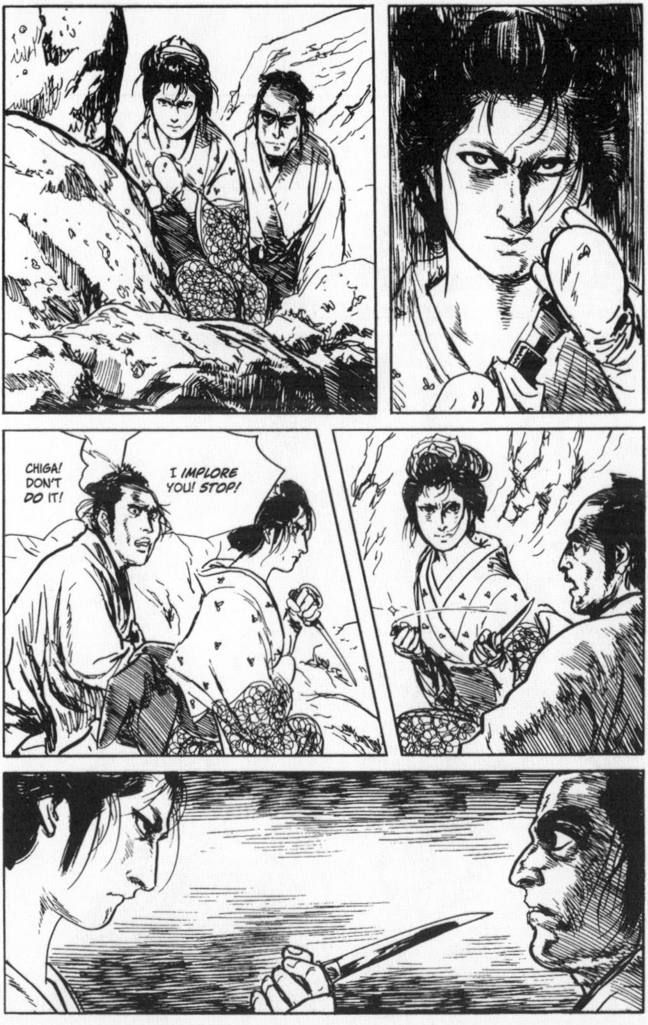
CHIGA! DON'T DO IT!
I IMPLORE YOU! STOP!

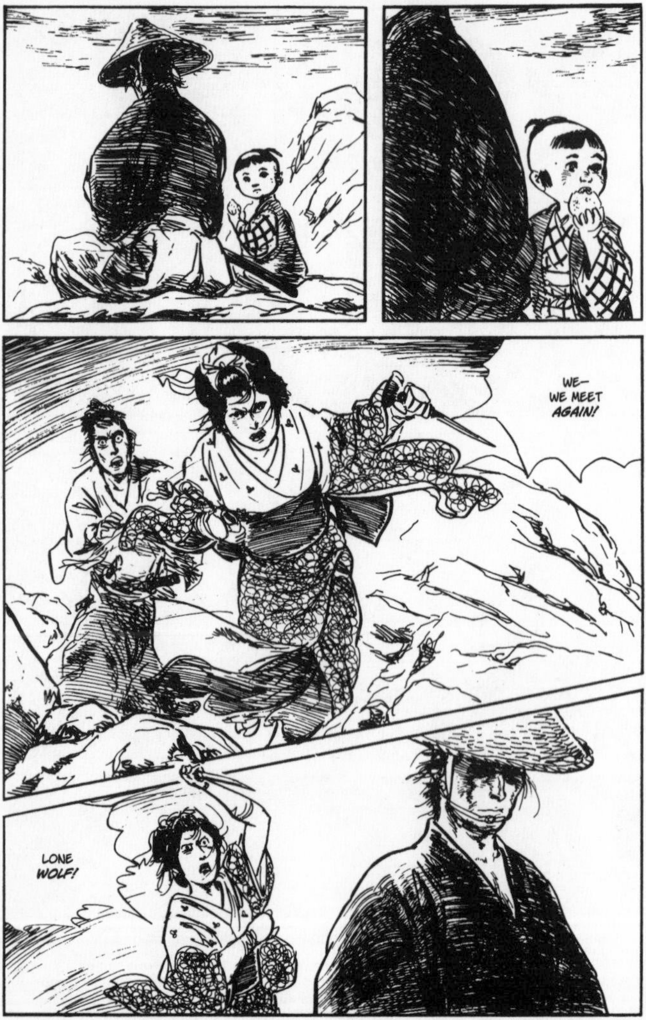
WE—
WE MEET AGAIN!
LONE WOLF!

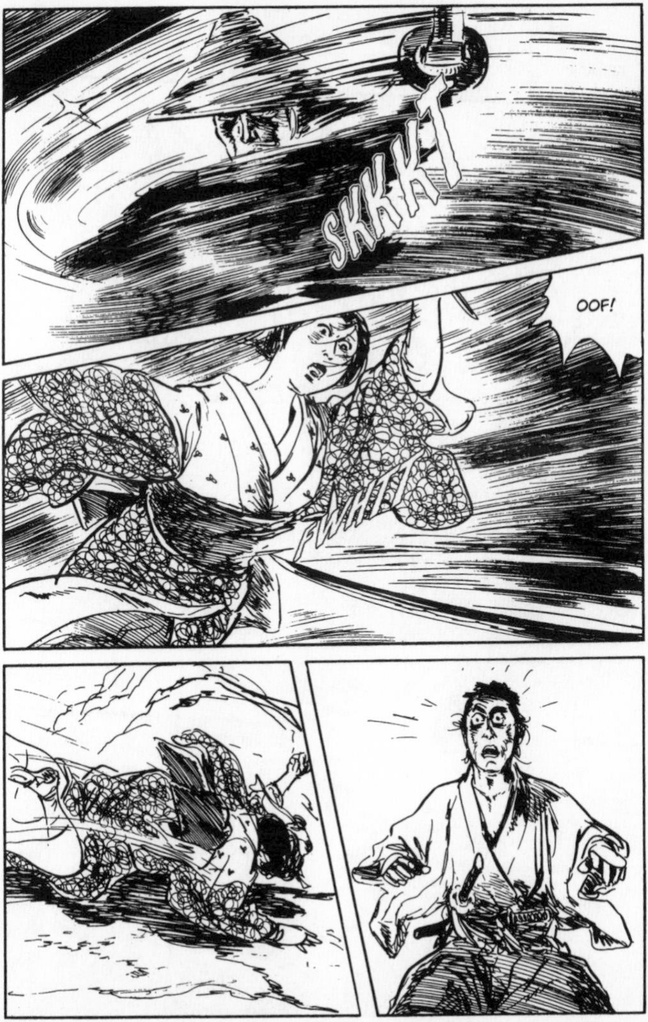
SKKKT
OOF!
FWHTT

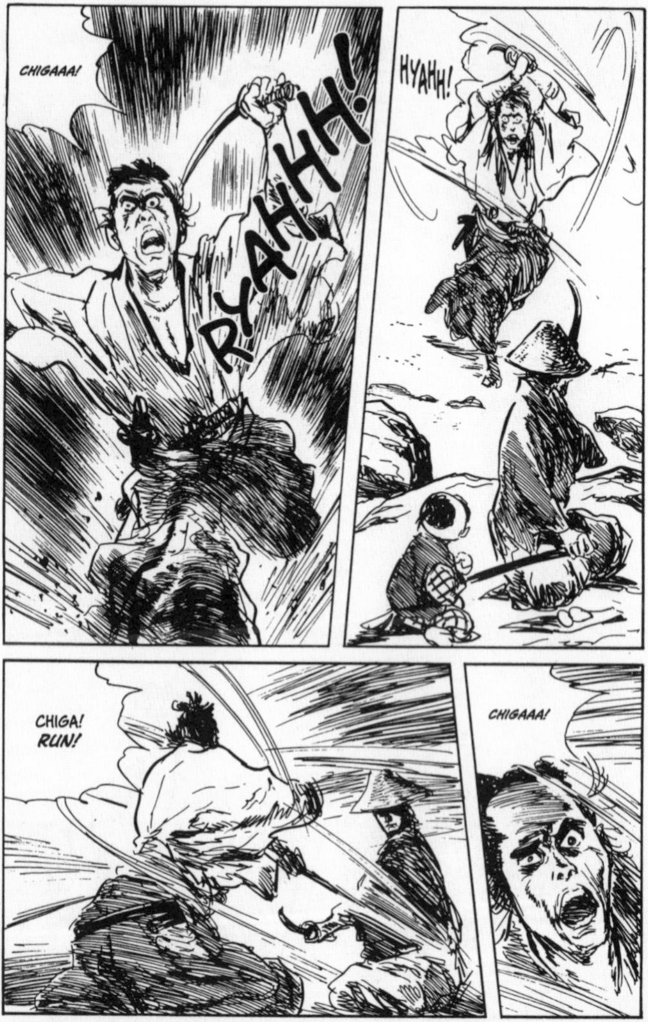
CHIGAAA!
RYAHHH!
HYAHH!
CHIGA! RUN!
CHIGAAA!

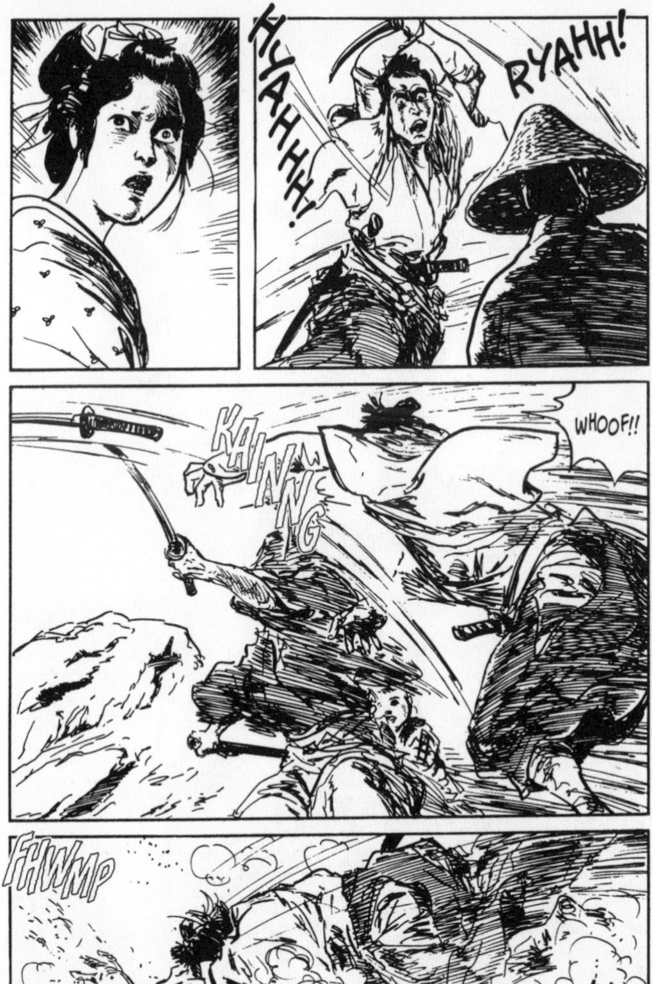
HYAHHH!
RYAHH!
KAINNNG
WHOOF!!
FHWMP

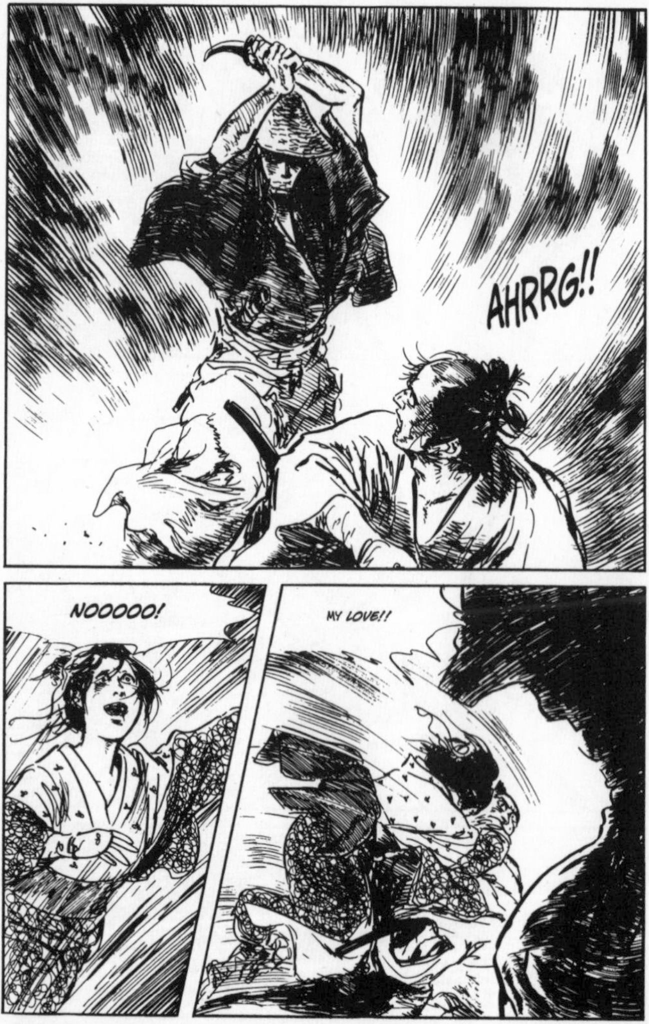
AHRRG!!
NOOOOO!
MY LOVE!!

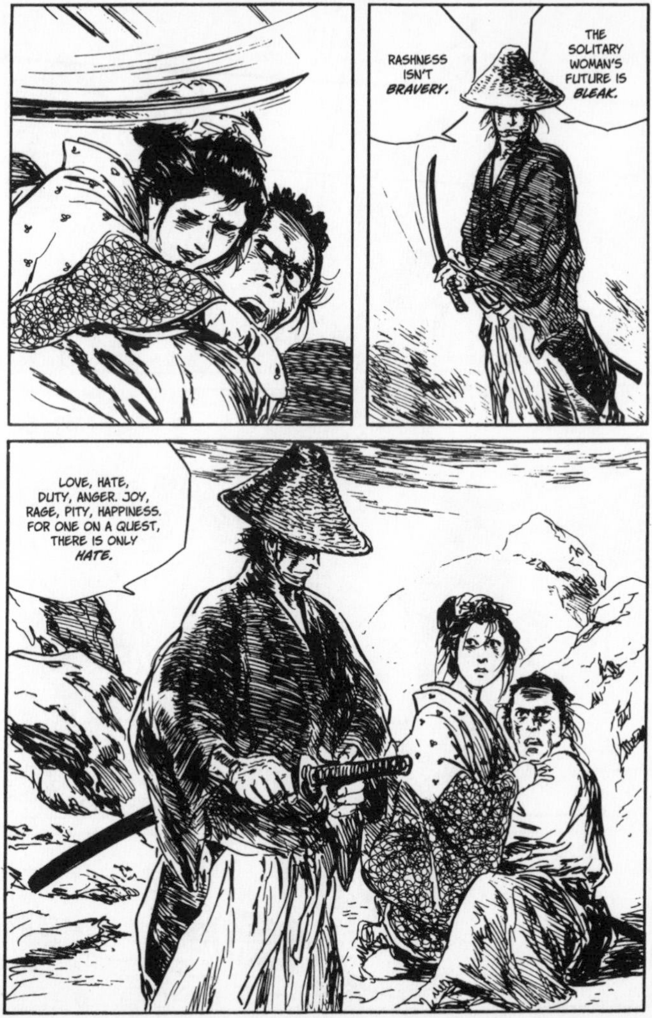
RASHNESS ISN'T *BRAVERY.*
THE SOLITARY WOMAN'S FUTURE IS *BLEAK.*
LOVE, HATE, DUTY, ANGER. JOY, RAGE, PITY, HAPPINESS. FOR ONE ON A QUEST, THERE IS ONLY *HATE.*

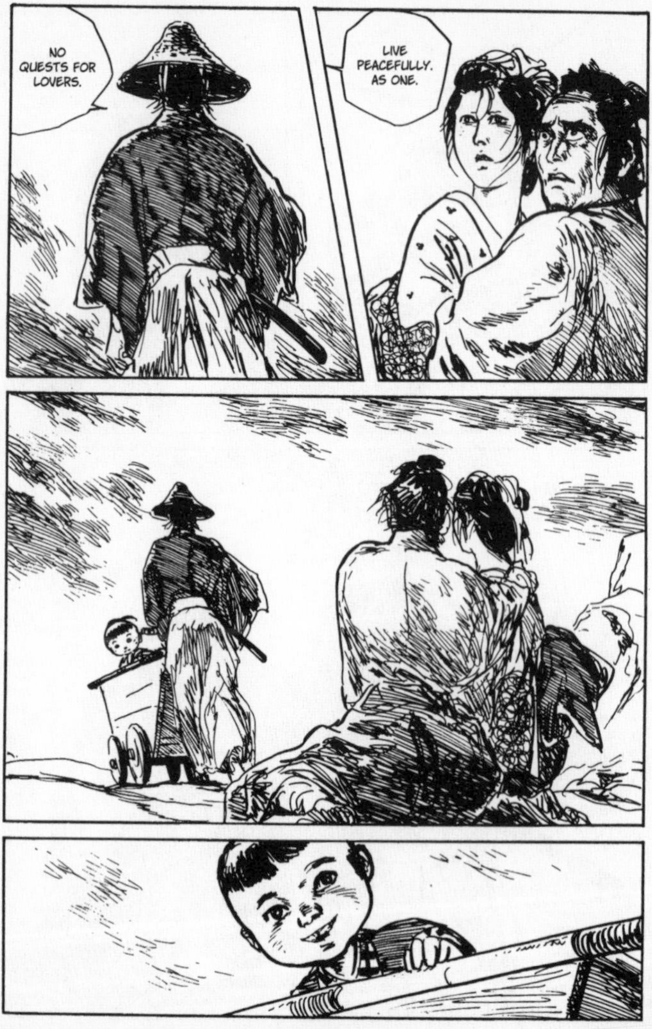
NO QUESTS FOR LOVERS.
LIVE PEACEFULLY. AS ONE.

the ninety-fifth

The Marksman

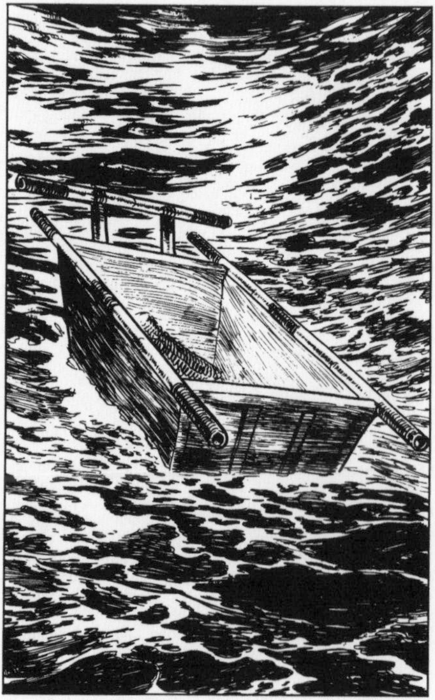

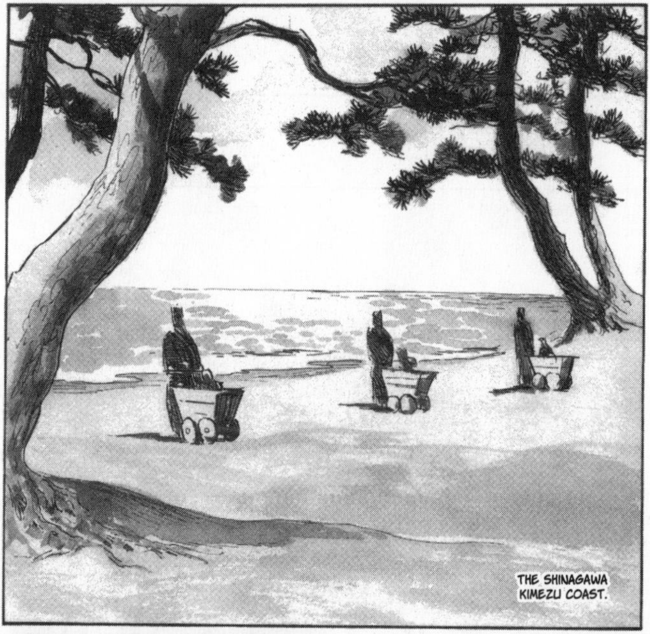
THE SHINAGAWA
KIMEZU COAST.
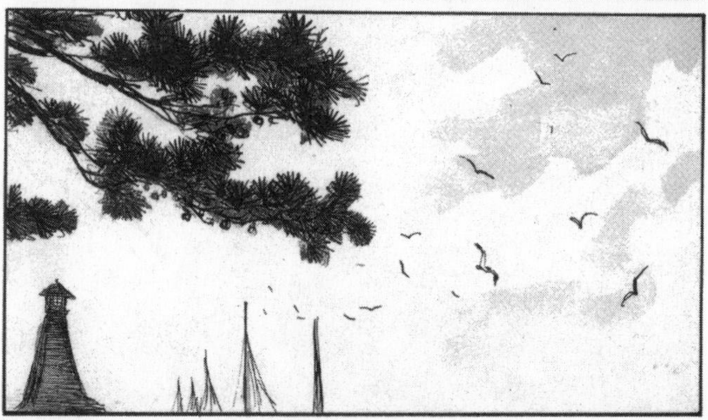

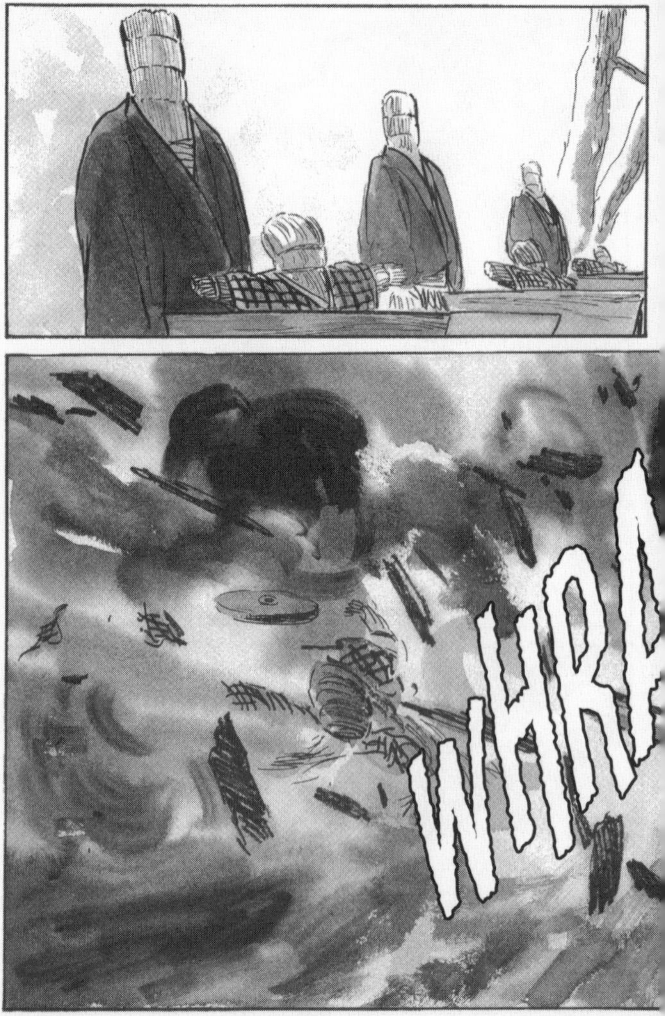
WHR

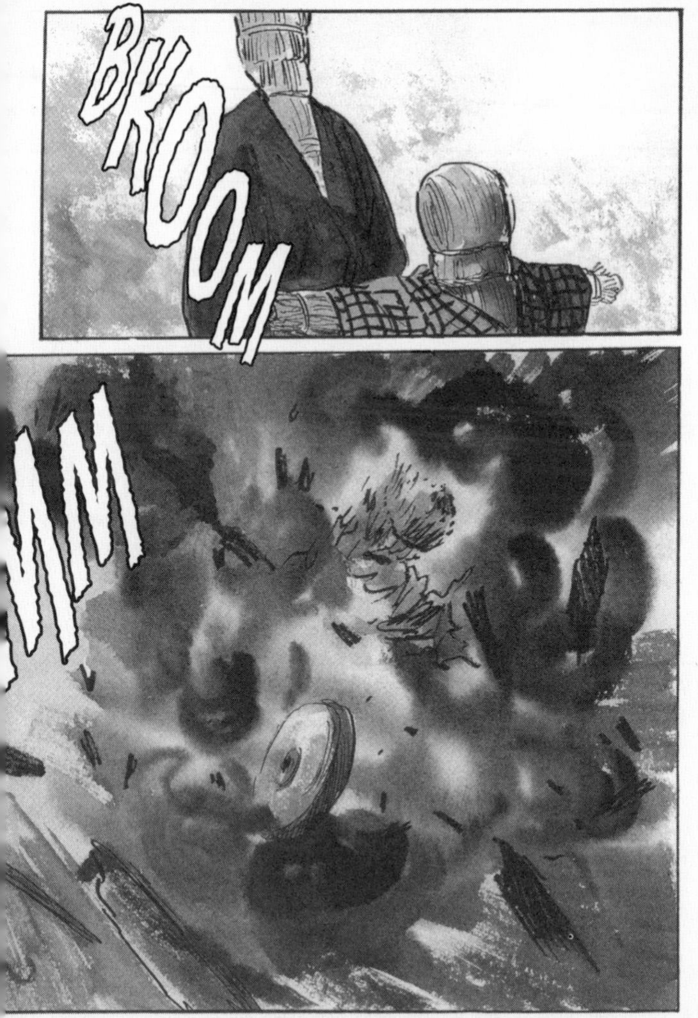
BKOOM

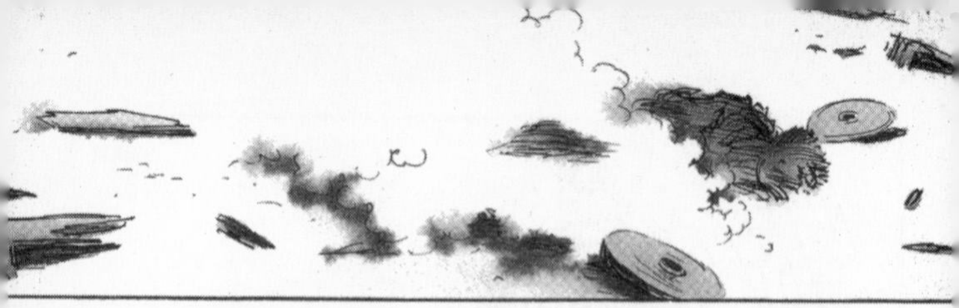

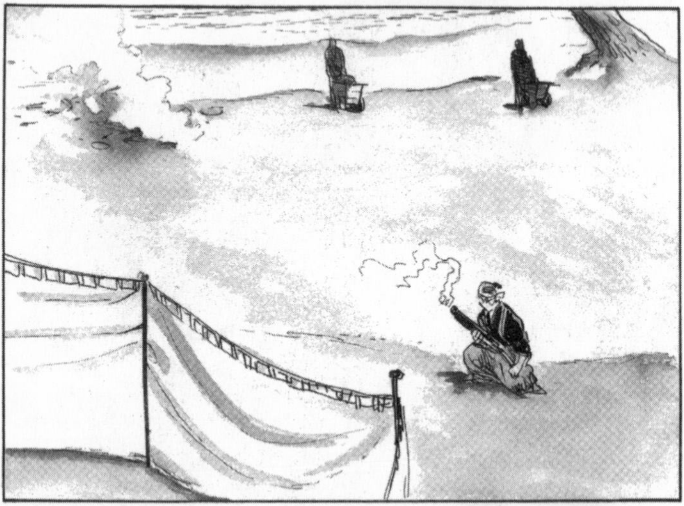

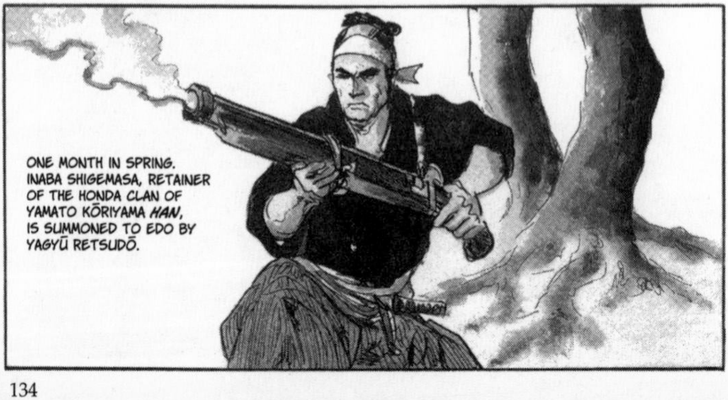
ONE MONTH IN SPRING. INABA SHIGEMASA, RETAINER OF THE HONDA CLAN OF YAMATO KŌRIYAMA *HAN*, IS SUMMONED TO EDO BY YAGYŪ RETSUDŌ.

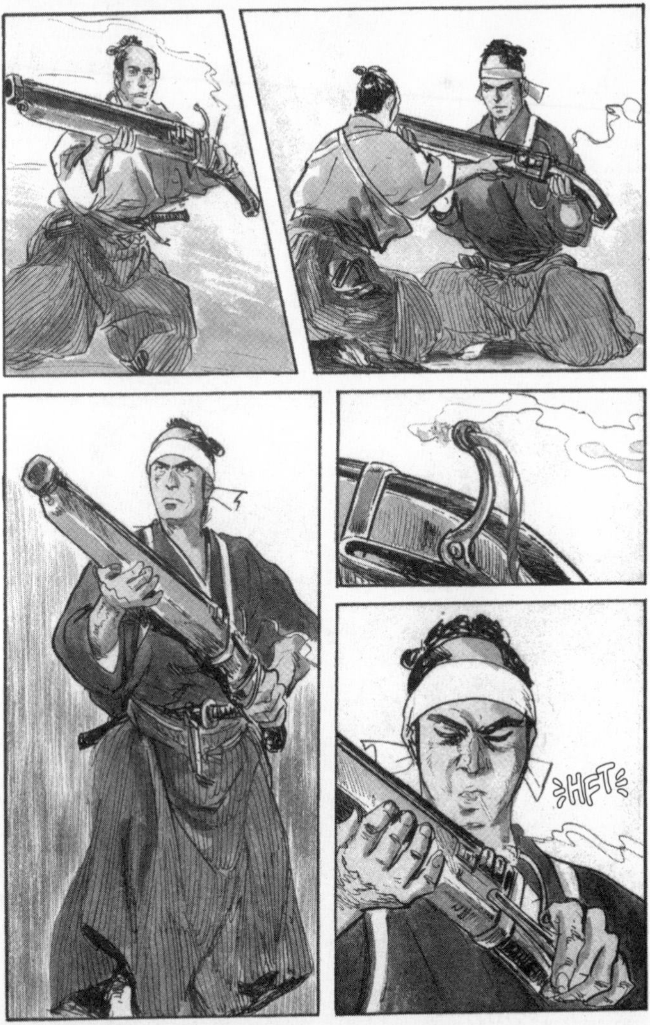
HFT

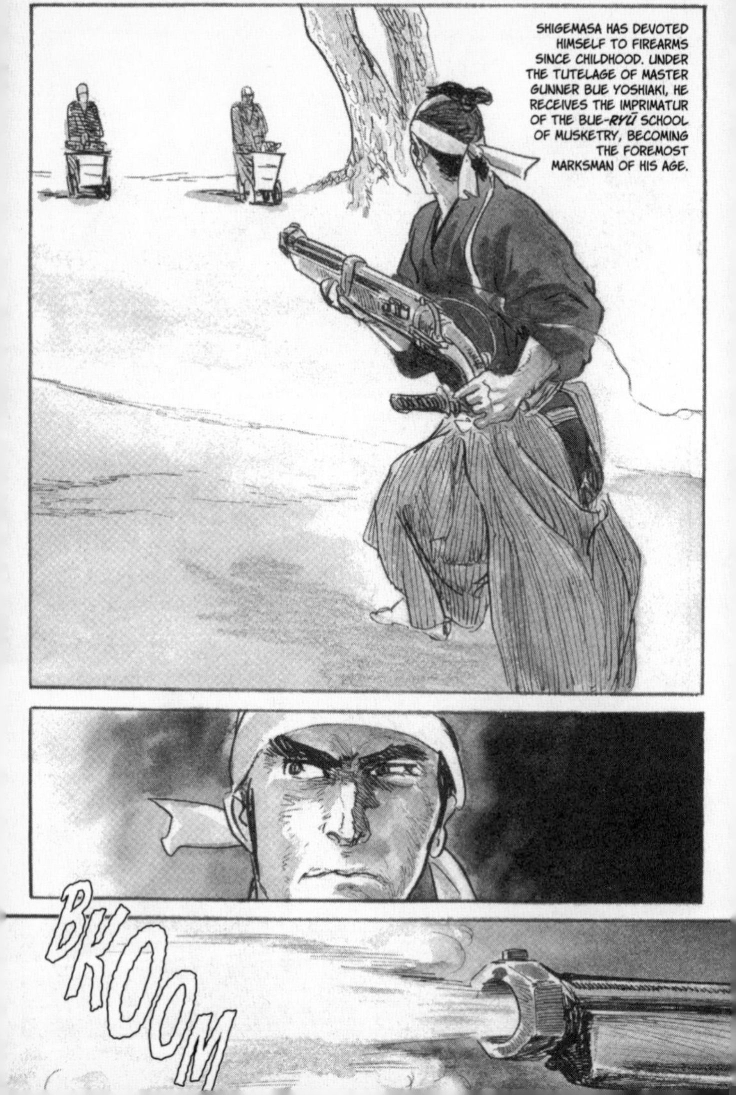
SHIGEMASA HAS DEVOTED HIMSELF TO FIREARMS SINCE CHILDHOOD. UNDER THE TUTELAGE OF MASTER GUNNER BUE YOSHIAKI, HE RECEIVES THE IMPRIMATUR OF THE BUE-*RYŪ* SCHOOL OF MUSKETRY, BECOMING THE FOREMOST MARKSMAN OF HIS AGE.
BKOOM

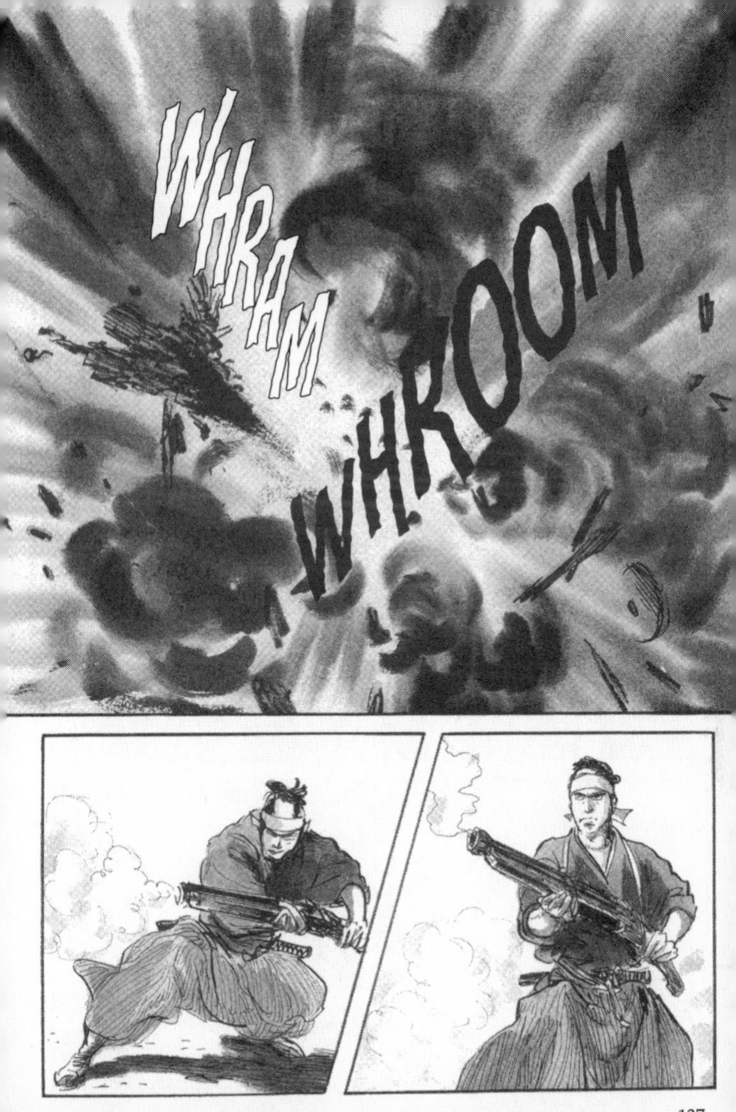
WHRAM
WHROOM

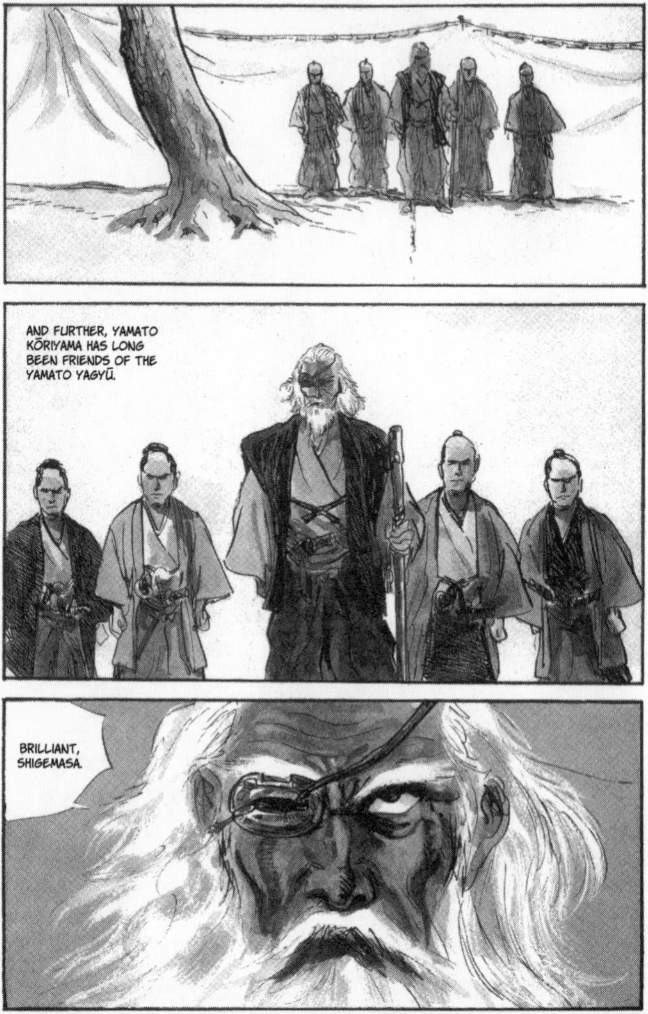
AND FURTHER, YAMATO KŌRIYAMA HAS LONG BEEN FRIENDS OF THE YAMATO YAGYŪ.
BRILLIANT, SHIGEMASA.

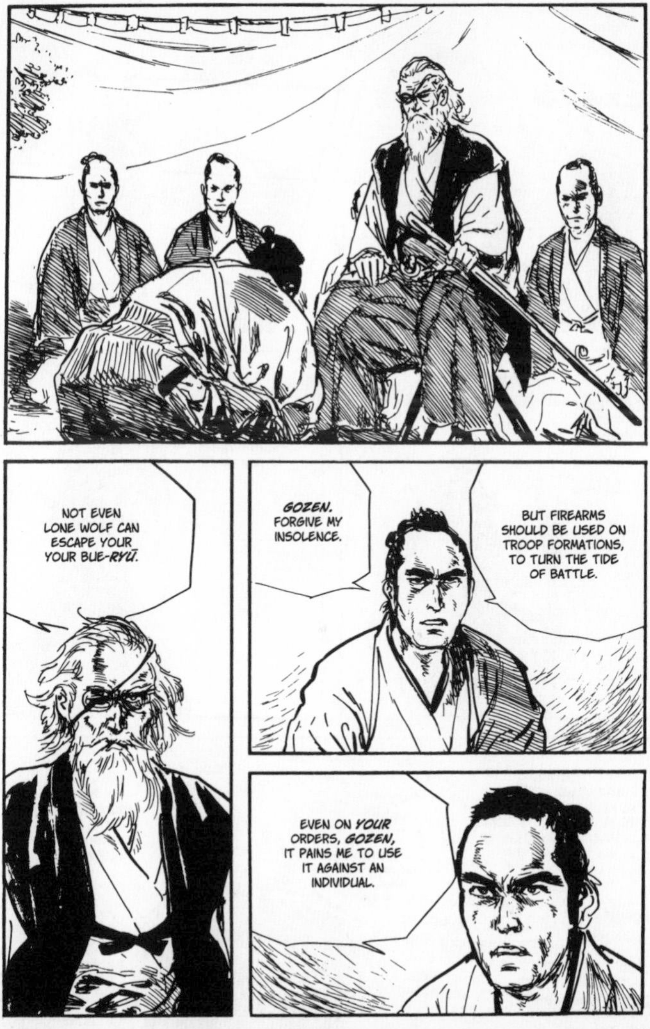
NOT EVEN LONE WOLF CAN ESCAPE YOUR YOUR BUE-RYŪ.
GOZEN. FORGIVE MY INSOLENCE.
BUT FIREARMS SHOULD BE USED ON TROOP FORMATIONS, TO TURN THE TIDE OF BATTLE.
EVEN ON YOUR ORDERS, GOZEN, IT PAINS ME TO USE IT AGAINST AN INDIVIDUAL.

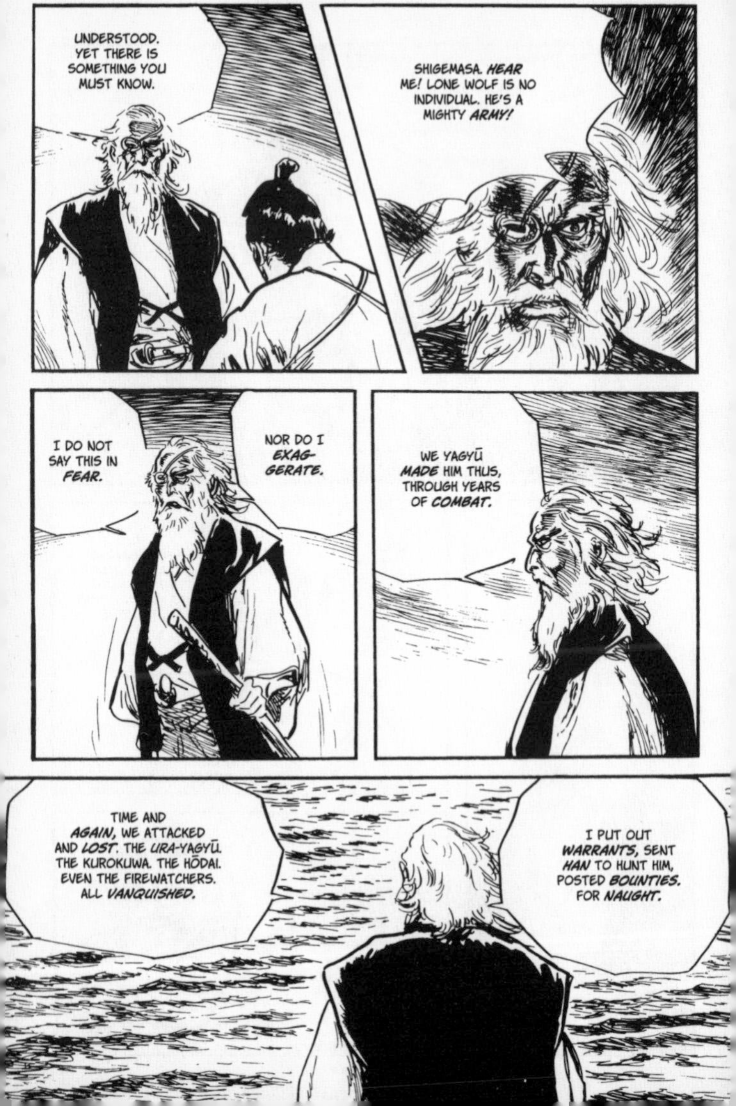
UNDERSTOOD. YET THERE IS SOMETHING YOU MUST KNOW.
SHIGEMASA. HEAR ME! LONE WOLF IS NO INDIVIDUAL. HE'S A MIGHTY ARMY!
I DO NOT SAY THIS IN FEAR.
NOR DO I EXAGGERATE.
WE YAGYŪ MADE HIM THUS, THROUGH YEARS OF COMBAT.
TIME AND AGAIN, WE ATTACKED AND LOST. THE URA-YAGYŪ. THE KUROKUWA. THE HŌDAI. EVEN THE FIREWATCHERS. ALL VANQUISHED.
I PUT OUT WARRANTS, SENT HAN TO HUNT HIM, POSTED BOUNTIES. FOR NAUGHT.

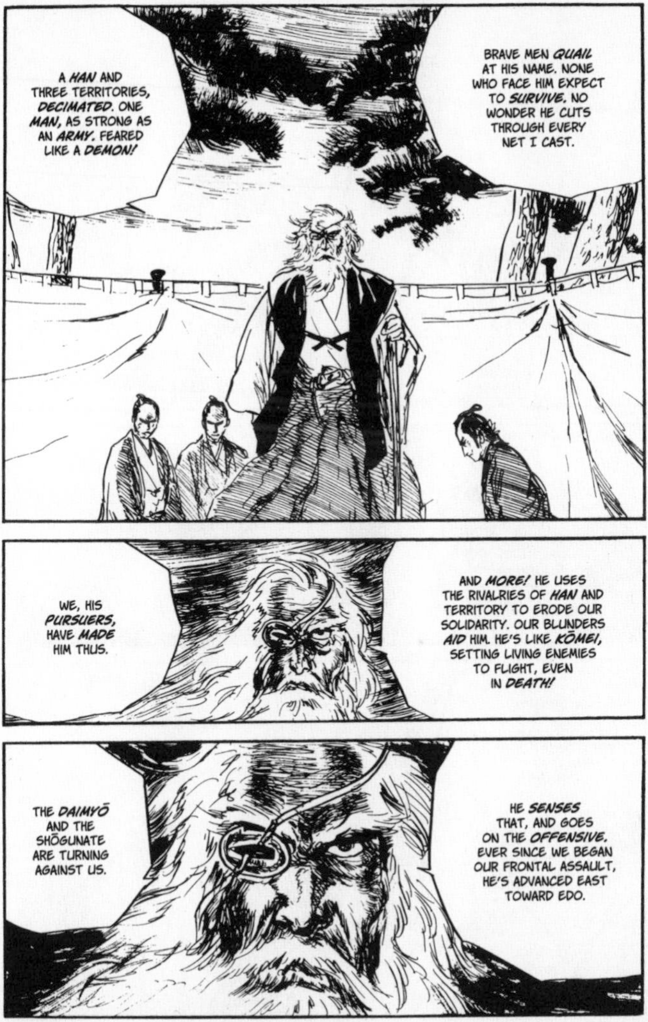
A HAN AND THREE TERRITORIES, DECIMATED. ONE MAN, AS STRONG AS AN ARMY. FEARED LIKE A DEMON!
BRAVE MEN QUAIL AT HIS NAME. NONE WHO FACE HIM EXPECT TO SURVIVE. NO WONDER HE CUTS THROUGH EVERY NET I CAST.
WE, HIS PURSUERS, HAVE MADE HIM THUS.
AND MORE! HE USES THE RIVALRIES OF HAN AND TERRITORY TO ERODE OUR SOLIDARITY. OUR BLUNDERS AID HIM. HE'S LIKE KŌMEI, SETTING LIVING ENEMIES TO FLIGHT, EVEN IN DEATH!
THE DAIMYŌ AND THE SHŌGUNATE ARE TURNING AGAINST US.
HE SENSES THAT, AND GOES ON THE OFFENSIVE. EVER SINCE WE BEGAN OUR FRONTAL ASSAULT, HE'S ADVANCED EAST TOWARD EDO.

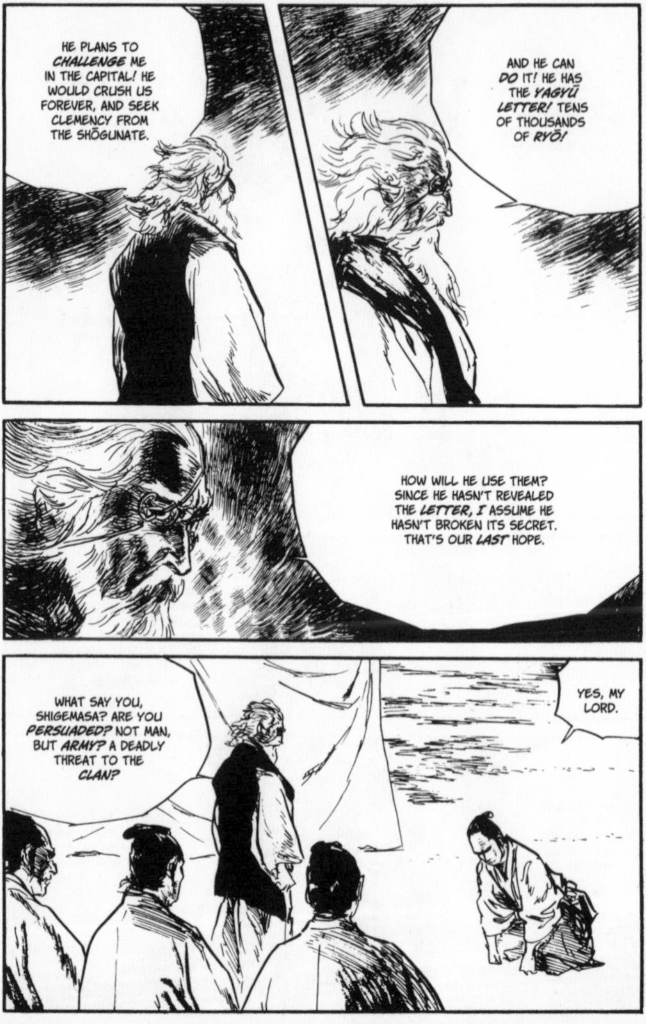
HE PLANS TO CHALLENGE ME IN THE CAPITAL! HE WOULD CRUSH US FOREVER, AND SEEK CLEMENCY FROM THE SHŌGUNATE.
AND HE CAN DO IT! HE HAS THE YAGYŪ LETTER! TENS OF THOUSANDS OF RYŌ!
HOW WILL HE USE THEM? SINCE HE HASN'T REVEALED THE LETTER, I ASSUME HE HASN'T BROKEN ITS SECRET. THAT'S OUR LAST HOPE.
WHAT SAY YOU, SHIGEMASA? ARE YOU PERSUADED? NOT MAN, BUT ARMY? A DEADLY THREAT TO THE CLAN?
YES, MY LORD.

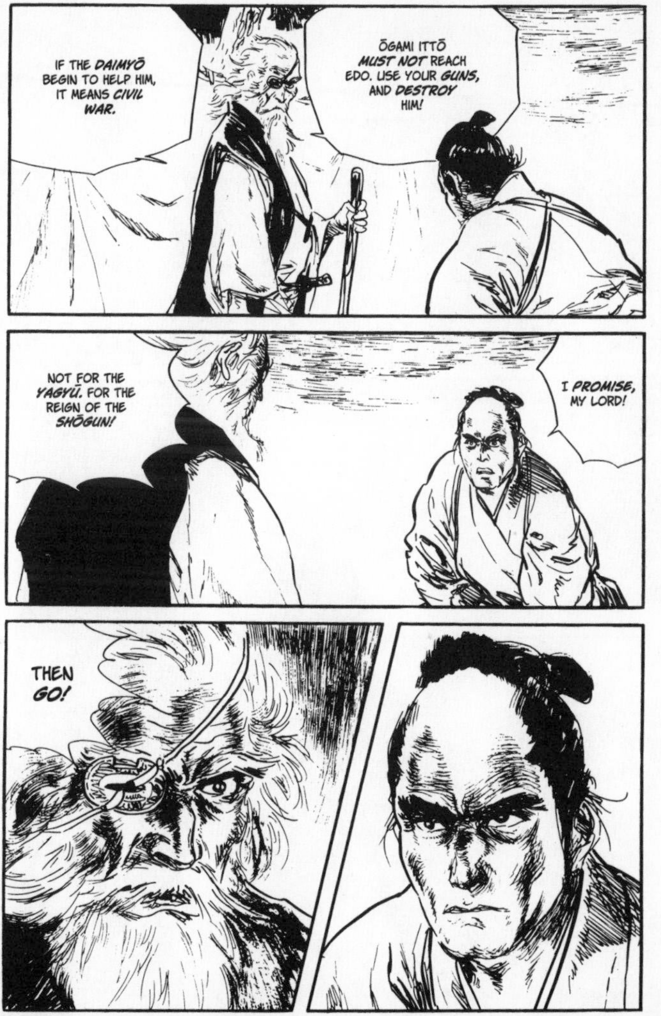
IF THE DAIMYŌ BEGIN TO HELP HIM, IT MEANS CIVIL WAR.
ŌGAMI ITTŌ MUST NOT REACH EDO. USE YOUR GUNS, AND DESTROY HIM!
NOT FOR THE YAGYŪ. FOR THE REIGN OF THE SHŌGUN!
I PROMISE, MY LORD!
THEN GO!

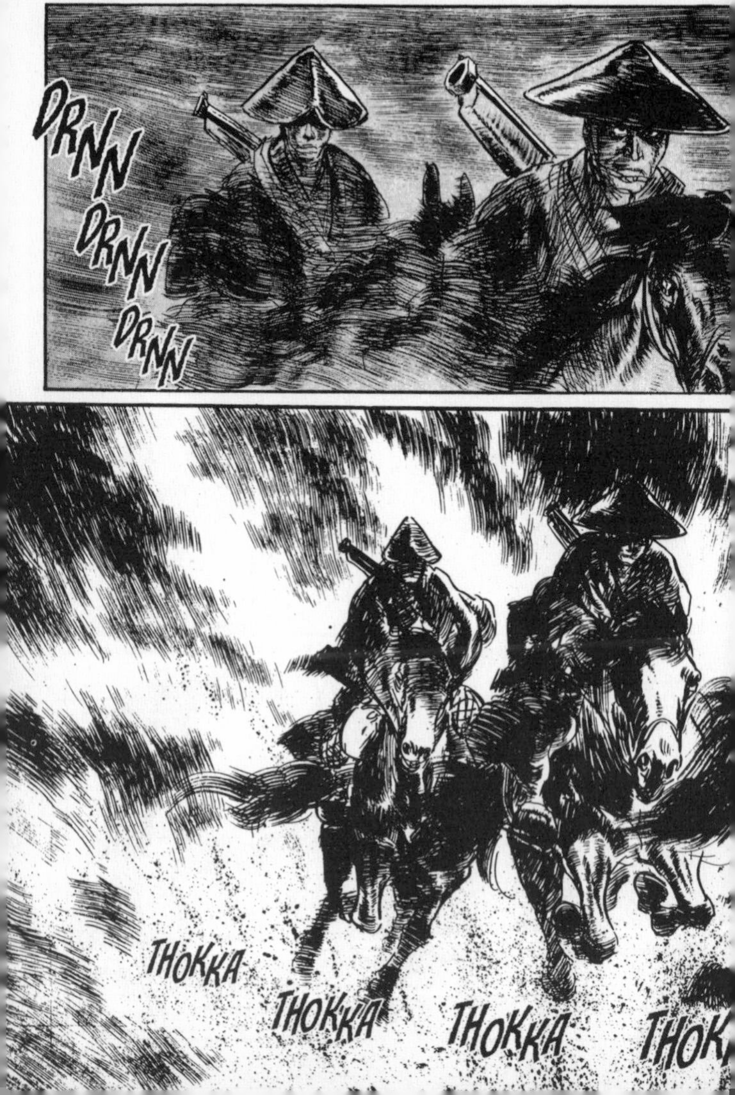
DRNN
DRNN
DRNN
THOKKA
THOKKA
THOKKA
THOK

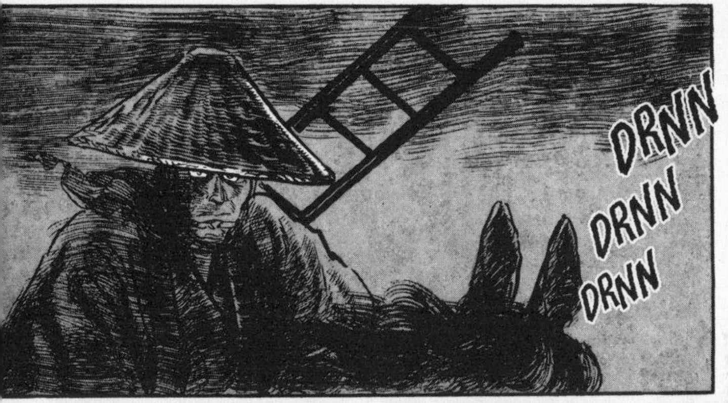
DRNN
DRNN
DRNN
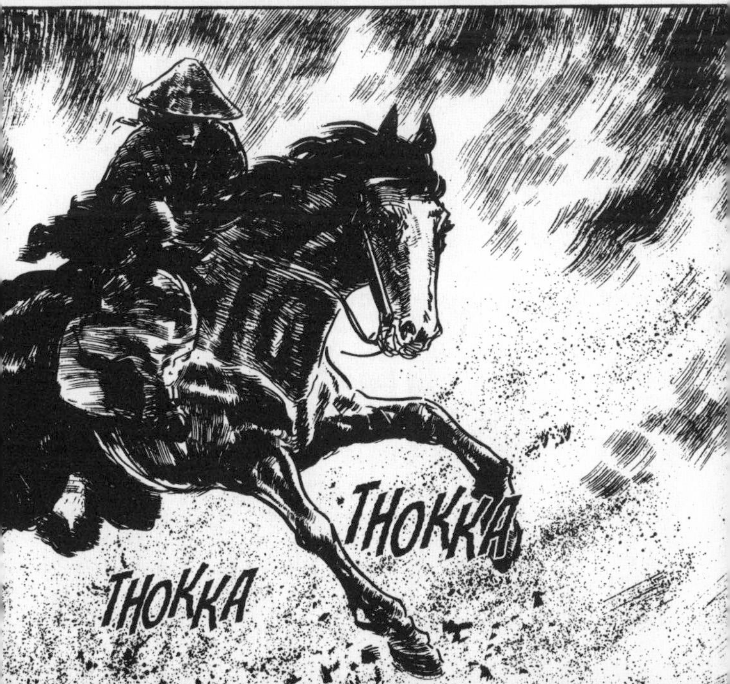
THOKKA
THOKKA

検見川代官所
*KEMIGAWA DAIKANSHO

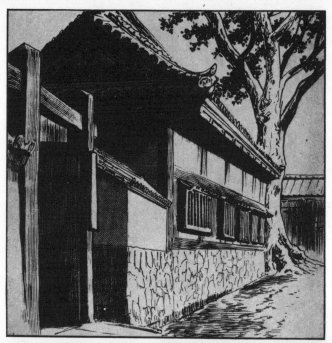

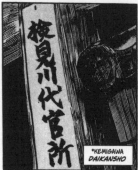

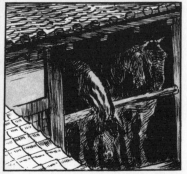

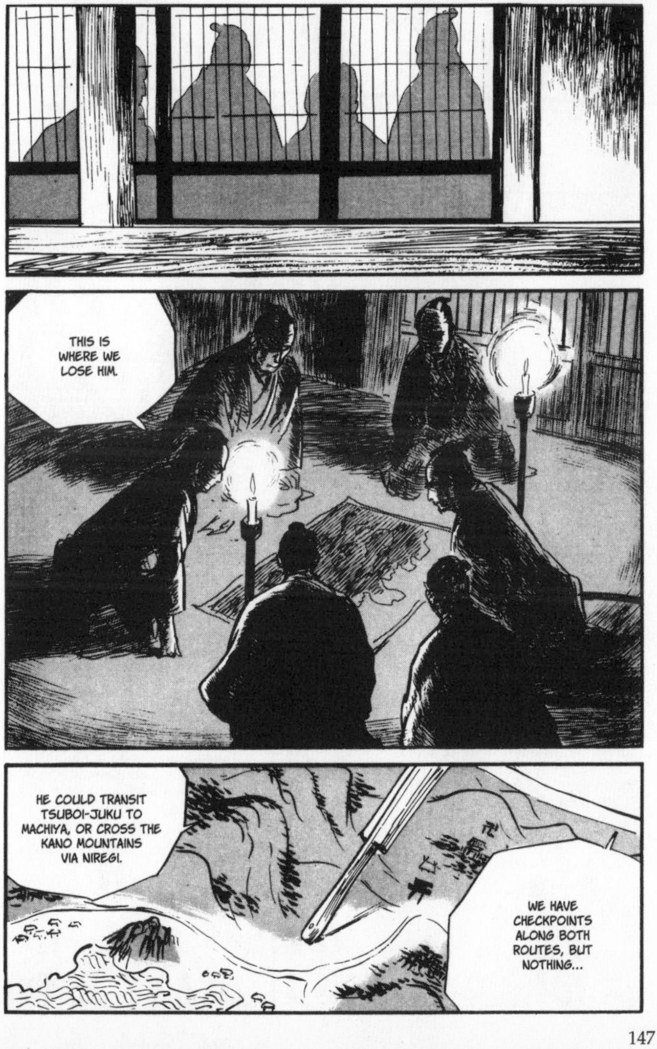
THIS IS WHERE WE LOSE HIM.
HE COULD TRANSIT TSUBOI-JUKU TO MACHIYA, OR CROSS THE KANO MOUNTAINS VIA NIREGI.
WE HAVE CHECKPOINTS ALONG BOTH ROUTES, BUT NOTHING...

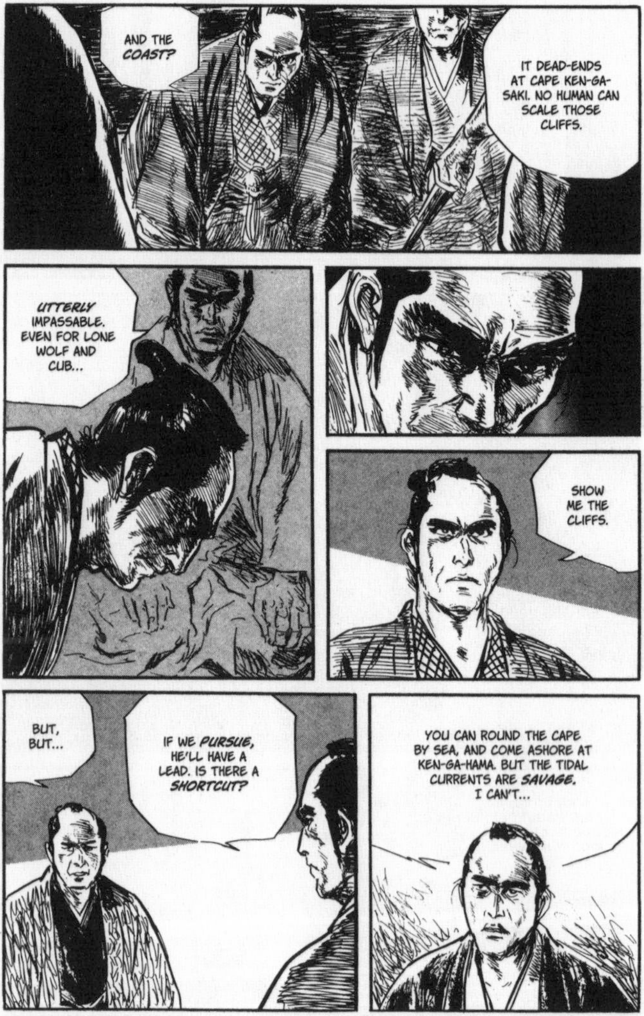
AND THE *COAST?*
IT DEAD-ENDS AT CAPE KEN-GA-SAKI. NO HUMAN CAN SCALE THOSE CLIFFS.
UTTERLY IMPASSABLE. EVEN FOR LONE WOLF AND CUB...
SHOW ME THE CLIFFS.
BUT, BUT...
IF WE *PURSUE,* HE'LL HAVE A LEAD. IS THERE A *SHORTCUT?*
YOU CAN ROUND THE CAPE BY SEA, AND COME ASHORE AT KEN-GA-HAMA. BUT THE TIDAL CURRENTS ARE *SAVAGE.* I CAN'T...

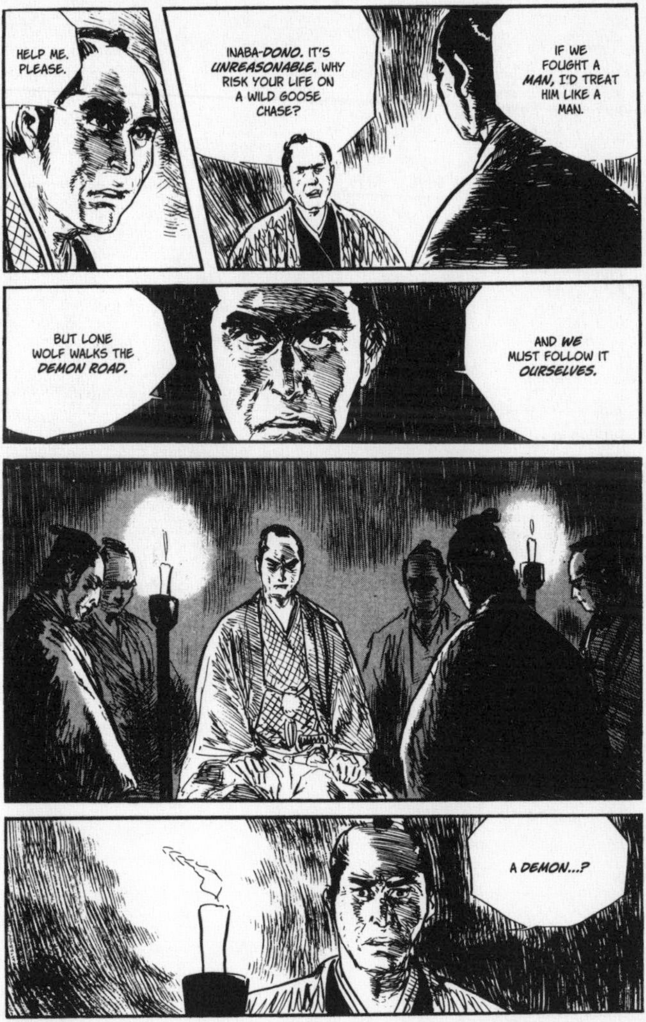
HELP ME. PLEASE.
INABA-DONO. IT'S UNREASONABLE. WHY RISK YOUR LIFE ON A WILD GOOSE CHASE?
IF WE FOUGHT A MAN, I'D TREAT HIM LIKE A MAN.
BUT LONE WOLF WALKS THE DEMON ROAD.
AND WE MUST FOLLOW IT OURSELVES.
A DEMON...?

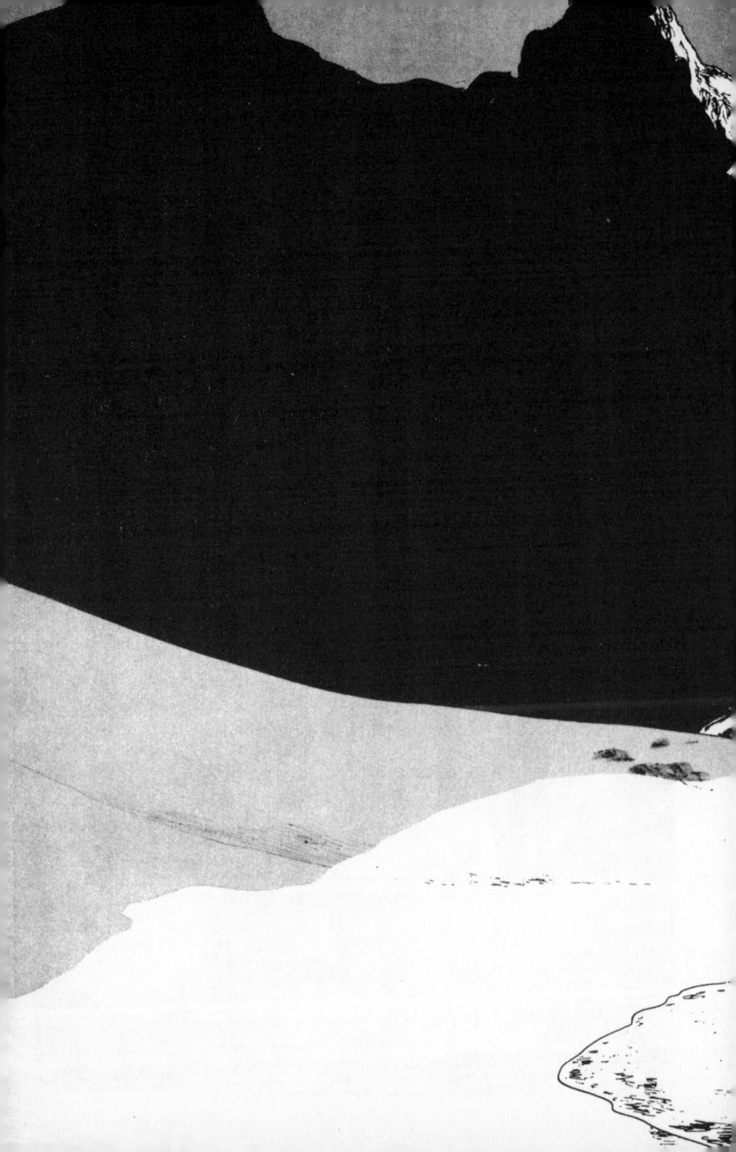

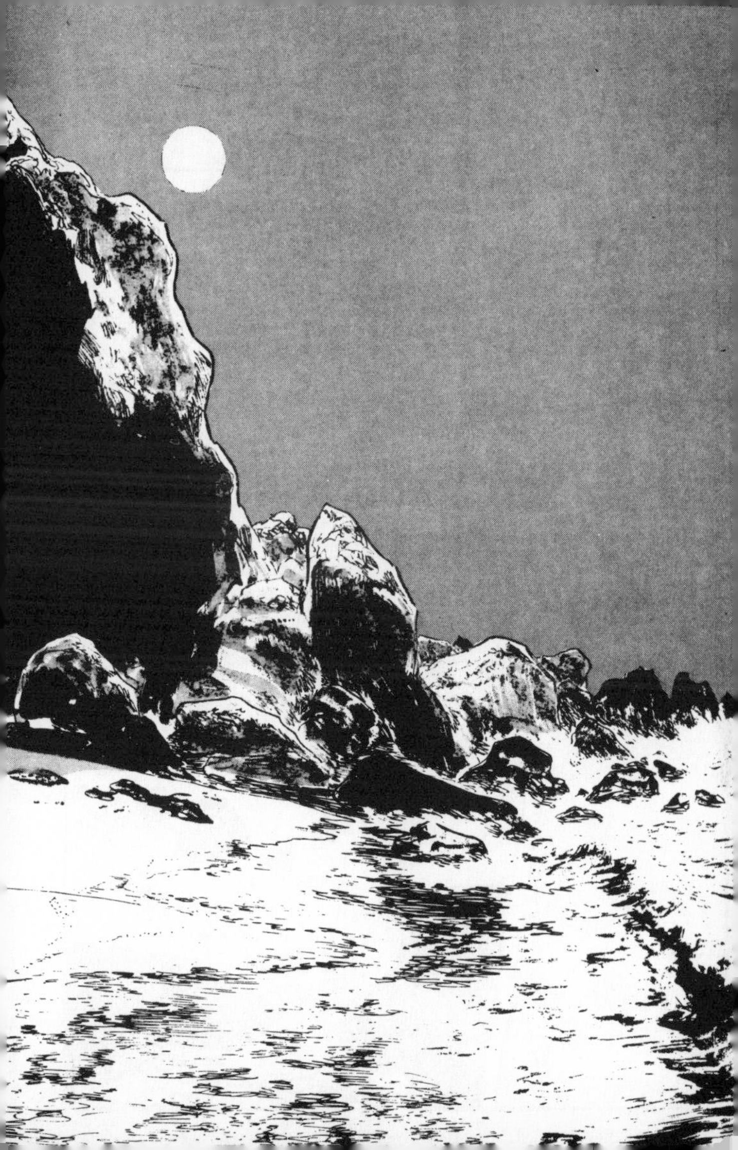

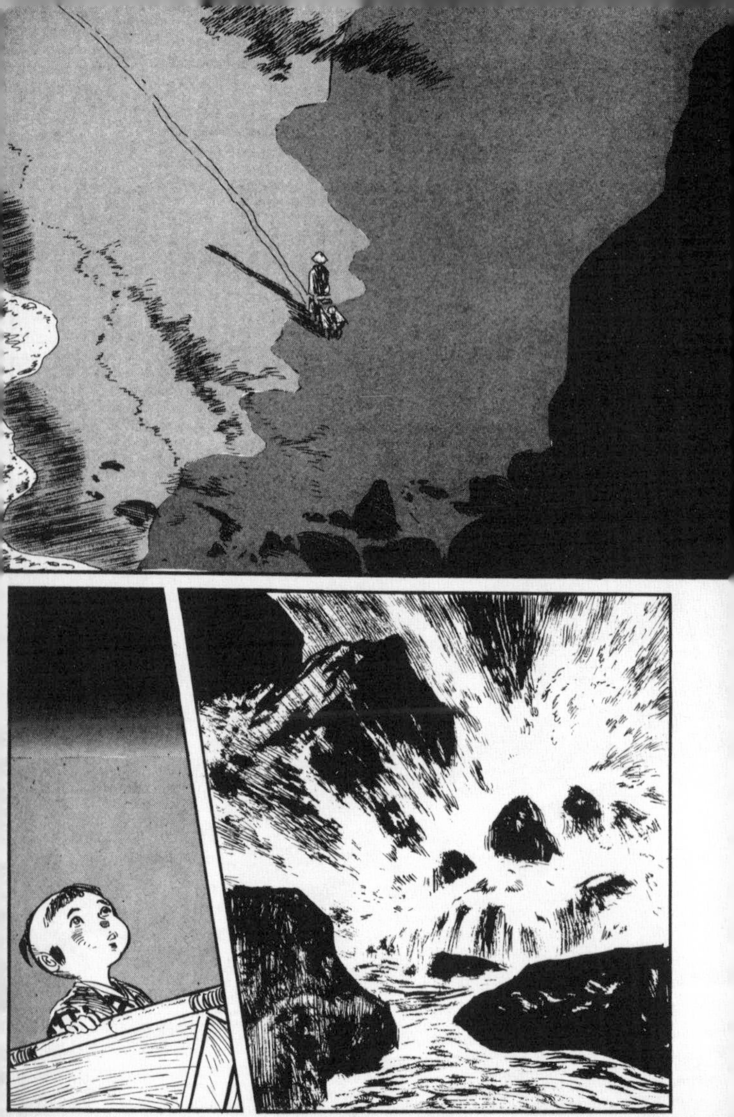

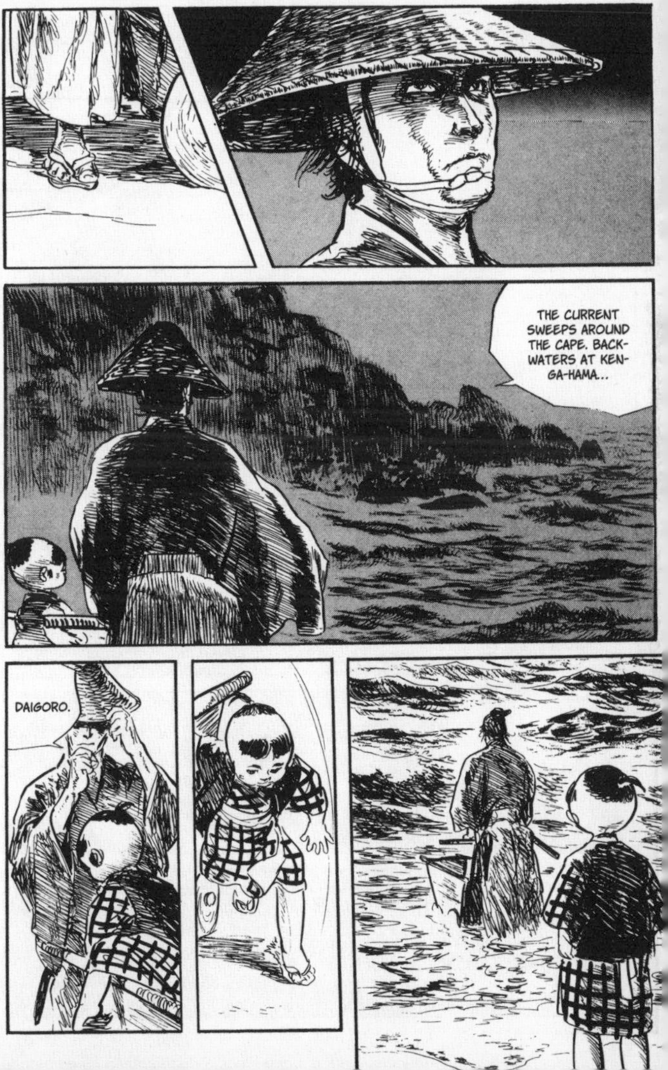THE CURRENT SWEEPS AROUND THE CAPE. BACK-WATERS AT KEN-GA-HAMA...
DAIGORO.

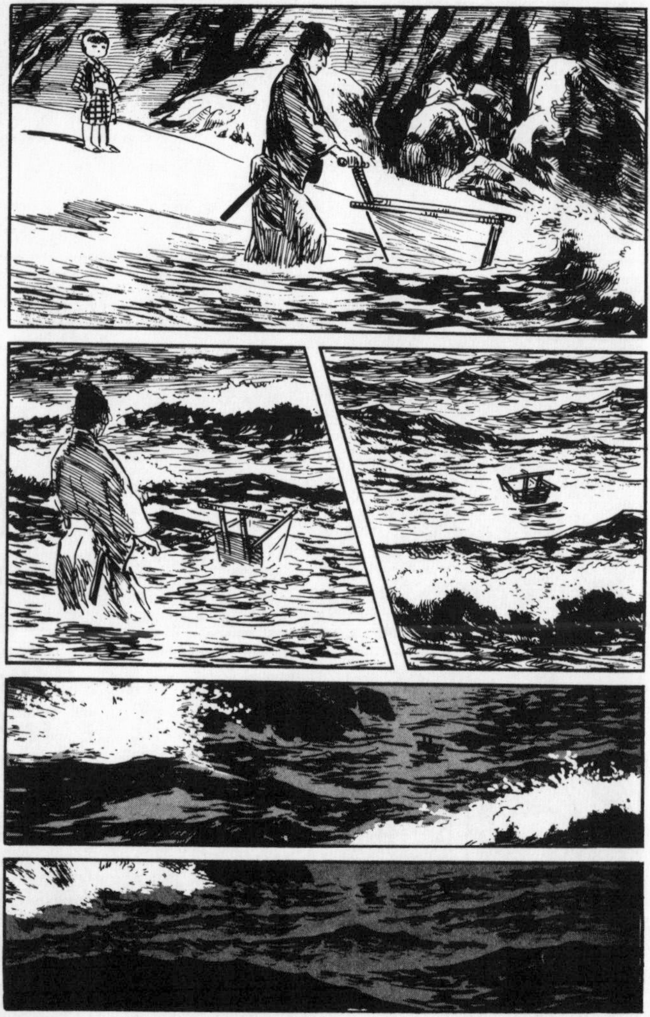

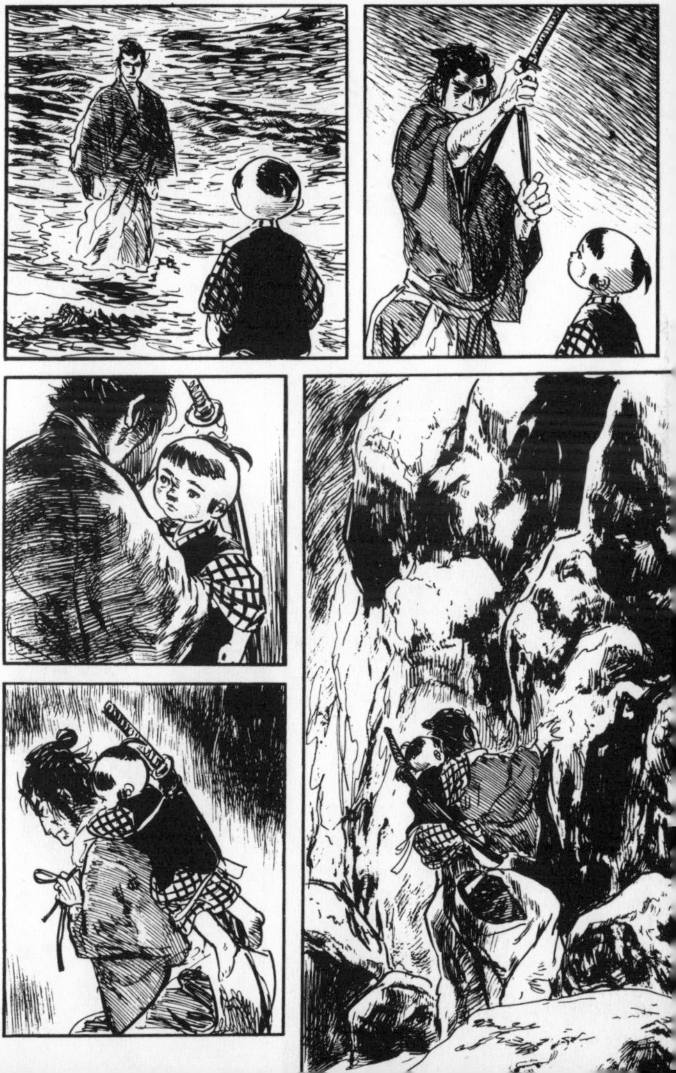

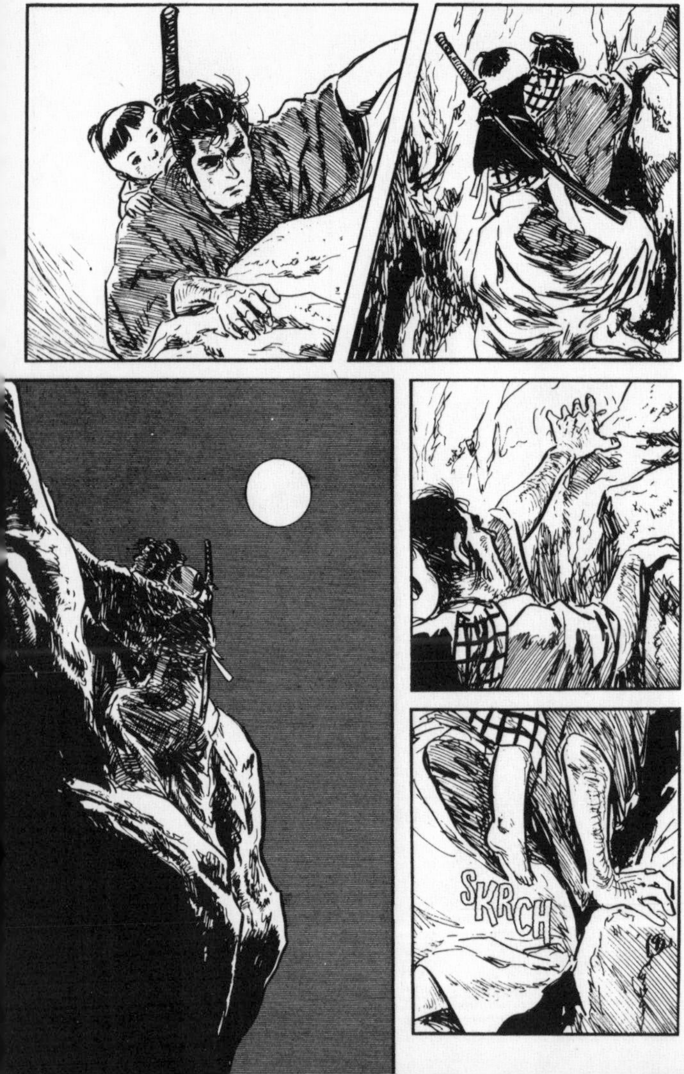
SKRCH

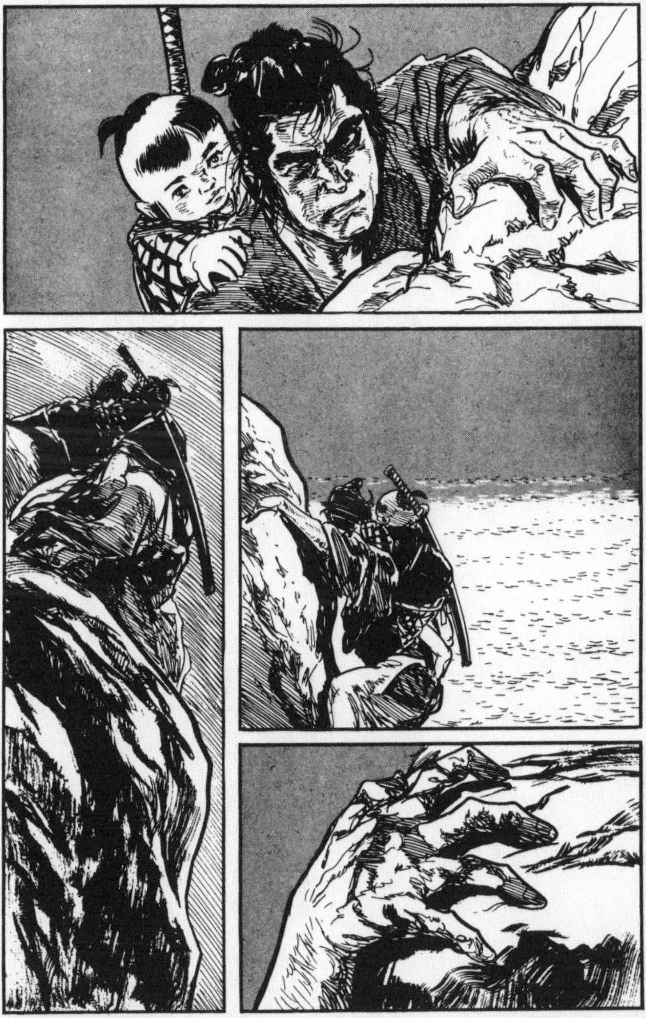

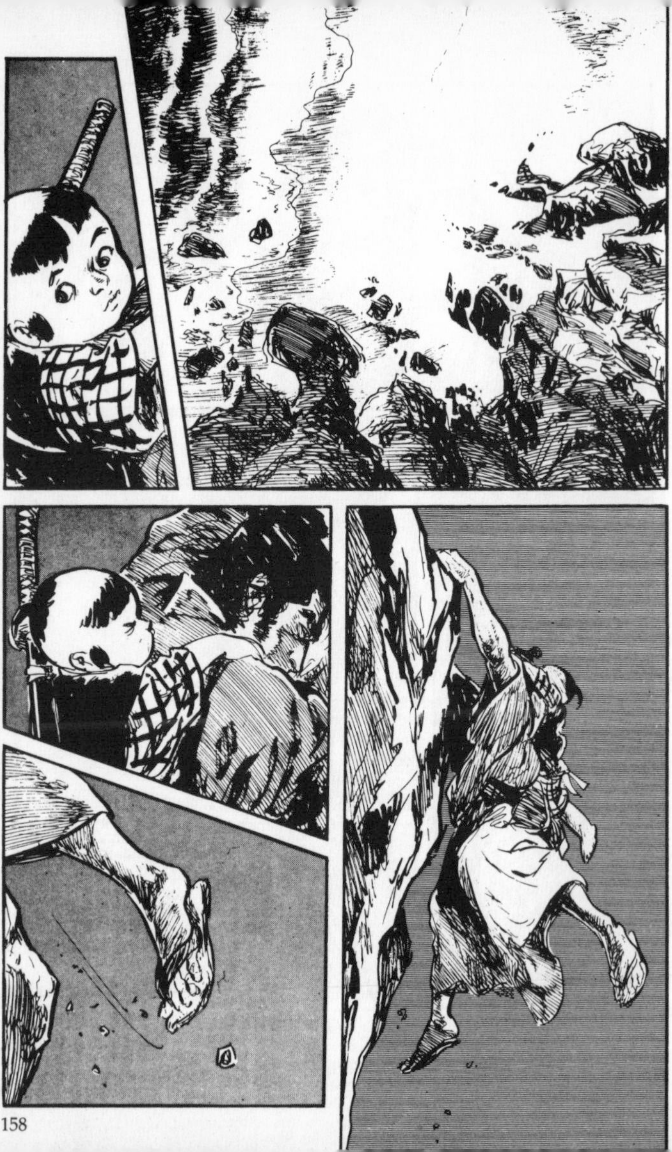

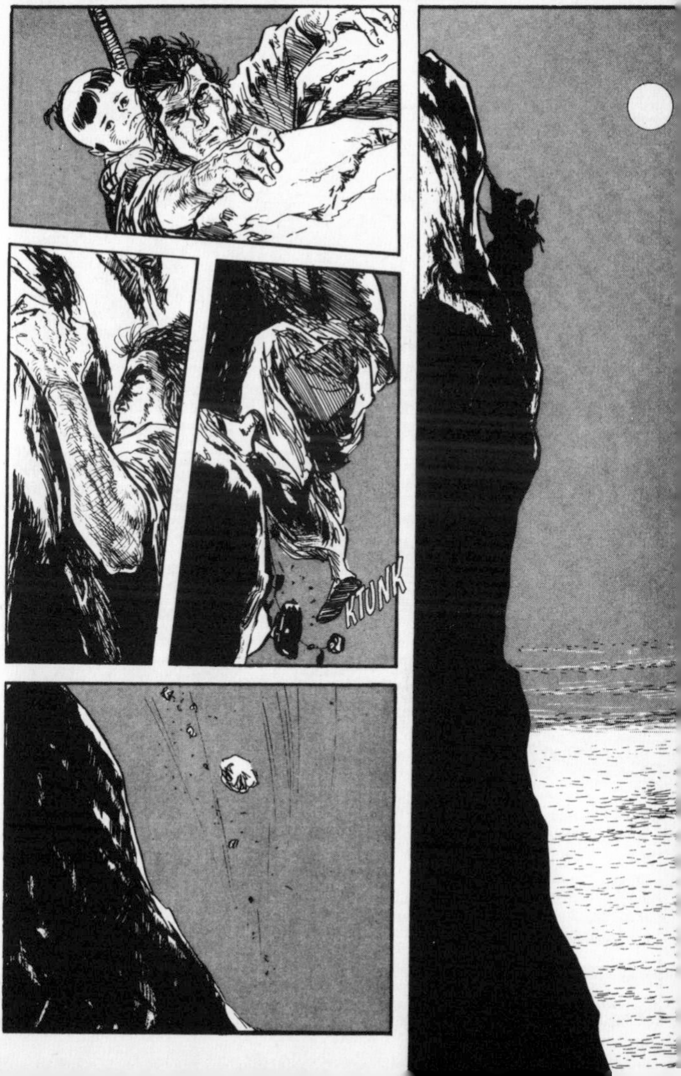
KTUNK

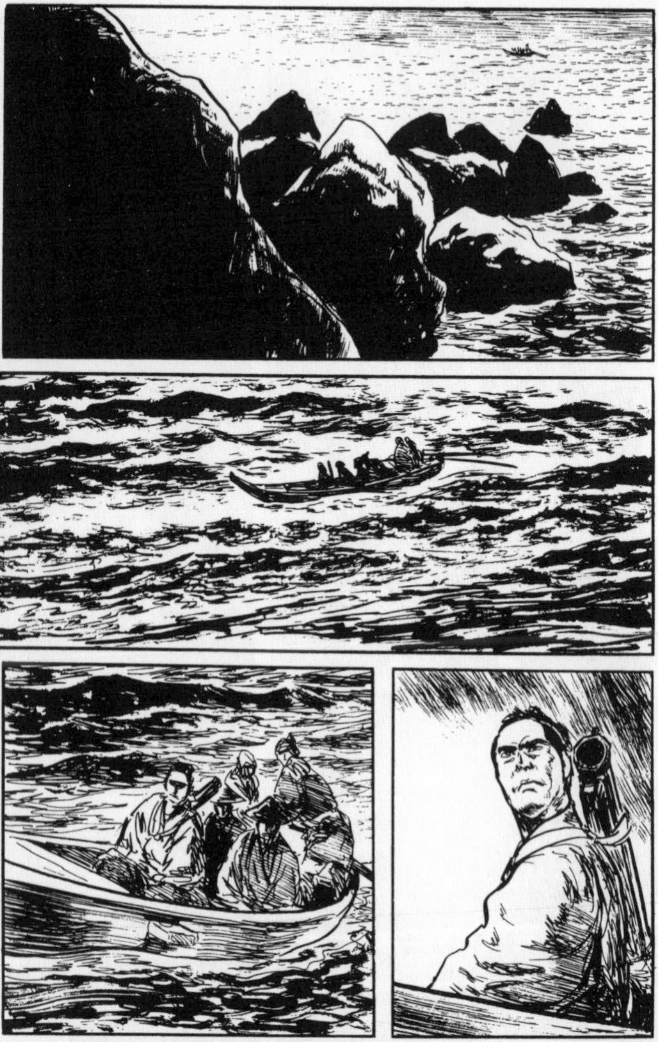

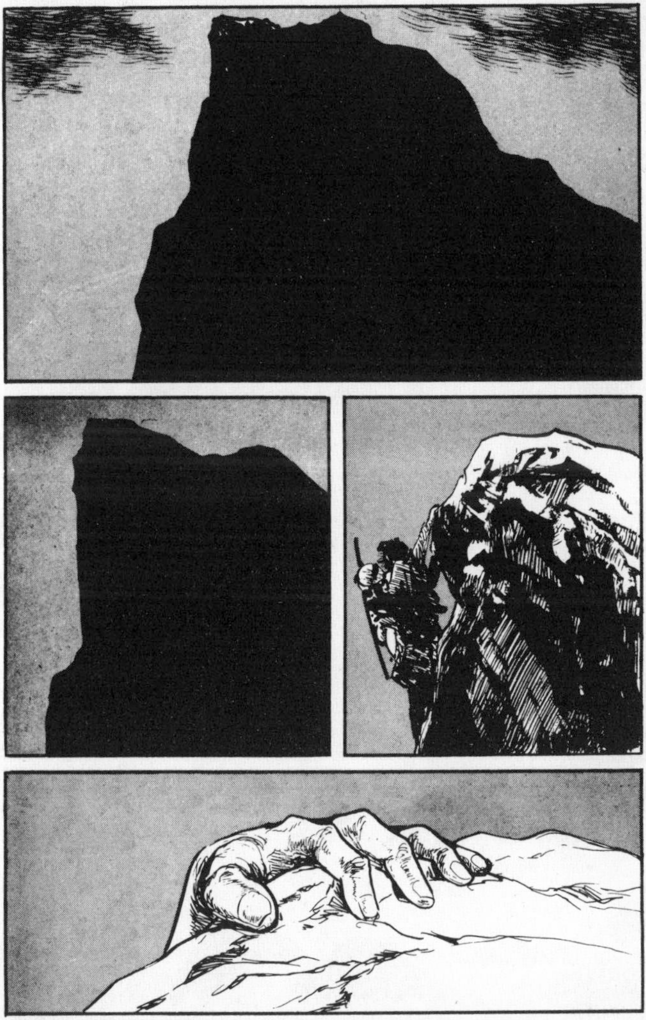

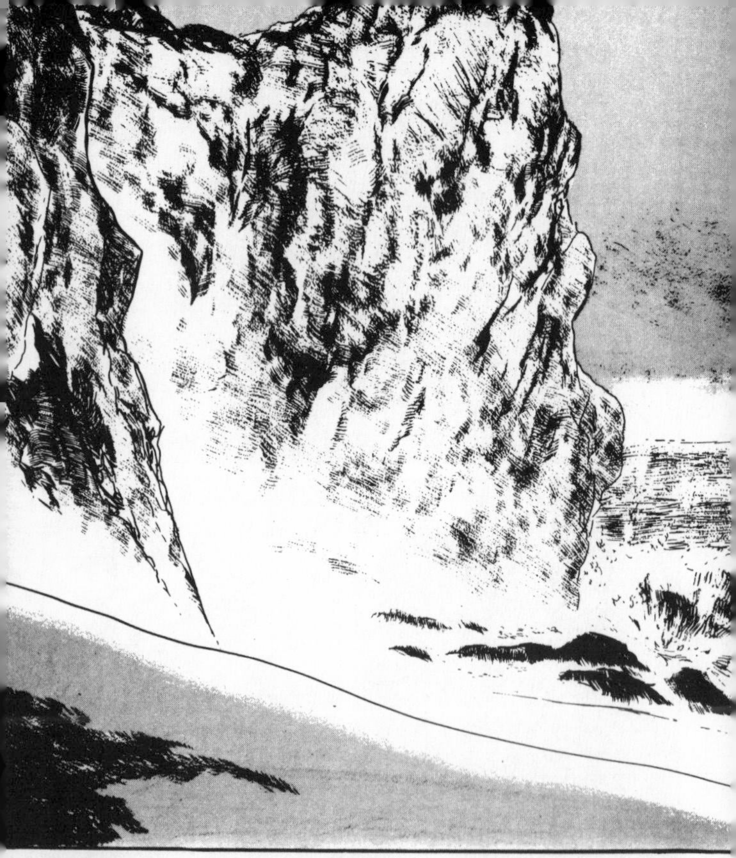

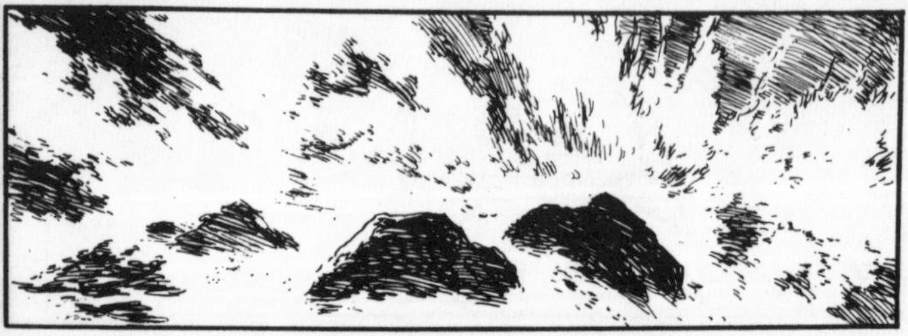

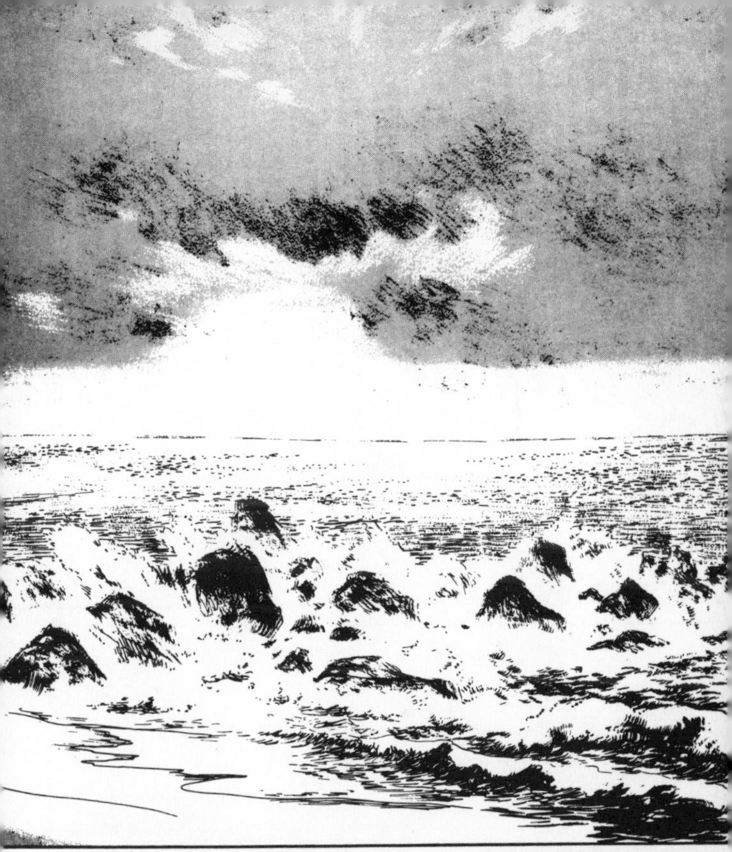
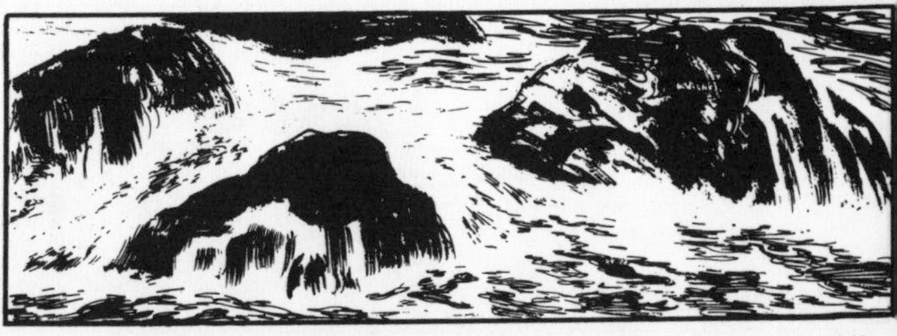

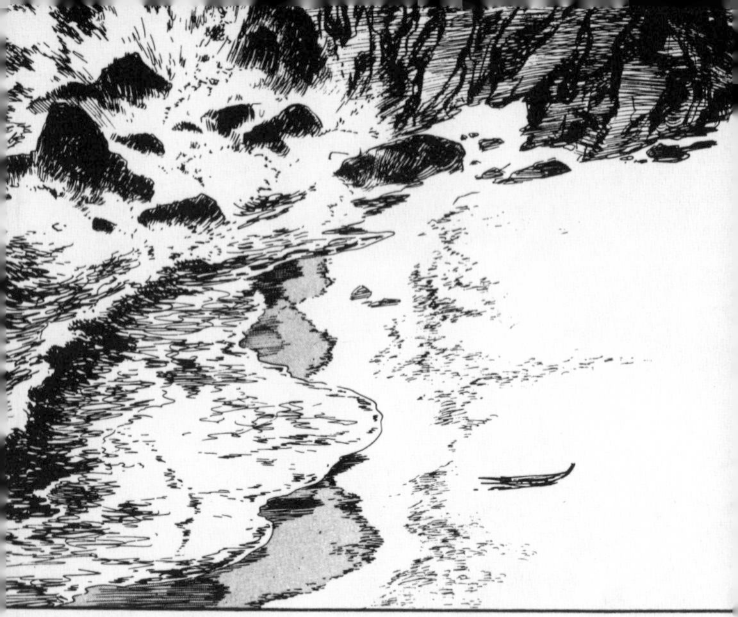
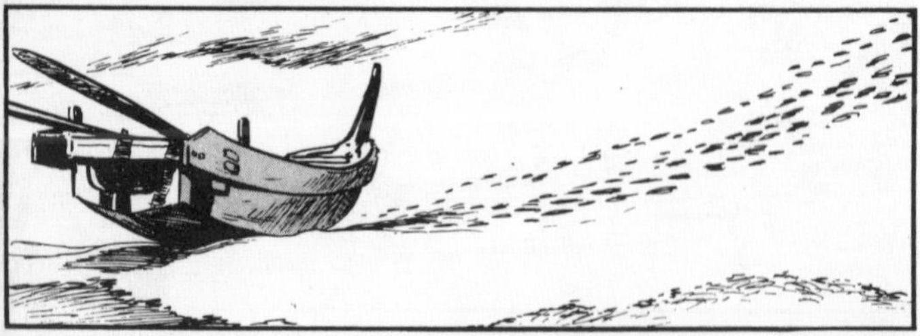
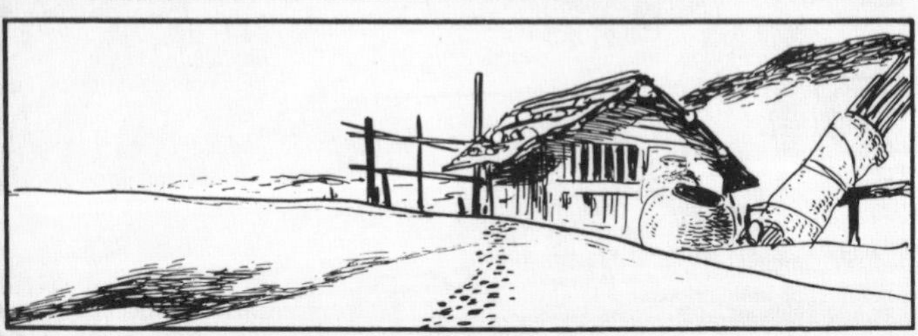

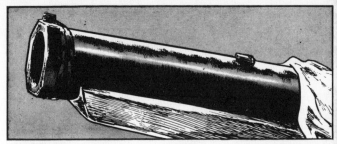

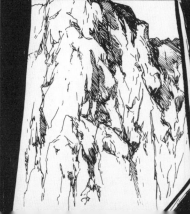

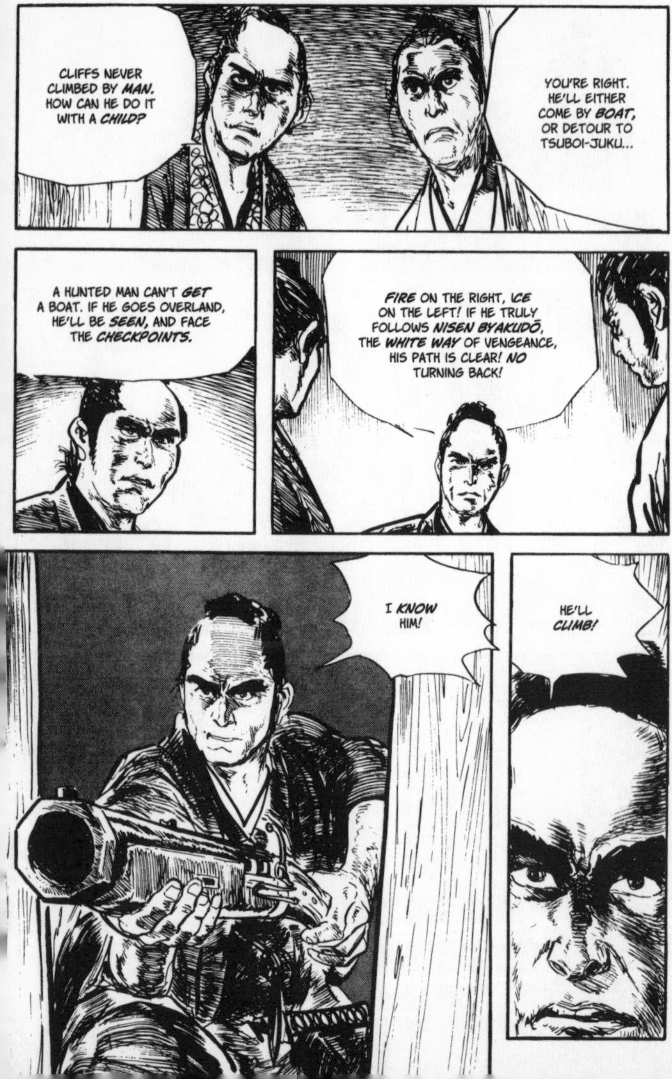

CLIFFS NEVER CLIMBED BY MAN. HOW CAN HE DO IT WITH A CHILD?
YOU'RE RIGHT. HE'LL EITHER COME BY BOAT, OR DETOUR TO TSUBOI-JUKU...
A HUNTED MAN CAN'T GET A BOAT. IF HE GOES OVERLAND, HE'LL BE SEEN, AND FACE THE CHECKPOINTS.
FIRE ON THE RIGHT, ICE ON THE LEFT! IF HE TRULY FOLLOWS NISEN BYAKUDŌ, THE WHITE WAY OF VENGEANCE, HIS PATH IS CLEAR! NO TURNING BACK!
I KNOW HIM!
HE'LL CLIMB!

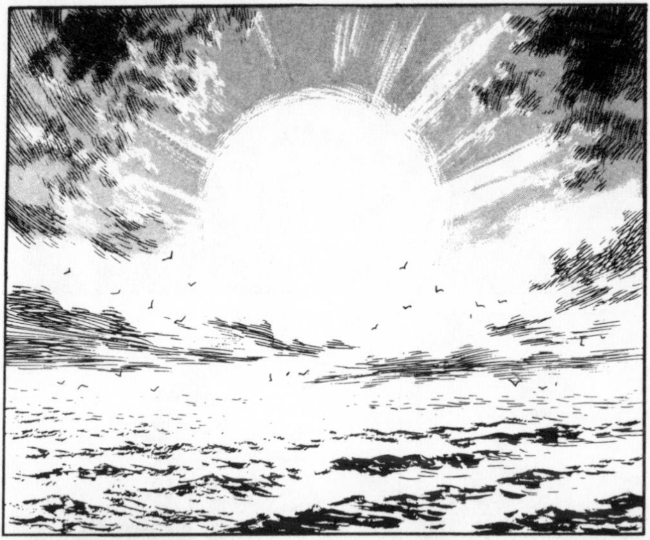
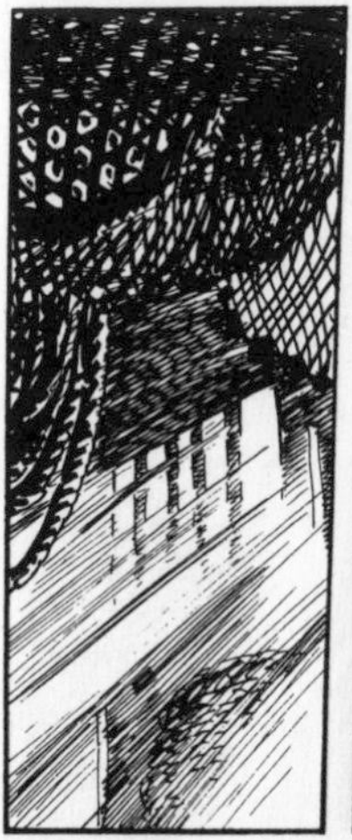
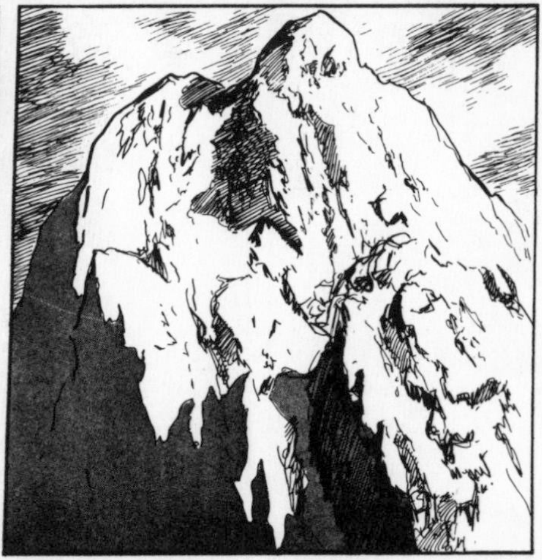

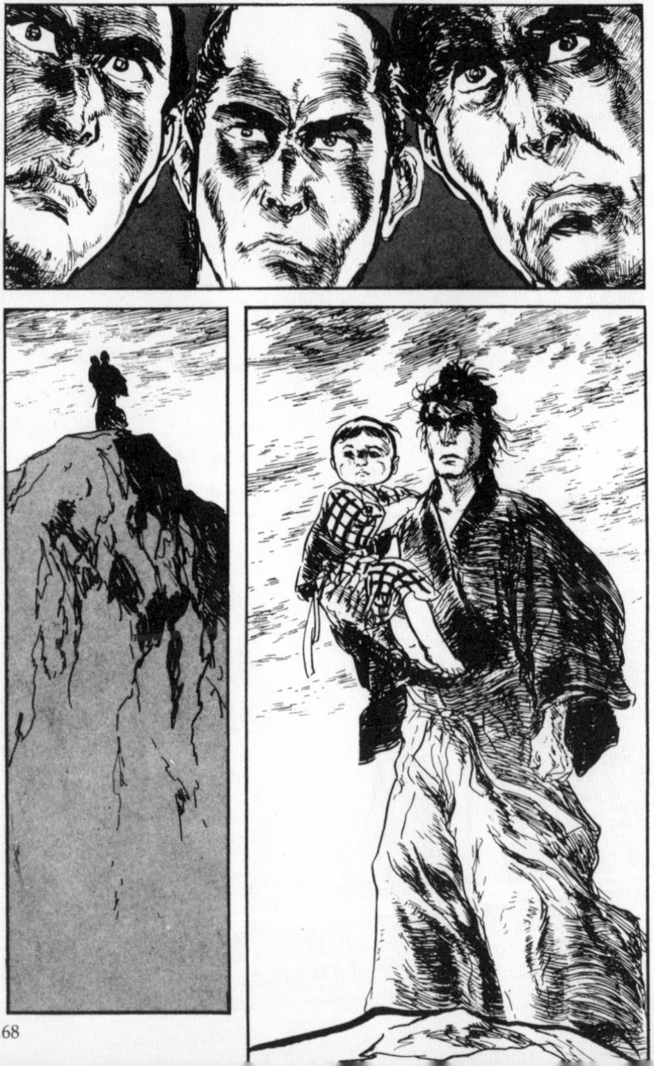

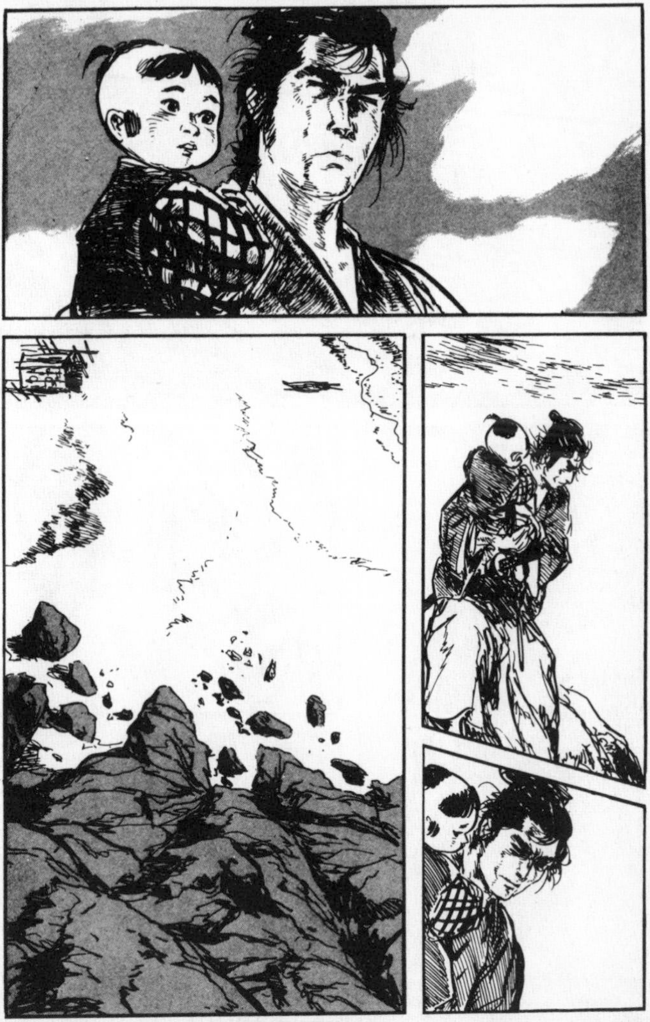

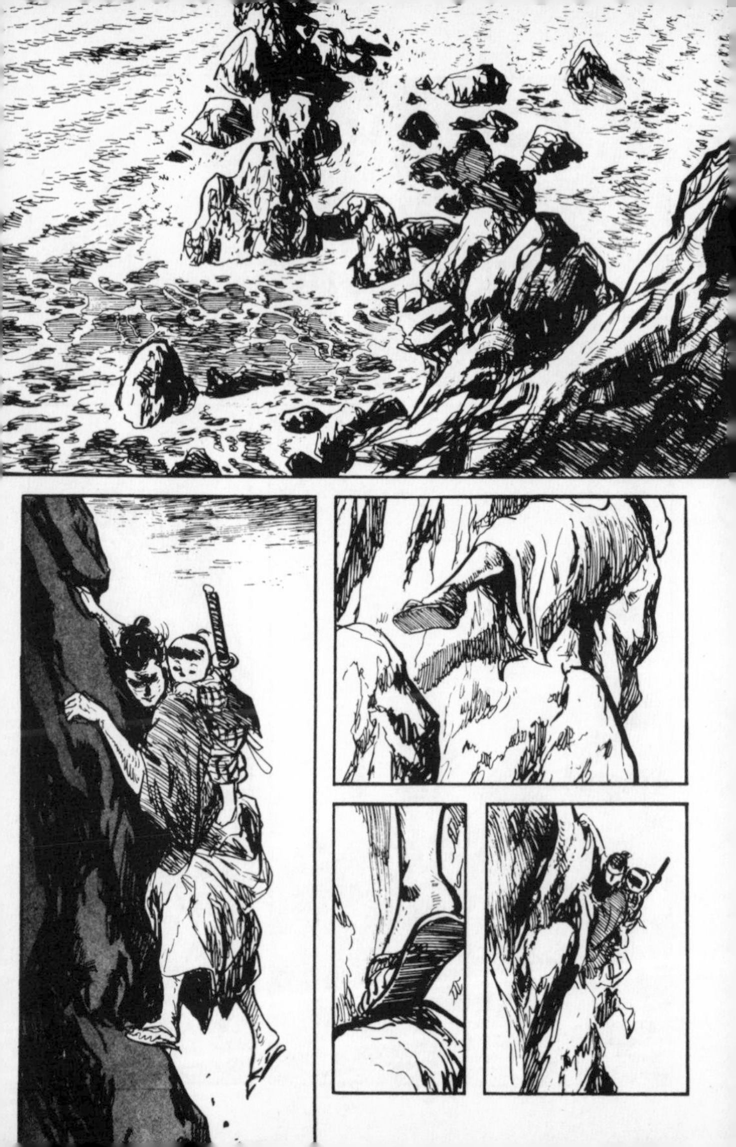

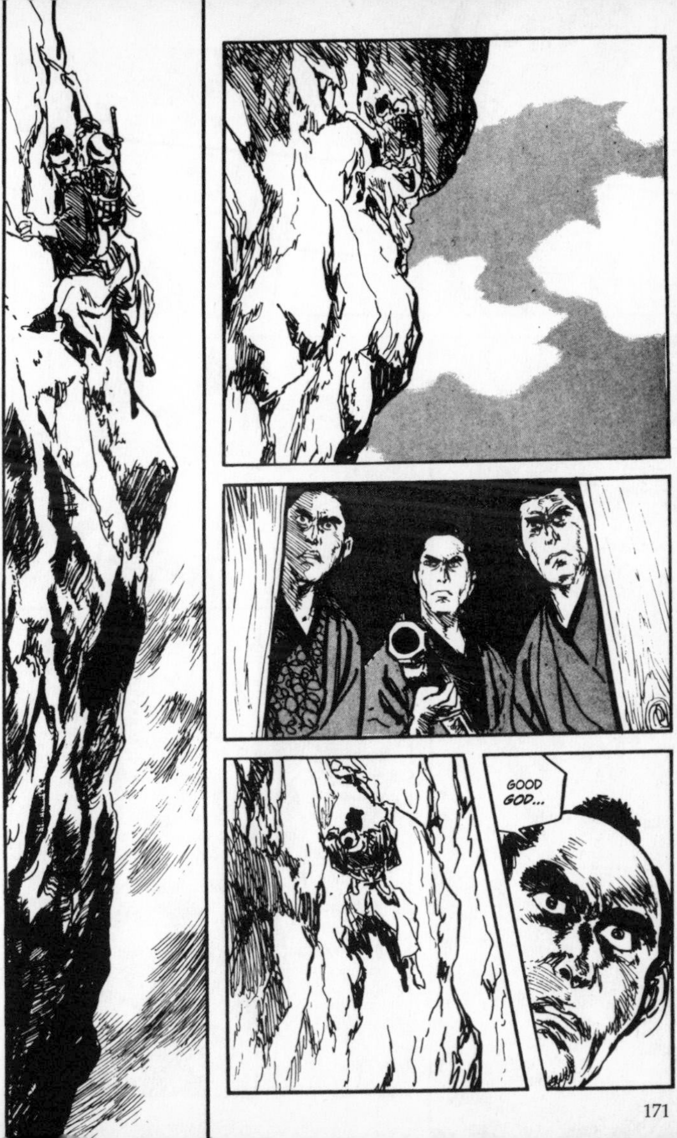
GOOD GOD...

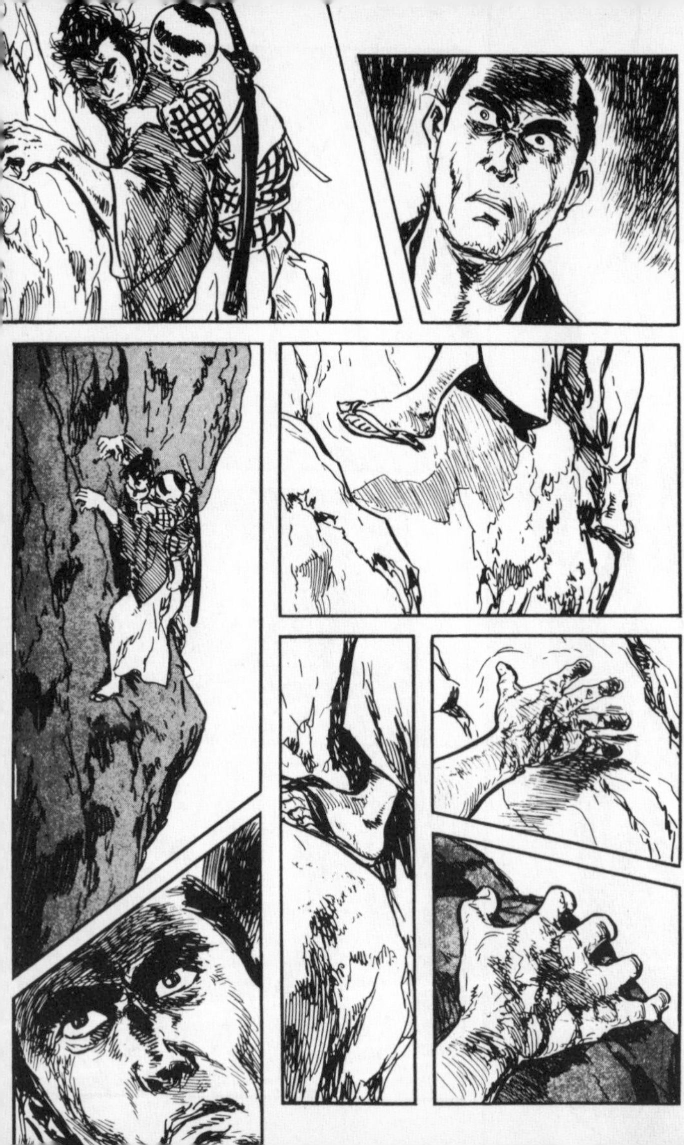

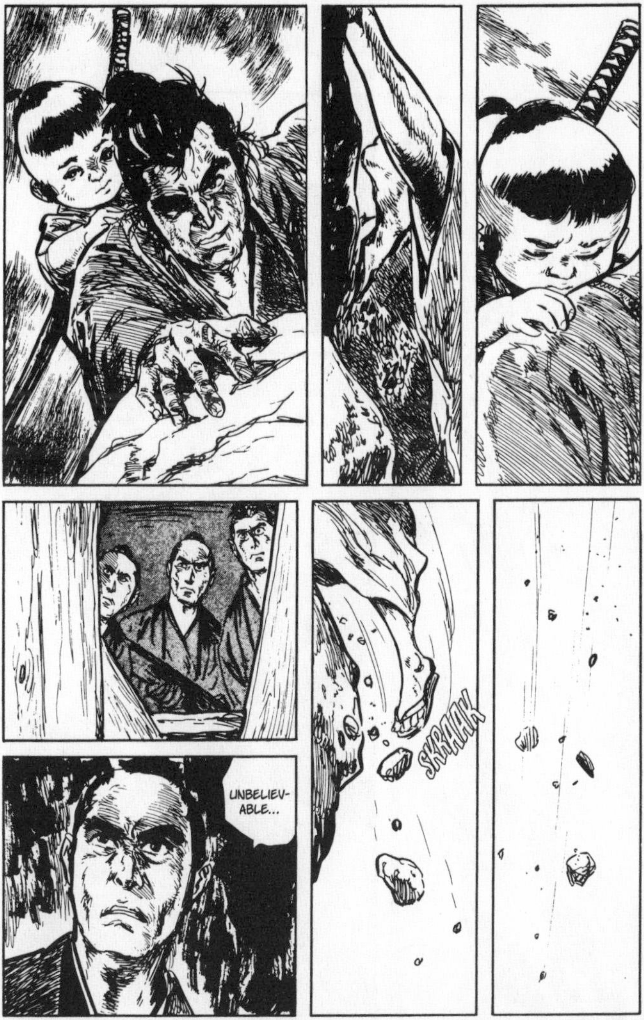
SKRAAK
UNBELIEV-
ABLE...

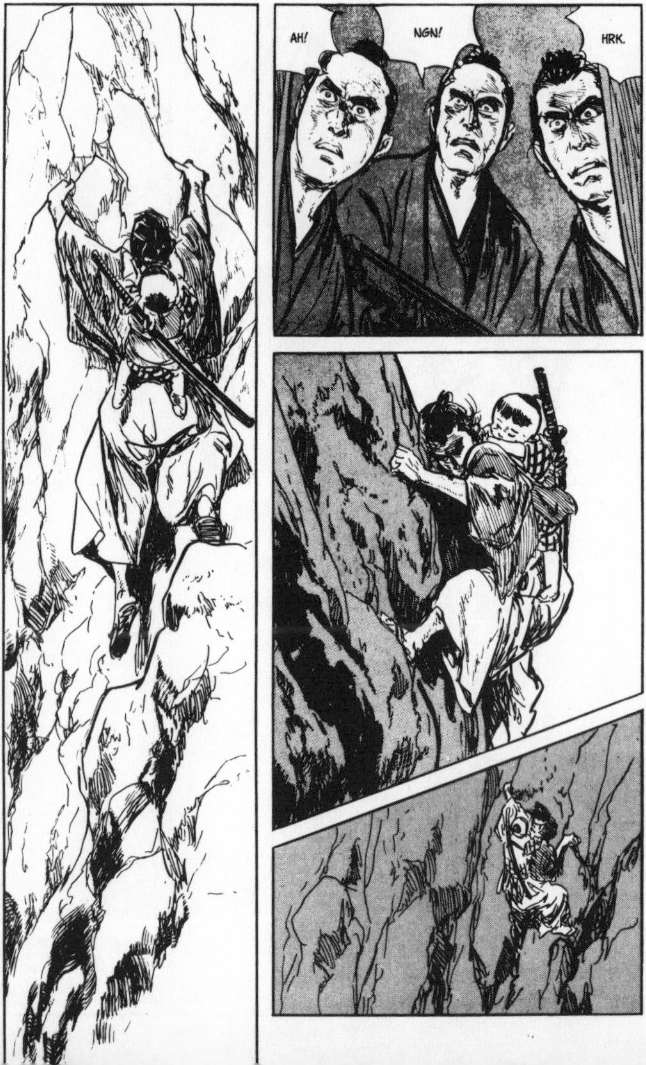
AH!
NGN!
HRK.

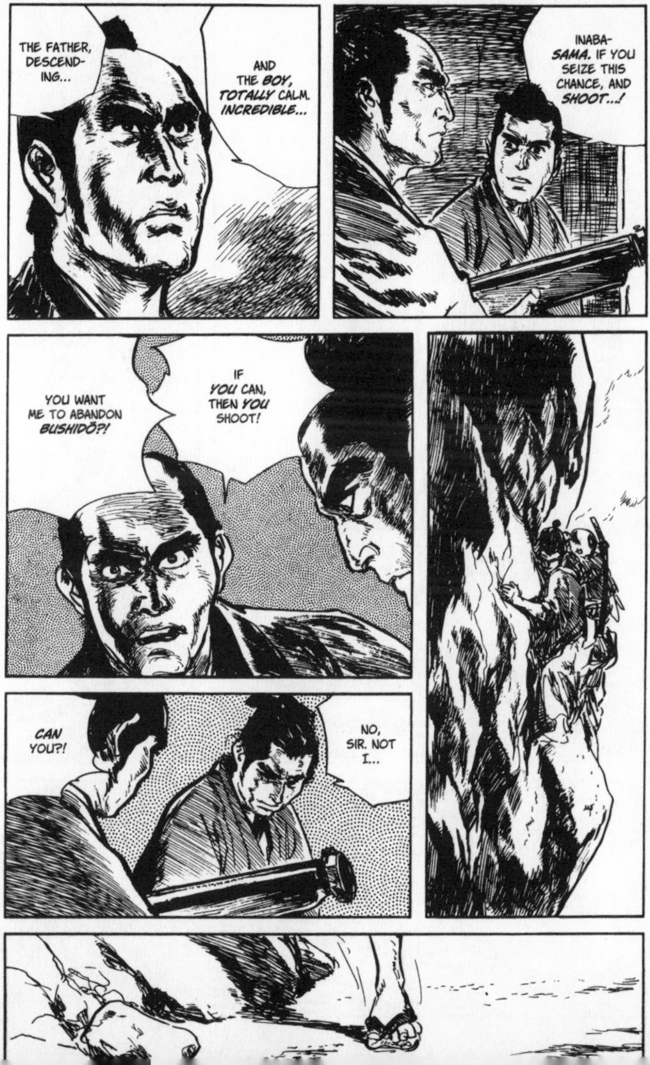
THE FATHER, DESCENDING...
AND THE BOY, TOTALLY CALM. INCREDIBLE...
INABA-SAMA. IF YOU SEIZE THIS CHANCE, AND SHOOT...!
YOU WANT ME TO ABANDON BUSHIDŌ?!
IF YOU CAN, THEN YOU SHOOT!
CAN YOU?!
NO, SIR. NOT I...

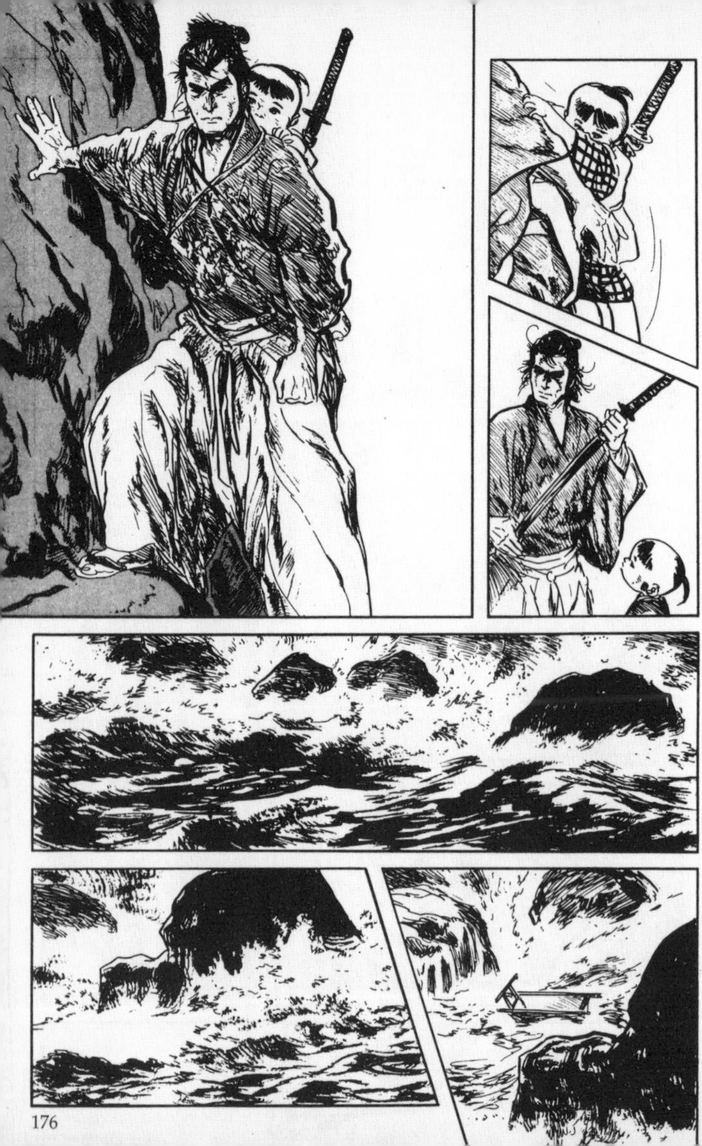

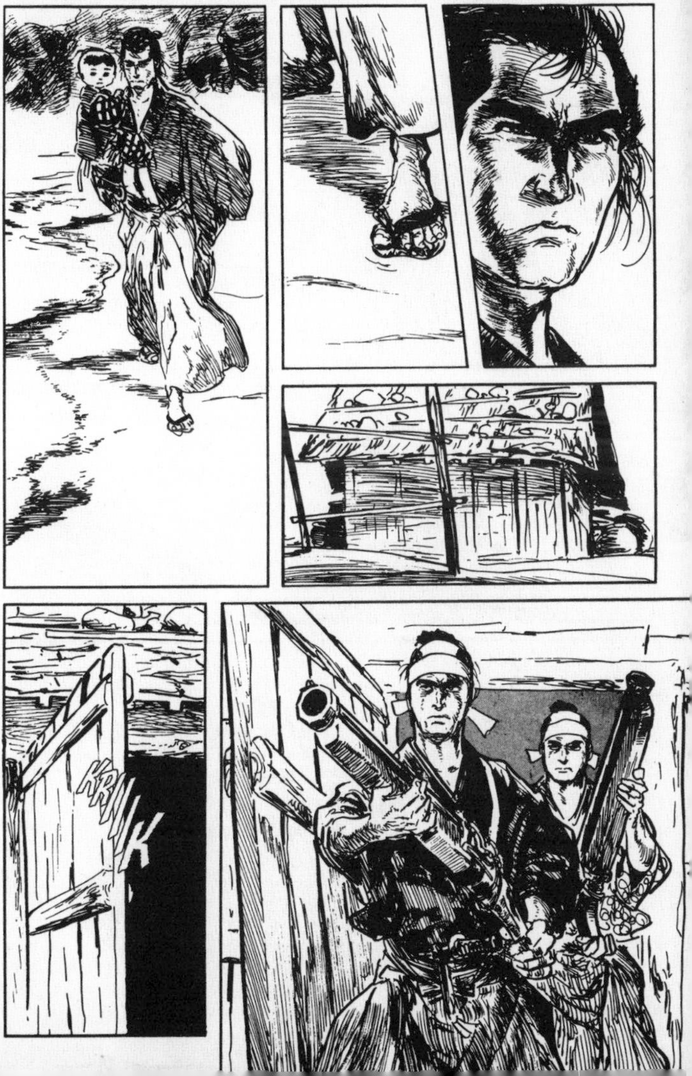
KRIIIK

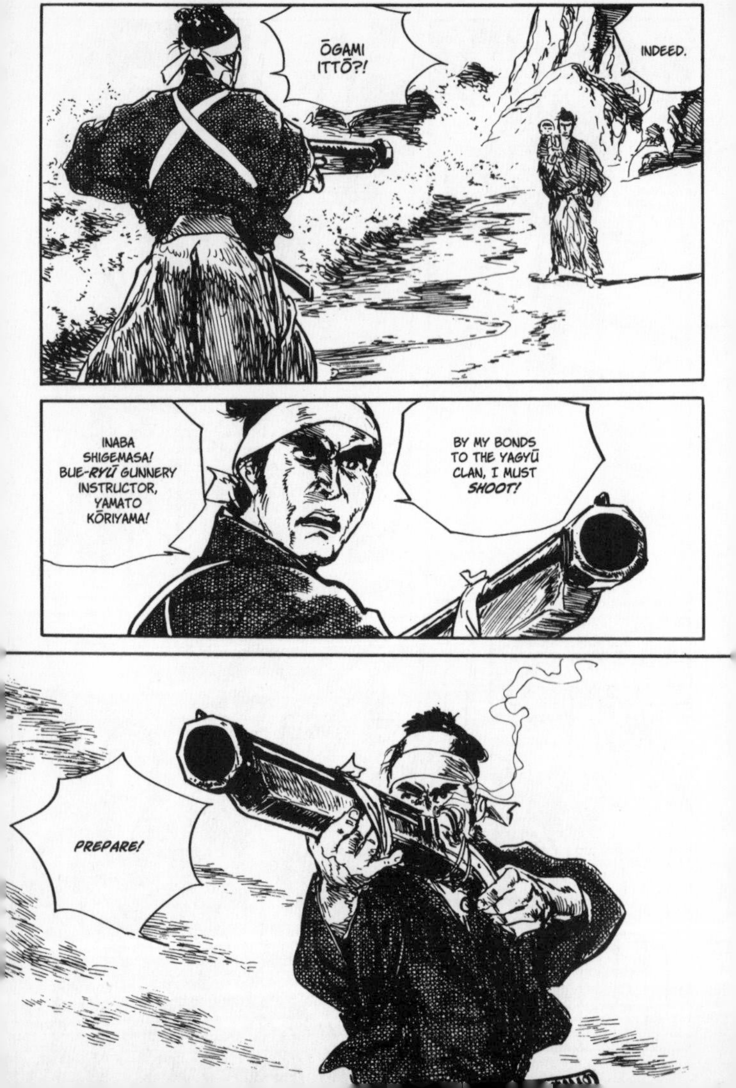
ŌGAMI ITTŌ?!
INDEED.
INABA SHIGEMASA! BUE-*RYŪ* GUNNERY INSTRUCTOR, YAMATO KŌRIYAMA!
BY MY BONDS TO THE YAGYŪ CLAN, I MUST *SHOOT!*
PREPARE!

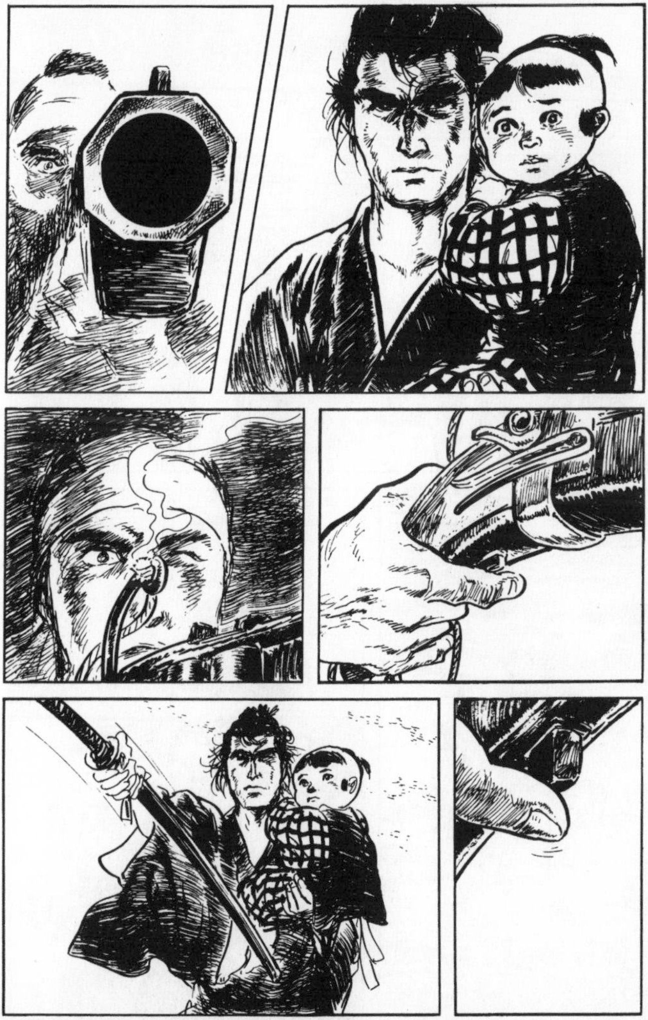

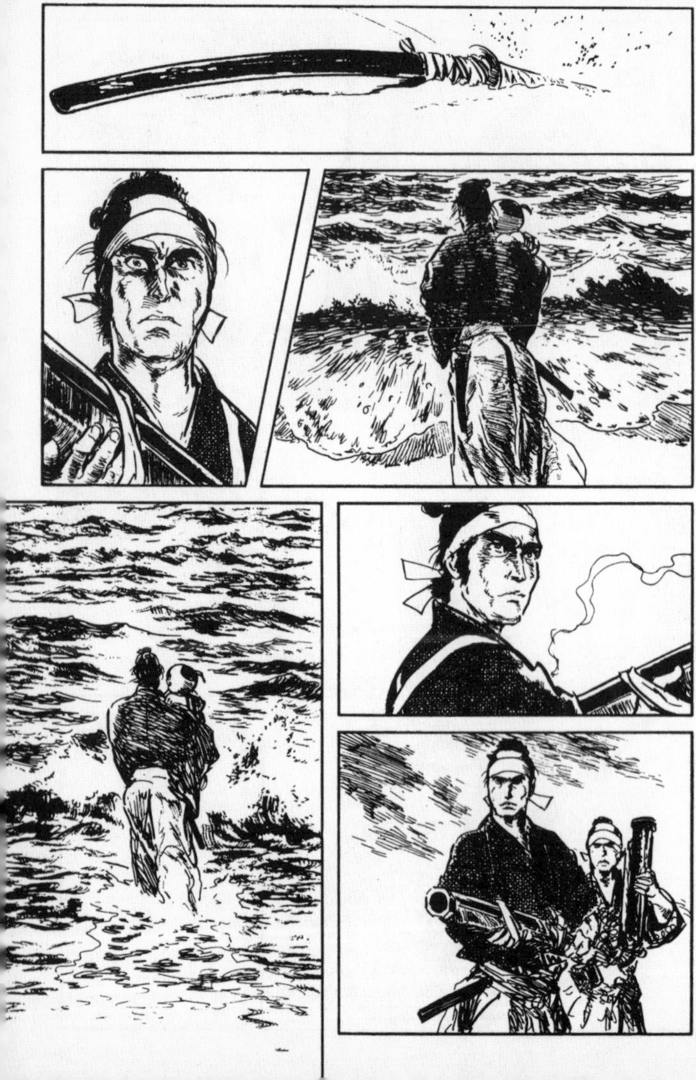

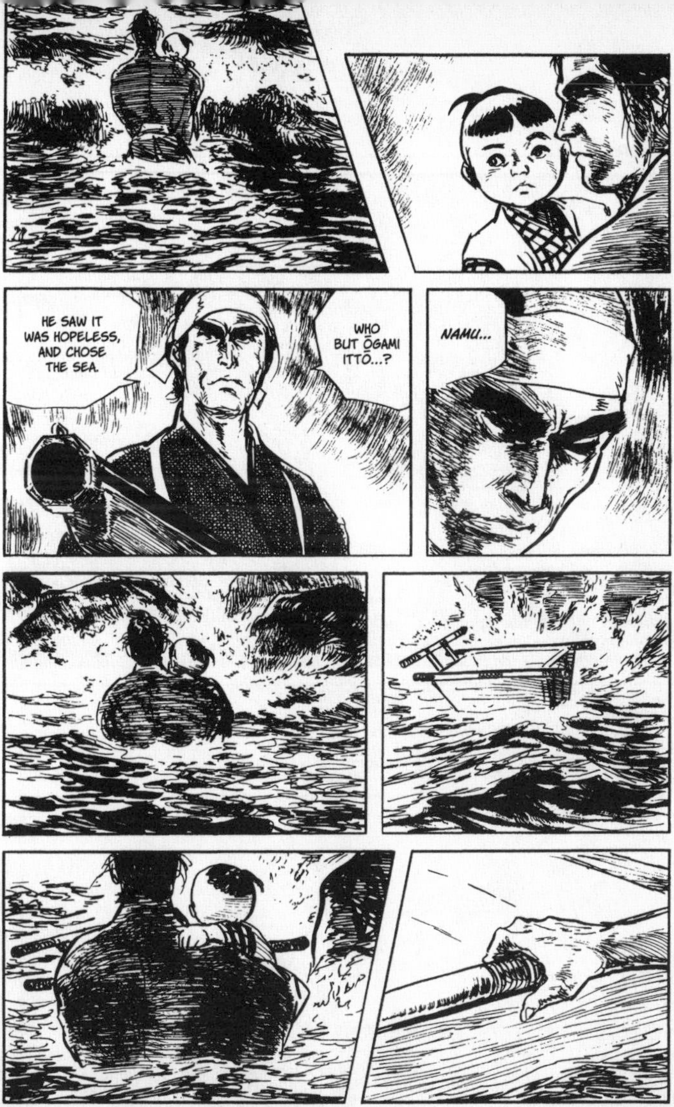
HE SAW IT WAS HOPELESS, AND CHOSE THE SEA.
WHO BUT ŌGAMI ITTŌ...?
NAMU...

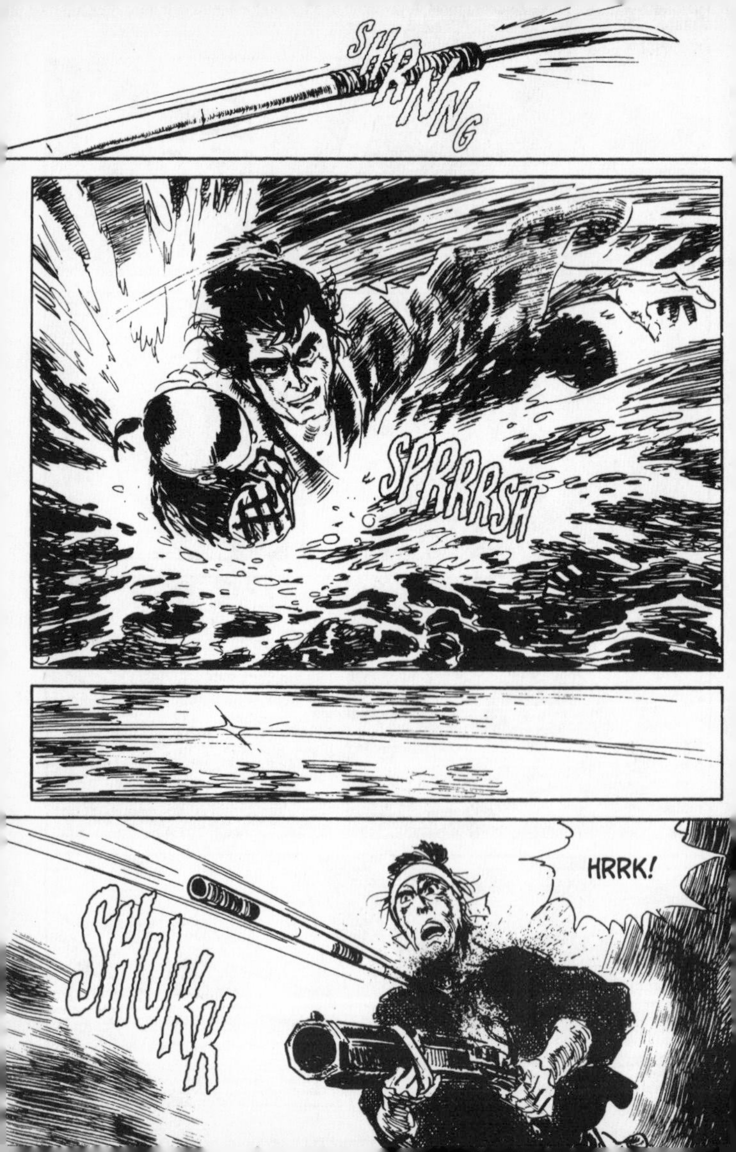
SHRNNG
SPRRRSH
SHUKK
HRRK!

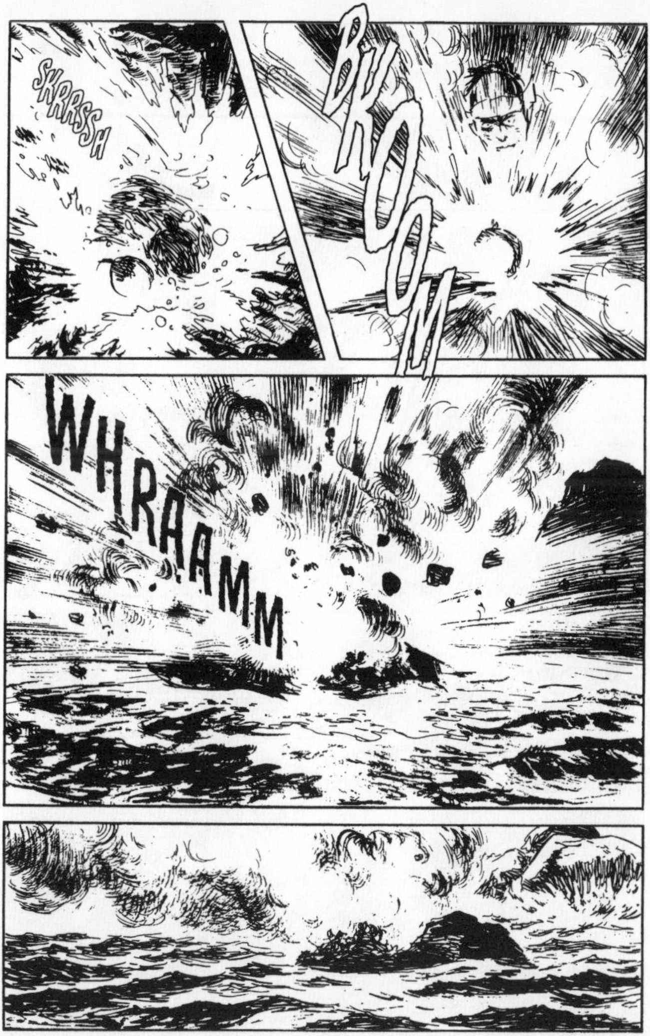
SKRRSSH
BROOOM
WHRAAMM

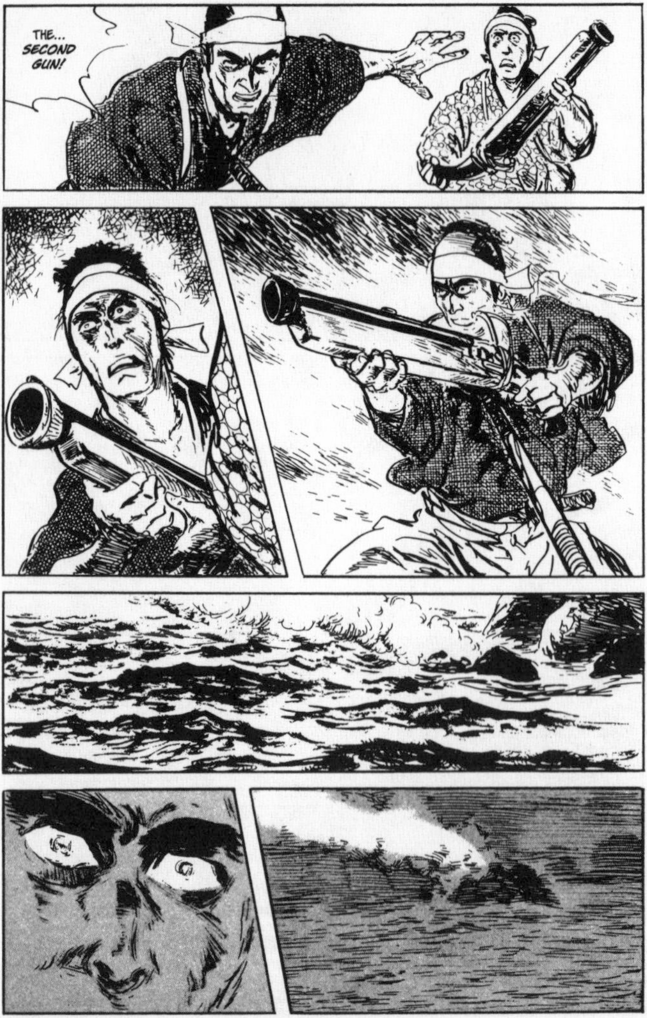
THE... SECOND GUN!

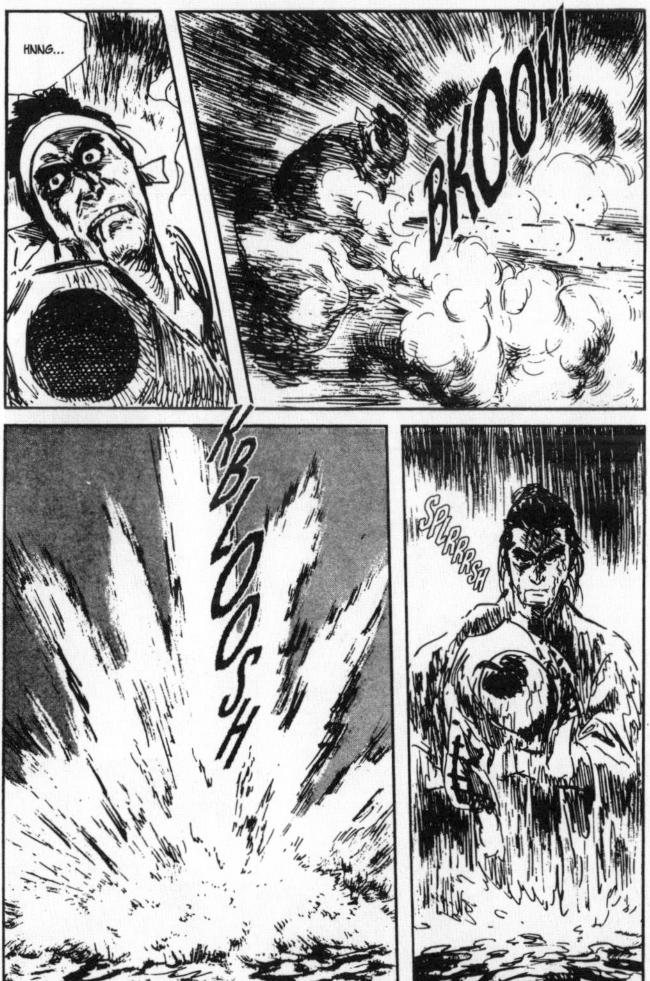
HNNG...
BKOOM
KBLOOSH
SPLRRRSH

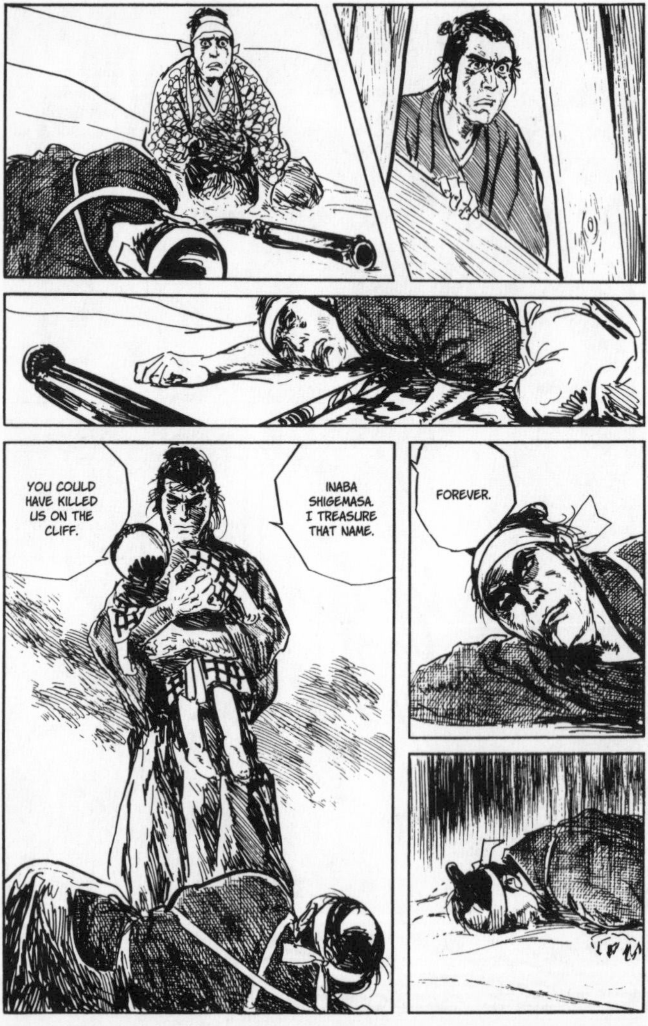
YOU COULD HAVE KILLED US ON THE CLIFF.
INABA SHIGEMASA. I TREASURE THAT NAME.
FOREVER.

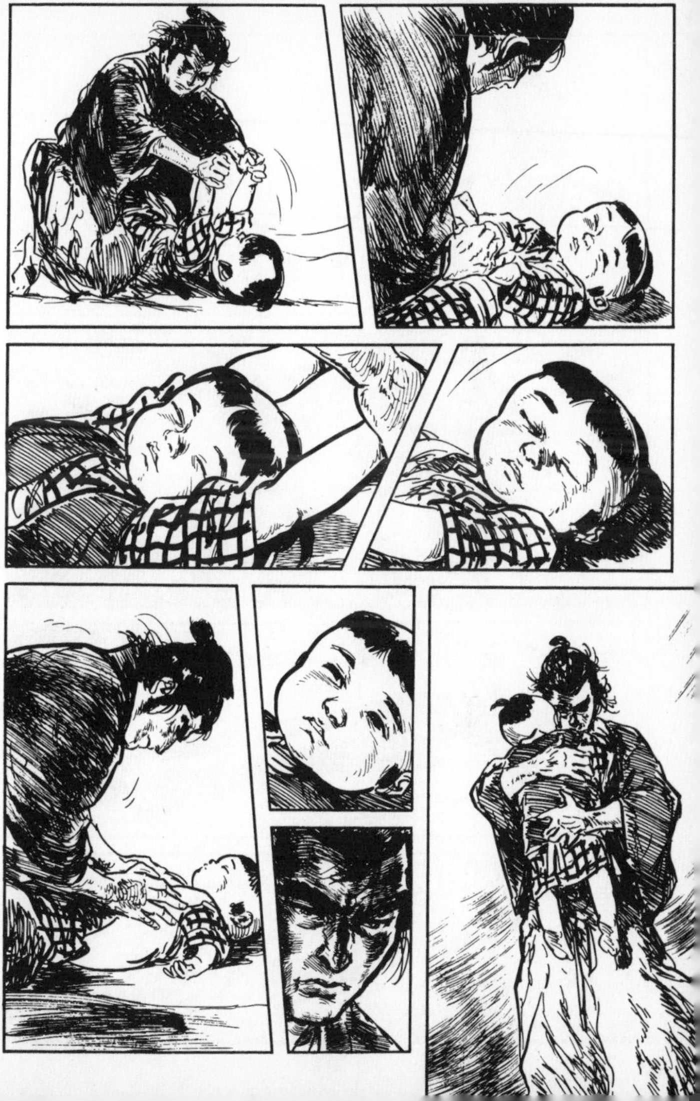

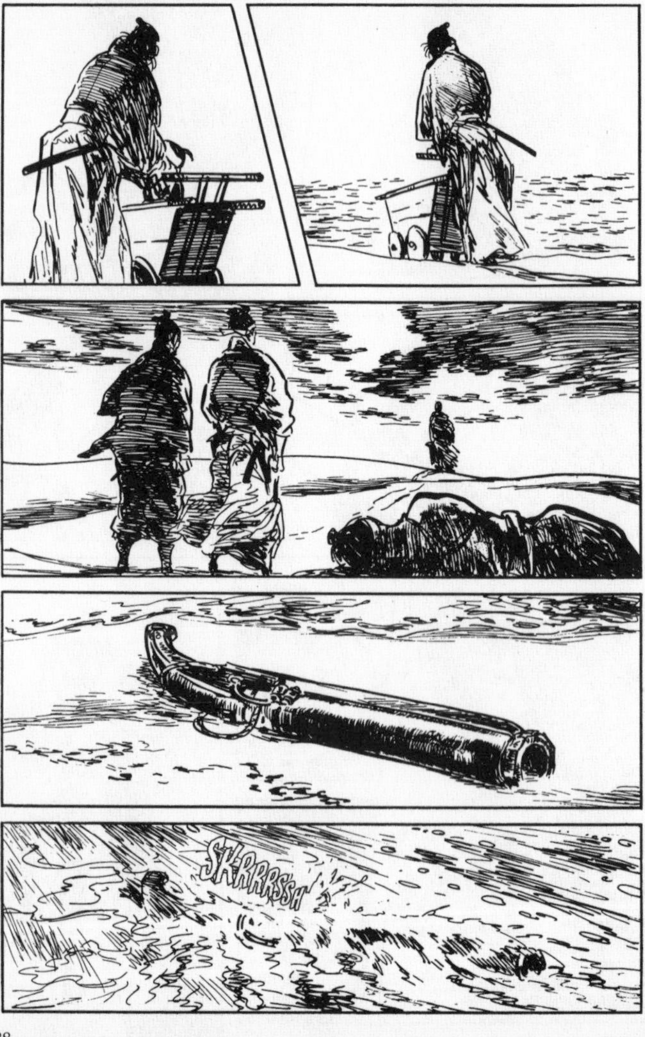
SKRRRSSH

the ninety-sixth

A Mother's Flavor

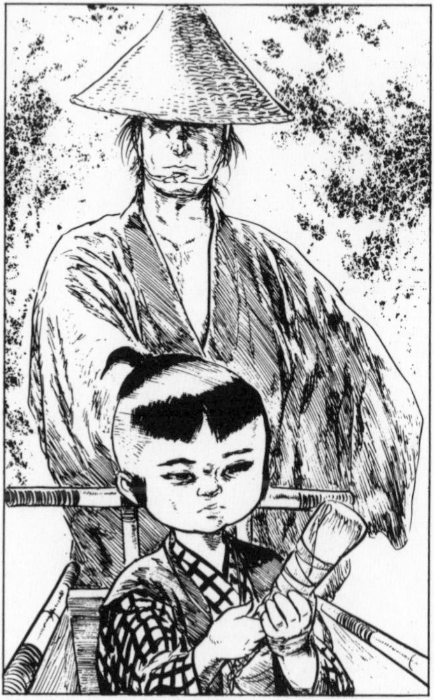

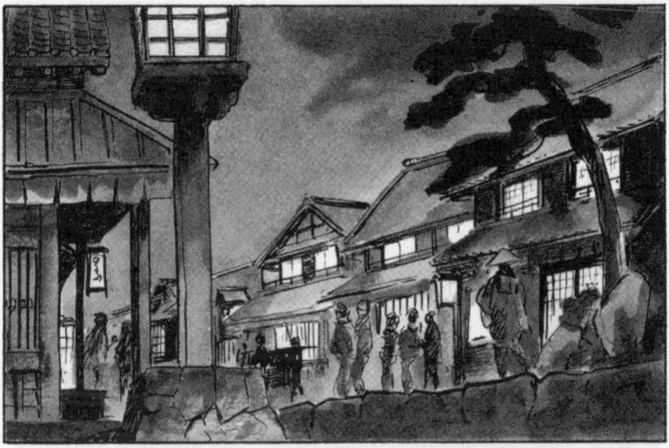

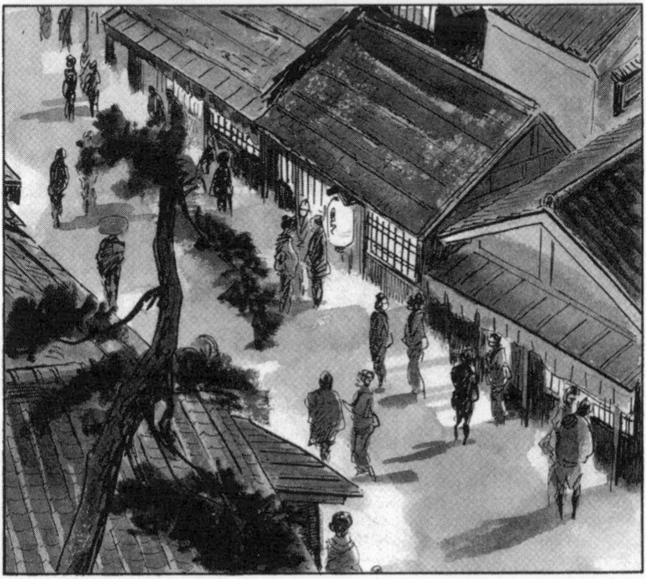

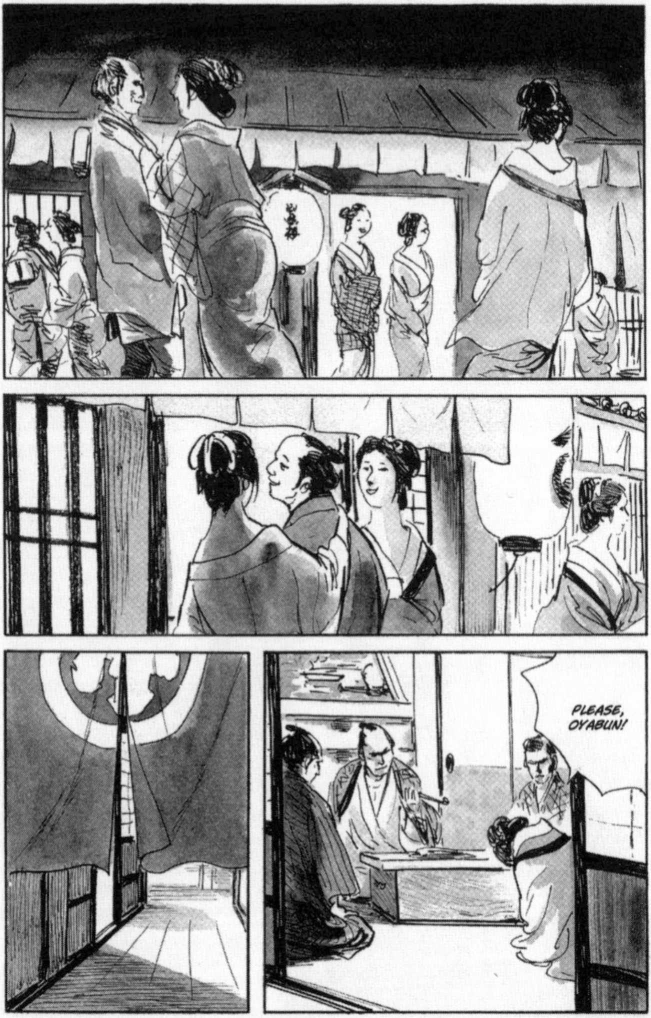
PLEASE, OYABUN!

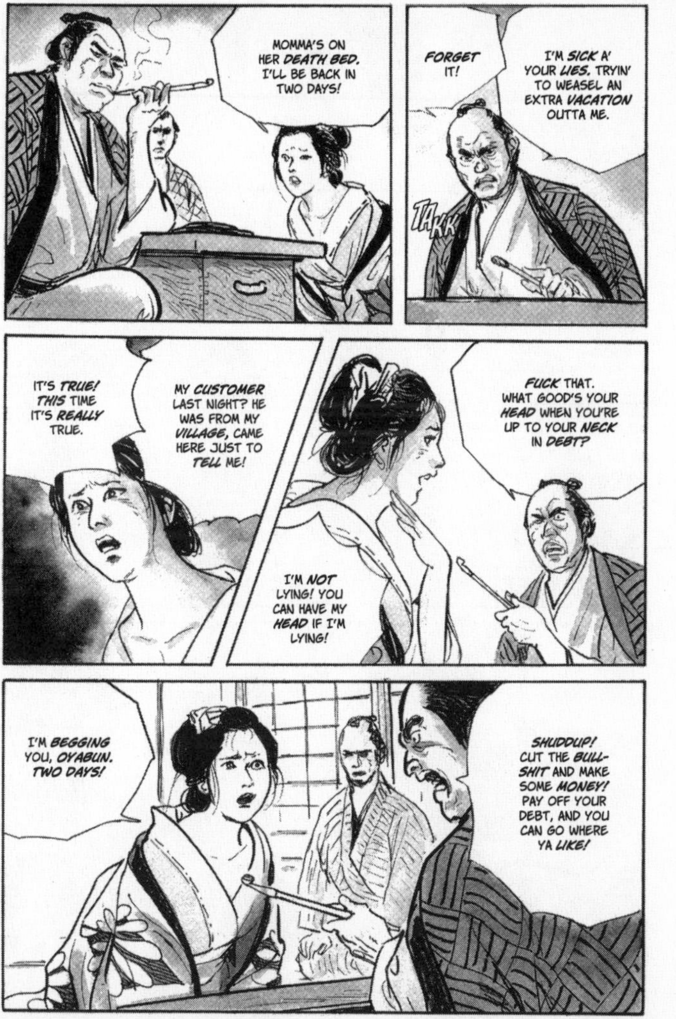
MOMMA'S ON HER DEATH BED. I'LL BE BACK IN TWO DAYS!
FORGET IT!
I'M SICK A' YOUR LIES. TRYIN' TO WEASEL AN EXTRA VACATION OUTTA ME.
TAKK
IT'S TRUE! THIS TIME IT'S REALLY TRUE.
MY CUSTOMER LAST NIGHT? HE WAS FROM MY VILLAGE, CAME HERE JUST TO TELL ME!
I'M NOT LYING! YOU CAN HAVE MY HEAD IF I'M LYING!
FUCK THAT. WHAT GOOD'S YOUR HEAD WHEN YOU'RE UP TO YOUR NECK IN DEBT?
I'M BEGGING YOU, OYABUN. TWO DAYS!
SHUDDUP! CUT THE BULL-SHIT AND MAKE SOME MONEY! PAY OFF YOUR DEBT, AND YOU CAN GO WHERE YA LIKE!

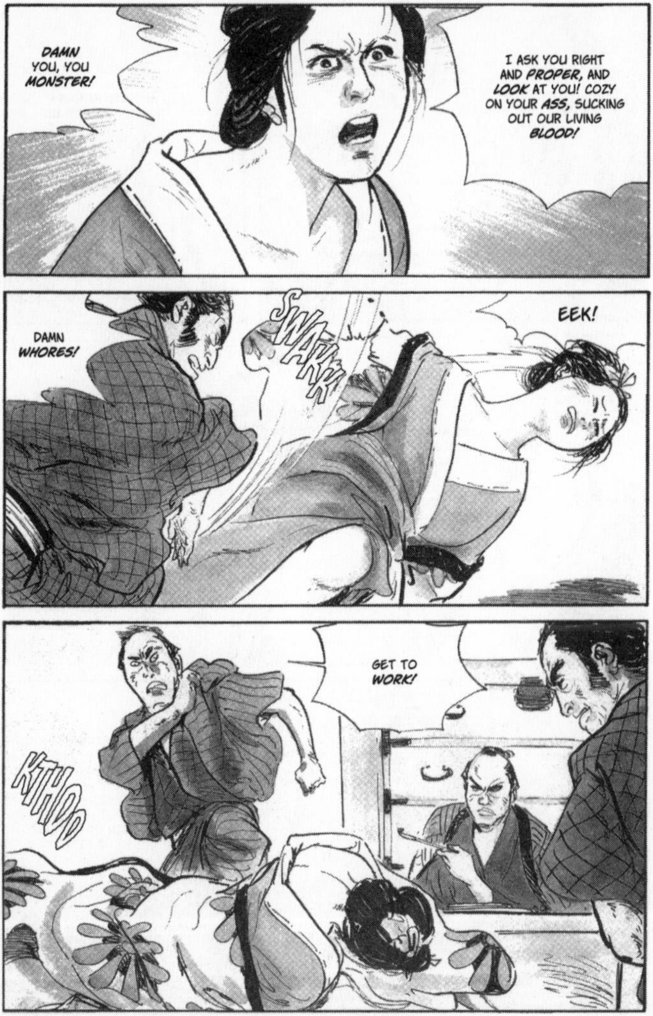
DAMN YOU, YOU MONSTER!
I ASK YOU RIGHT AND PROPER, AND LOOK AT YOU! COZY ON YOUR ASS, SUCKING OUT OUR LIVING BLOOD!
DAMN WHORES!
SWAKK
EEK!
KTHOO
GET TO WORK!

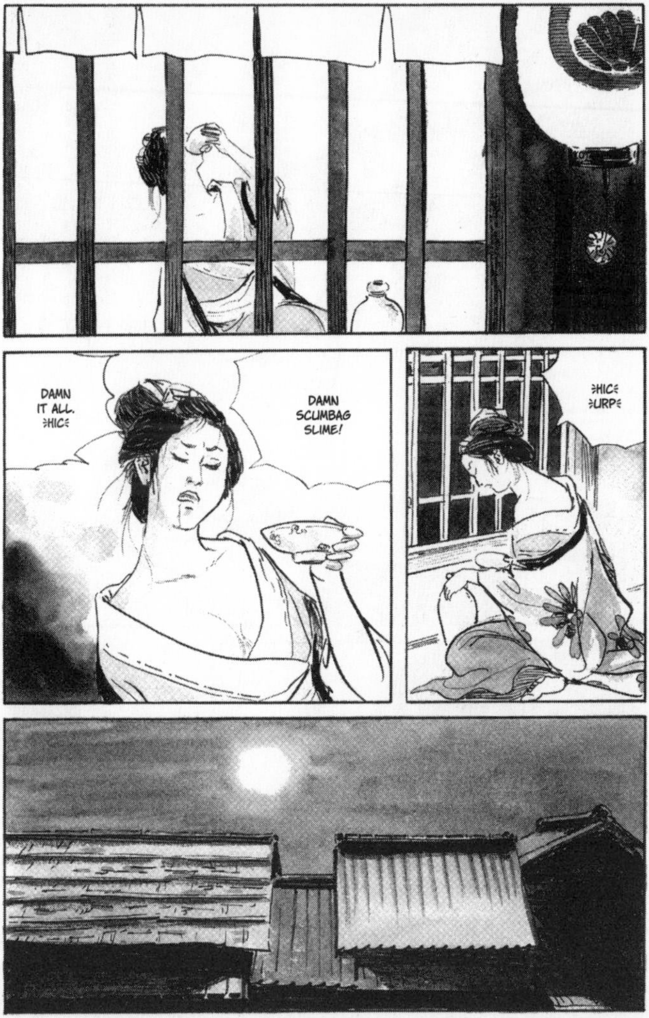
DAMN IT ALL. ≡HIC≡
DAMN SCUMBAG SLIME!
≡HIC≡ ≡URP≡

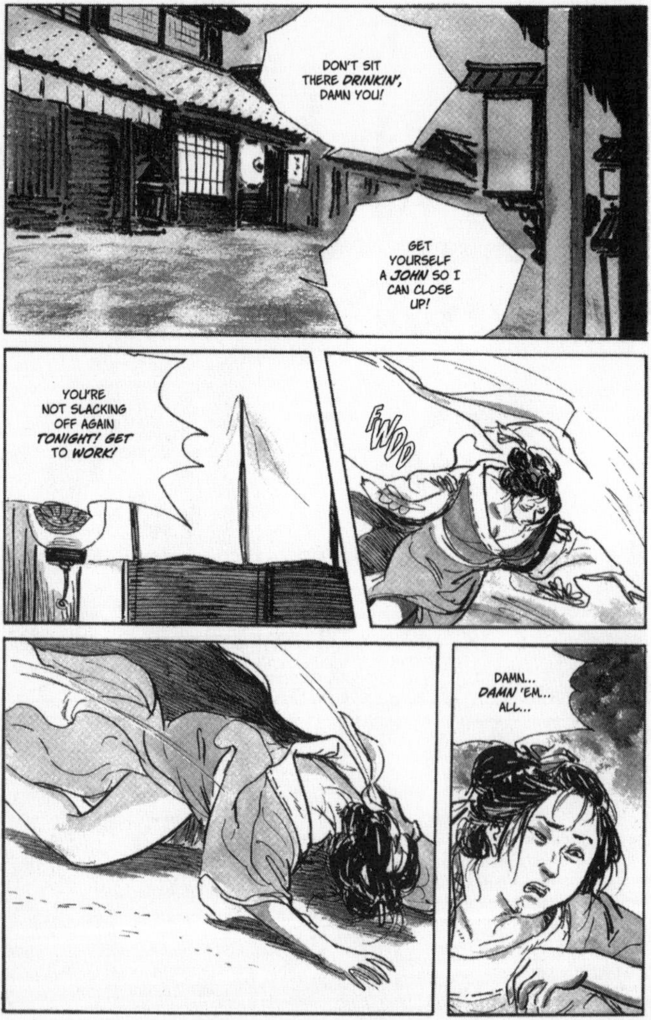
DON'T SIT THERE *DRINKIN'*, DAMN YOU!
GET YOURSELF A *JOHN* SO I CAN CLOSE UP!
YOU'RE NOT SLACKING OFF AGAIN *TONIGHT!* GET TO *WORK!*
FWOO
DAMN... *DAMN* 'EM... ALL...

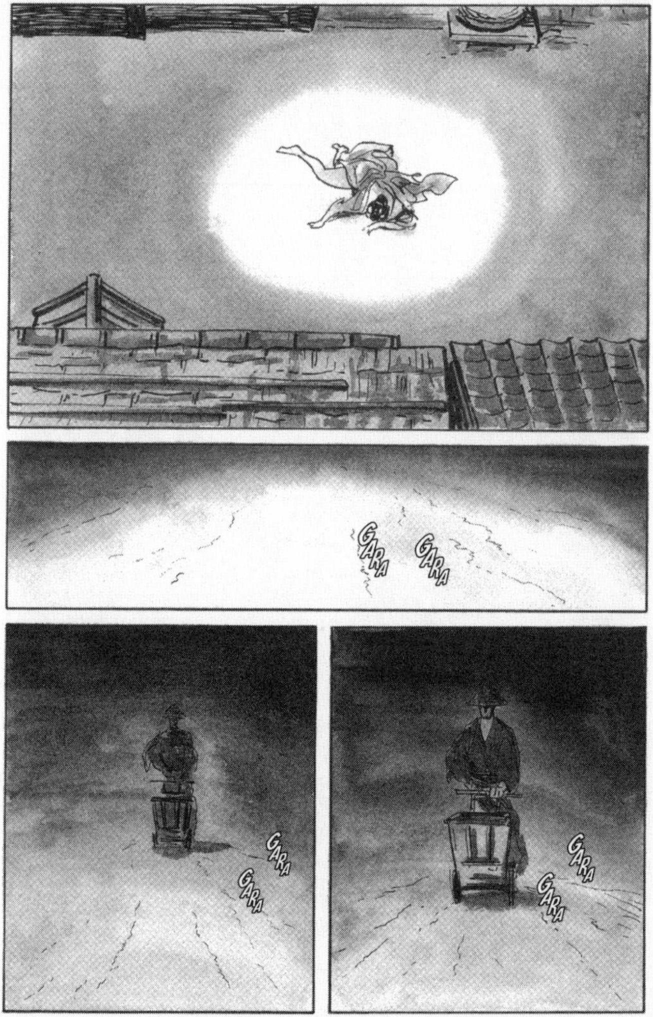
GARA
GARA
GARA
GARA
GARA
GARA

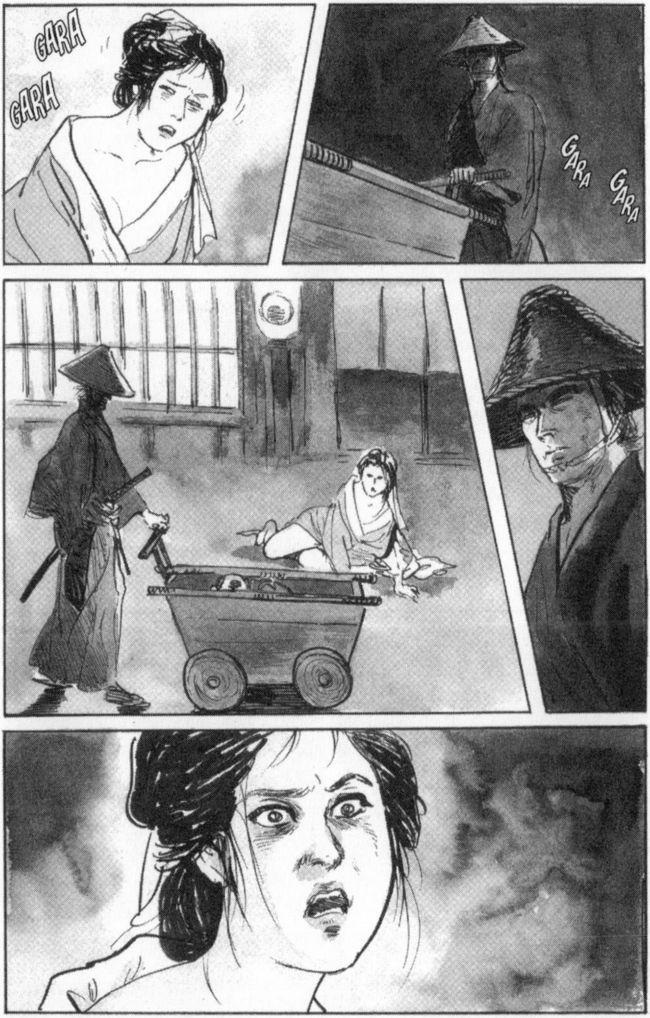
GARA
GARA
GARA
GARA

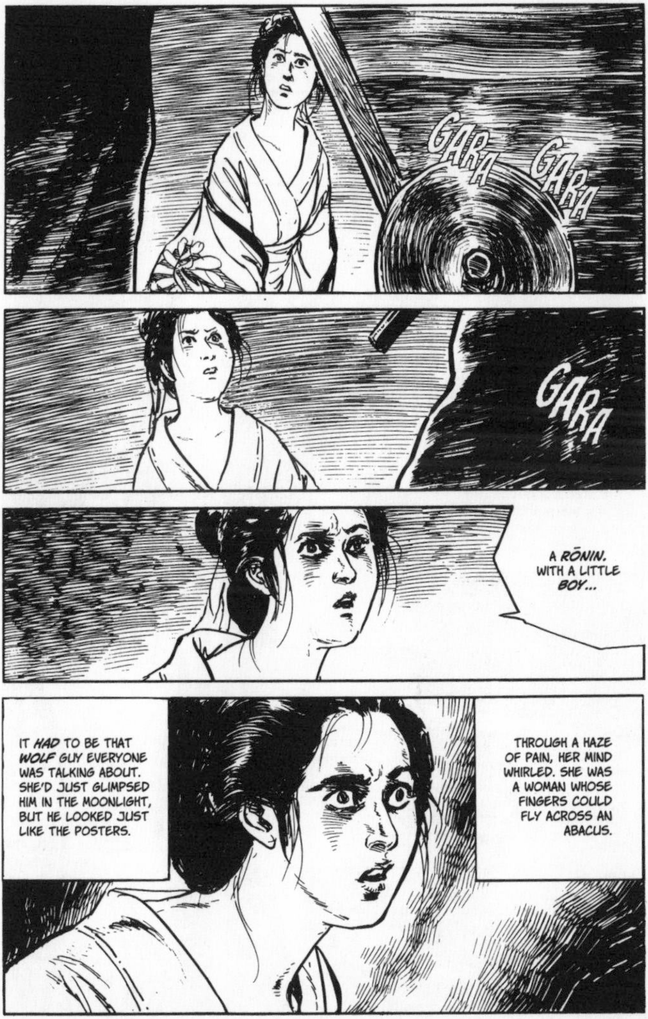
GARA GARA
GARA
A *RŌNIN.* WITH A LITTLE *BOY*...
IT *HAD* TO BE THAT *WOLF* GUY EVERYONE WAS TALKING ABOUT. SHE'D JUST GLIMPSED HIM IN THE MOONLIGHT, BUT HE LOOKED JUST LIKE THE POSTERS.
THROUGH A HAZE OF PAIN, HER MIND WHIRLED. SHE WAS A WOMAN WHOSE FINGERS COULD FLY ACROSS AN ABACUS.

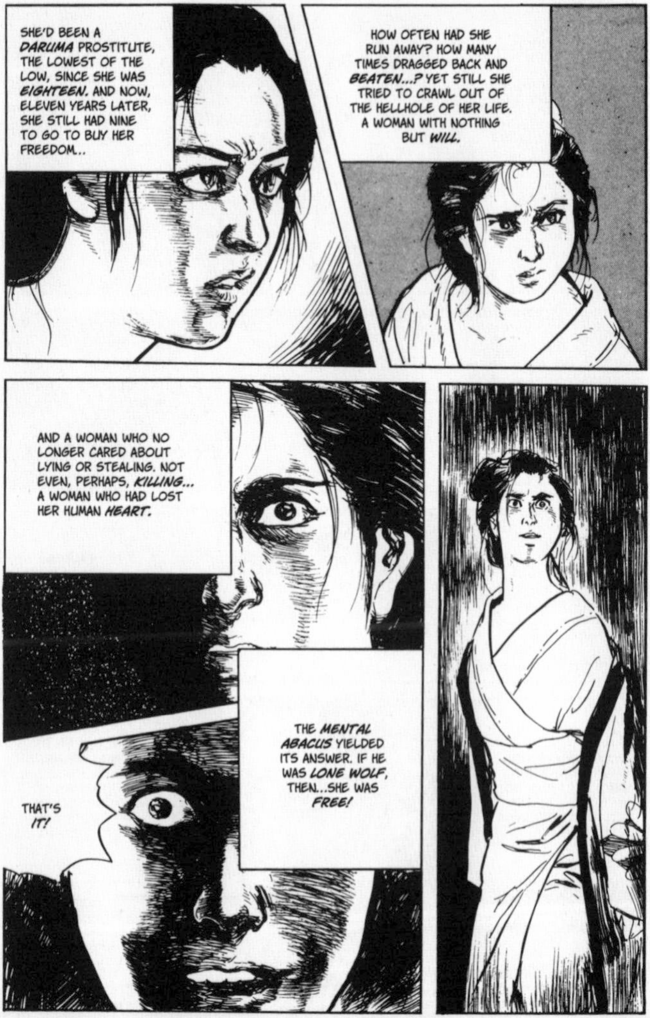
SHE'D BEEN A *DARUMA* PROSTITUTE, THE LOWEST OF THE LOW, SINCE SHE WAS *EIGHTEEN.* AND NOW, ELEVEN YEARS LATER, SHE STILL HAD NINE TO GO TO BUY HER FREEDOM..
HOW OFTEN HAD SHE RUN AWAY? HOW MANY TIMES DRAGGED BACK AND *BEATEN...?* YET STILL SHE TRIED TO CRAWL OUT OF THE HELLHOLE OF HER LIFE. A WOMAN WITH NOTHING BUT *WILL.*
AND A WOMAN WHO NO LONGER CARED ABOUT LYING OR STEALING. NOT EVEN, PERHAPS, *KILLING...* A WOMAN WHO HAD LOST HER HUMAN *HEART.*
THAT'S *IT!*
THE *MENTAL ABACUS* YIELDED ITS ANSWER. IF HE WAS *LONE WOLF,* THEN...SHE WAS *FREE!*

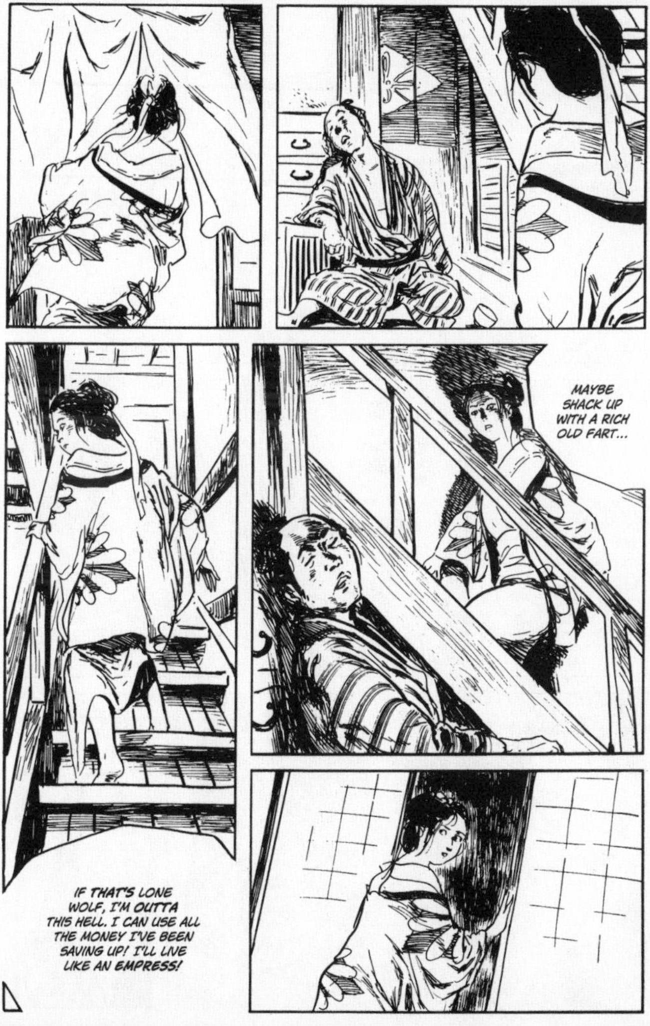
MAYBE SHACK UP WITH A RICH OLD FART...
IF THAT'S LONE WOLF, I'M OUTTA THIS HELL. I CAN USE ALL THE MONEY I'VE BEEN SAVING UP! I'LL LIVE LIKE AN EMPRESS!

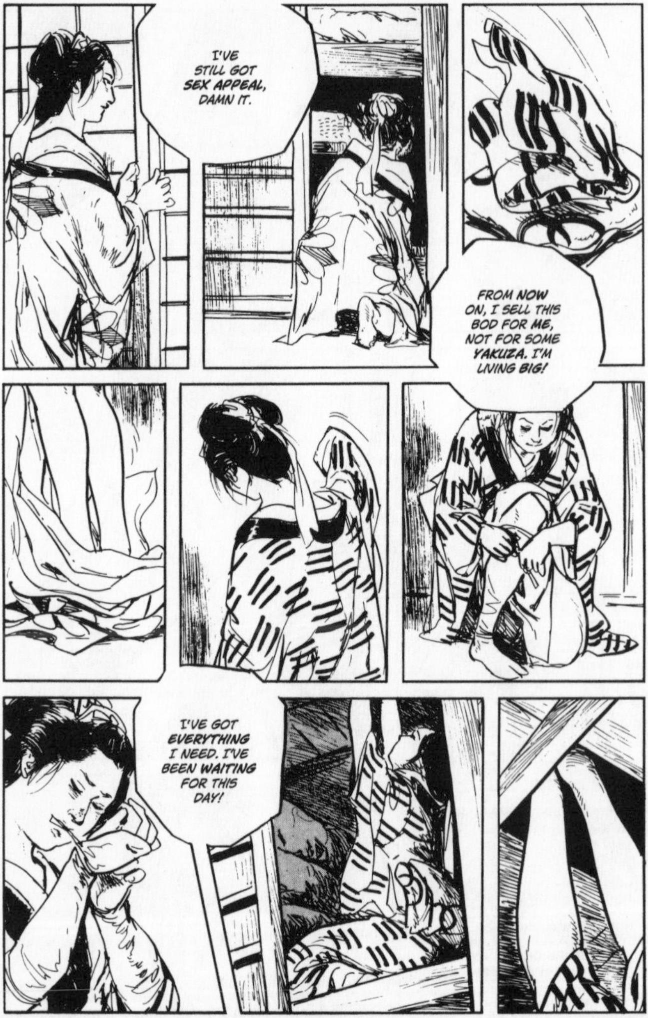
I'VE STILL GOT SEX APPEAL, DAMN IT.
FROM NOW ON, I SELL THIS BOD FOR ME, NOT FOR SOME YAKUZA. I'M LIVING BIG!
I'VE GOT EVERYTHING I NEED. I'VE BEEN WAITING FOR THIS DAY!

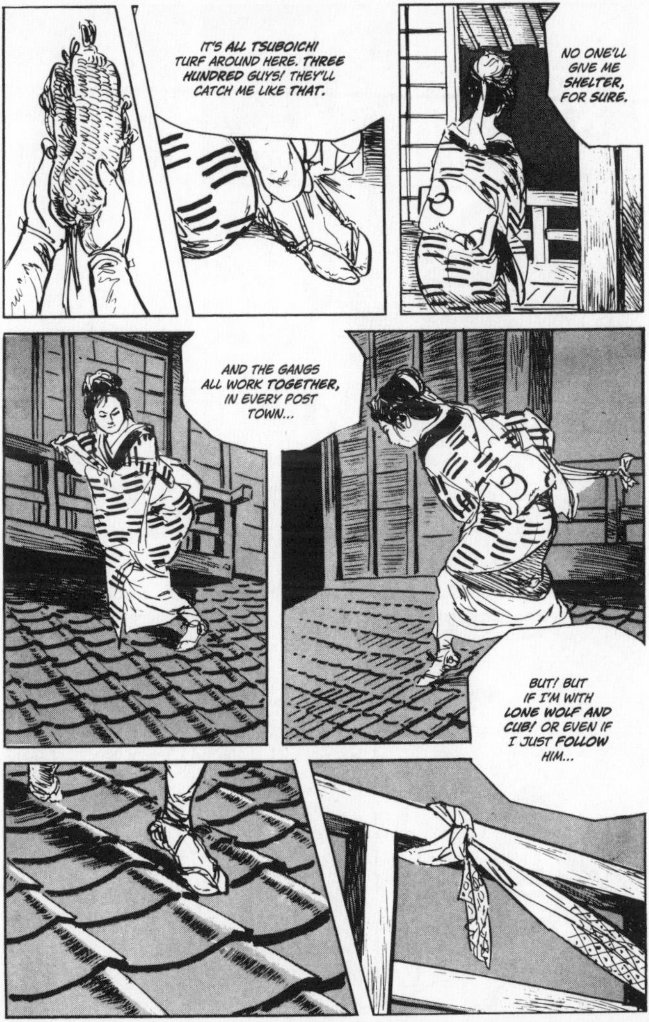
IT'S ALL TSUBOICHI TURF AROUND HERE. THREE HUNDRED GUYS! THEY'LL CATCH ME LIKE THAT.
NO ONE'LL GIVE ME SHELTER, FOR SURE.
AND THE GANGS ALL WORK TOGETHER, IN EVERY POST TOWN...
BUT! BUT IF I'M WITH LONE WOLF AND CUB! OR EVEN IF I JUST FOLLOW HIM...

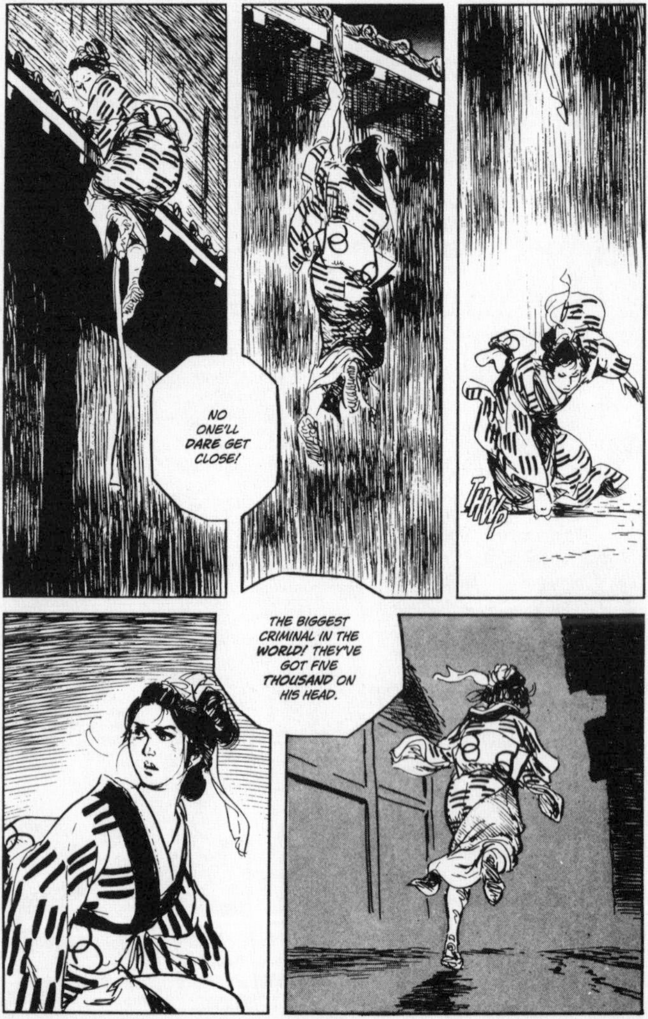
NO ONE'LL DARE GET CLOSE!
THWP
THE BIGGEST CRIMINAL IN THE WORLD! THEY'VE GOT FIVE THOUSAND ON HIS HEAD.

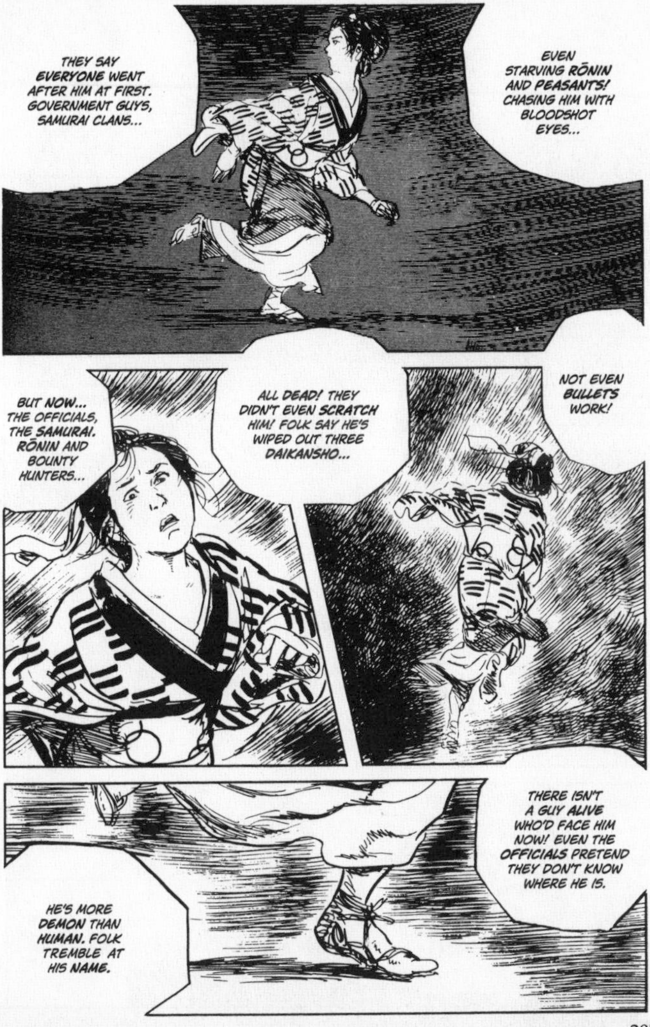
THEY SAY EVERYONE WENT AFTER HIM AT FIRST. GOVERNMENT GUYS, SAMURAI CLANS...
EVEN STARVING RŌNIN AND PEASANTS! CHASING HIM WITH BLOODSHOT EYES...
BUT NOW... THE OFFICIALS, THE SAMURAI. RŌNIN AND BOUNTY HUNTERS...
ALL DEAD! THEY DIDN'T EVEN SCRATCH HIM! FOLK SAY HE'S WIPED OUT THREE DAIKANSHO...
NOT EVEN BULLETS WORK!
THERE ISN'T A GUY ALIVE WHO'D FACE HIM NOW! EVEN THE OFFICIALS PRETEND THEY DON'T KNOW WHERE HE IS.
HE'S MORE DEMON THAN HUMAN. FOLK TREMBLE AT HIS NAME.

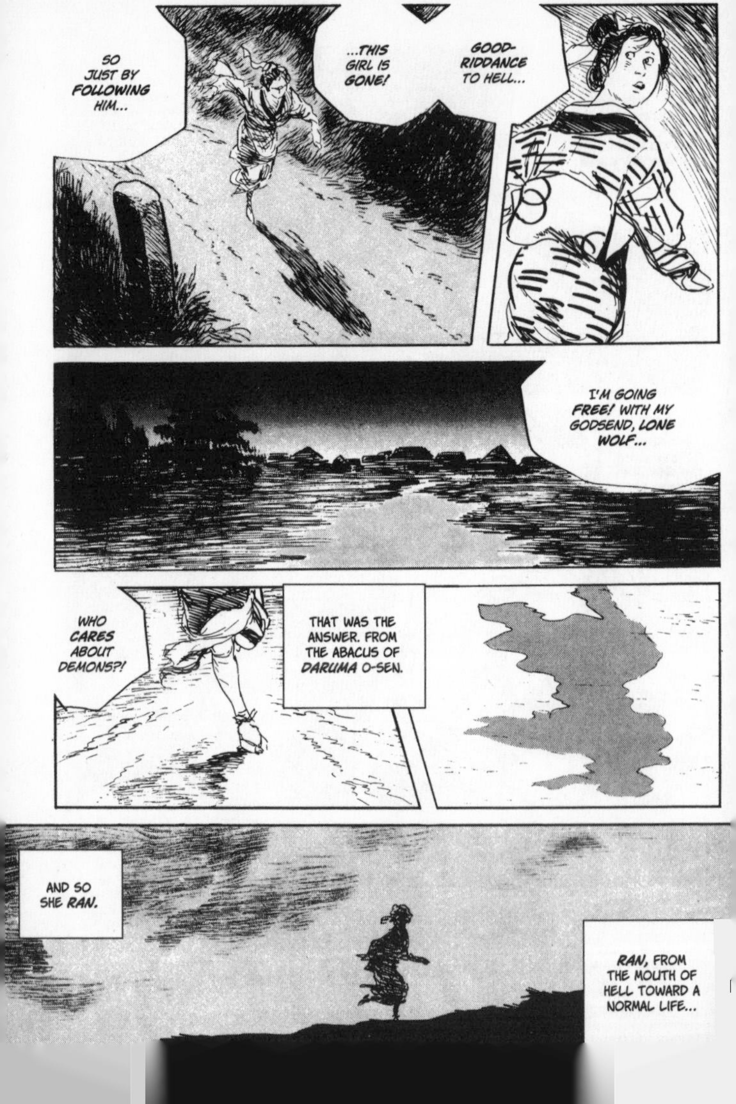
SO JUST BY FOLLOWING HIM...
...THIS GIRL IS GONE!
GOOD-RIDDANCE TO HELL...
I'M GOING FREE! WITH MY GODSEND, LONE WOLF...
WHO CARES ABOUT DEMONS?!
THAT WAS THE ANSWER. FROM THE ABACUS OF DARUMA O-SEN.
AND SO SHE RAN.
RAN, FROM THE MOUTH OF HELL TOWARD A NORMAL LIFE...

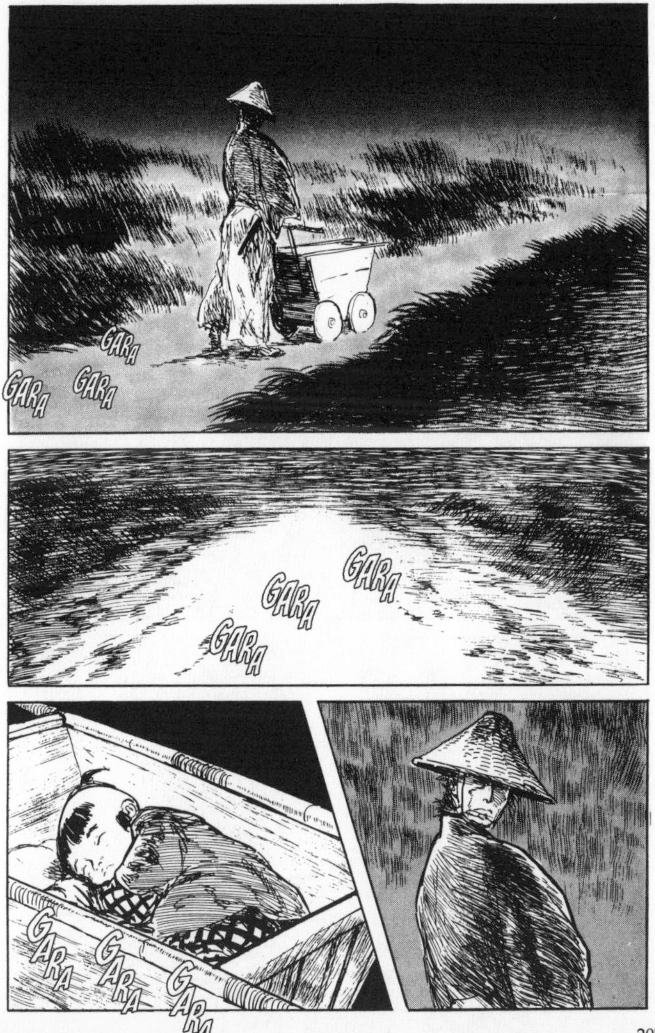
GARA
GARA
GARA
GARA
GARA
GARA
GARA
GARA
GARA

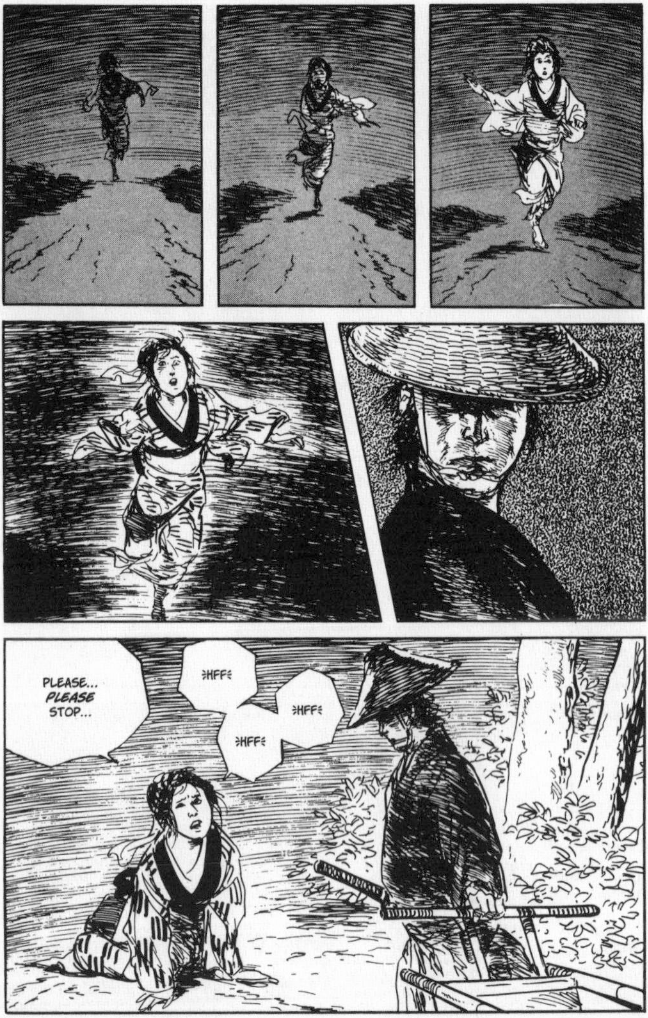
PLEASE...
PLEASE
STOP...
HFF
HFF
HFF

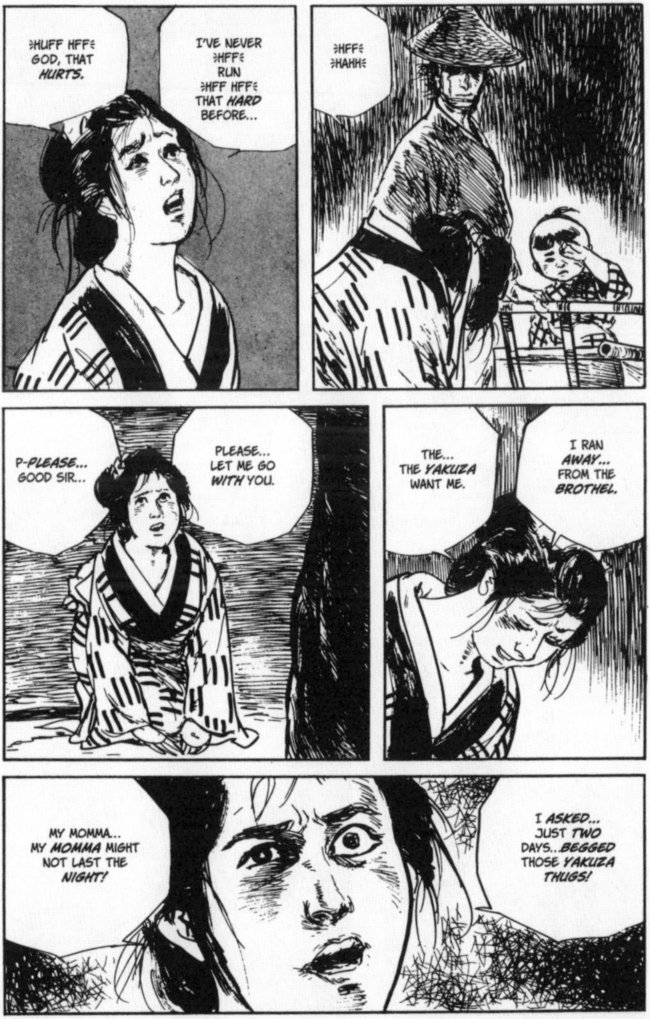
⋟HUFF HFF⋞ GOD, THAT *HURTS.*
I'VE NEVER ⋟HFF⋞ RUN ⋟HFF HFF⋞ THAT *HARD* BEFORE...
⋟HFF⋞ ⋟HAHH⋞
P-*PLEASE...* GOOD SIR...
PLEASE... LET ME GO *WITH* YOU.
THE... THE *YAKUZA* WANT ME.
I RAN *AWAY...* FROM THE *BROTHEL.*
MY MOMMA... MY *MOMMA* MIGHT NOT LAST THE *NIGHT!*
I *ASKED...* JUST *TWO* DAYS...*BEGGED* THOSE *YAKUZA* *THUGS!*

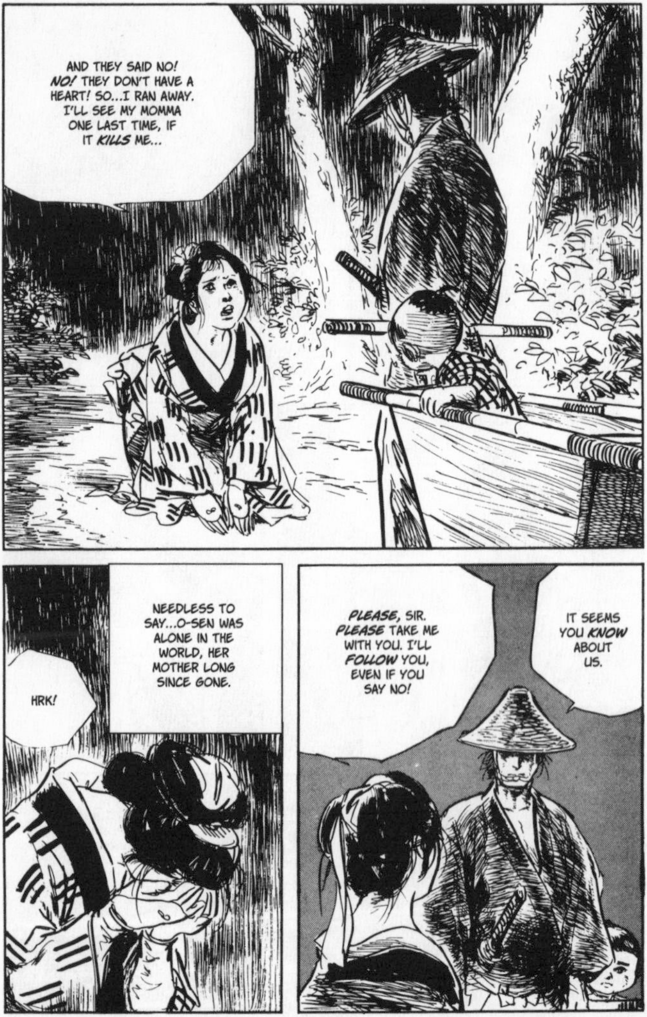
AND THEY SAID NO! *NO!* THEY DON'T HAVE A HEART! SO...I RAN AWAY. I'LL SEE MY MOMMA ONE LAST TIME, IF IT *KILLS* ME...
NEEDLESS TO SAY...O-SEN WAS ALONE IN THE WORLD, HER MOTHER LONG SINCE GONE.
HRK!
PLEASE, SIR. *PLEASE* TAKE ME WITH YOU. I'LL *FOLLOW* YOU, EVEN IF YOU SAY NO!
IT SEEMS YOU *KNOW* ABOUT US.

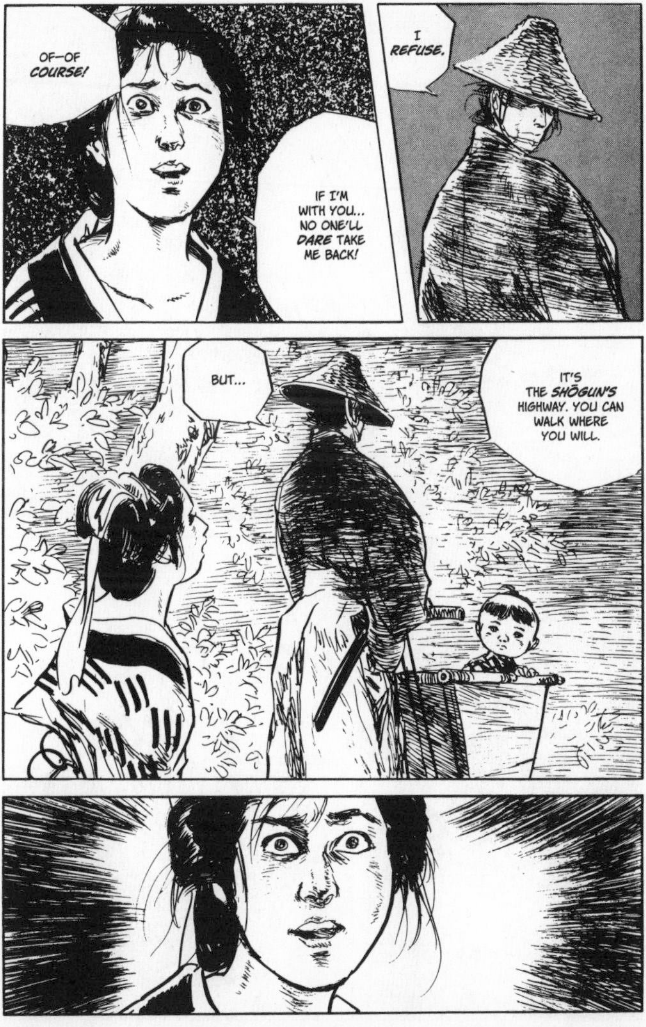
OF—OF COURSE!
I REFUSE.
IF I'M WITH YOU... NO ONE'LL DARE TAKE ME BACK!
BUT...
IT'S THE SHŌGUN'S HIGHWAY. YOU CAN WALK WHERE YOU WILL.

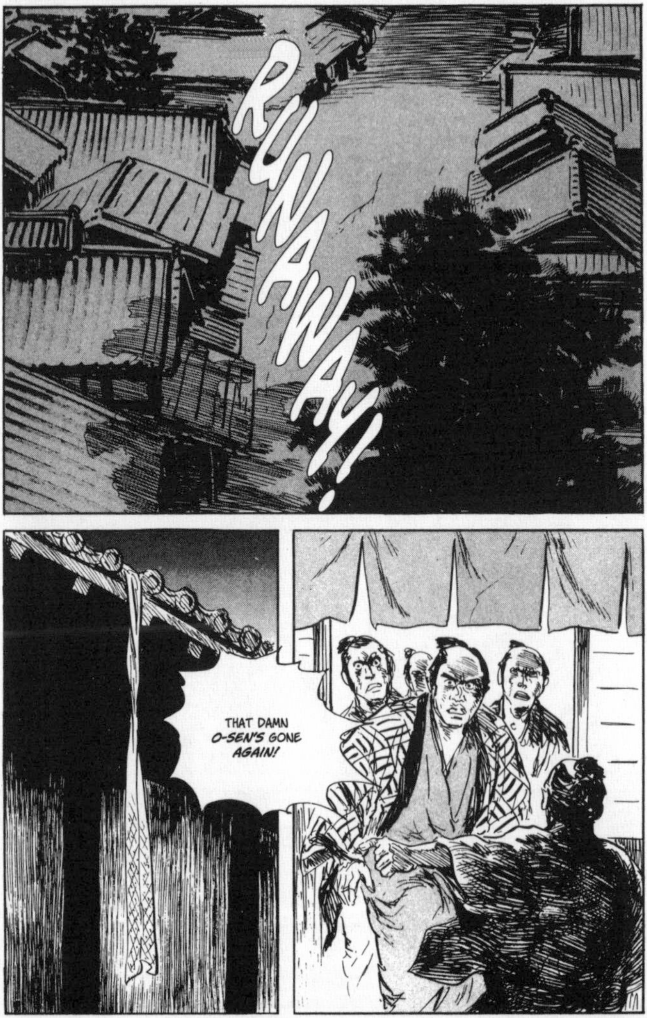
RUNAWAY!
THAT DAMN O-SEN'S GONE AGAIN!

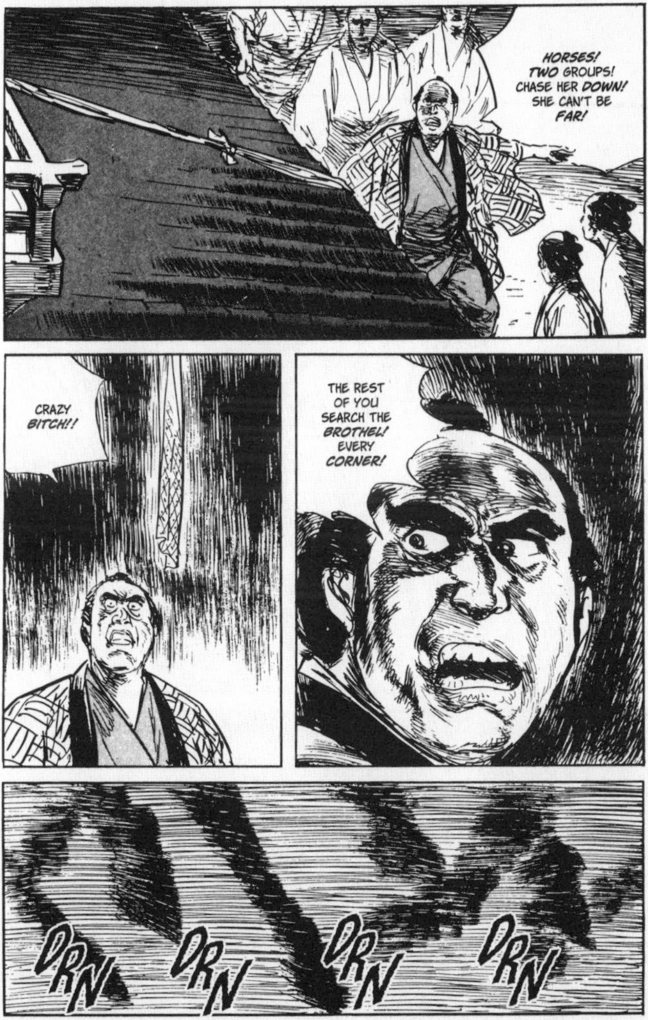
HORSES! TWO GROUPS! CHASE HER DOWN! SHE CAN'T BE FAR!
CRAZY BITCH!!
THE REST OF YOU SEARCH THE BROTHEL! EVERY CORNER!
DRN
DRN
DRN
DRN

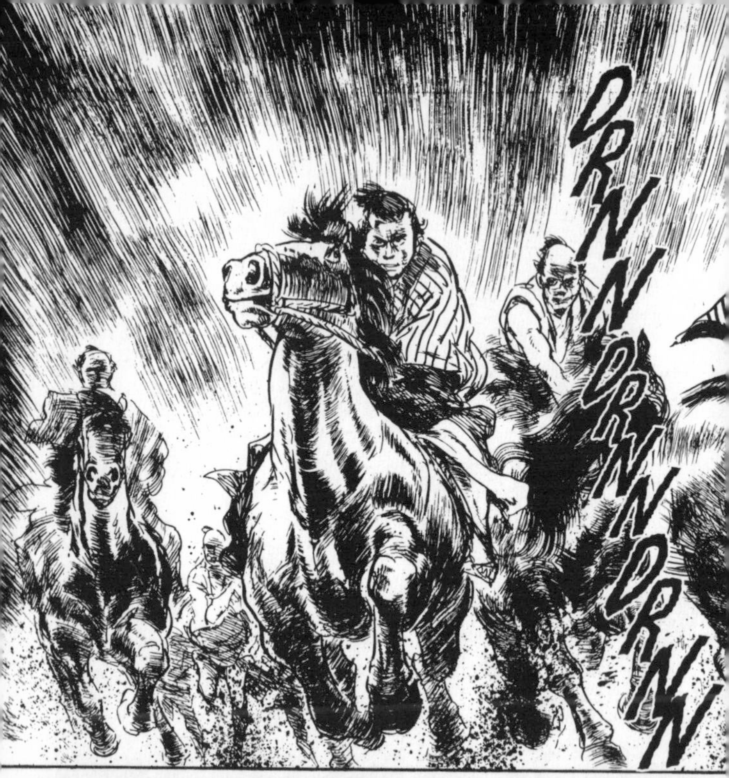
DRNN DRNN DRNN
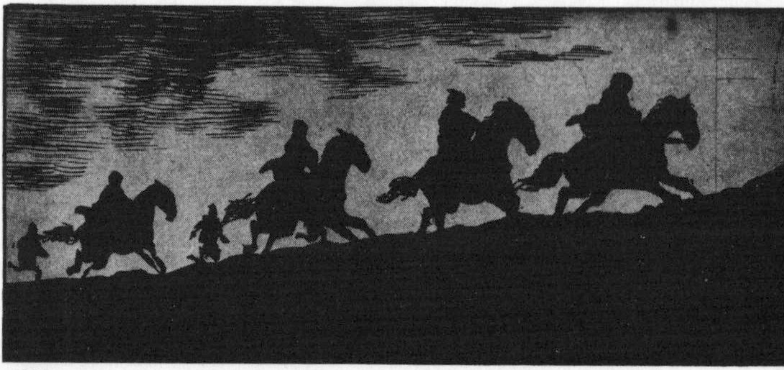

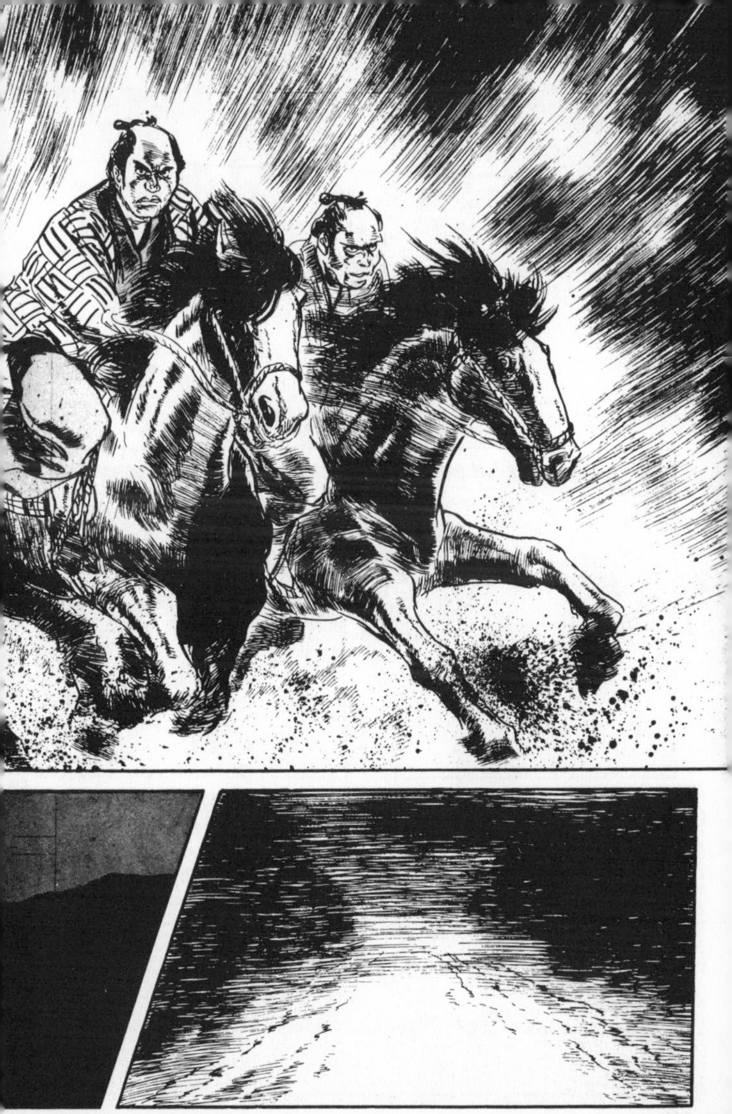

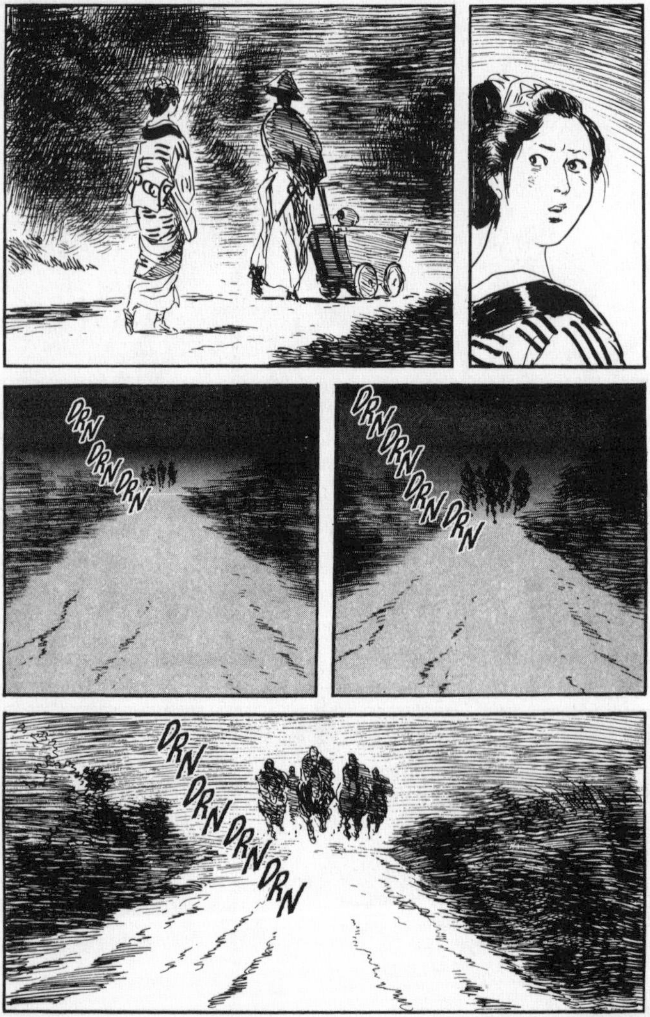
DRN DRN DRN DRN
DRN DRN DRN DRN DRN
DRN DRN DRN DRN DRN

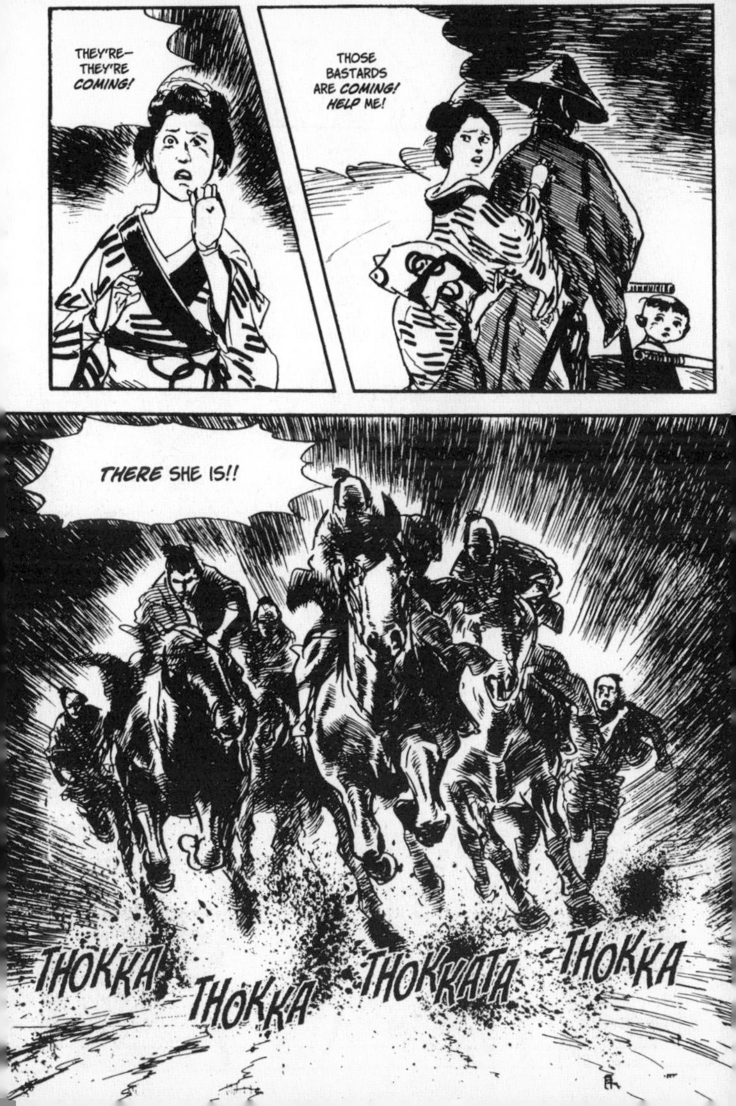
THEY'RE— THEY'RE *COMING!*
THOSE BASTARDS ARE *COMING! HELP* ME!
THERE SHE IS!!
THOKKA
THOKKA
THOKKATA
THOKKA

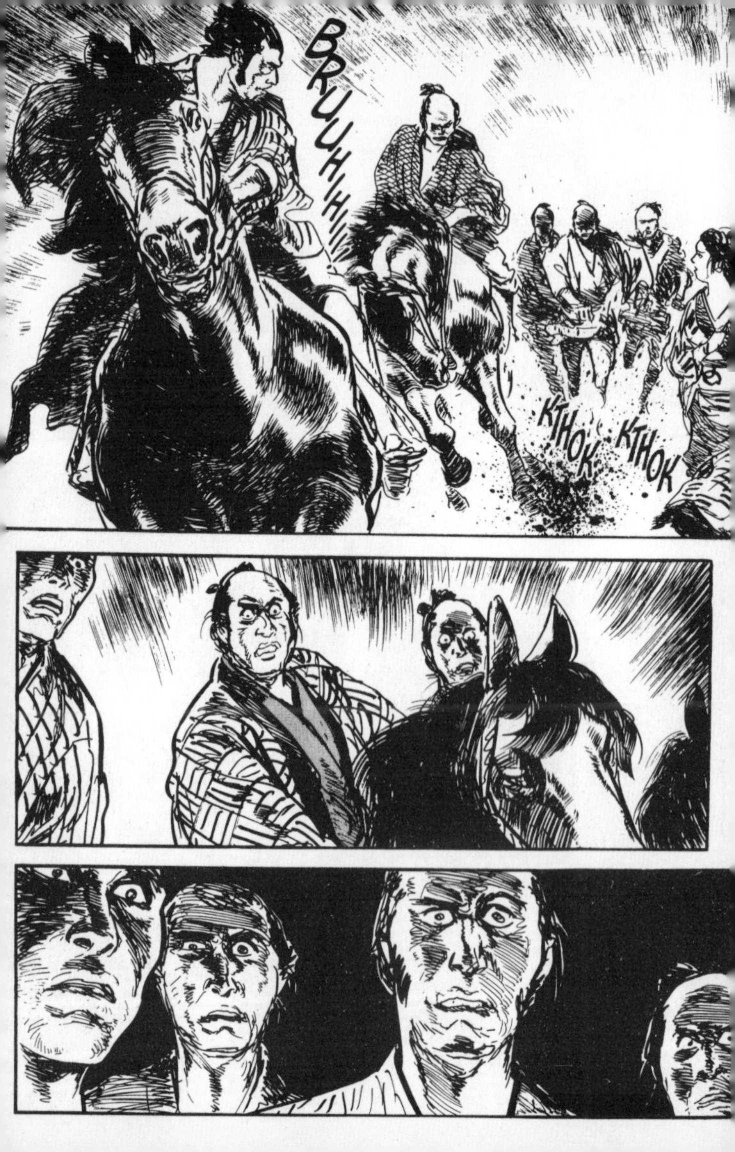
BRUUHHH
KTHOK KTHOK

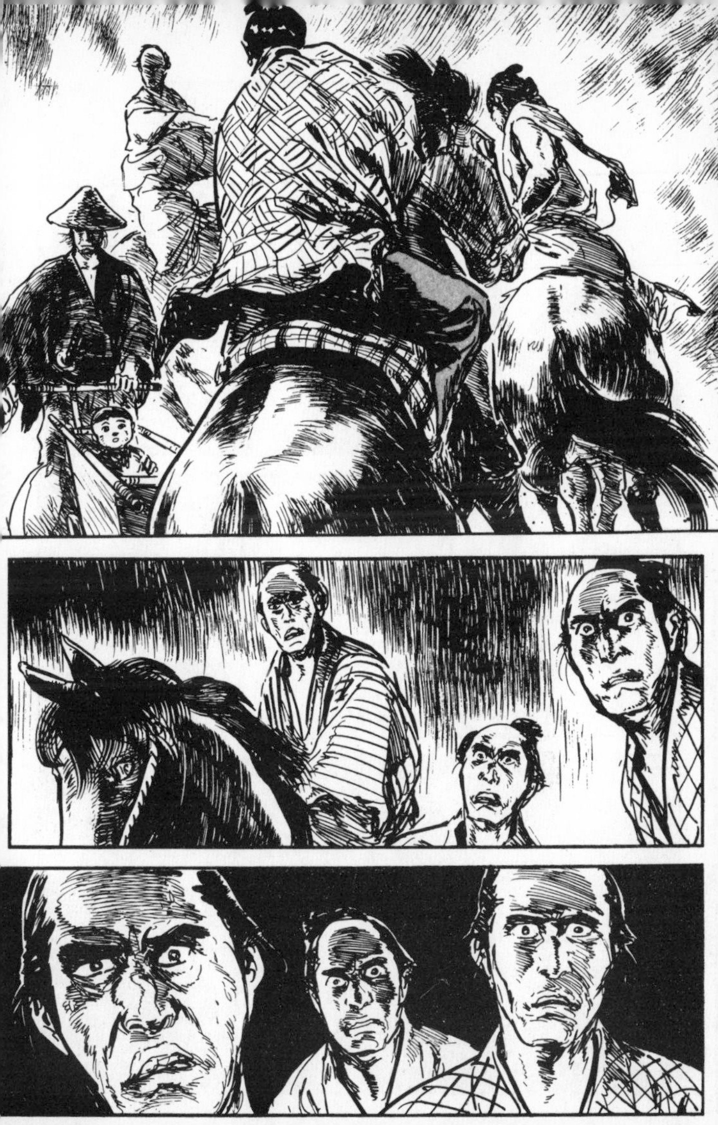

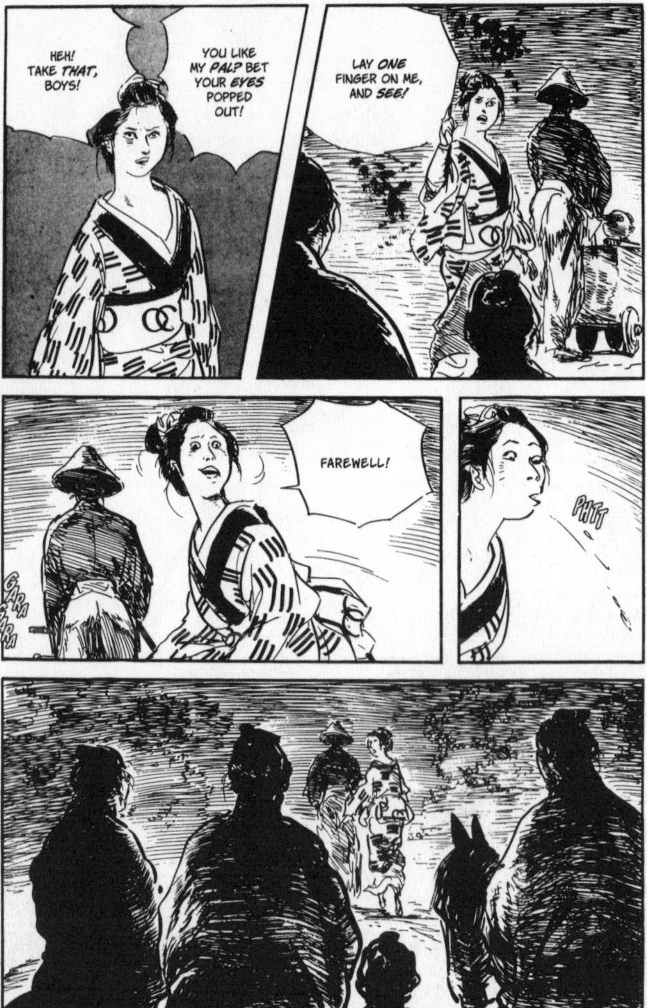
HEH! TAKE THAT, BOYS!
YOU LIKE MY PAL? BET YOUR EYES POPPED OUT!
LAY ONE FINGER ON ME, AND SEE!
GARA GARA
FAREWELL!
PHTT

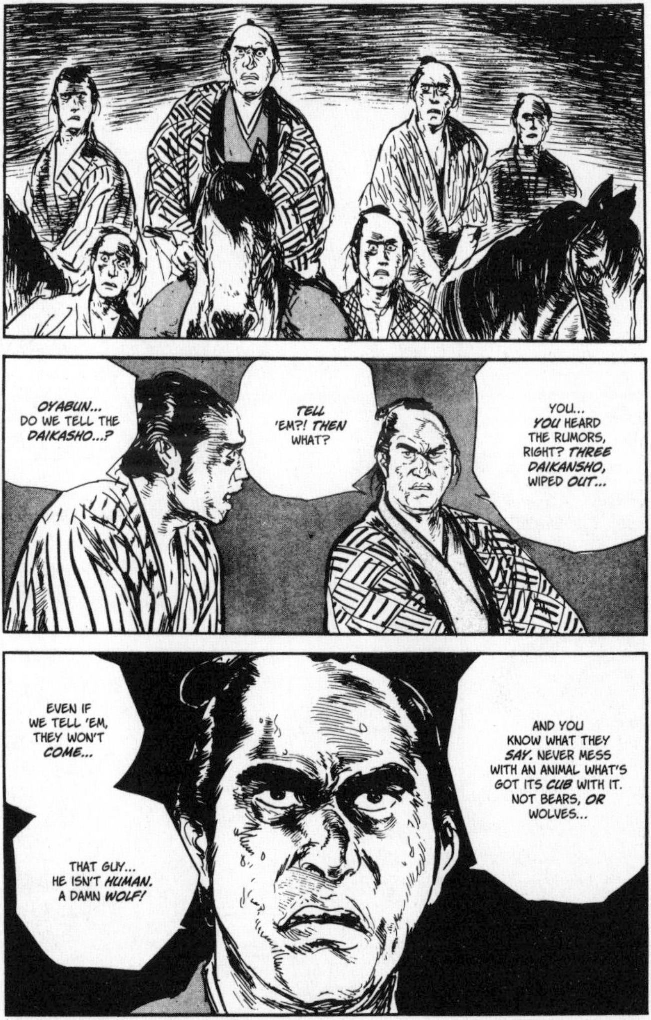
OYABUN... DO WE TELL THE DAIKASHO...?
TELL 'EM?! THEN WHAT?
YOU... YOU HEARD THE RUMORS, RIGHT? THREE DAIKANSHO, WIPED OUT...
EVEN IF WE TELL 'EM, THEY WON'T COME...
AND YOU KNOW WHAT THEY SAY. NEVER MESS WITH AN ANIMAL WHAT'S GOT ITS CUB WITH IT. NOT BEARS, OR WOLVES...
THAT GUY... HE ISN'T HUMAN. A DAMN WOLF!

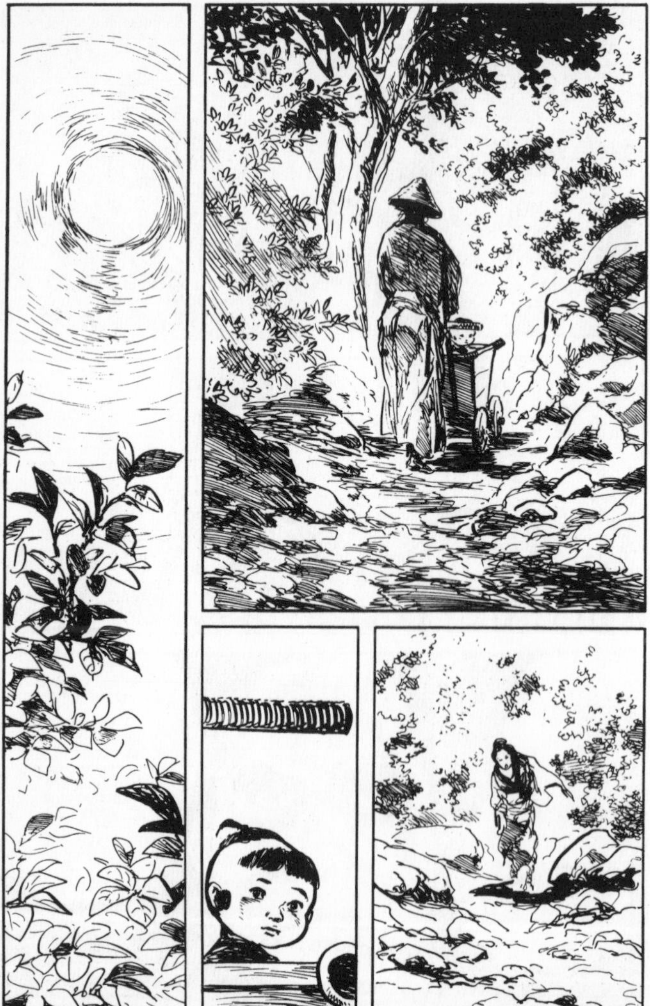

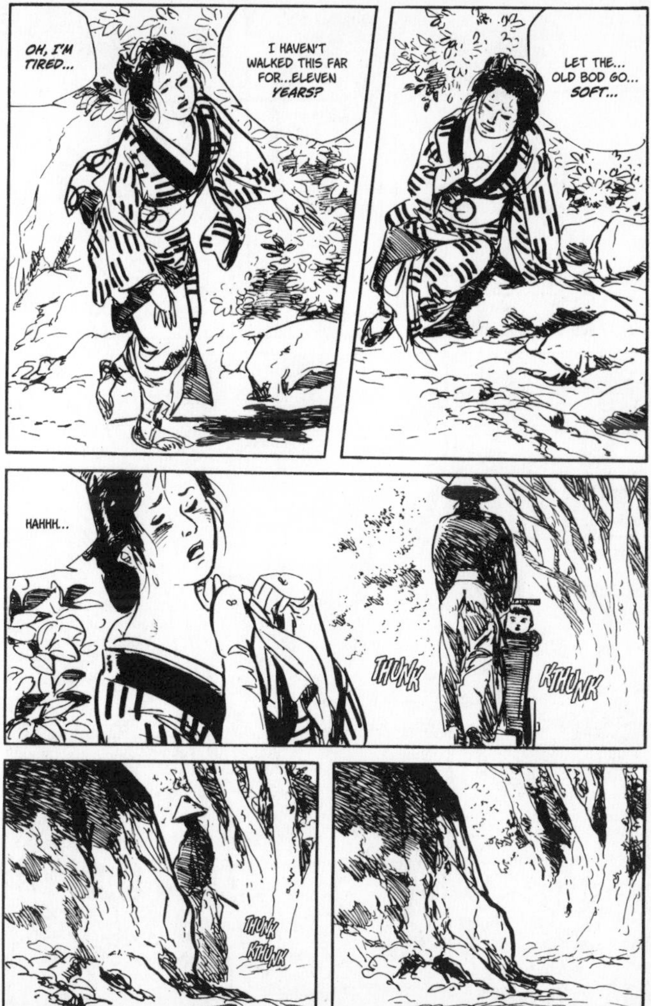
OH, I'M TIRED...
I HAVEN'T WALKED THIS FAR FOR...ELEVEN YEARS?
LET THE... OLD BOD GO... SOFT...
HAHHH...
THUNK
KTHUNK
THUNK
KTHUNK

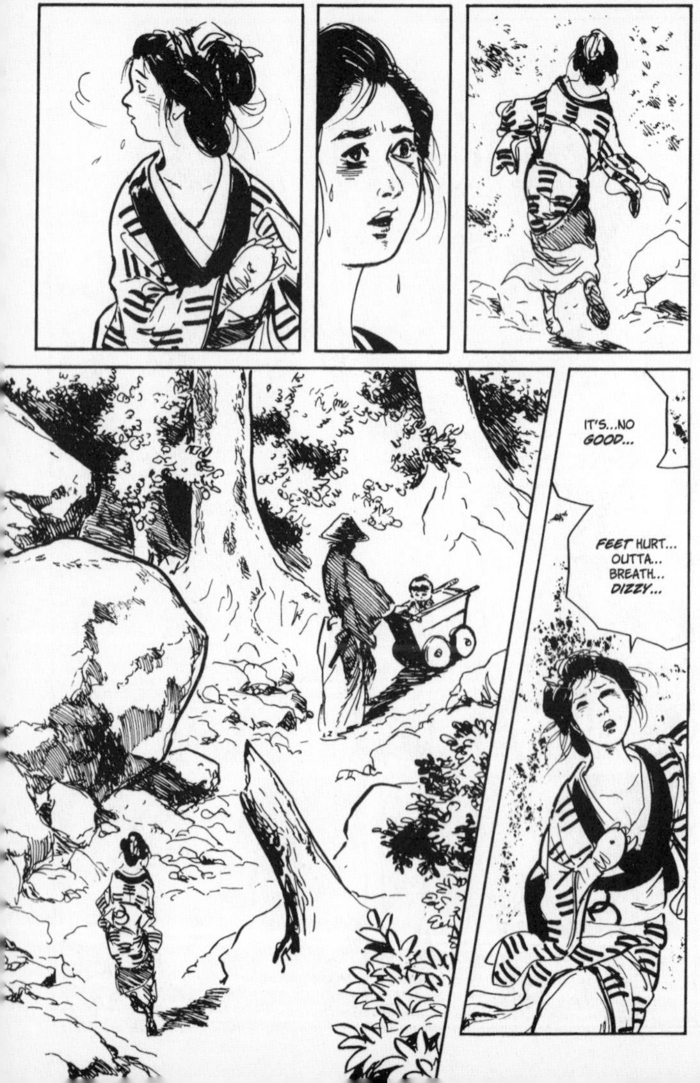
IT'S...NO GOOD...
FEET HURT... OUTTA... BREATH... DIZZY...

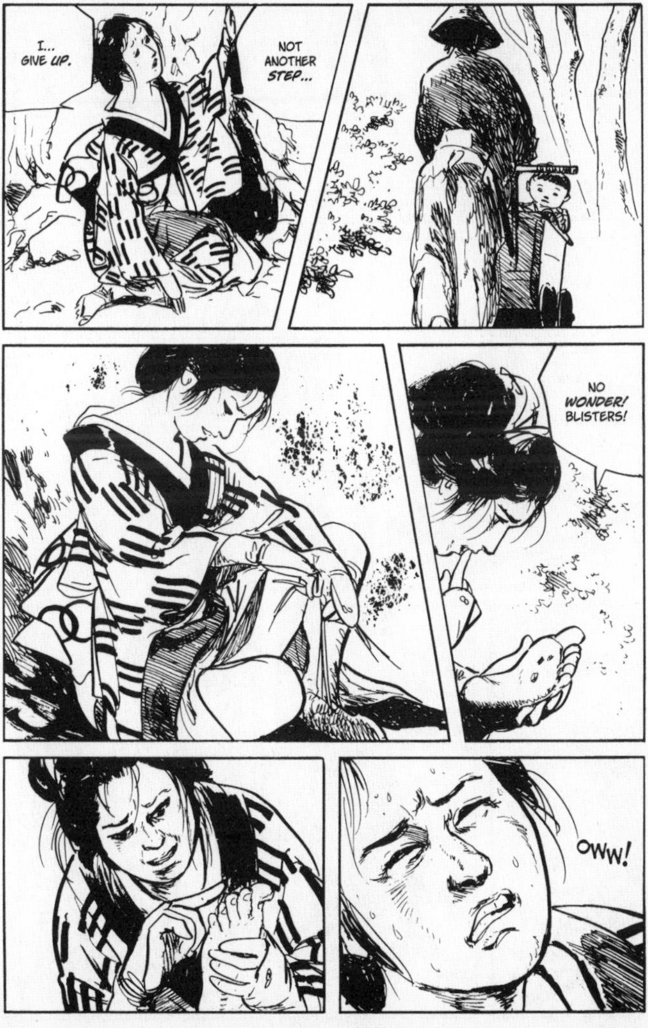
I... GIVE UP.
NOT ANOTHER STEP...
NO WONDER! BLISTERS!
OWW!

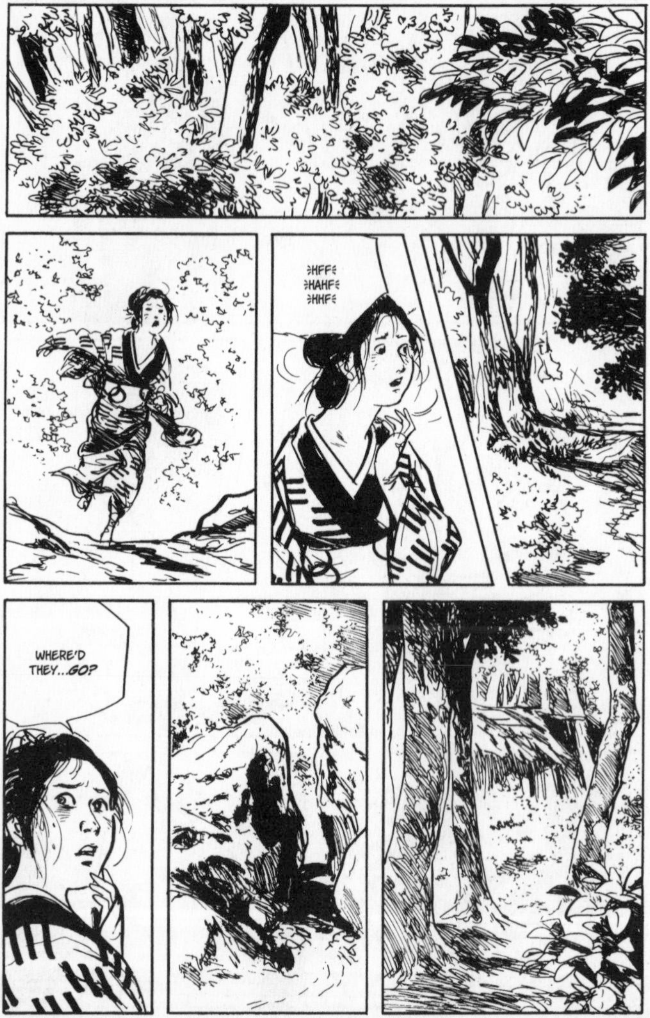

HFF
HAHF
HHF
WHERE'D THEY...GO?

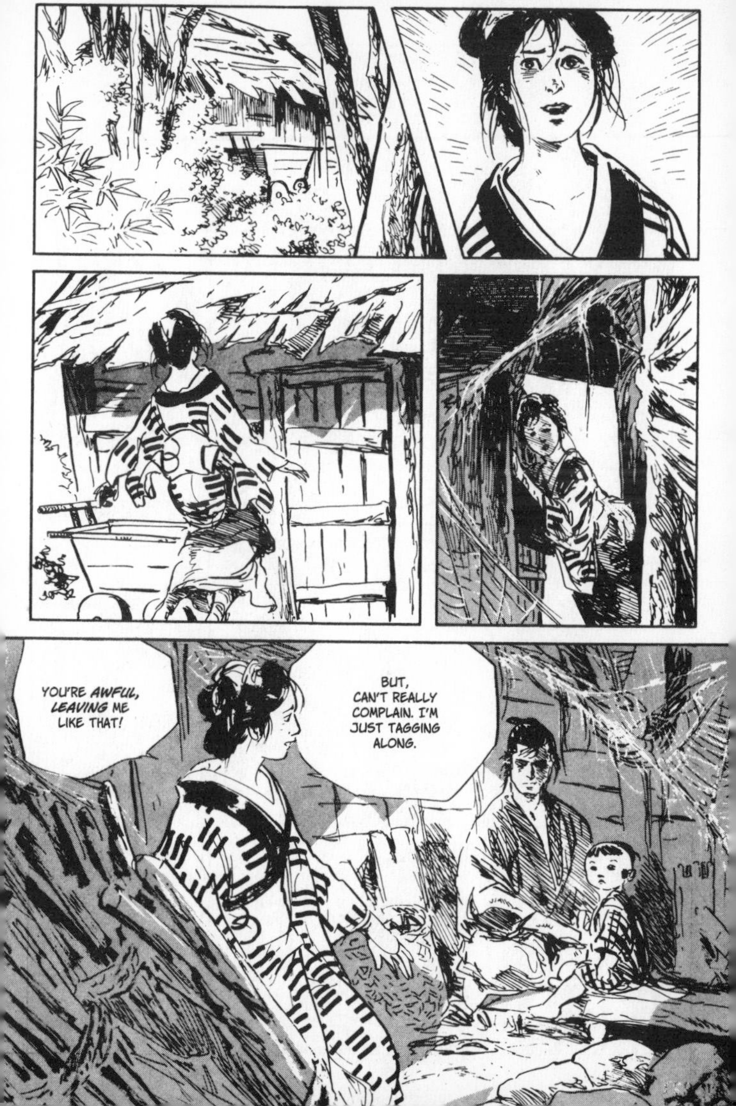
YOU'RE AWFUL, LEAVING ME LIKE THAT!
BUT, CAN'T REALLY COMPLAIN. I'M JUST TAGGING ALONG.

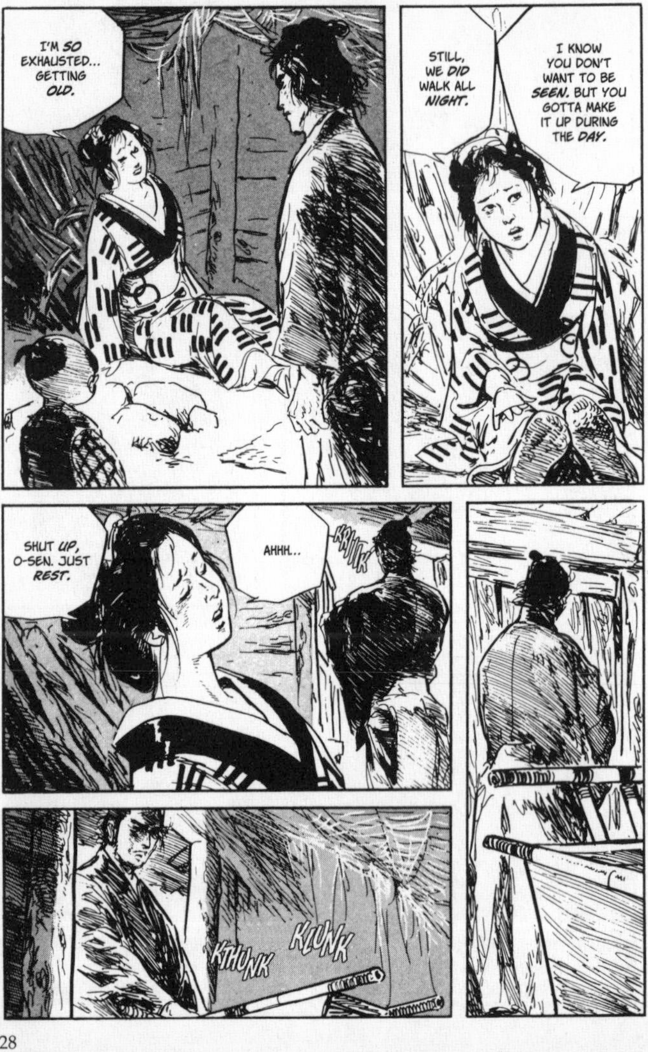

I'M SO EXHAUSTED... GETTING OLD.
STILL, WE DID WALK ALL NIGHT.
I KNOW YOU DON'T WANT TO BE SEEN. BUT YOU GOTTA MAKE IT UP DURING THE DAY.
SHUT UP, O-SEN. JUST REST.
AHHH...
KRIIK
KTHUNK
KLUNK

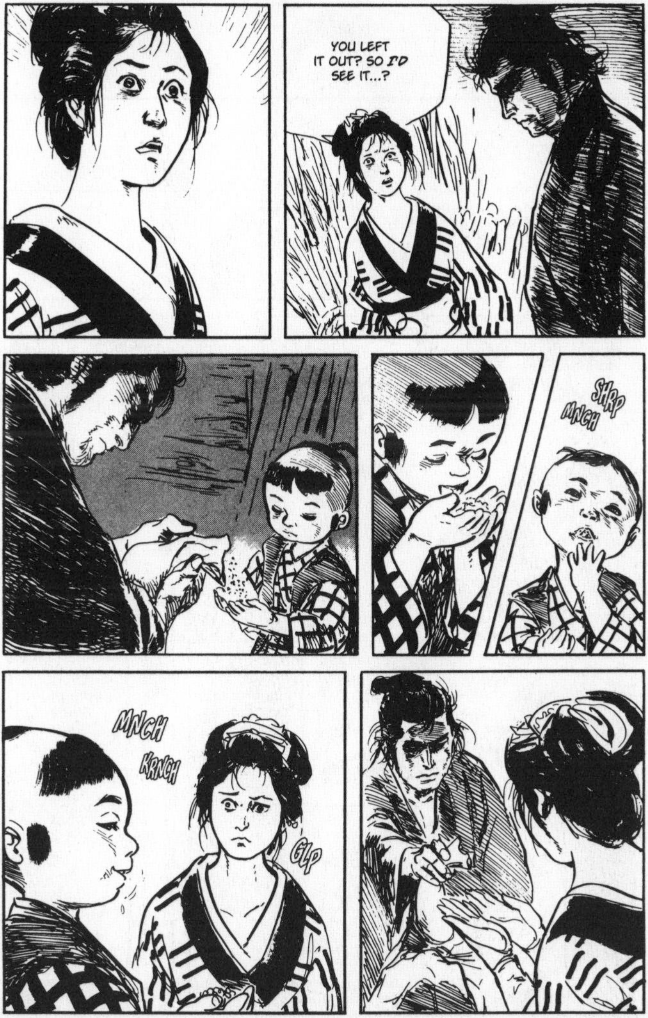
YOU LEFT IT OUT? SO I'D SEE IT...?
SHRP
MNCH
MNCH
KRNCH
GLP

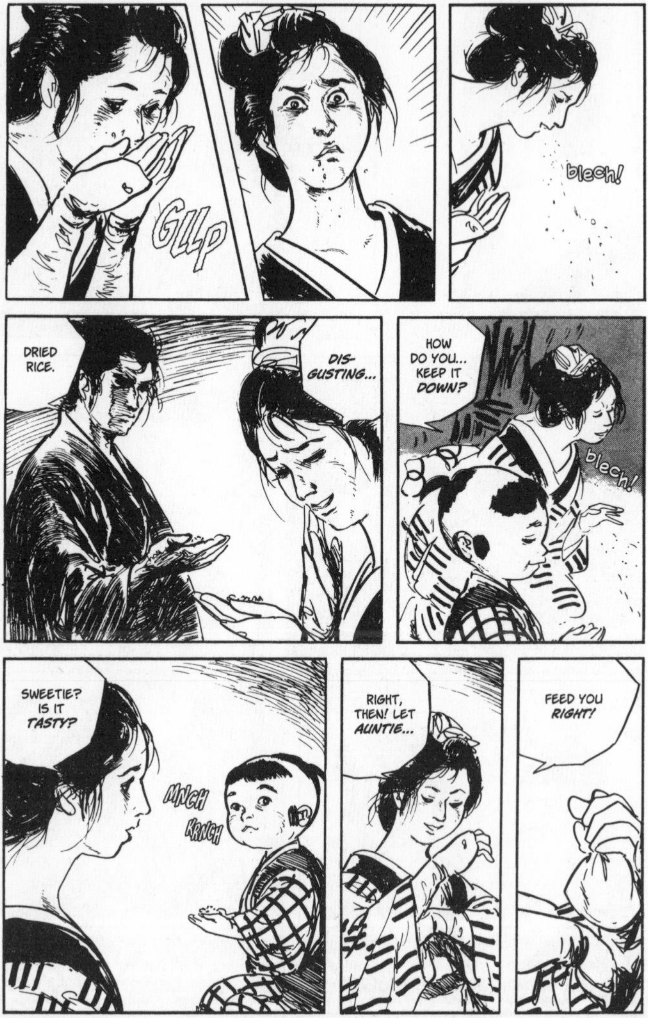
GULP
blech!
DRIED RICE.
DIS-GUSTING...
HOW DO YOU... KEEP IT DOWN?
blech!
SWEETIE? IS IT TASTY?
MNCH
KRNCH
RIGHT, THEN! LET AUNTIE...
FEED YOU RIGHT!

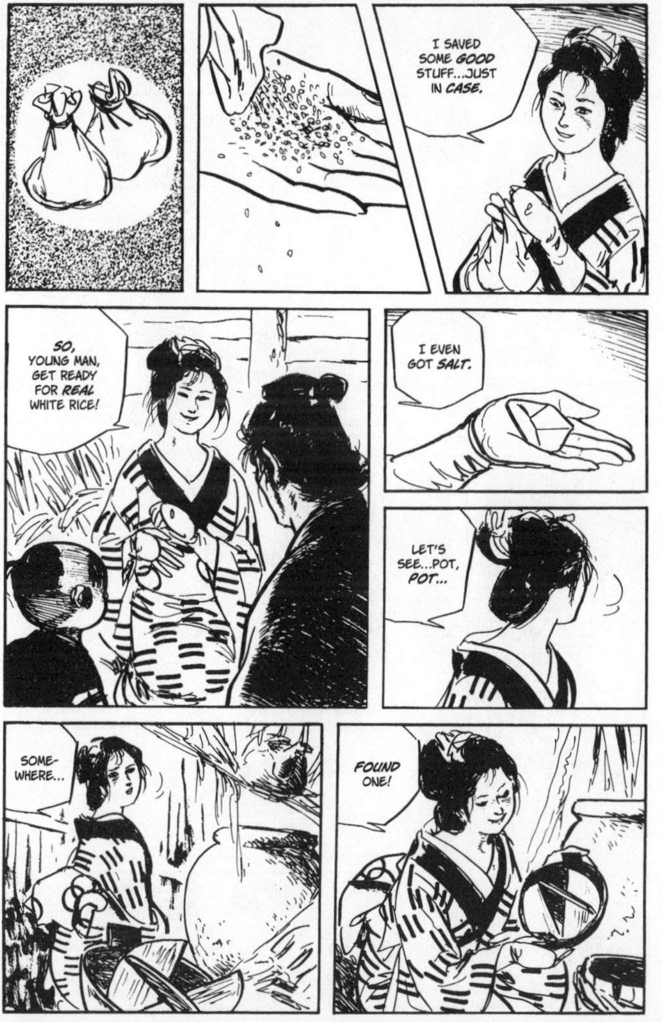
I SAVED SOME GOOD STUFF...JUST IN CASE.
SO, YOUNG MAN, GET READY FOR REAL WHITE RICE!
I EVEN GOT SALT.
LET'S SEE...POT, POT...
SOME-WHERE...
FOUND ONE!

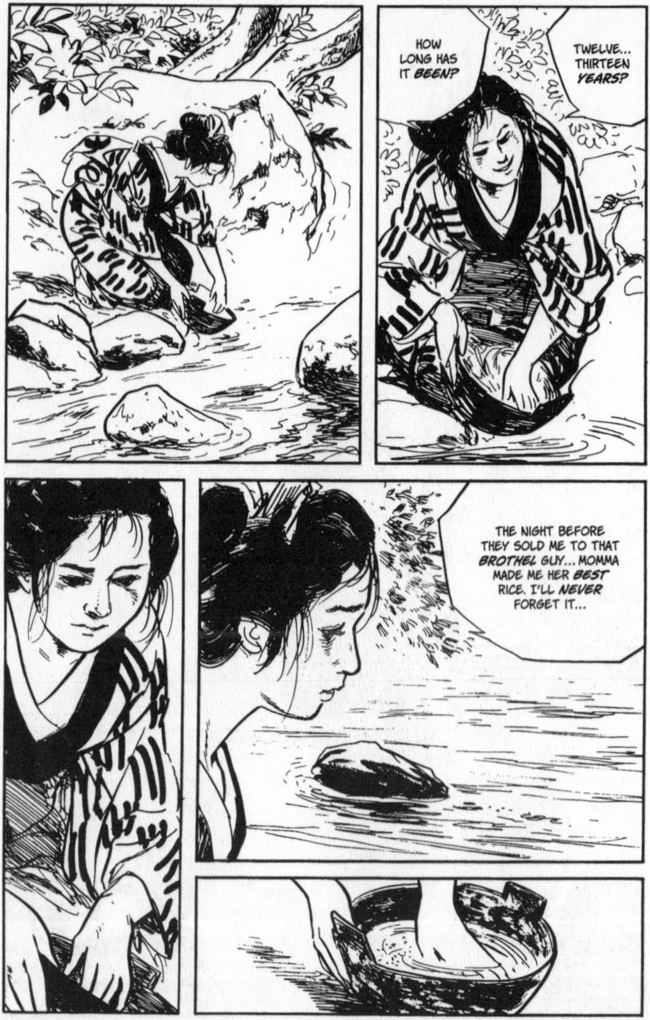
HOW LONG HAS IT *BEEN?*
TWELVE... THIRTEEN *YEARS?*
THE NIGHT BEFORE THEY SOLD ME TO THAT *BROTHEL* GUY... MOMMA MADE ME HER *BEST* RICE. I'LL *NEVER* FORGET IT...

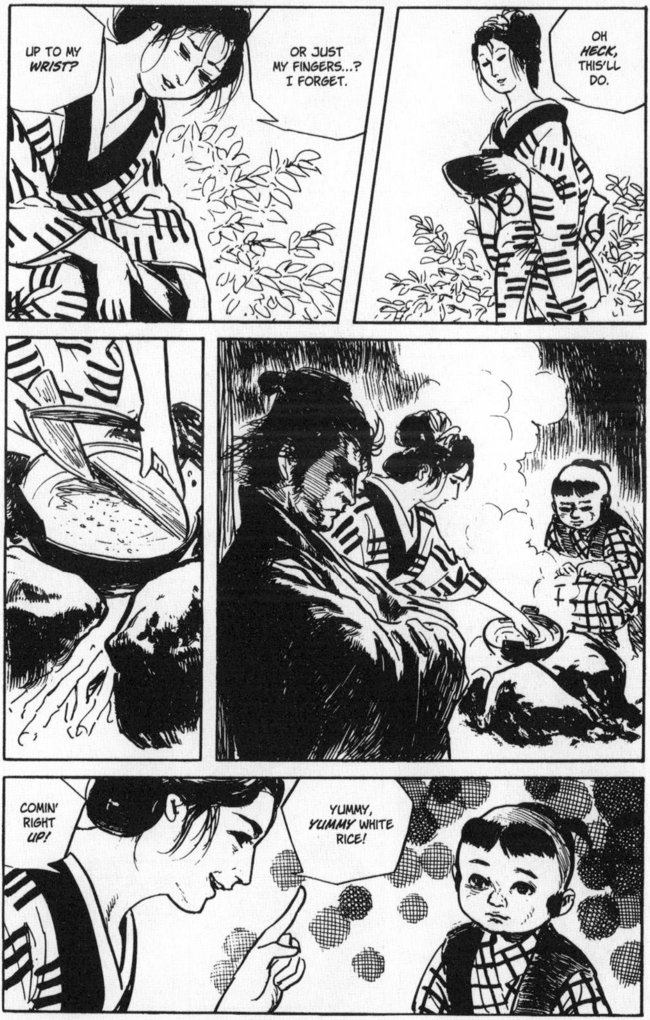
UP TO MY *WRIST?*
OR JUST MY FINGERS...? I FORGET.
OH *HECK,* THIS'LL DO.
COMIN' RIGHT *UP!*
YUMMY, *YUMMY* WHITE RICE!

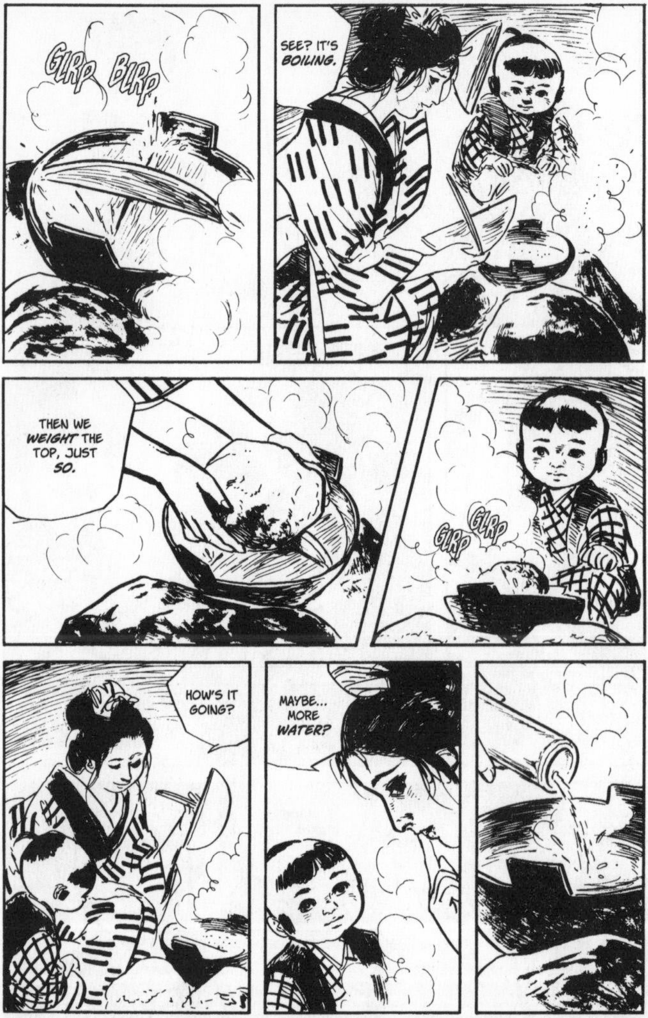
GLRP BLRP
SEE? IT'S BOILING.
THEN WE WEIGHT THE TOP, JUST SO.
GLRP
GLRP
HOW'S IT GOING?
MAYBE... MORE WATER?

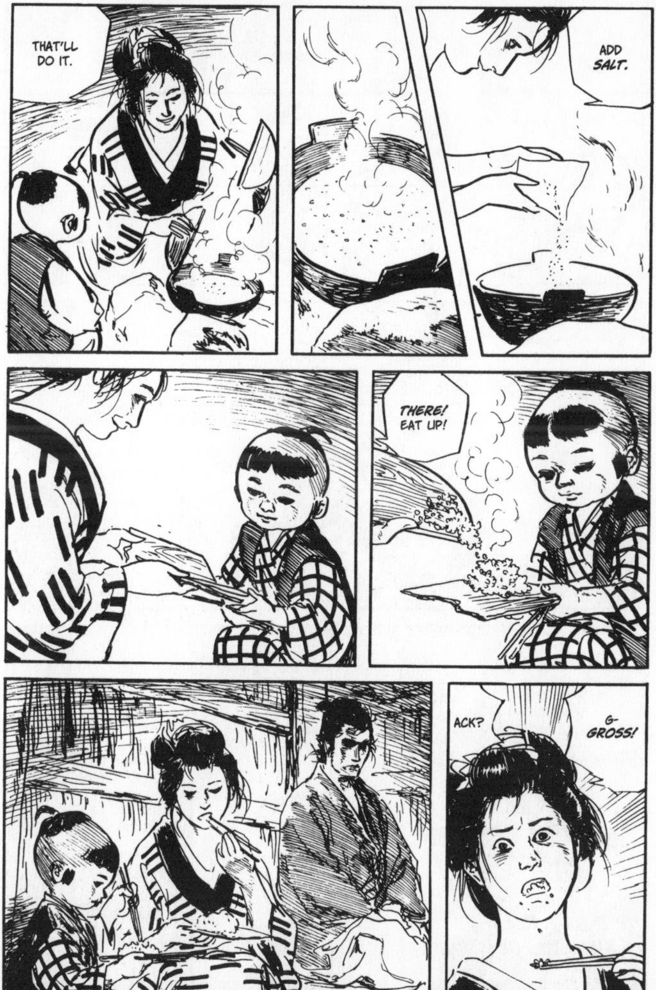
THAT'LL DO IT.
ADD SALT.
THERE! EAT UP!
ACK?
G-GROSS!

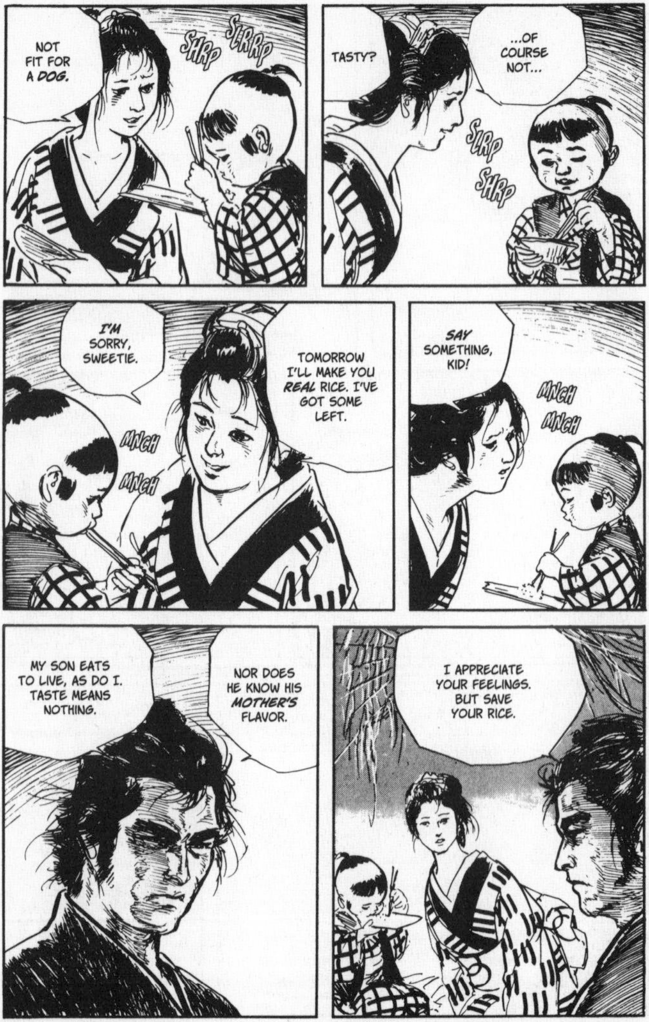
NOT FIT FOR A *DOG.*
SHRP
SLRRP
TASTY?
...OF COURSE NOT...
SLRP
SHRP
I'M SORRY, SWEETIE.
TOMORROW I'LL MAKE YOU *REAL* RICE. I'VE GOT SOME LEFT.
MNCH
MNCH
SAY SOMETHING, KID!
MNCH
MNCH
MY SON EATS TO LIVE, AS DO I. TASTE MEANS NOTHING.
NOR DOES HE KNOW HIS *MOTHER'S* FLAVOR.
I APPRECIATE YOUR FEELINGS. BUT SAVE YOUR RICE.

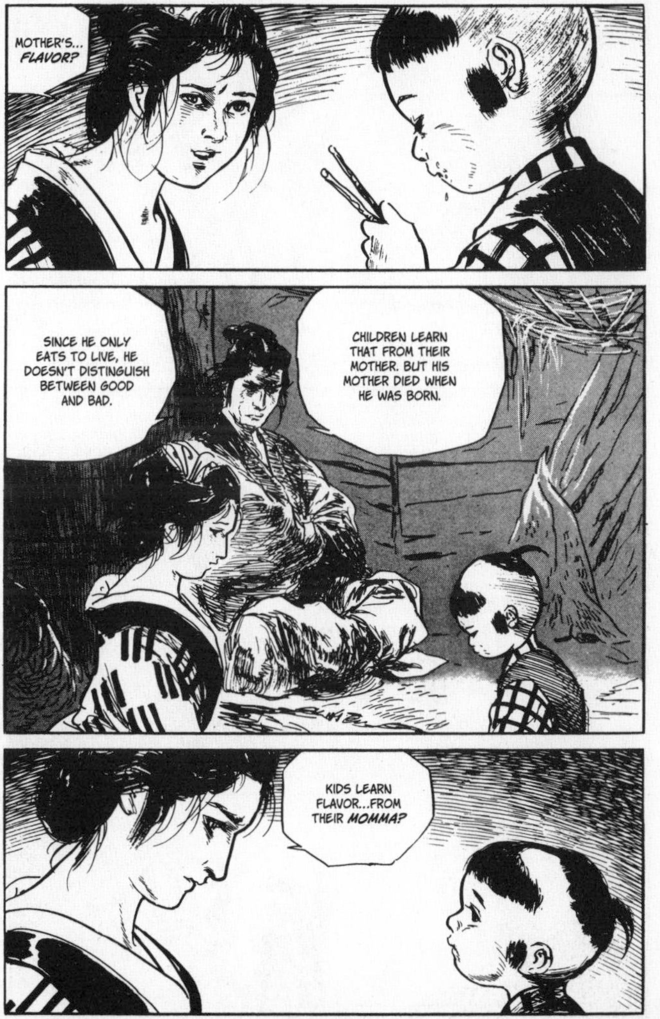
MOTHER'S... *FLAVOR?*
SINCE HE ONLY EATS TO LIVE, HE DOESN'T DISTINGUISH BETWEEN GOOD AND BAD.
CHILDREN LEARN THAT FROM THEIR MOTHER. BUT HIS MOTHER DIED WHEN HE WAS BORN.
KIDS LEARN FLAVOR...FROM THEIR *MOMMA?*

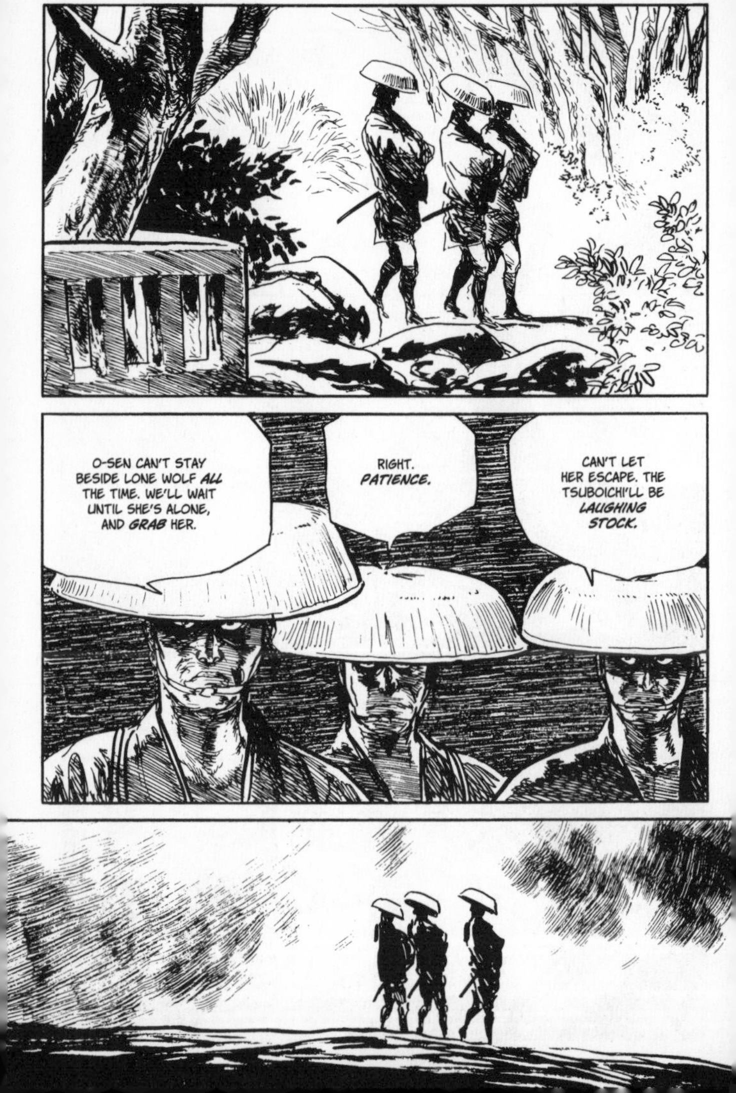
O-SEN CAN'T STAY BESIDE LONE WOLF *ALL* THE TIME. WE'LL WAIT UNTIL SHE'S ALONE, AND *GRAB* HER.
RIGHT. *PATIENCE.*
CAN'T LET HER ESCAPE. THE TSUBOICHI'LL BE *LAUGHING STOCK.*

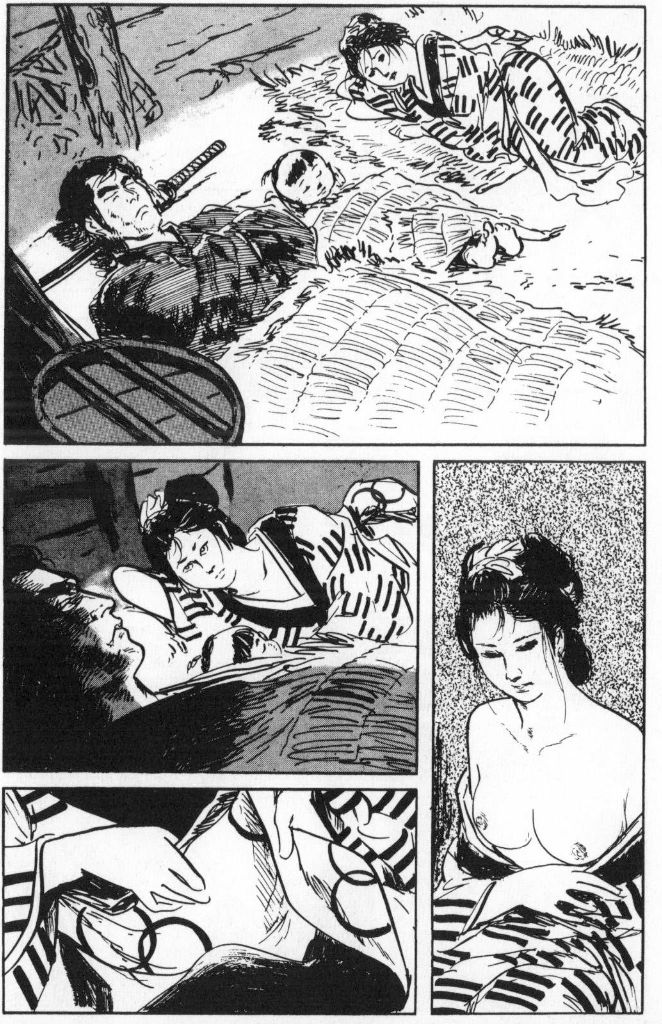

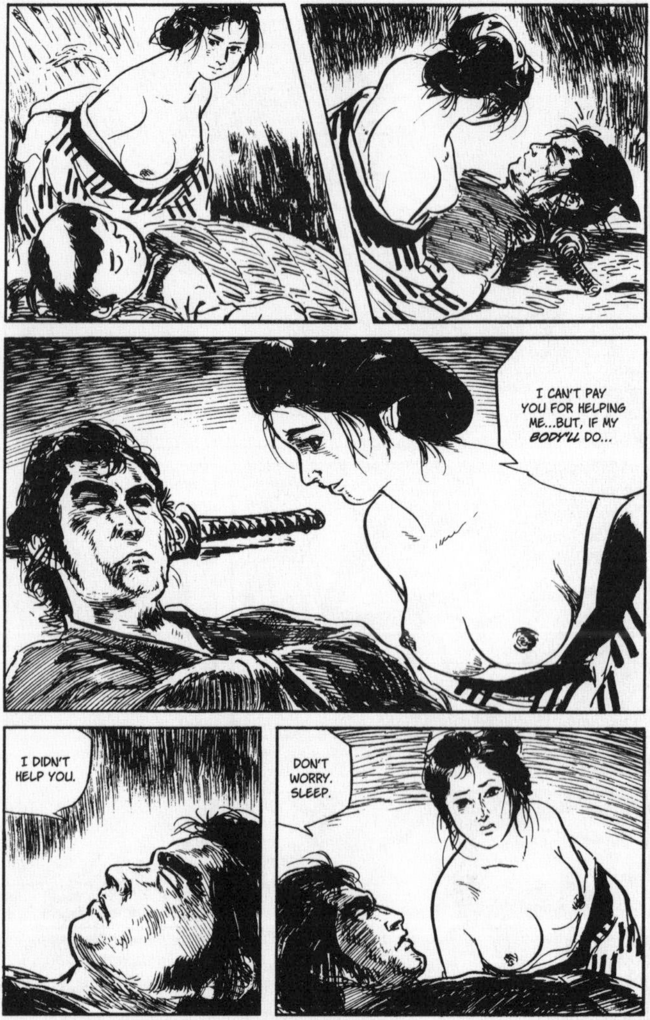
I CAN'T PAY YOU FOR HELPING ME...BUT, IF MY *BODY'LL* DO...
I DIDN'T HELP YOU.
DON'T WORRY. SLEEP.

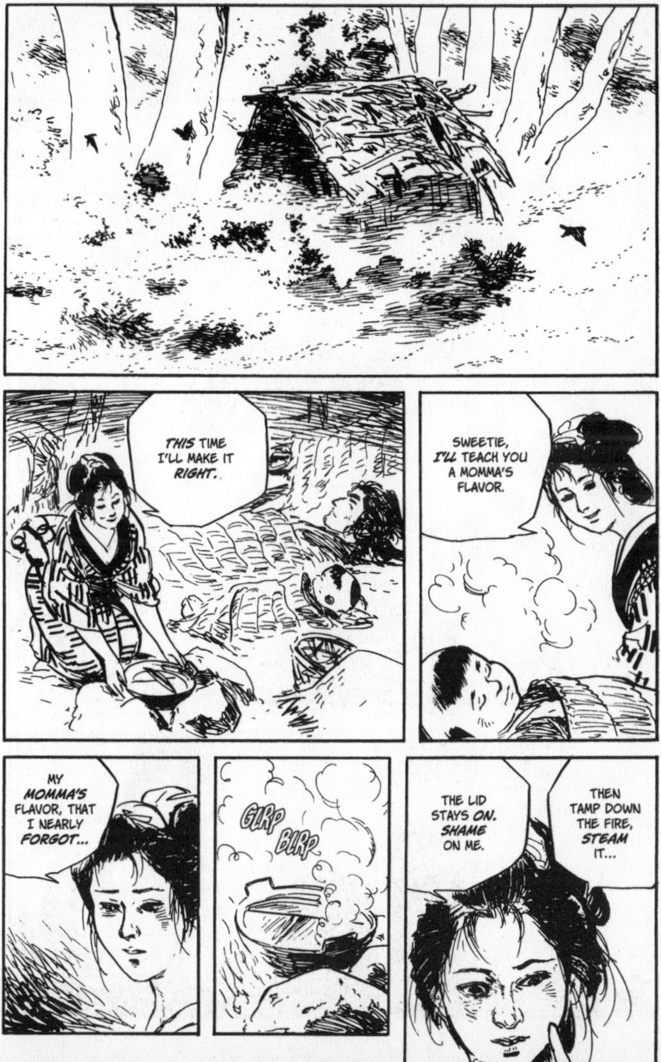
THIS TIME I'LL MAKE IT RIGHT.
SWEETIE, I'LL TEACH YOU A MOMMA'S FLAVOR.
MY MOMMA'S FLAVOR, THAT I NEARLY FORGOT...
GIRP
BLIRP
THE LID STAYS ON. SHAME ON ME.
THEN TAMP DOWN THE FIRE, STEAM IT...

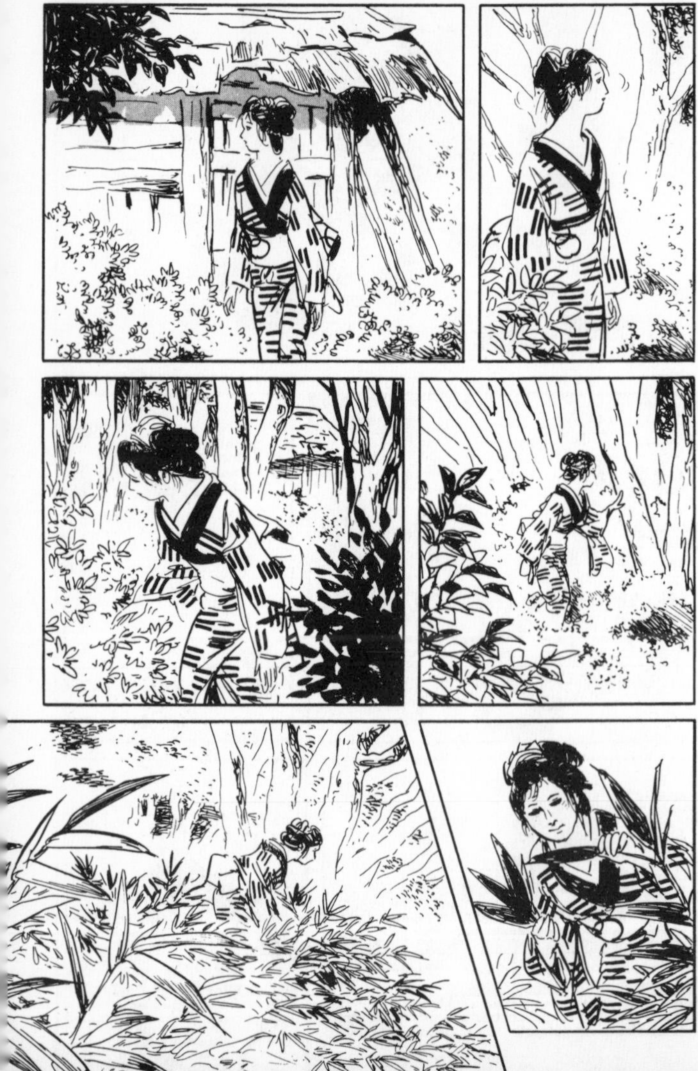

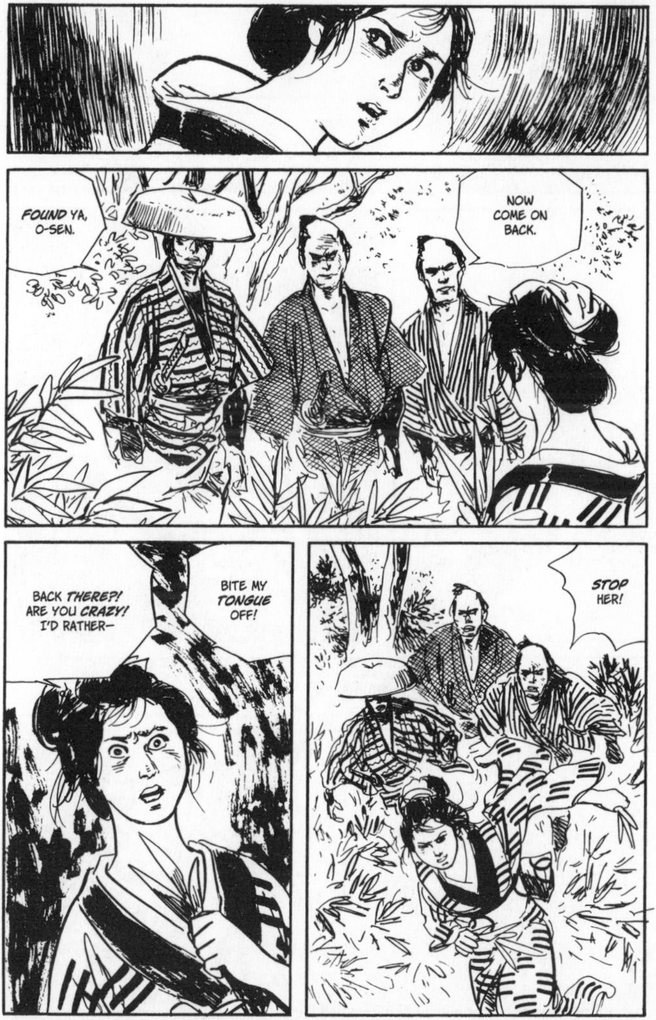
FOUND YA, O-SEN.
NOW COME ON BACK.
BACK THERE?! ARE YOU CRAZY! I'D RATHER—
BITE MY TONGUE OFF!
STOP HER!

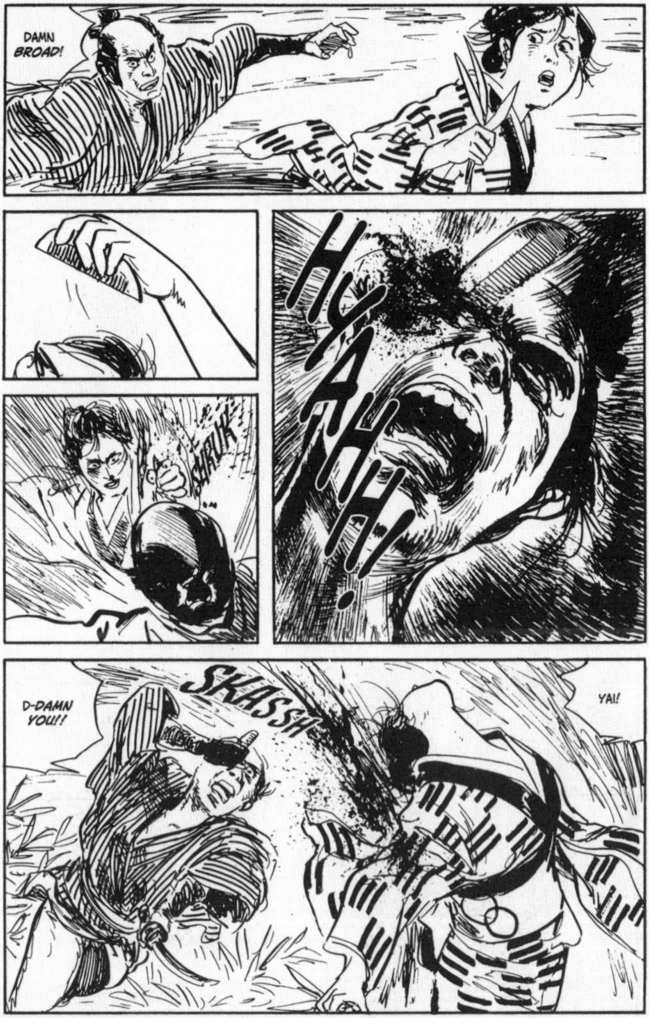
DAMN BROAD!
SHRUK
..
HYAAHH!
D-DAMN YOU!!
SKASSH
YAI!

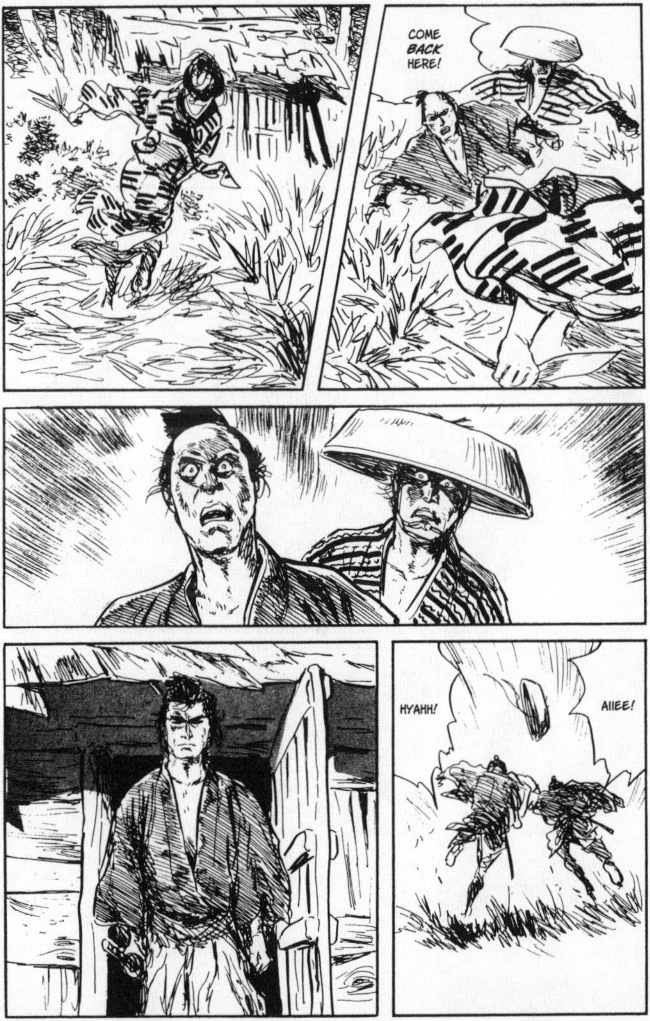
COME BACK HERE!
HYAHH!
AIIEE!

URNN...

HNG...

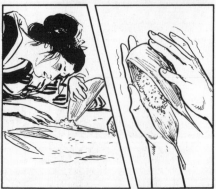

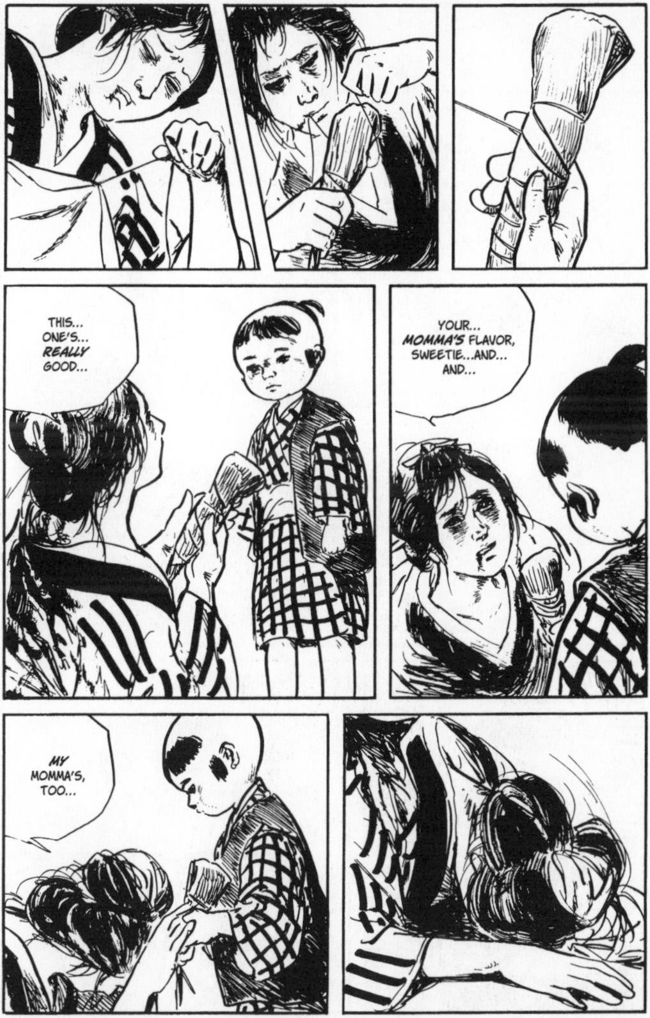
THIS... ONE'S... REALLY GOOD...
YOUR... MOMMA'S FLAVOR, SWEETIE...AND... AND...
MY MOMMA'S, TOO...

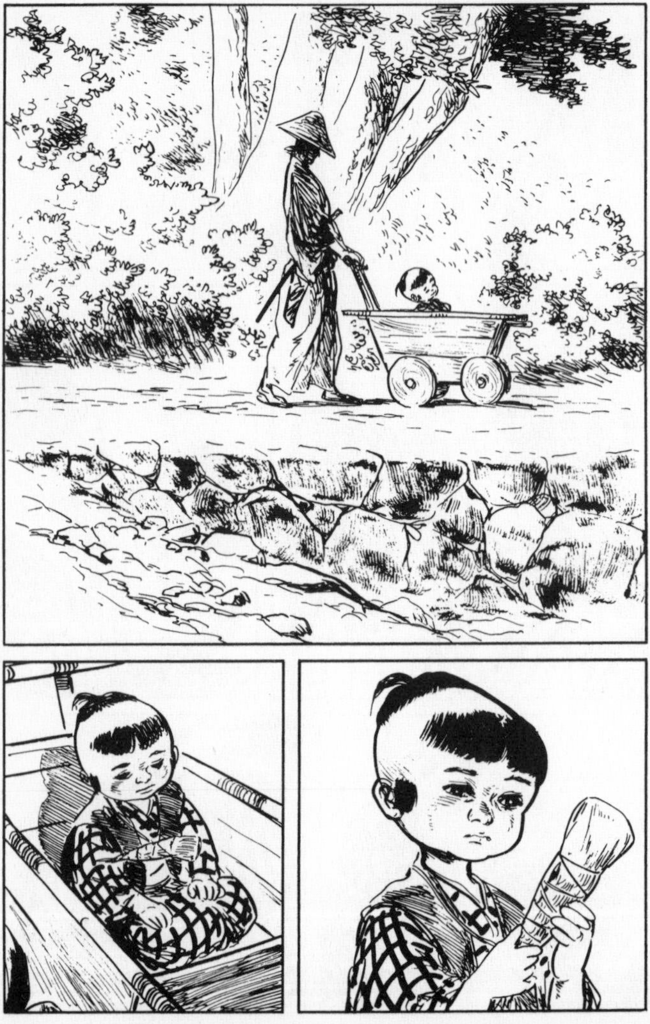

the ninety-seventh

The Moon in Our Hearts

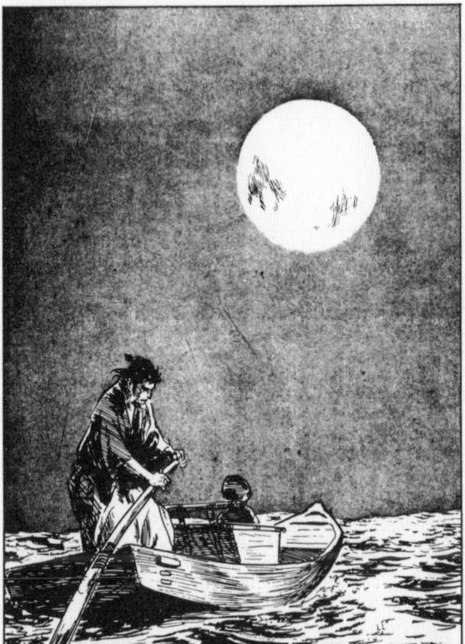

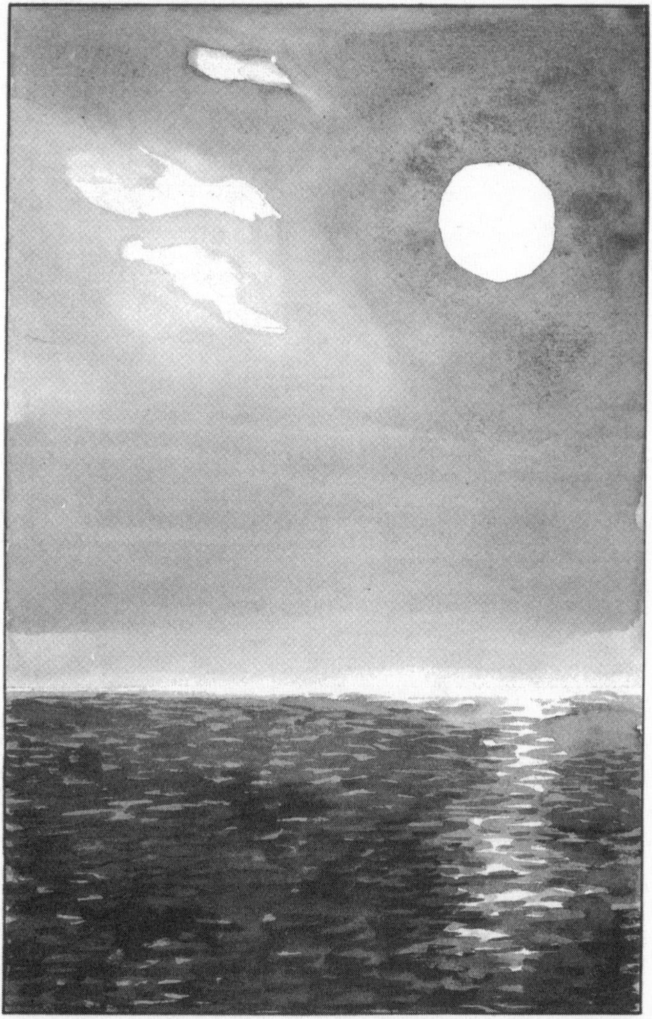

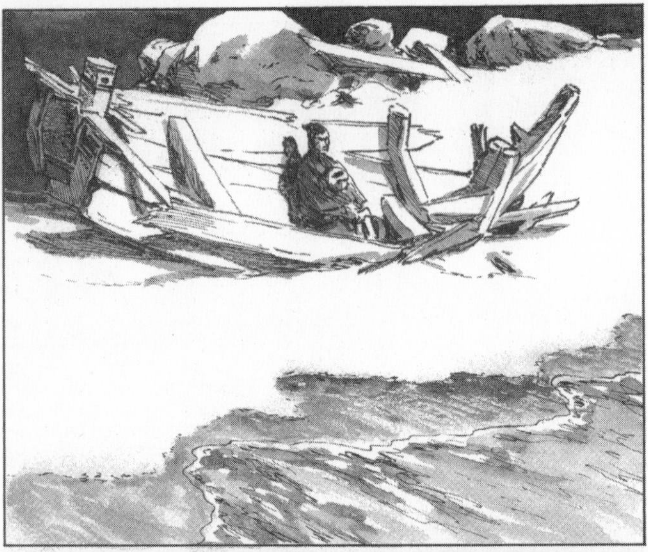

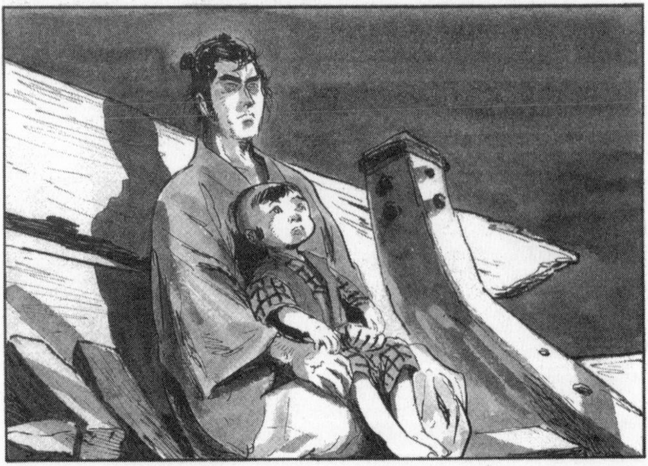

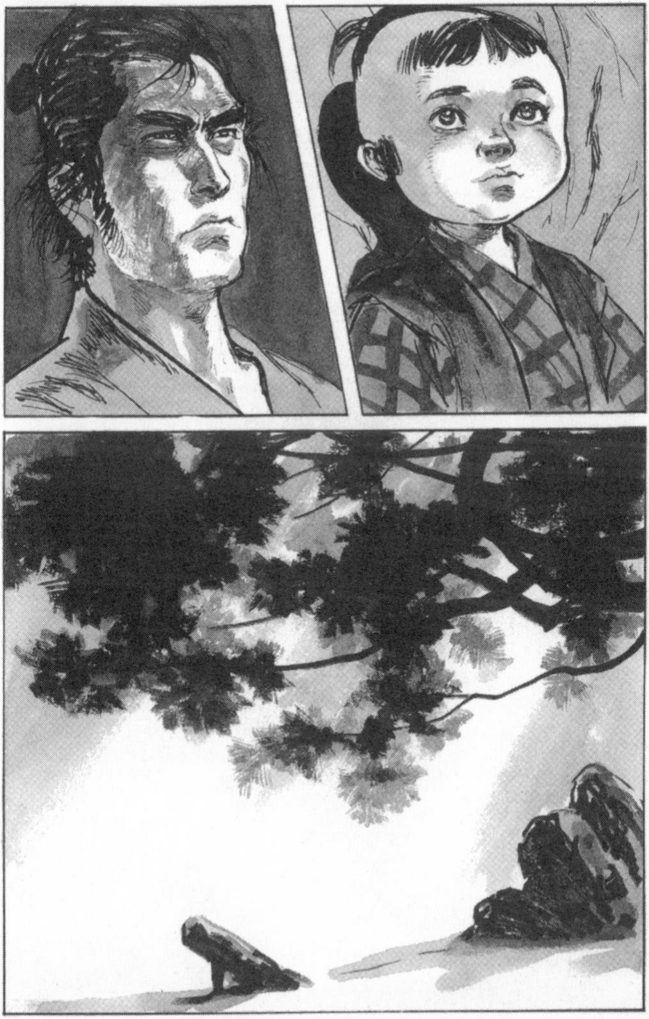

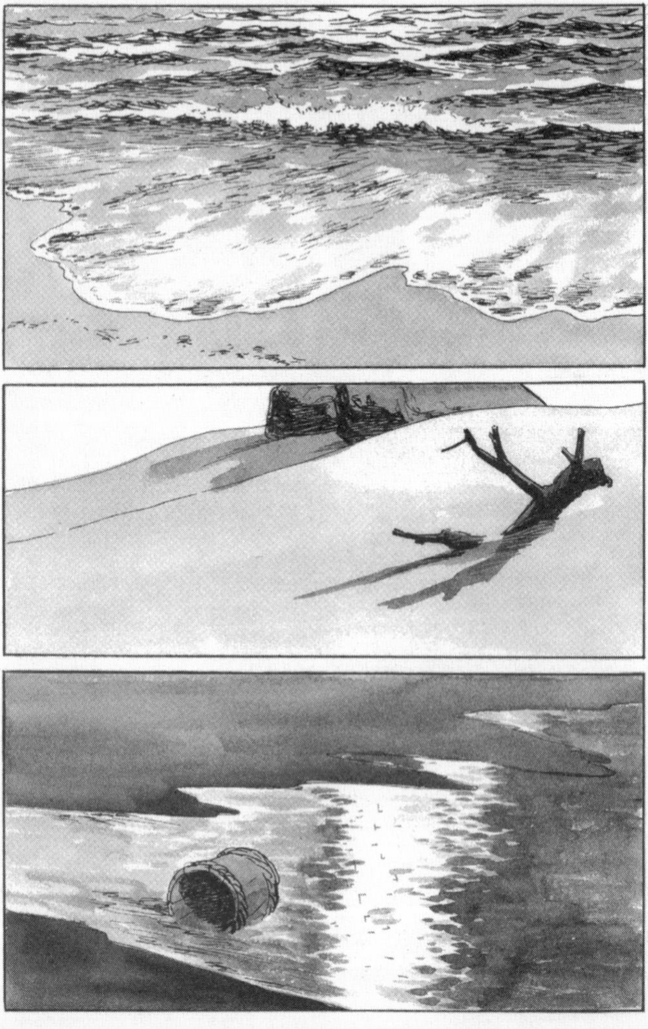

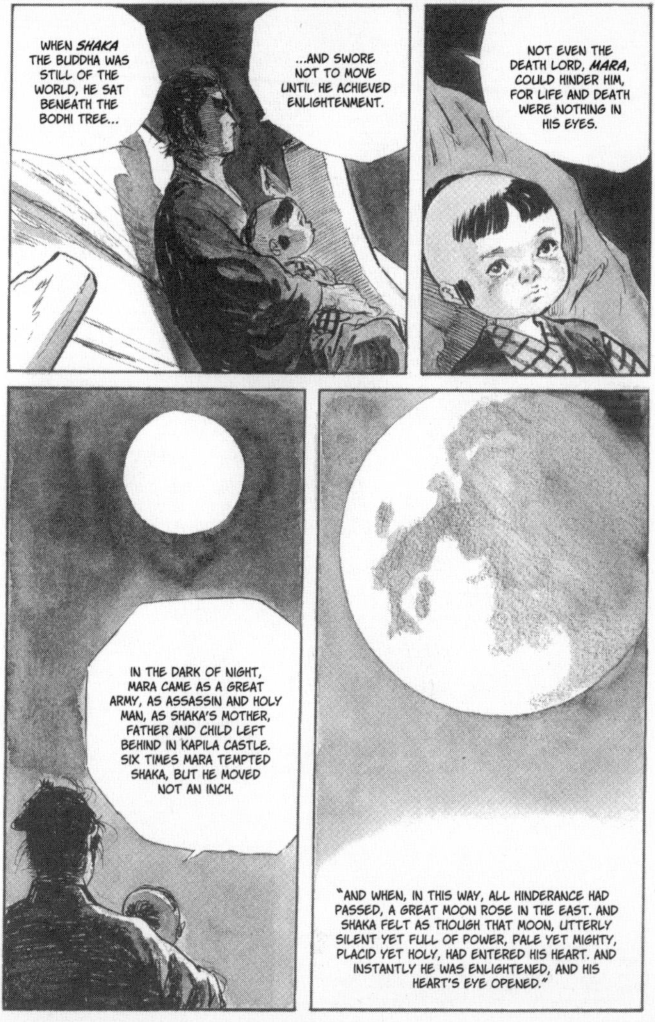

WHEN *SHAKA* THE BUDDHA WAS STILL OF THE WORLD, HE SAT BENEATH THE BODHI TREE...
...AND SWORE NOT TO MOVE UNTIL HE ACHIEVED ENLIGHTENMENT.
NOT EVEN THE DEATH LORD, *MARA*, COULD HINDER HIM, FOR LIFE AND DEATH WERE NOTHING IN HIS EYES.
IN THE DARK OF NIGHT, MARA CAME AS A GREAT ARMY, AS ASSASSIN AND HOLY MAN, AS SHAKA'S MOTHER, FATHER AND CHILD LEFT BEHIND IN KAPILA CASTLE. SIX TIMES MARA TEMPTED SHAKA, BUT HE MOVED NOT AN INCH.
"AND WHEN, IN THIS WAY, ALL HINDERANCE HAD PASSED, A GREAT MOON ROSE IN THE EAST. AND SHAKA FELT AS THOUGH THAT MOON, UTTERLY SILENT YET FULL OF POWER, PALE YET MIGHTY, PLACID YET HOLY, HAD ENTERED HIS HEART. AND INSTANTLY HE WAS ENLIGHTENED, AND HIS HEART'S EYE OPENED."

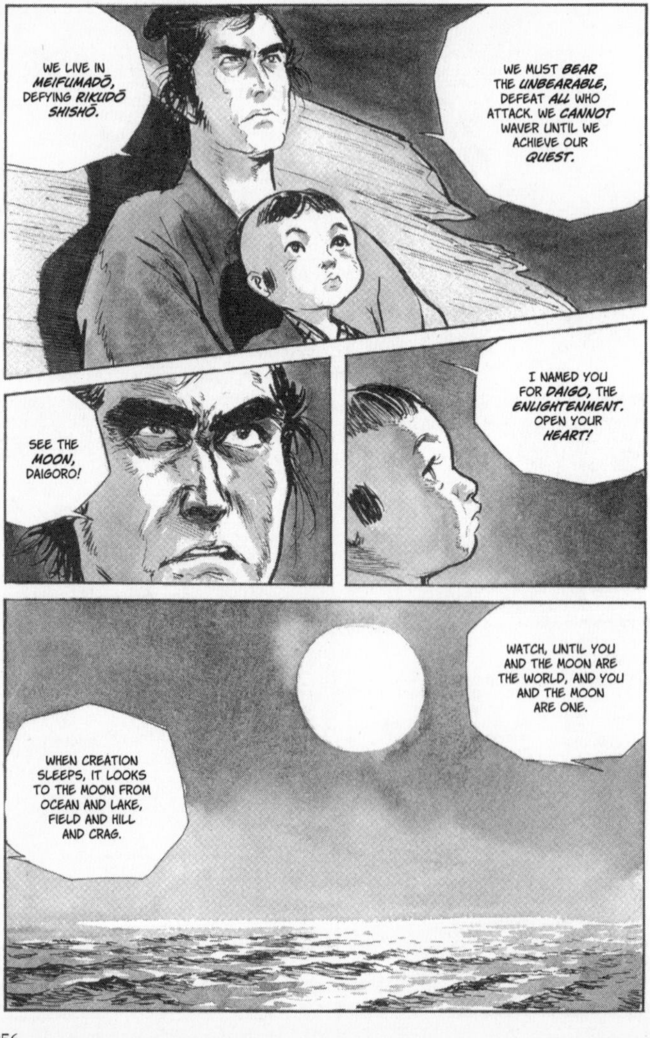

WE LIVE IN MEIFUMADŌ, DEFYING RIKUDŌ SHISHŌ.
WE MUST BEAR THE UNBEARABLE, DEFEAT ALL WHO ATTACK. WE CANNOT WAVER UNTIL WE ACHIEVE OUR QUEST.
SEE THE MOON, DAIGORO!
I NAMED YOU FOR DAIGO, THE ENLIGHTENMENT. OPEN YOUR HEART!
WHEN CREATION SLEEPS, IT LOOKS TO THE MOON FROM OCEAN AND LAKE, FIELD AND HILL AND CRAG.
WATCH, UNTIL YOU AND THE MOON ARE THE WORLD, AND YOU AND THE MOON ARE ONE.

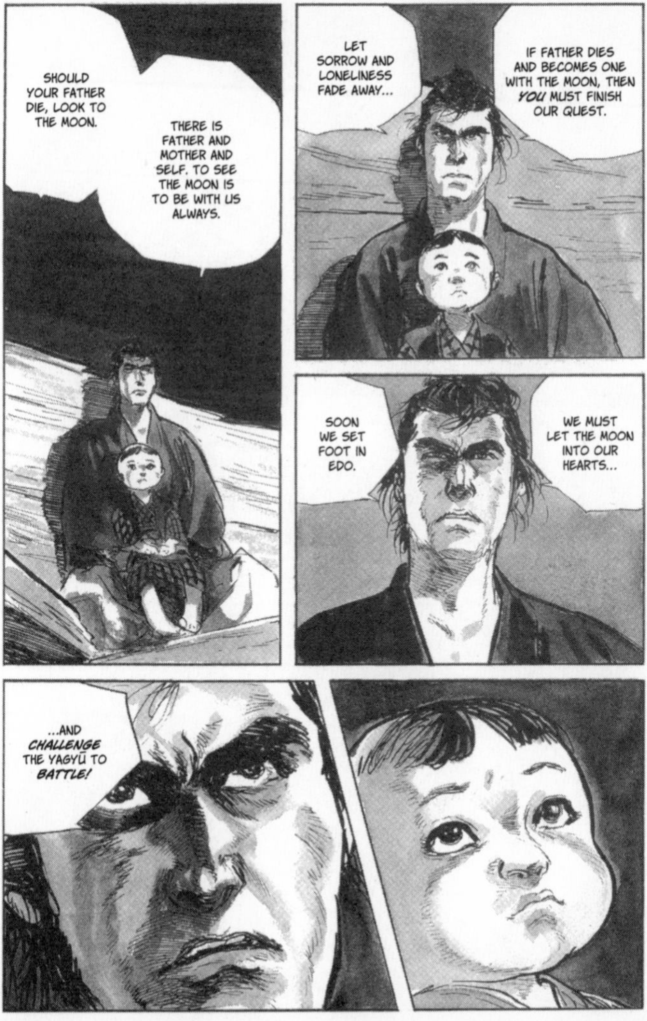
SHOULD YOUR FATHER DIE, LOOK TO THE MOON.
THERE IS FATHER AND MOTHER AND SELF. TO SEE THE MOON IS TO BE WITH US ALWAYS.
LET SORROW AND LONELINESS FADE AWAY...
IF FATHER DIES AND BECOMES ONE WITH THE MOON, THEN *YOU* MUST FINISH OUR QUEST.
SOON WE SET FOOT IN EDO.
WE MUST LET THE MOON INTO OUR HEARTS...
...AND *CHALLENGE* THE YAGYŪ TO *BATTLE!*

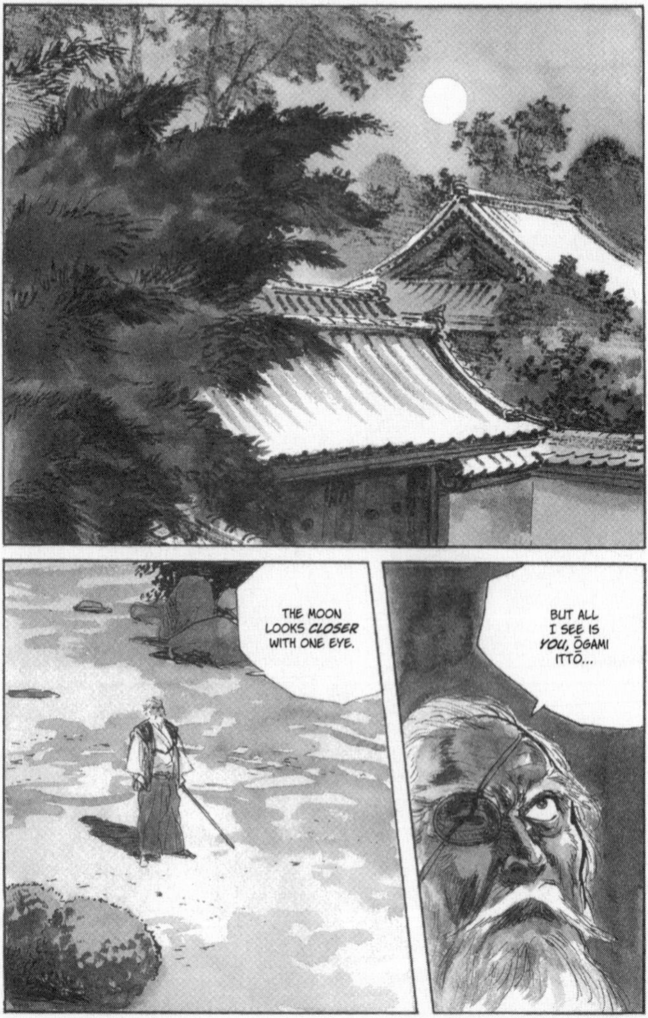
THE MOON LOOKS CLOSER WITH ONE EYE.
BUT ALL I SEE IS YOU, ŌGAMI ITTŌ...

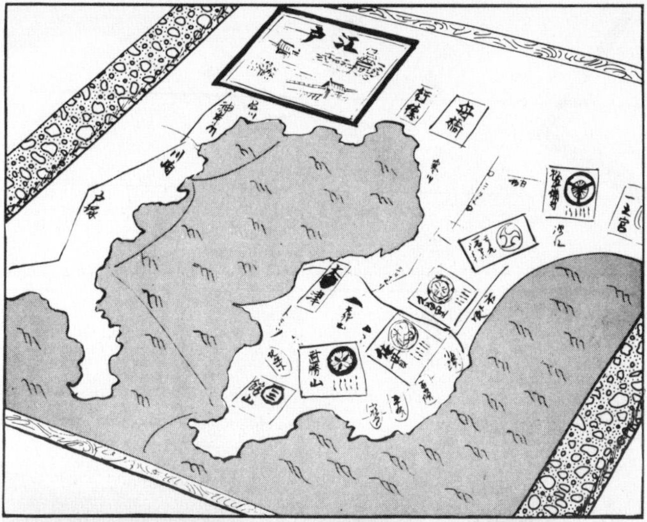

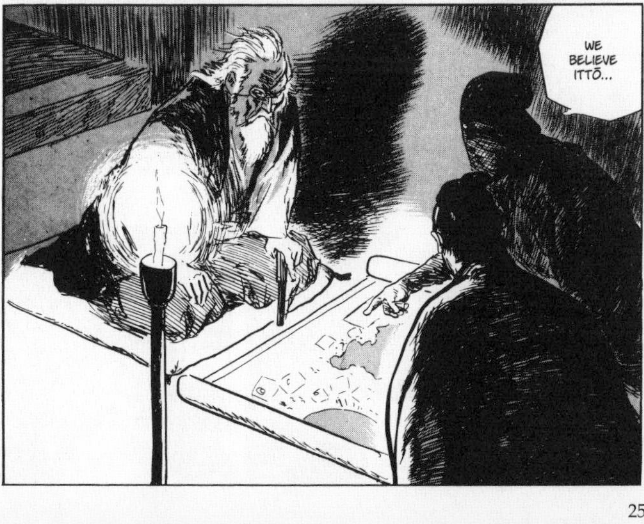
WE BELIEVE ITTŌ...

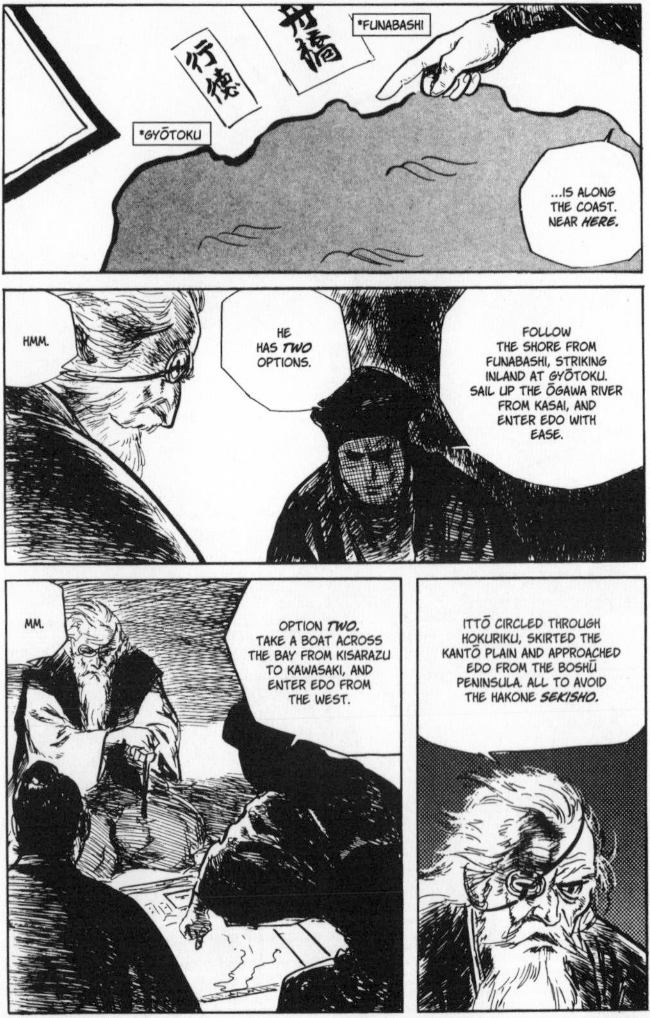

行徳
*FUNABASHI
*GYŌTOKU
...IS ALONG THE COAST. NEAR *HERE.*
HMM.
HE HAS *TWO* OPTIONS.
FOLLOW THE SHORE FROM FUNABASHI, STRIKING INLAND AT GYŌTOKU. SAIL UP THE ŌGAWA RIVER FROM KASAI, AND ENTER EDO WITH EASE.
MM.
OPTION *TWO.* TAKE A BOAT ACROSS THE BAY FROM KISARAZU TO KAWASAKI, AND ENTER EDO FROM THE WEST.
ITTŌ CIRCLED THROUGH HOKURIKU, SKIRTED THE KANTŌ PLAIN AND APPROACHED EDO FROM THE BOSHŪ PENINSULA. ALL TO AVOID THE HAKONE *SEKISHO.*

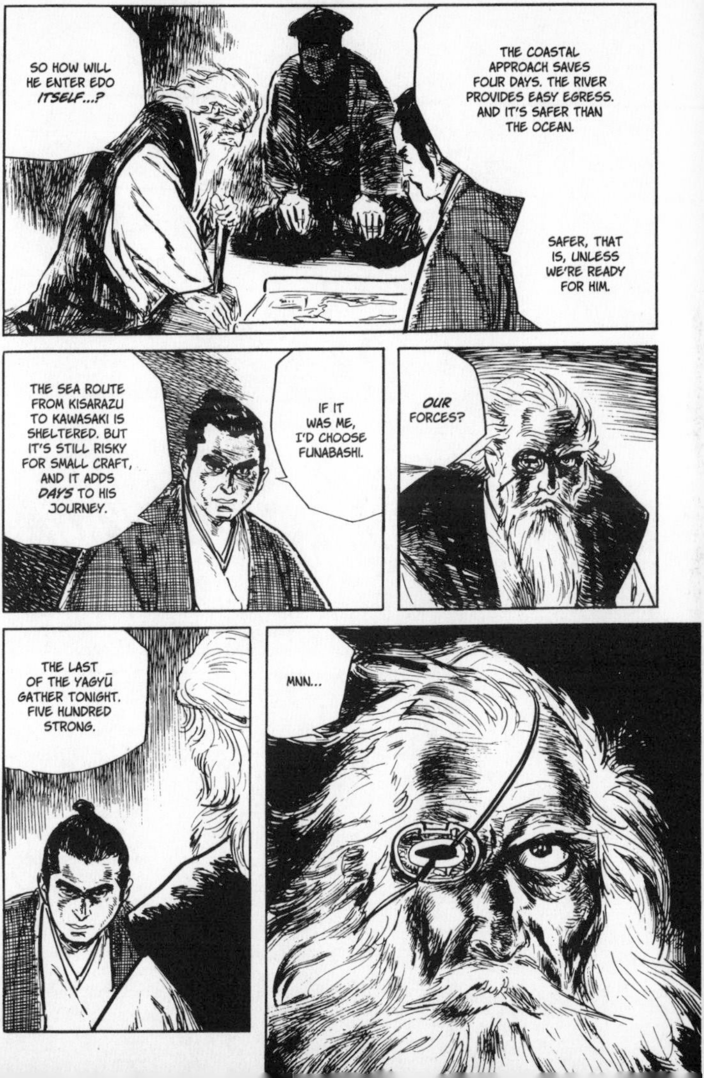
SO HOW WILL HE ENTER EDO *ITSELF...?*
THE COASTAL APPROACH SAVES FOUR DAYS. THE RIVER PROVIDES EASY EGRESS. AND IT'S SAFER THAN THE OCEAN.
SAFER, THAT IS, UNLESS WE'RE READY FOR HIM.
THE SEA ROUTE FROM KISARAZU TO KAWASAKI IS SHELTERED. BUT IT'S STILL RISKY FOR SMALL CRAFT, AND IT ADDS *DAYS* TO HIS JOURNEY.
IF IT WAS ME, I'D CHOOSE FUNABASHI.
OUR FORCES?
THE LAST OF THE YAGYŪ GATHER TONIGHT. FIVE HUNDRED STRONG.
MNN...

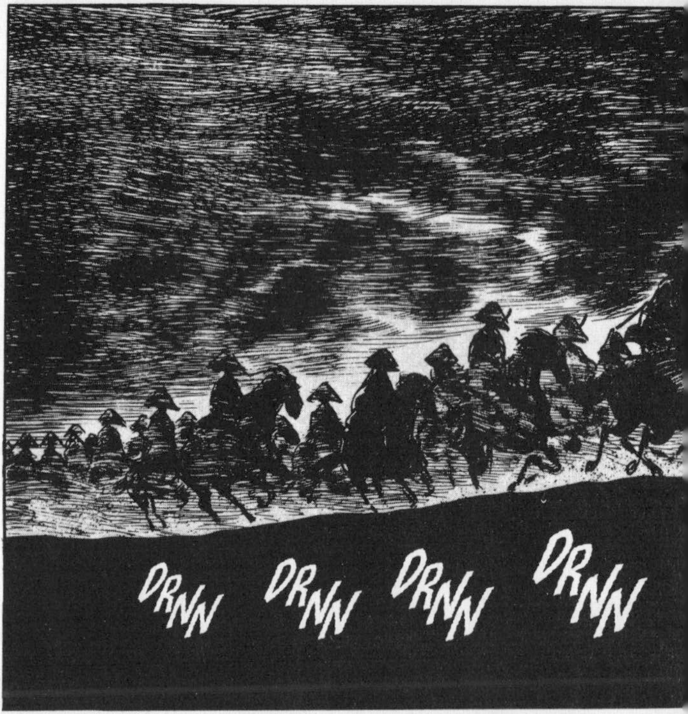
DRNN
DRNN
DRNN
DRNN
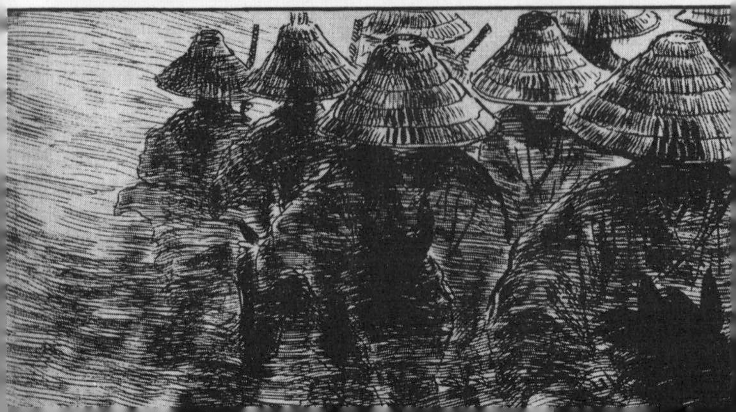

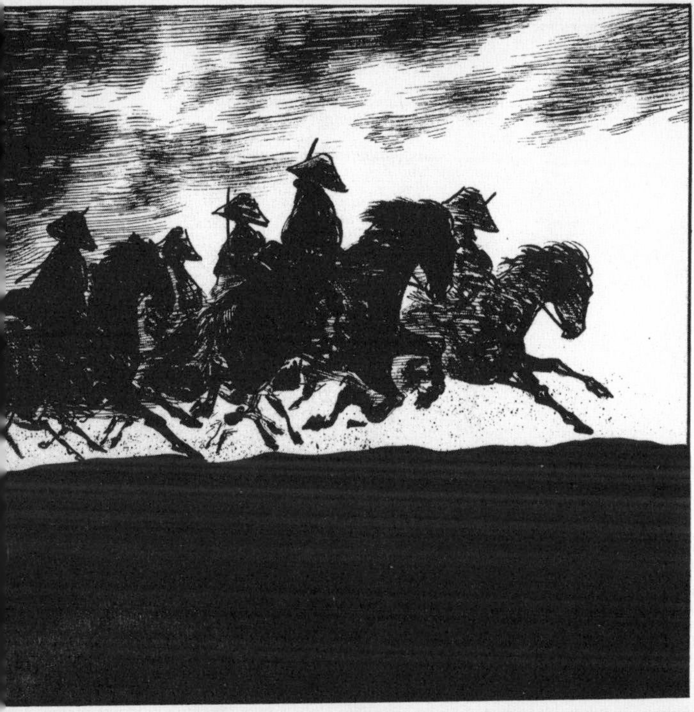
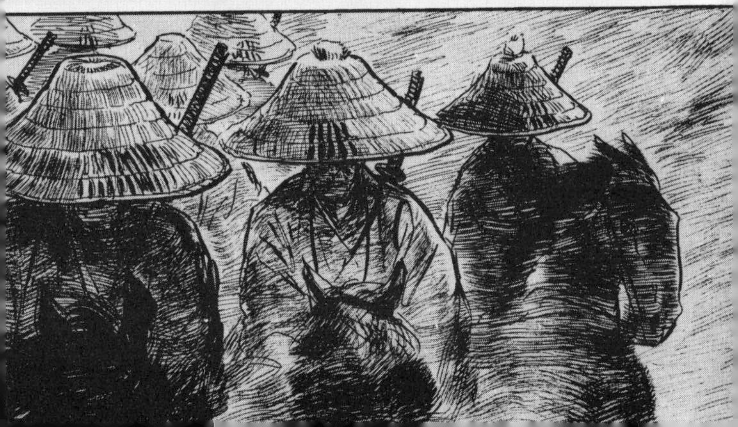

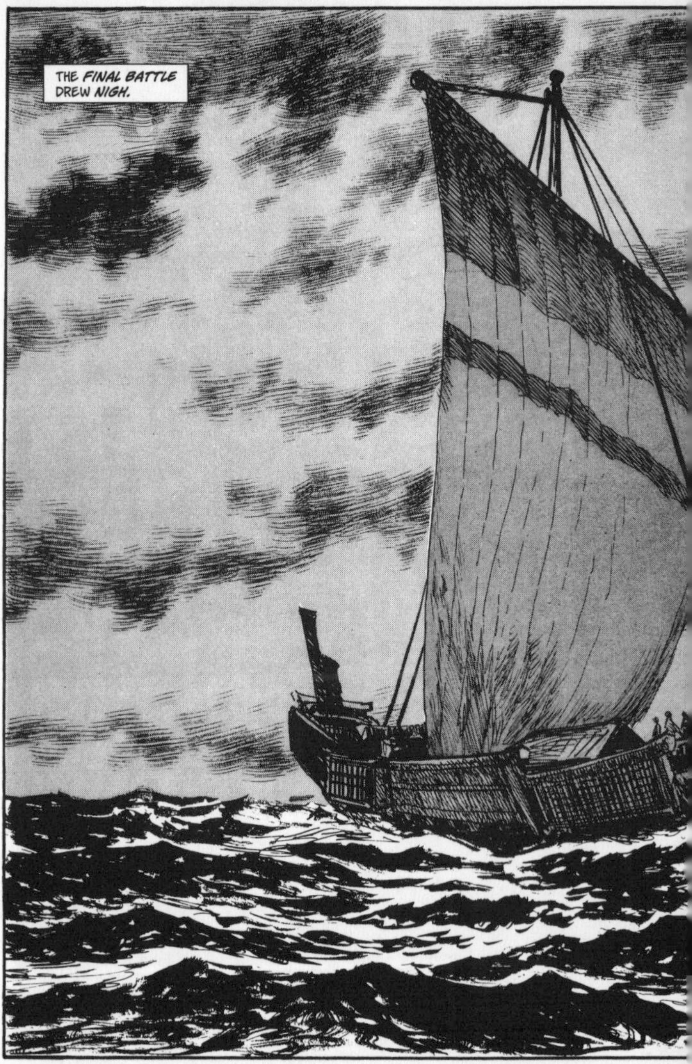
THE *FINAL BATTLE* DREW *NIGH.*

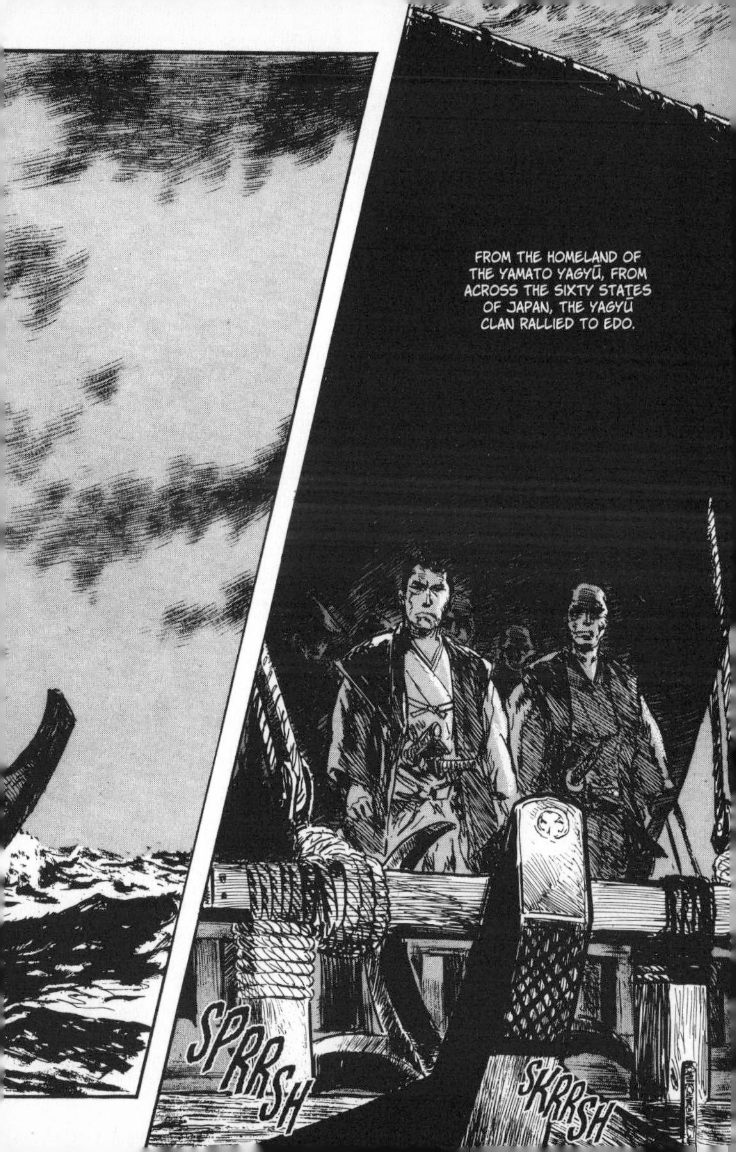
FROM THE HOMELAND OF THE YAMATO YAGYŪ, FROM ACROSS THE SIXTY STATES OF JAPAN, THE YAGYŪ CLAN RALLIED TO EDO.
SPRRSH
SKRRSH

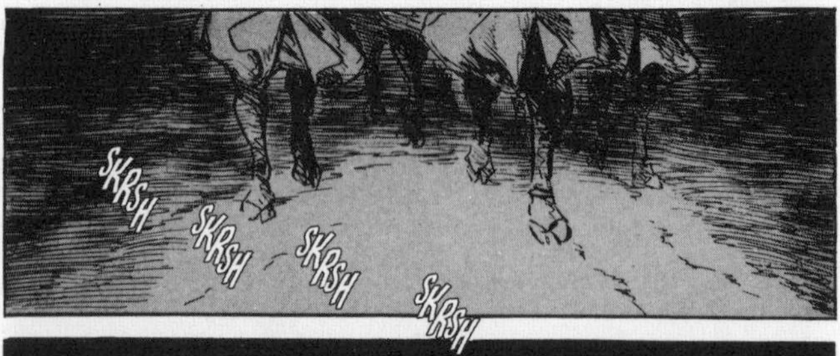
SKRSH
SKRSH
SKRSH
SKRSH

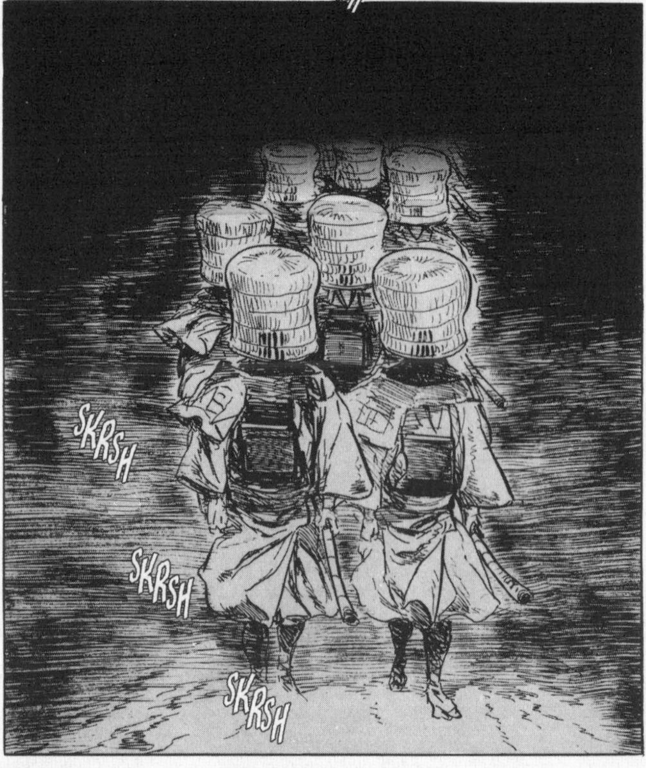
SKRSH
SKRSH
SKRSH

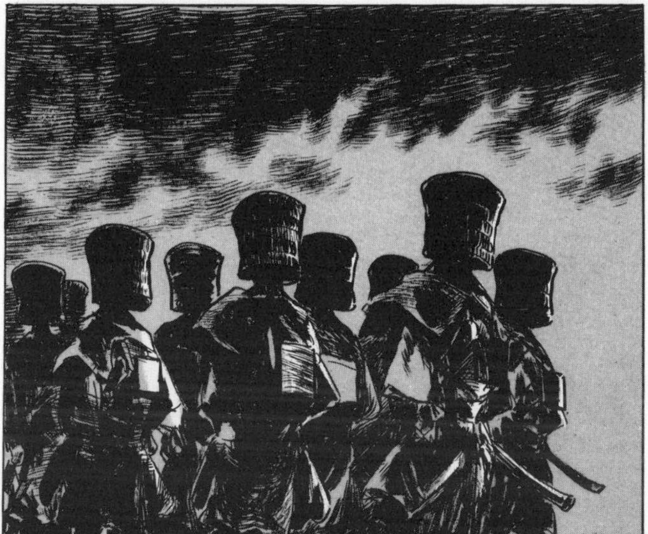

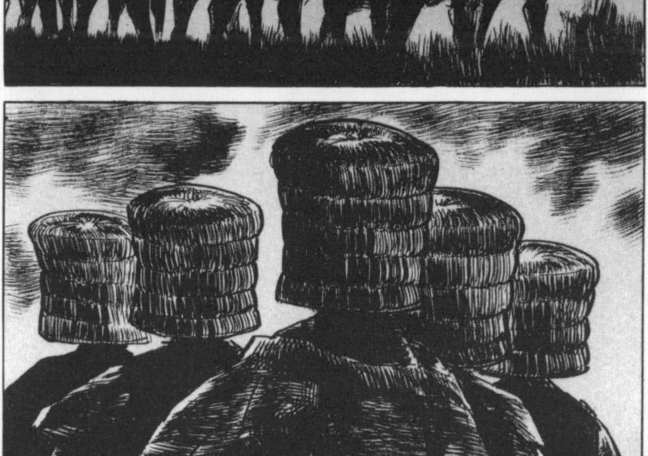

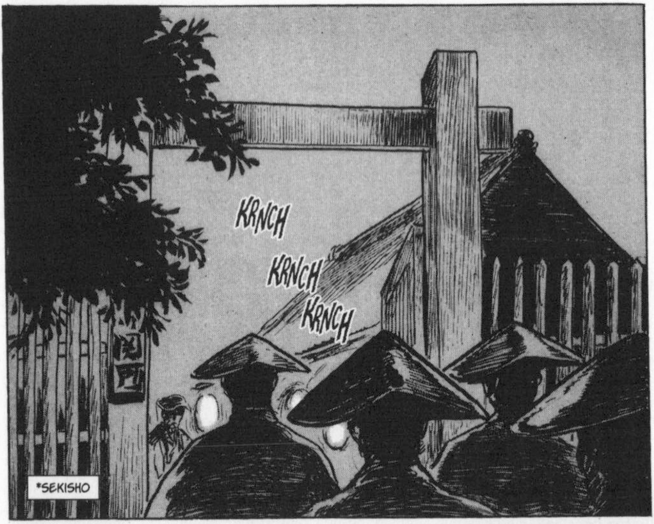
KRNCH
KRNCH
KRNCH
*SEKISHO
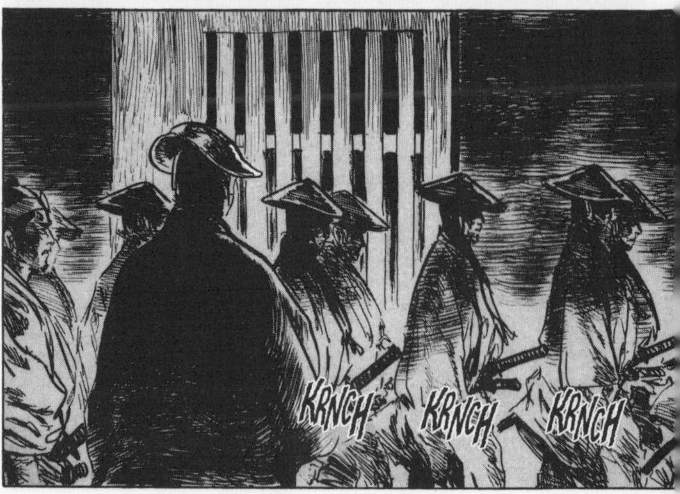
KRNCH
KRNCH
KRNCH

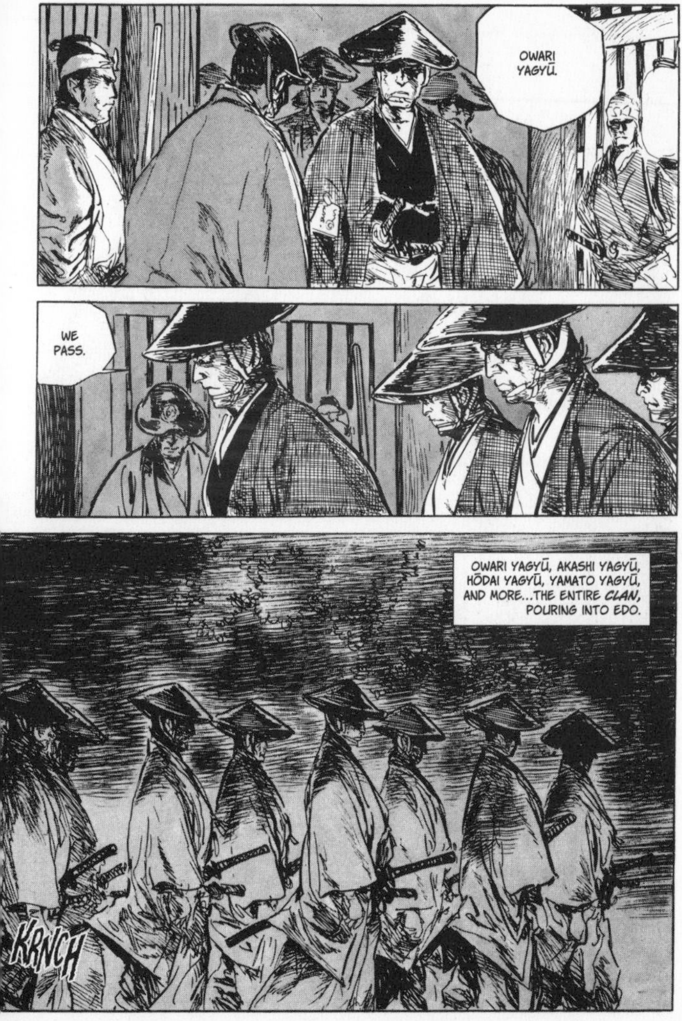
OWARI YAGYŪ.
WE PASS.
OWARI YAGYŪ, AKASHI YAGYŪ, HŌDAI YAGYŪ, YAMATO YAGYŪ, AND MORE...THE ENTIRE *CLAN,* POURING INTO EDO.
KRNCH

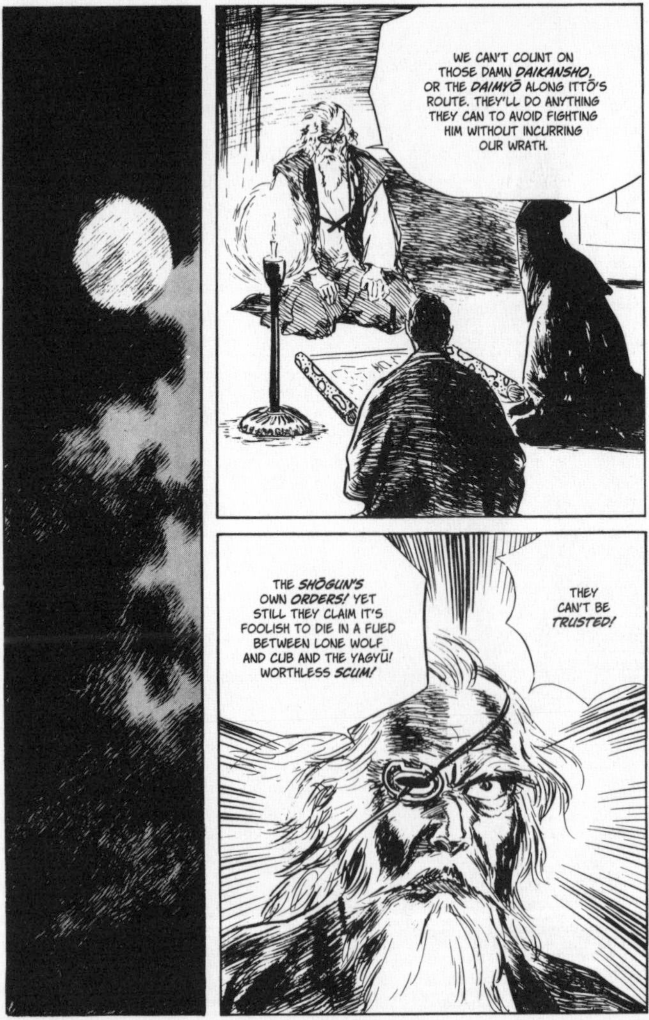
WE CAN'T COUNT ON THOSE DAMN *DAIKANSHO*, OR THE *DAIMYŌ* ALONG ITTŌ'S ROUTE. THEY'LL DO ANYTHING THEY CAN TO AVOID FIGHTING HIM WITHOUT INCURRING OUR WRATH.
THE *SHŌGUN'S* OWN *ORDERS!* YET STILL THEY CLAIM IT'S FOOLISH TO DIE IN A FUED BETWEEN LONE WOLF AND CUB AND THE YAGYŪ! WORTHLESS *SCUM!*
THEY CAN'T BE *TRUSTED!*

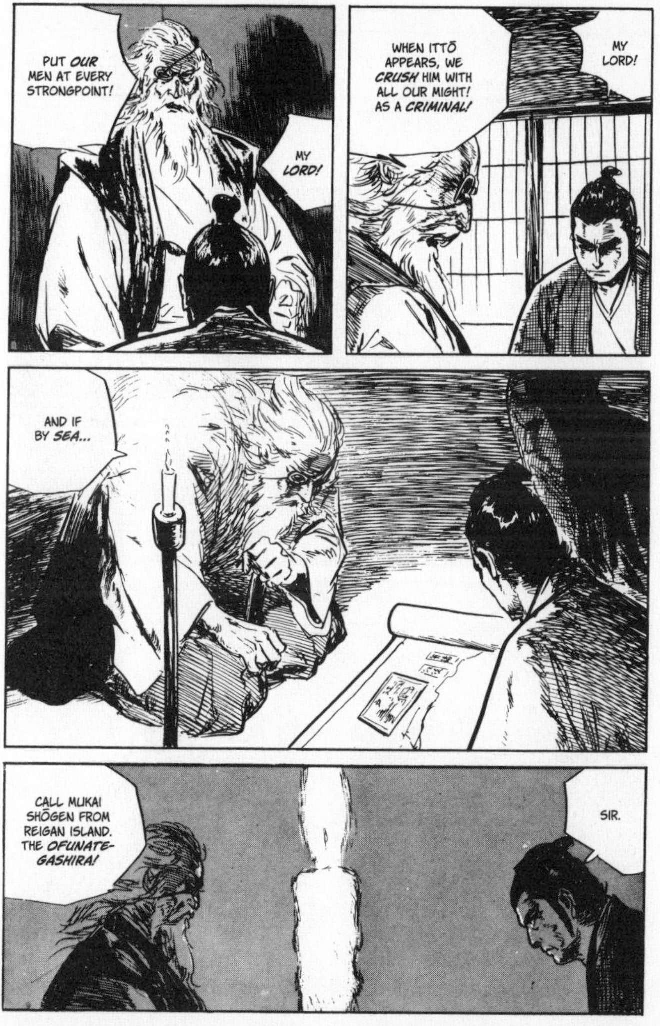
PUT OUR MEN AT EVERY STRONGPOINT!
MY LORD!
WHEN ITTŌ APPEARS, WE CRUSH HIM WITH ALL OUR MIGHT! AS A CRIMINAL!
MY LORD!
AND IF BY SEA...
CALL MUKAI SHŌGEN FROM REIGAN ISLAND. THE OFUNATE-GASHIRA!
SIR.

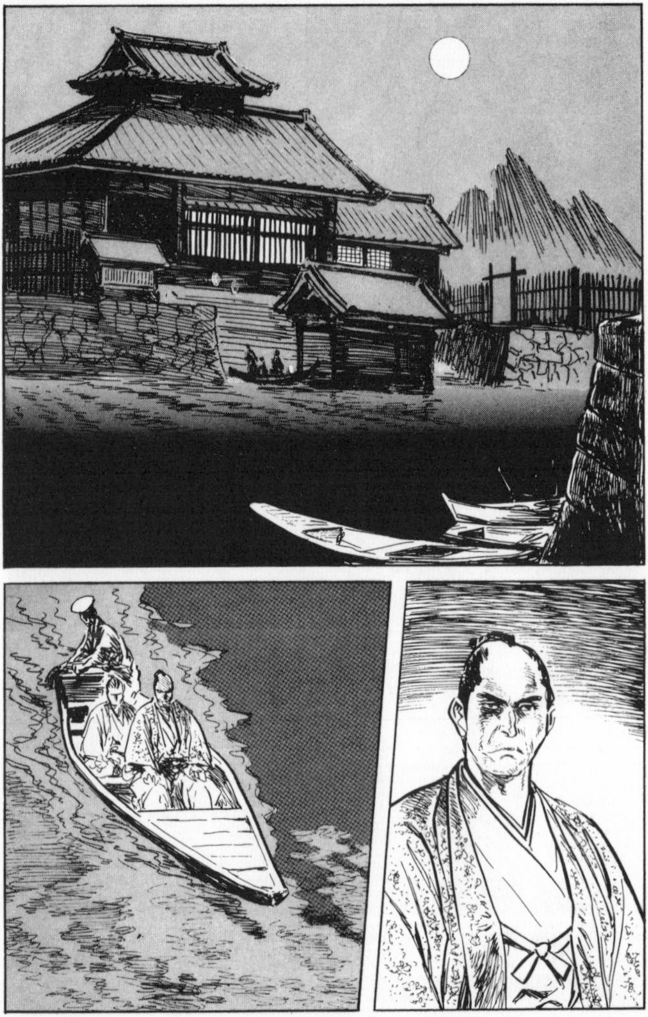

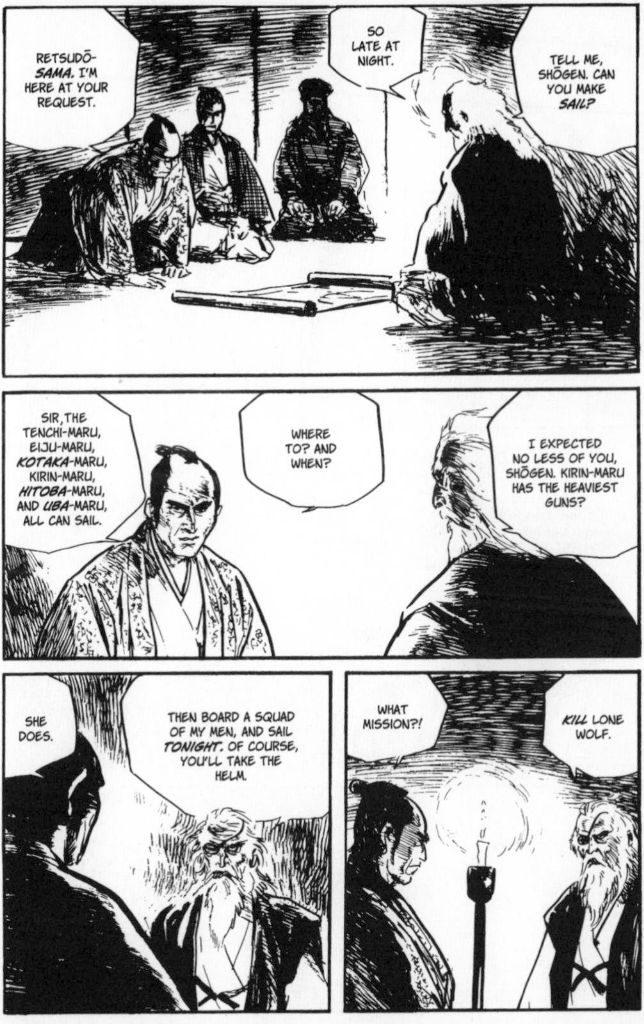

RETSUDŌ-*SAMA.* I'M HERE AT YOUR REQUEST.
SO LATE AT NIGHT.
TELL ME, SHŌGEN. CAN YOU MAKE *SAIL?*
SIR, THE TENCHI-MARU, EIJU-MARU, *KOTAKA*-MARU, KIRIN-MARU, *HITOBA*-MARU, AND *UBA*-MARU, ALL CAN SAIL.
WHERE TO? AND WHEN?
I EXPECTED NO LESS OF YOU, SHŌGEN. KIRIN-MARU HAS THE HEAVIEST GUNS?
SHE DOES.
THEN BOARD A SQUAD OF MY MEN, AND SAIL *TONIGHT.* OF COURSE, YOU'LL TAKE THE HELM.
WHAT MISSION?!
KILL LONE WOLF.

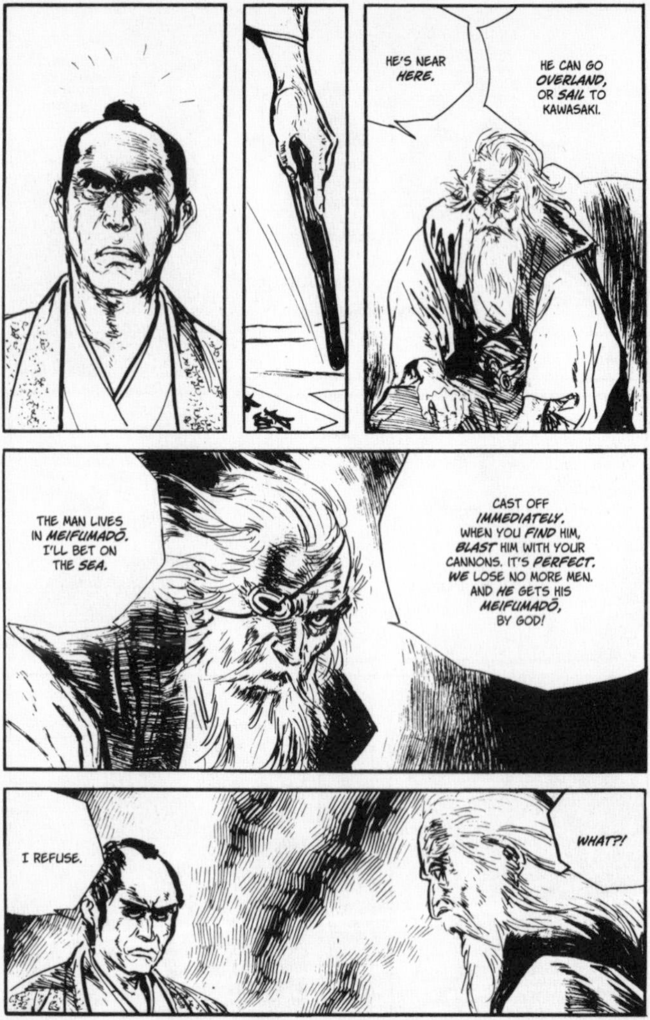
HE'S NEAR HERE.
HE CAN GO OVERLAND, OR SAIL TO KAWASAKI.
THE MAN LIVES IN MEIFUMADŌ. I'LL BET ON THE SEA.
CAST OFF IMMEDIATELY. WHEN YOU FIND HIM, BLAST HIM WITH YOUR CANNONS. IT'S PERFECT. WE LOSE NO MORE MEN. AND HE GETS HIS MEIFUMADŌ, BY GOD!
I REFUSE.
WHAT?!

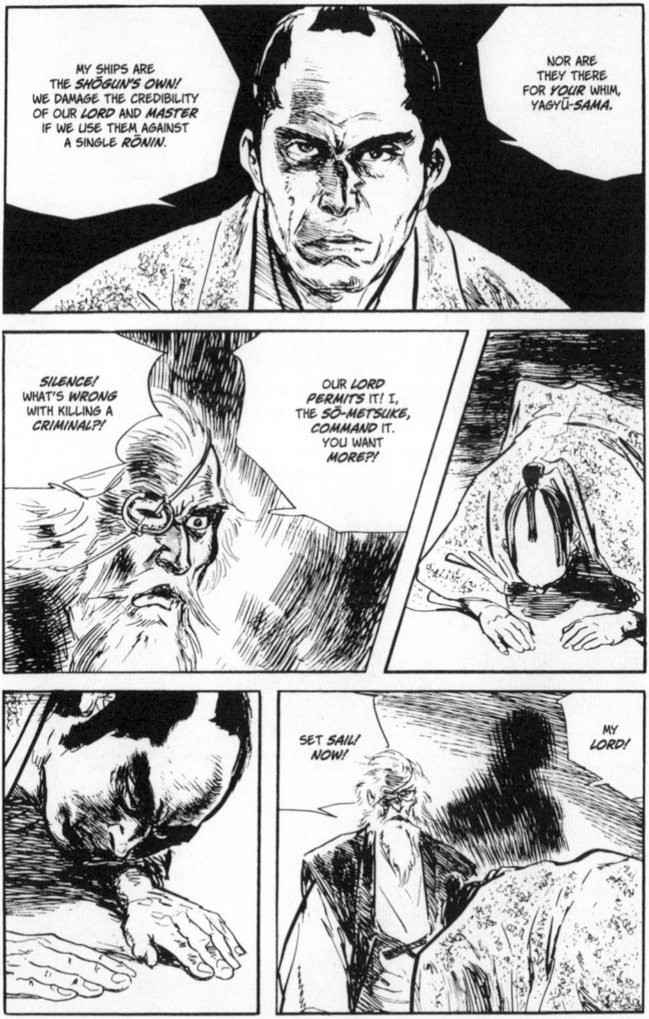
MY SHIPS ARE THE SHŌGUN'S OWN! WE DAMAGE THE CREDIBILITY OF OUR LORD AND MASTER IF WE USE THEM AGAINST A SINGLE RŌNIN.
NOR ARE THEY THERE FOR YOUR WHIM, YAGYŪ-SAMA.
SILENCE! WHAT'S WRONG WITH KILLING A CRIMINAL?!
OUR LORD PERMITS IT! I, THE SŌ-METSUKE, COMMAND IT. YOU WANT MORE?!
SET SAIL! NOW!
MY LORD!

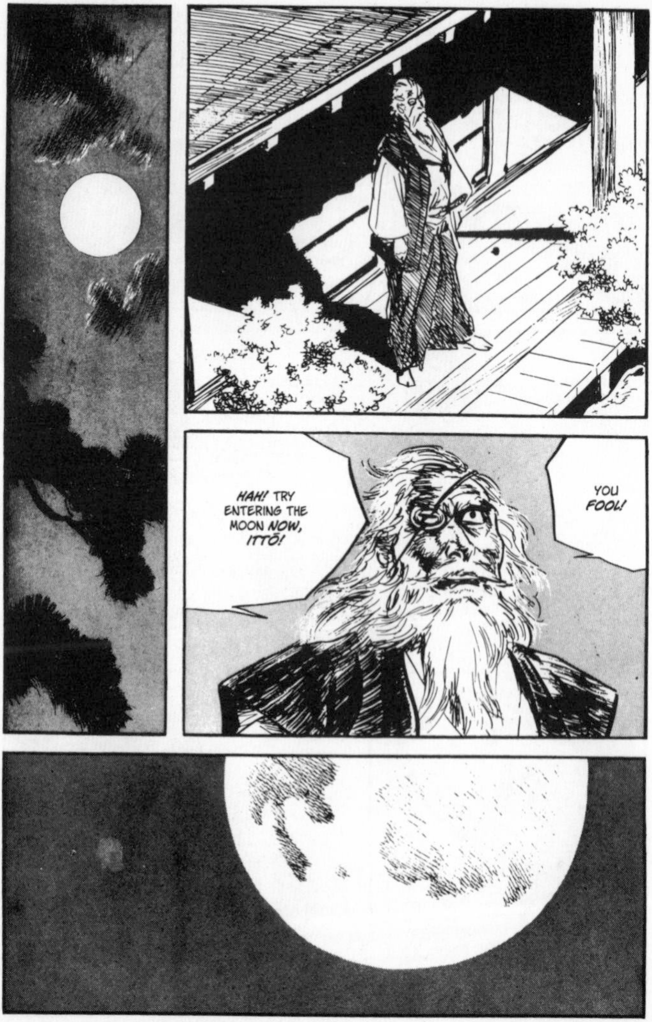
HAH! TRY ENTERING THE MOON NOW, ITTŌ!
YOU FOOL!

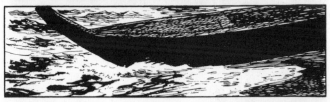

277

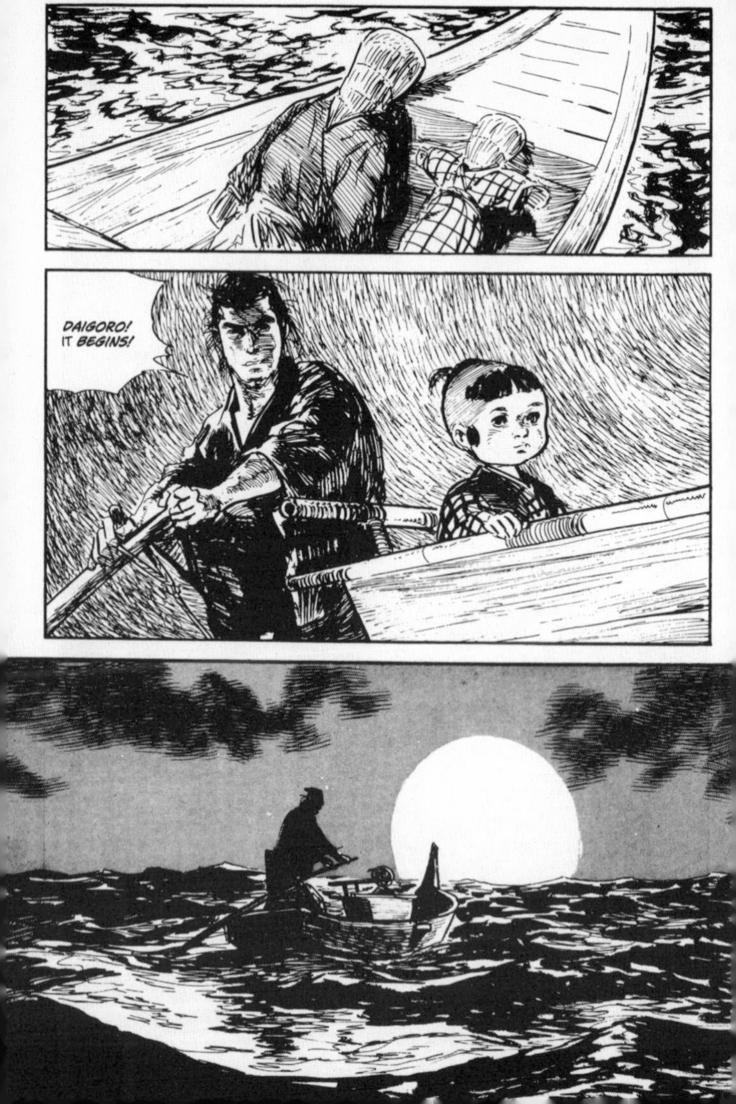
DAIGORO! IT BEGINS!

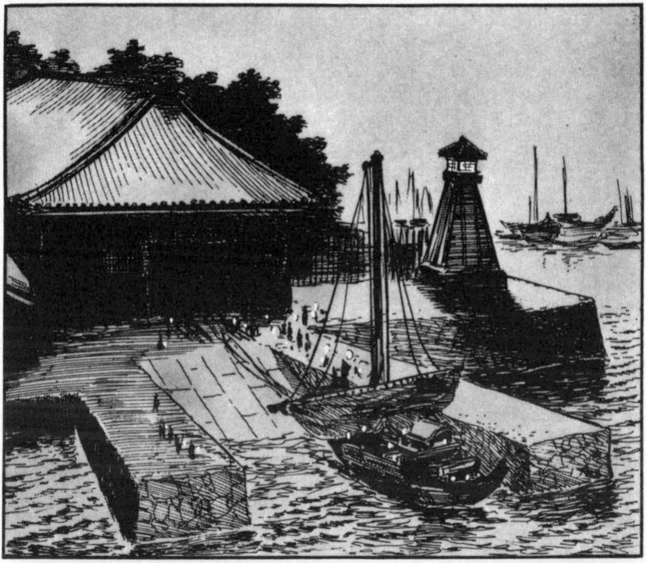

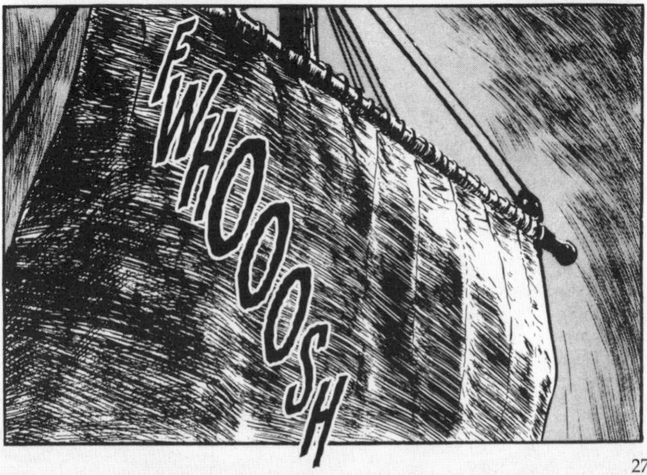
FWHOOOSH

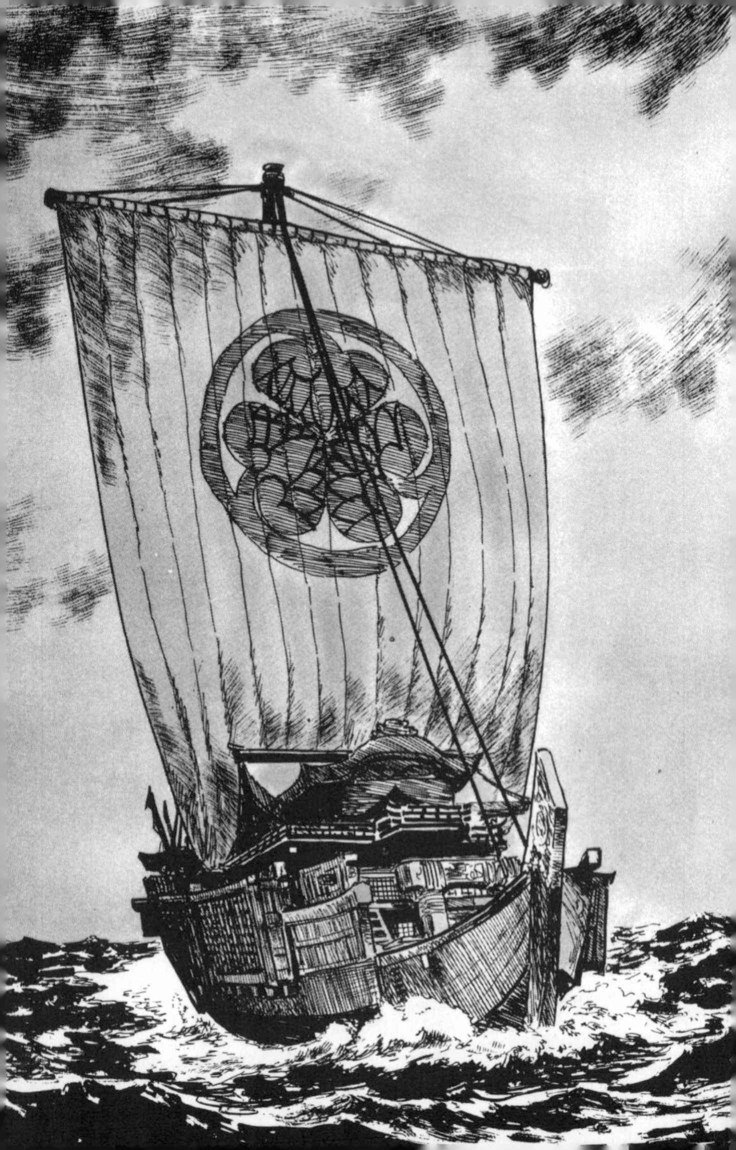

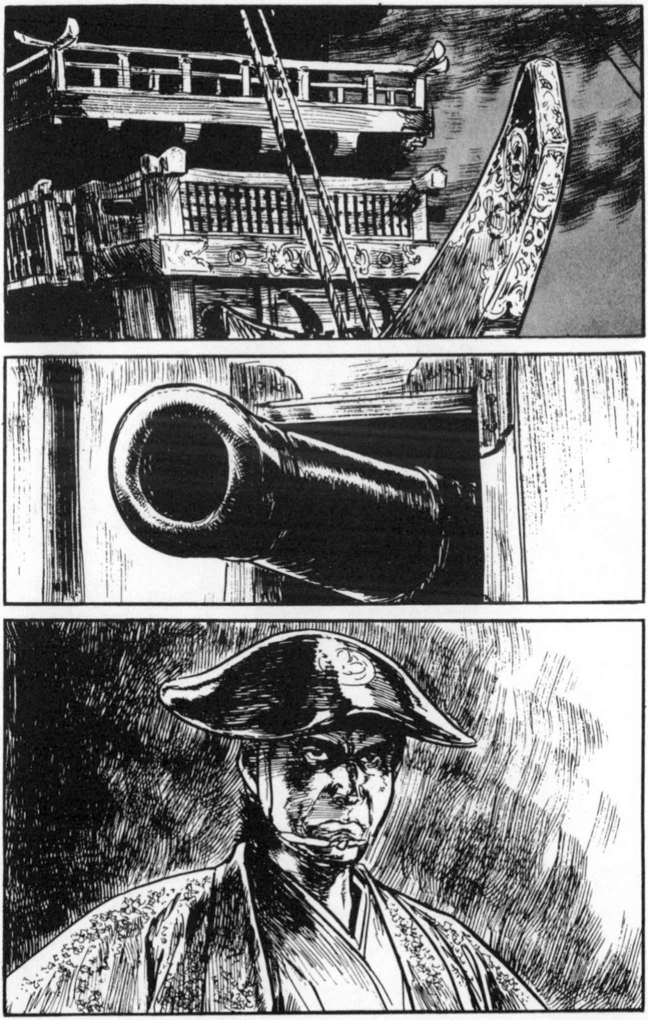

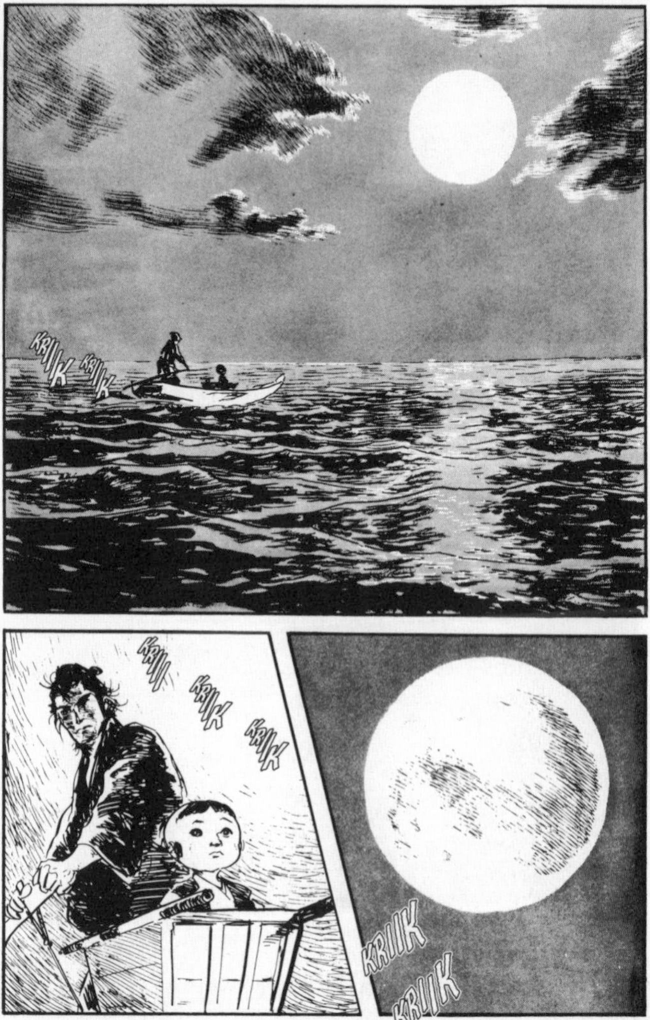
KRIIK
KRIIK
KRIII
KRIIK
KRIIK
KRIIK
KRIIK

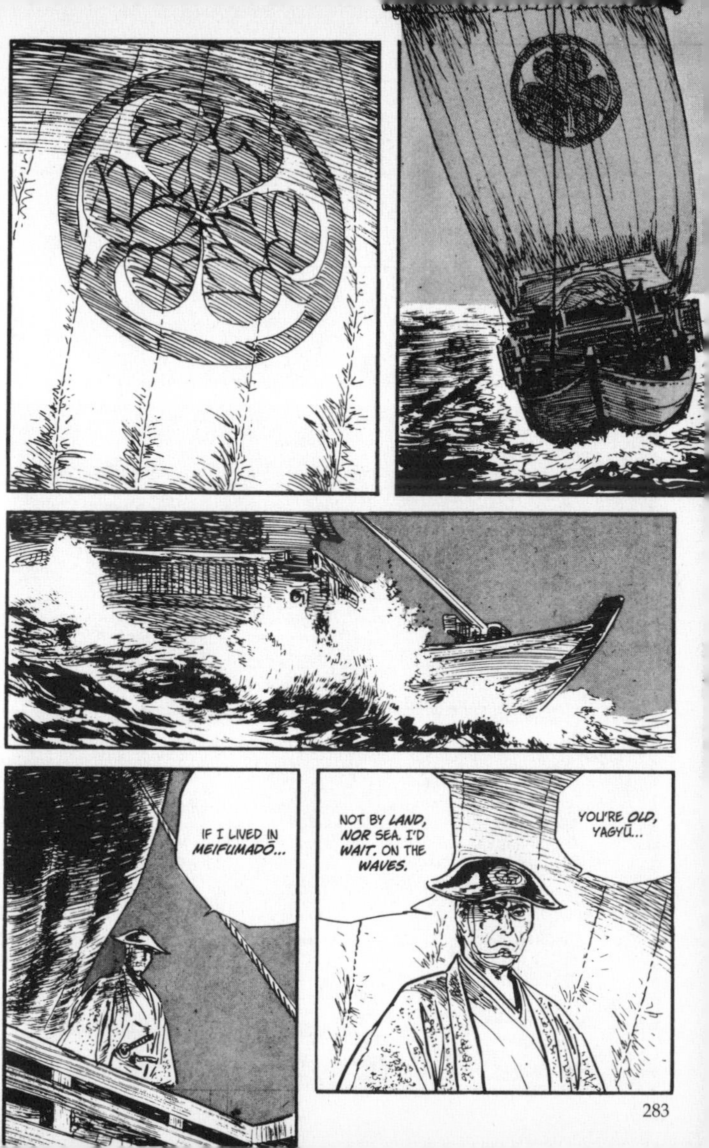
IF I LIVED IN
MEIFUMADŌ...
NOT BY LAND,
NOR SEA. I'D
WAIT. ON THE
WAVES.
YOU'RE OLD,
YAGYŪ...

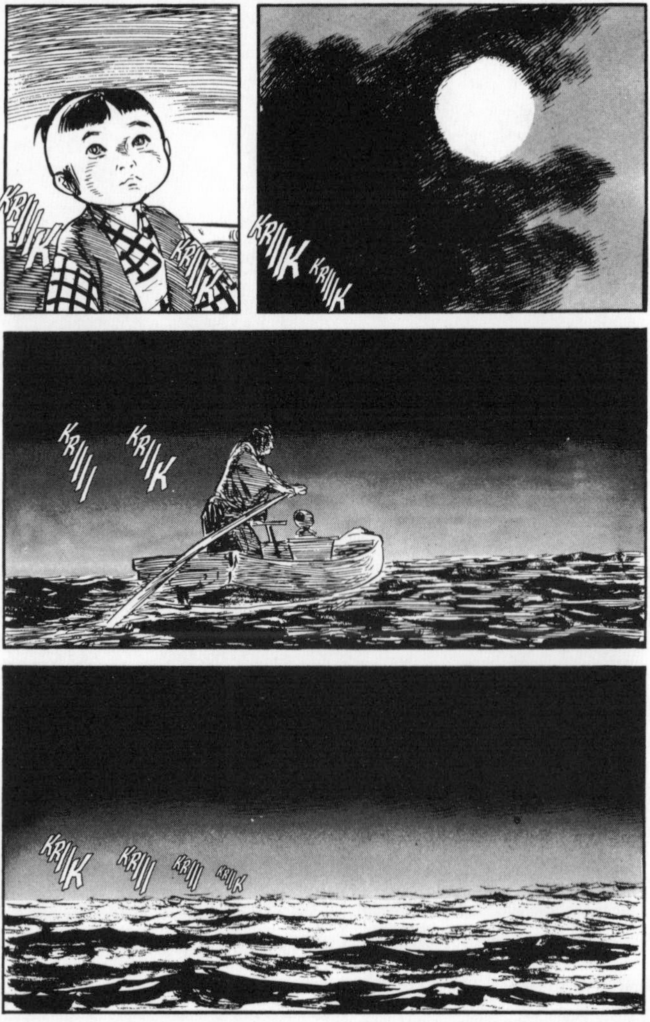
KRIIIK
KRIIIK
KRIIIK
KRIIIK
KRIIII
KRIIK
KRIIK
KRIII
KRIII
KRIIK

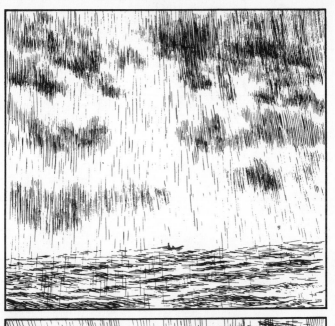

285

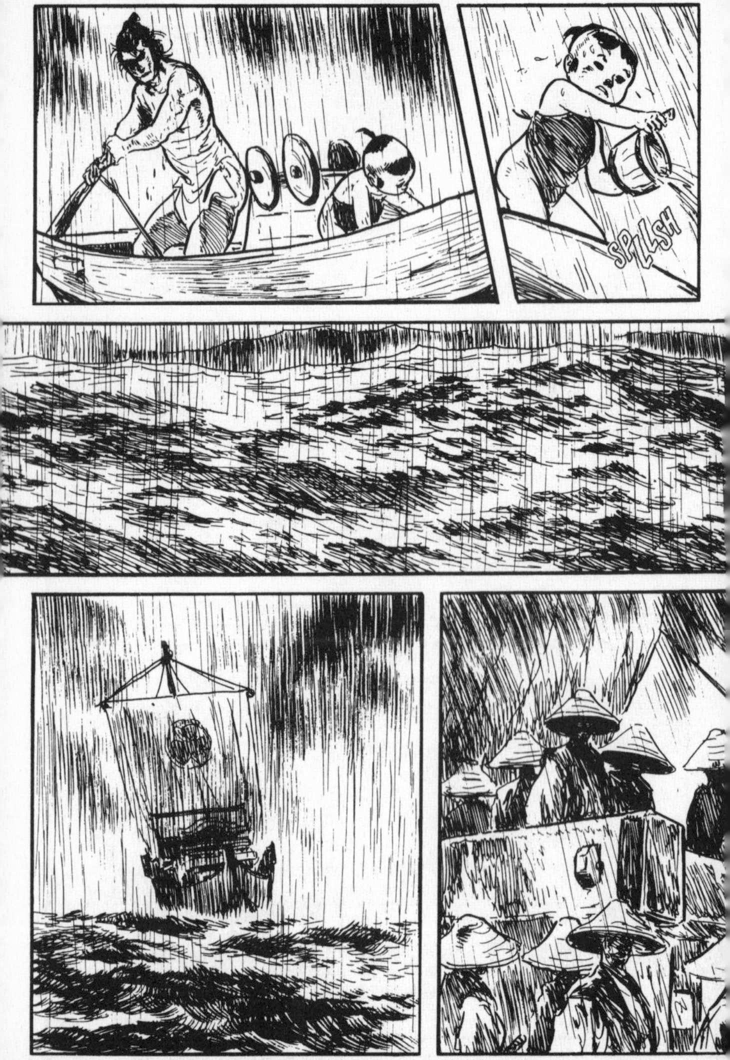
SPLLSH

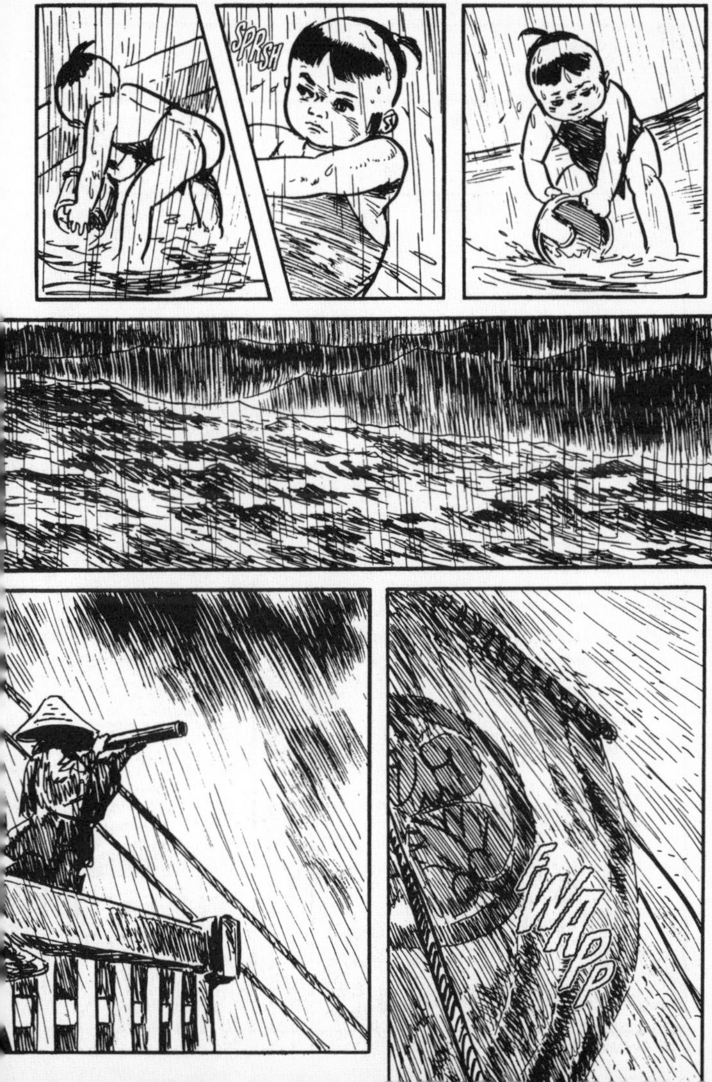

SPRSH
FWAPP

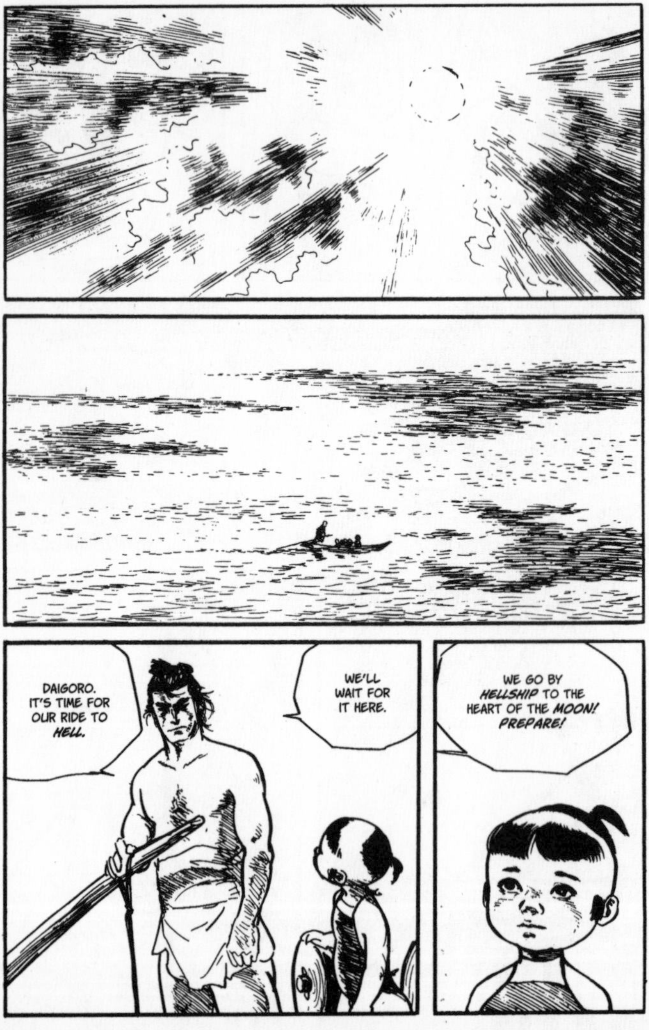
DAIGORO. IT'S TIME FOR OUR RIDE TO HELL.
WE'LL WAIT FOR IT HERE.
WE GO BY HELLSHIP TO THE HEART OF THE MOON! PREPARE!

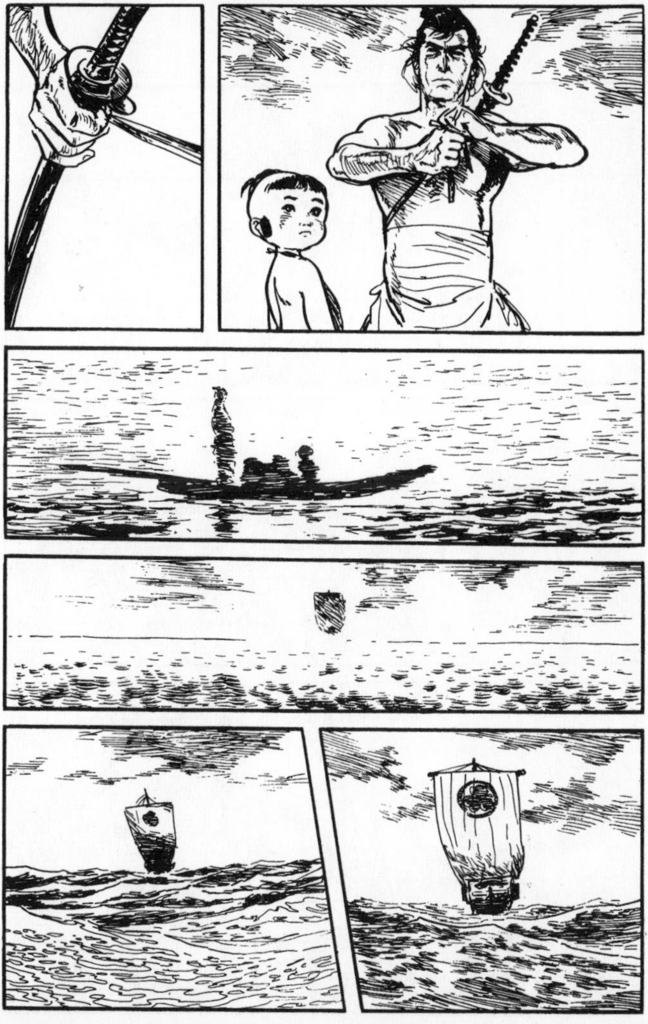

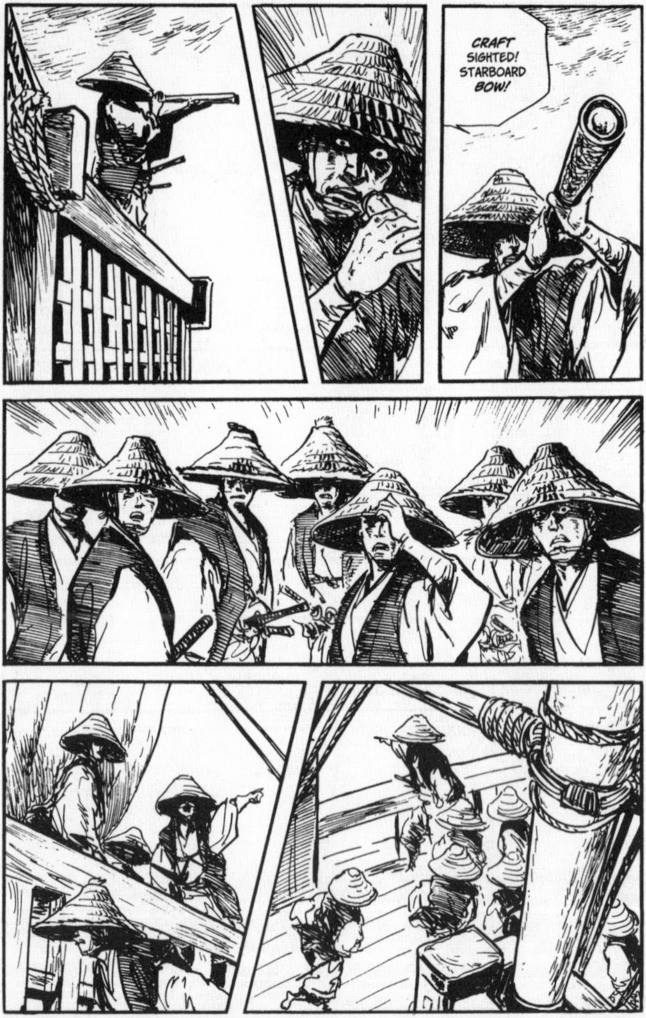
CRAFT SIGHTED! STARBOARD BOW!

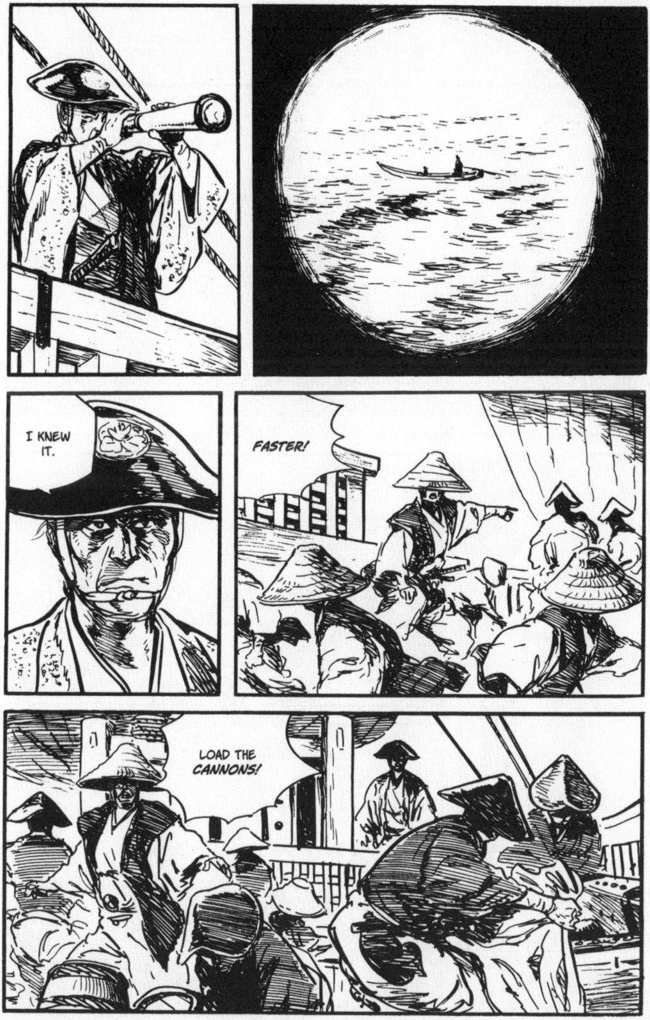
I KNEW IT.
FASTER!
LOAD THE CANNONS!

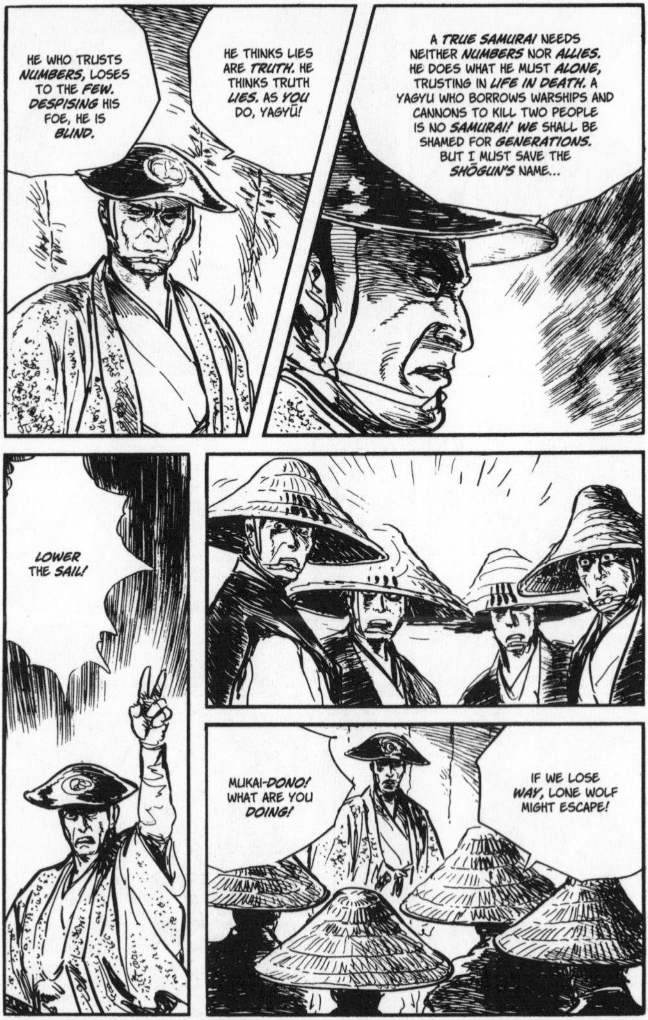
HE WHO TRUSTS NUMBERS, LOSES TO THE FEW. DESPISING HIS FOE, HE IS BLIND.
HE THINKS LIES ARE TRUTH. HE THINKS TRUTH LIES. AS YOU DO, YAGYŪ!
A TRUE SAMURAI NEEDS NEITHER NUMBERS NOR ALLIES. HE DOES WHAT HE MUST ALONE, TRUSTING IN LIFE IN DEATH. A YAGYU WHO BORROWS WARSHIPS AND CANNONS TO KILL TWO PEOPLE IS NO SAMURAI! WE SHALL BE SHAMED FOR GENERATIONS. BUT I MUST SAVE THE SHŌGUN'S NAME...
LOWER THE SAIL!
MUKAI-DONO! WHAT ARE YOU DOING!
IF WE LOSE WAY, LONE WOLF MIGHT ESCAPE!

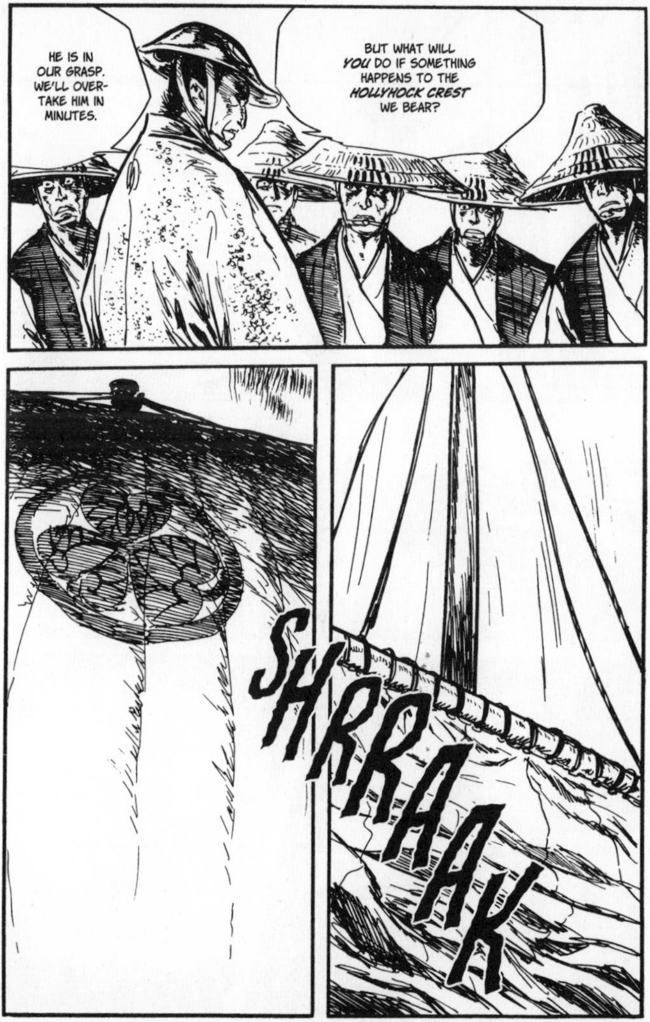
HE IS IN OUR GRASP. WE'LL OVER-TAKE HIM IN MINUTES.
BUT WHAT WILL *YOU* DO IF SOMETHING HAPPENS TO THE ***HOLLYHOCK CREST*** WE BEAR?
SHRRAAK

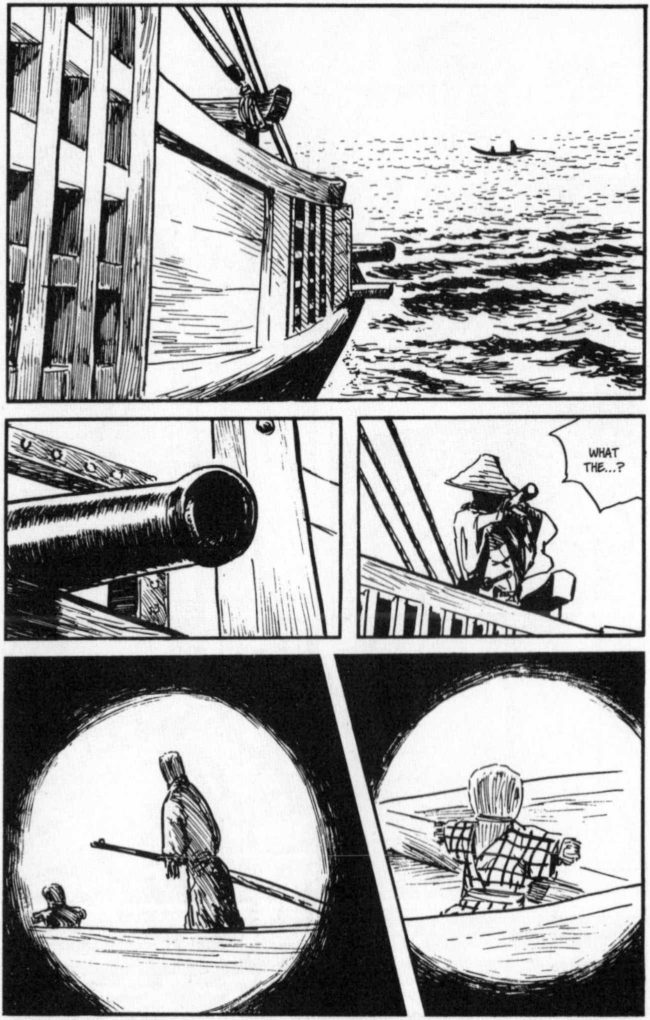
WHAT THE...?

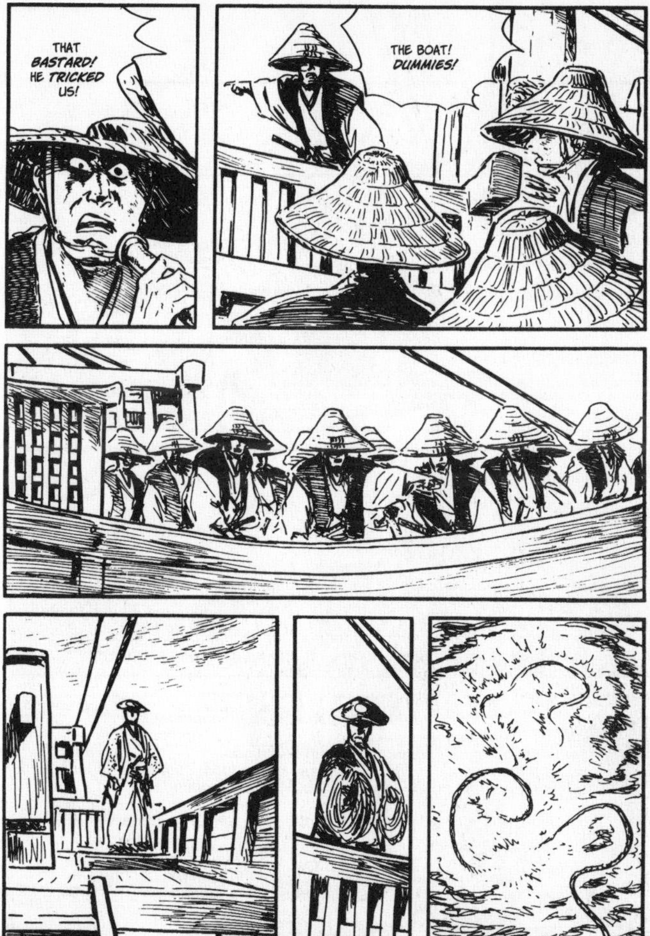
THAT *BASTARD!* HE *TRICKED* US!
THE BOAT! *DUMMIES!*

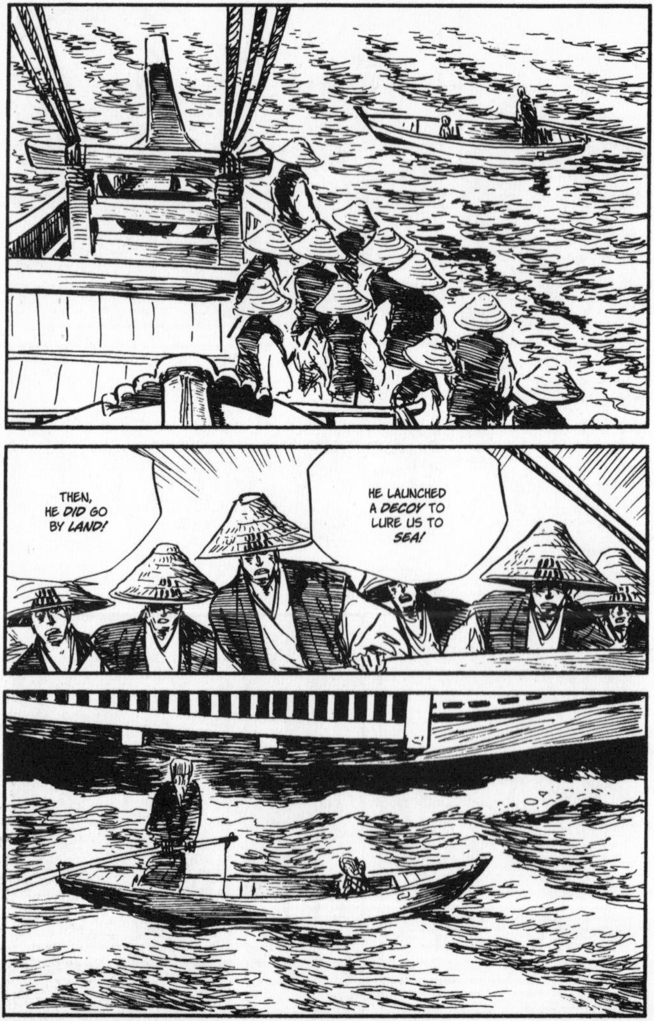
THEN, HE DID GO BY LAND!
HE LAUNCHED A DECOY TO LURE US TO SEA!

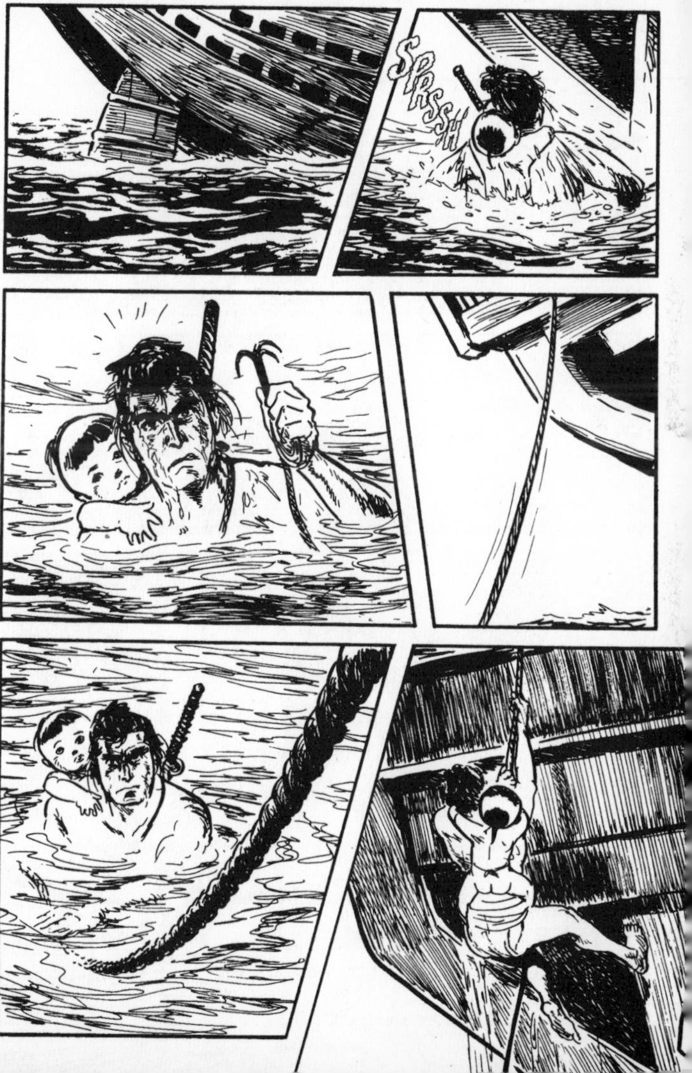
SPRSSSH

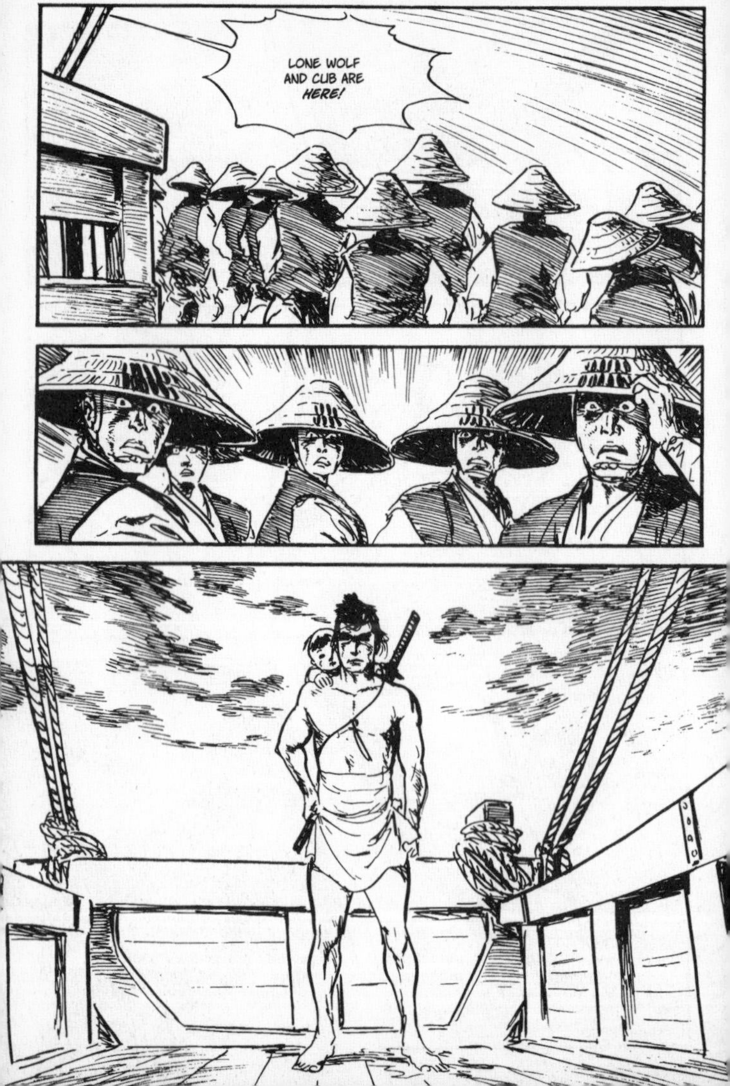
LONE WOLF AND CUB ARE *HERE!*

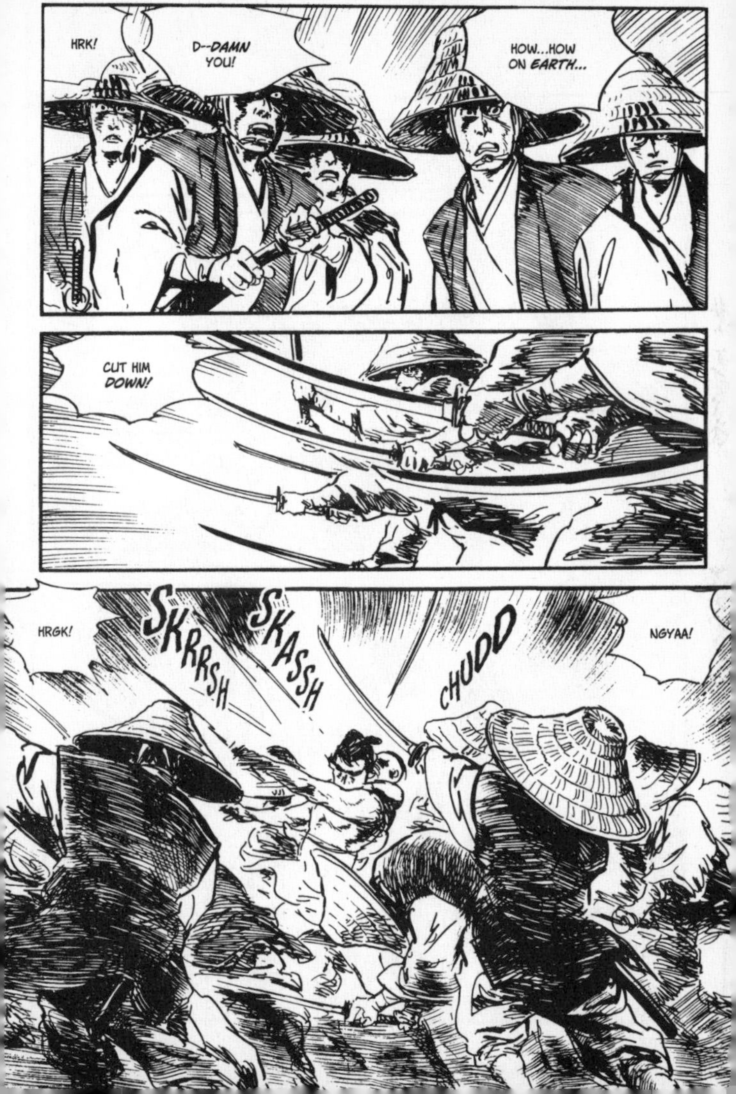
HRK!
D--*DAMN* YOU!
HOW...HOW ON *EARTH*...
CUT HIM *DOWN!*
HRGK!
SKRRSH
SKASSH
CHUDD
NGYAA!

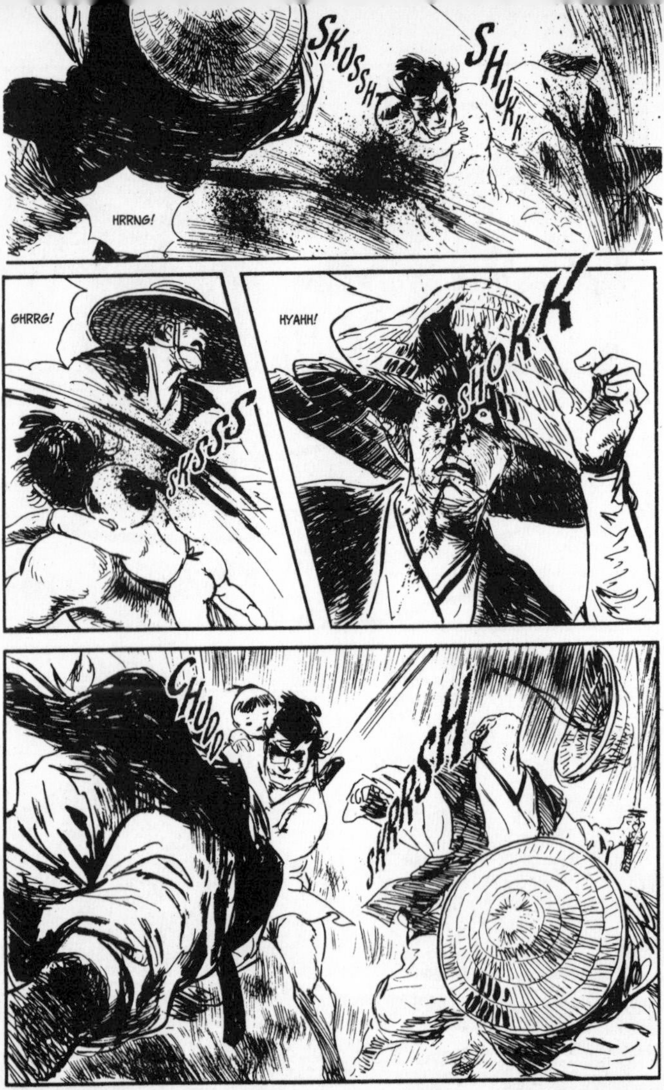
SKUSSH
SHUKK
HRRNG!
GHRRG!
SKSSS
HYAHH!
SHOKK
SHRRSH

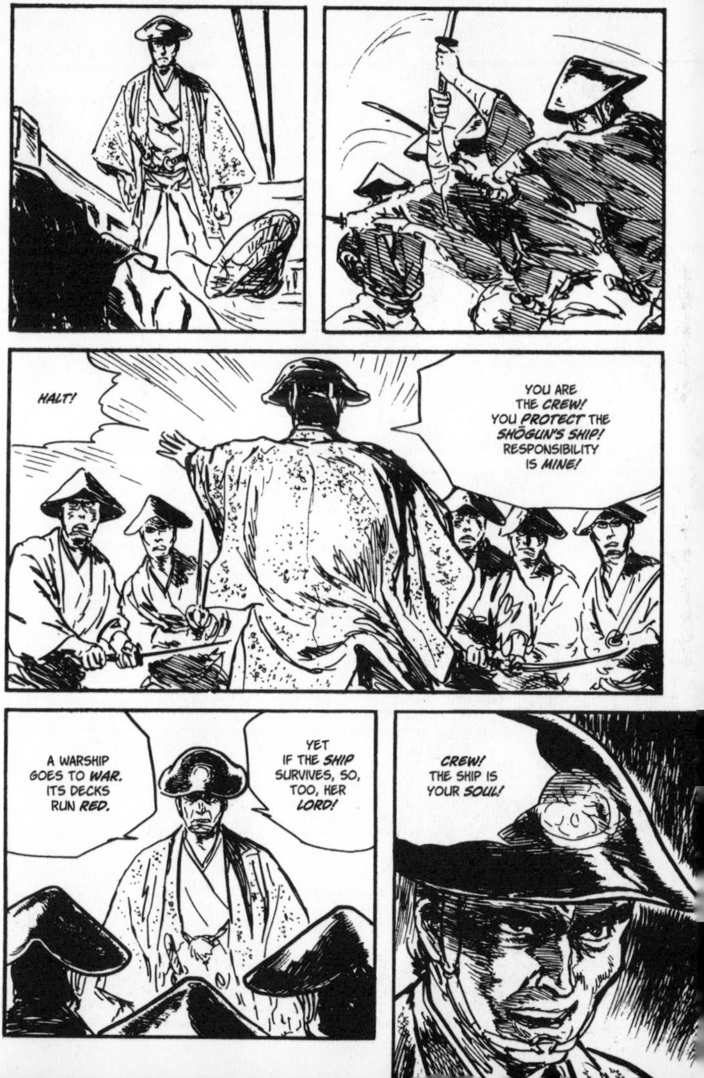
HALT!
YOU ARE THE CREW! YOU PROTECT THE SHŌGUN'S SHIP! RESPONSIBILITY IS MINE!
A WARSHIP GOES TO WAR. ITS DECKS RUN RED.
YET IF THE SHIP SURVIVES, SO, TOO, HER LORD!
CREW! THE SHIP IS YOUR SOUL!

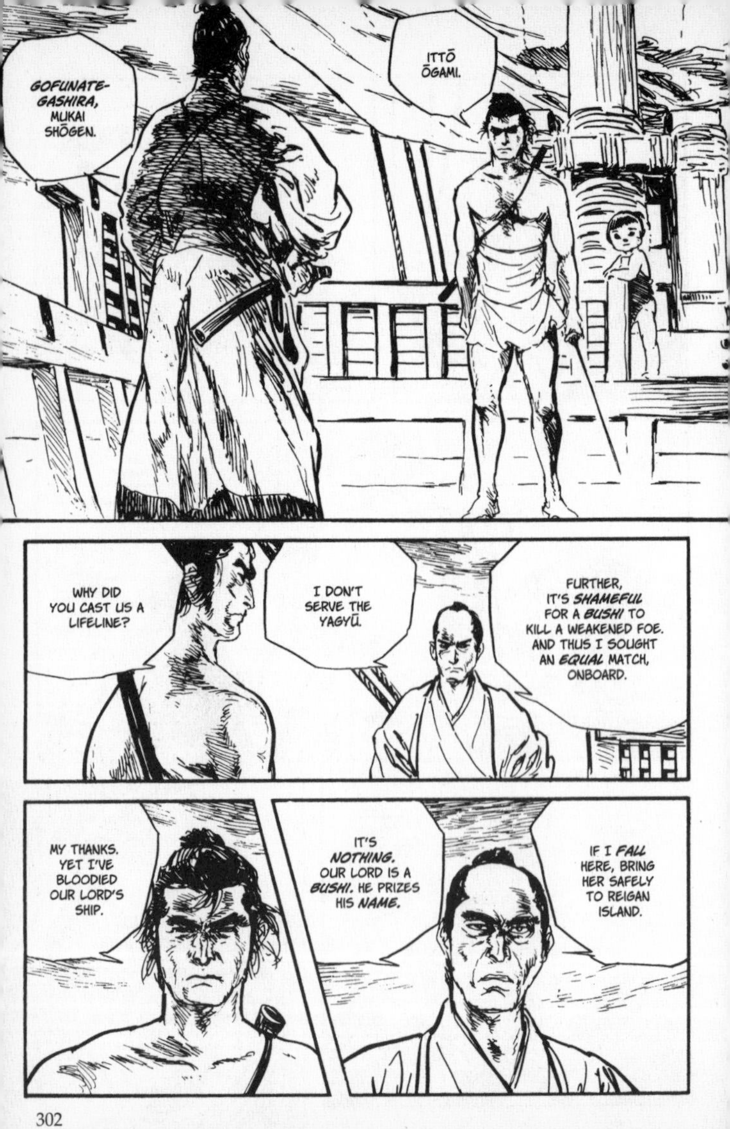
GOFUNATE-GASHIRA, MUKAI SHŌGEN.
ITTŌ ŌGAMI.
WHY DID YOU CAST US A LIFELINE?
I DON'T SERVE THE YAGYŪ.
FURTHER, IT'S *SHAMEFUL* FOR A *BUSHI* TO KILL A WEAKENED FOE. AND THUS I SOUGHT AN *EQUAL* MATCH, ONBOARD.
MY THANKS. YET I'VE BLOODIED OUR LORD'S SHIP.
IT'S *NOTHING.* OUR LORD IS A *BUSHI.* HE PRIZES HIS *NAME.*
IF I *FALL* HERE, BRING HER SAFELY TO REIGAN ISLAND.

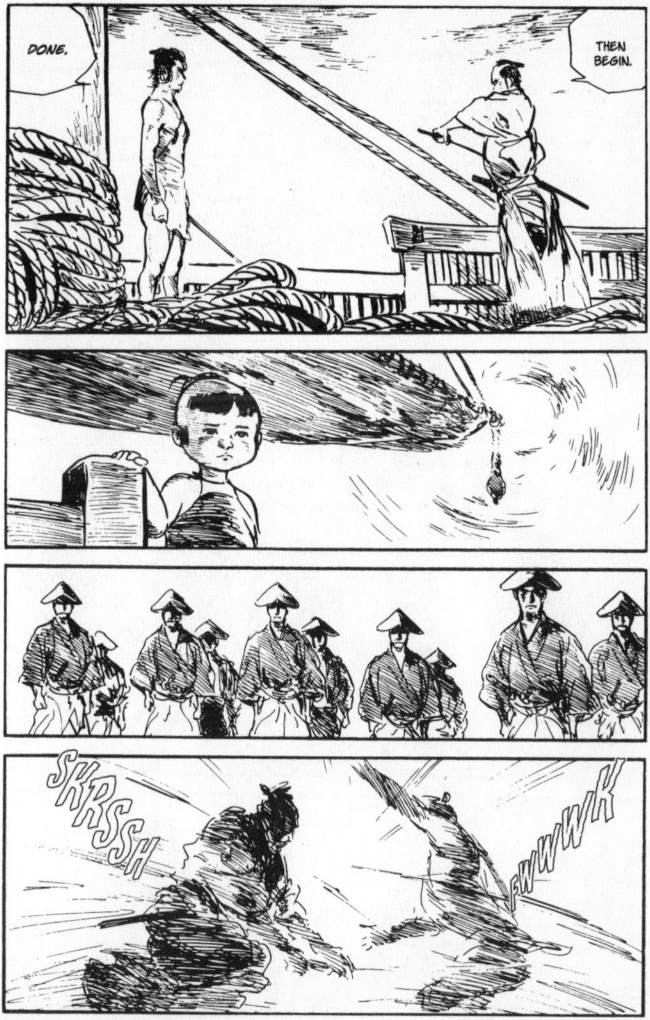

DONE.
THEN BEGIN.
SKRSSH
FWWWK

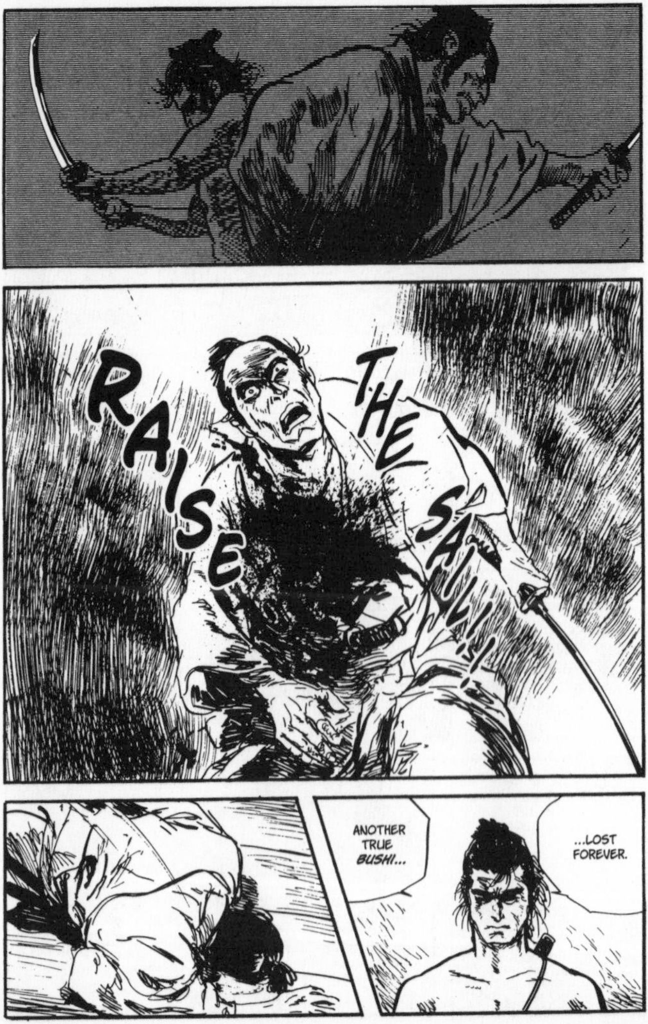
RAISE THE SAIL!!
ANOTHER TRUE BUSHI...
...LOST FOREVER.

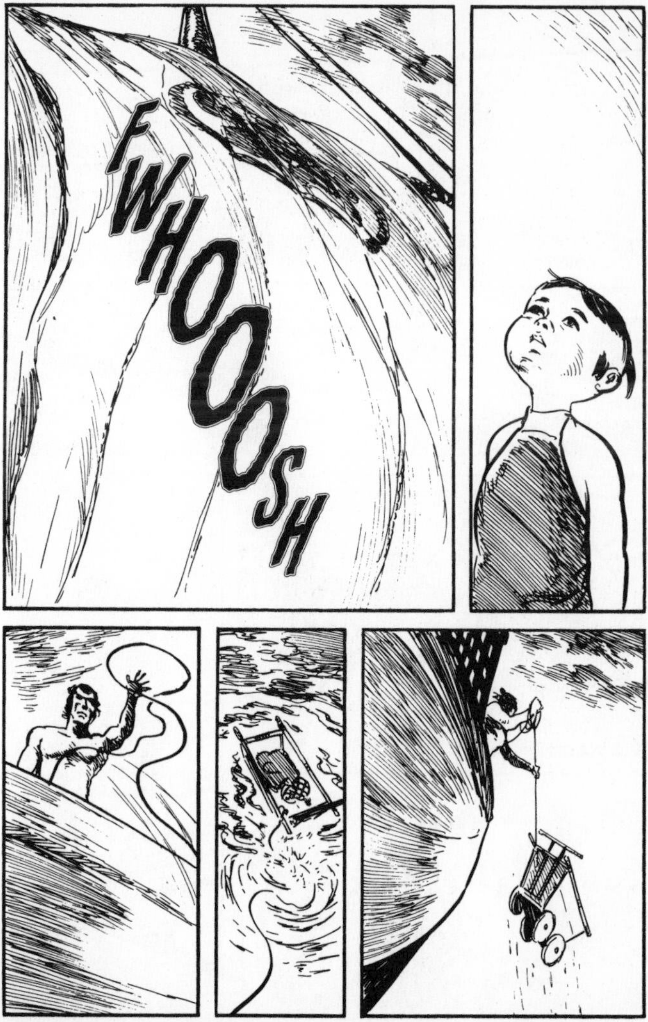
FWHOOOSH

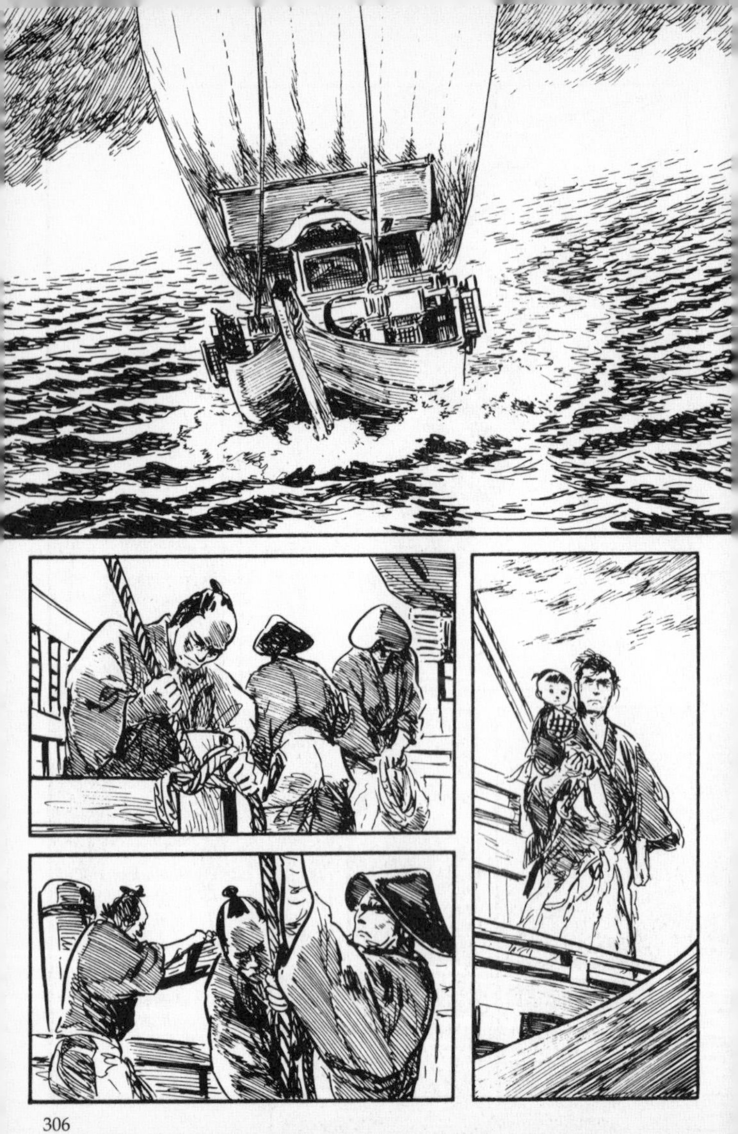

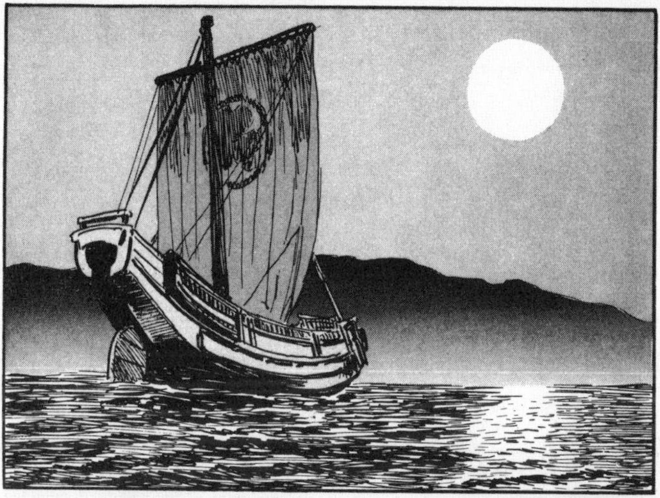
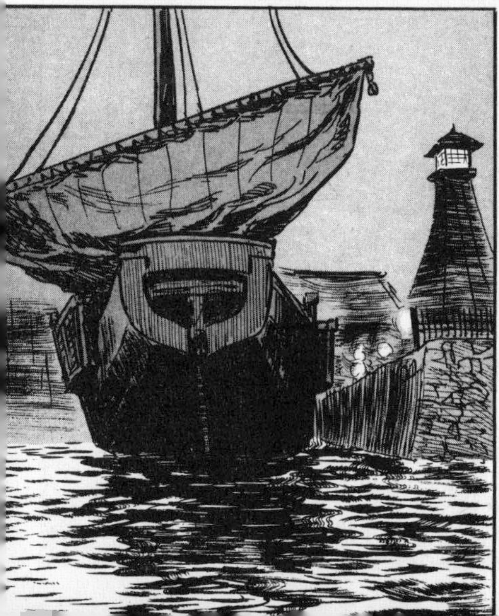
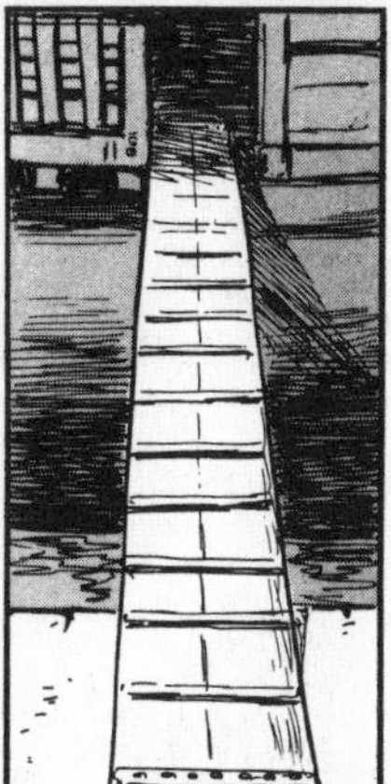

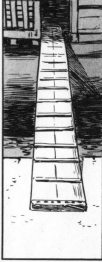

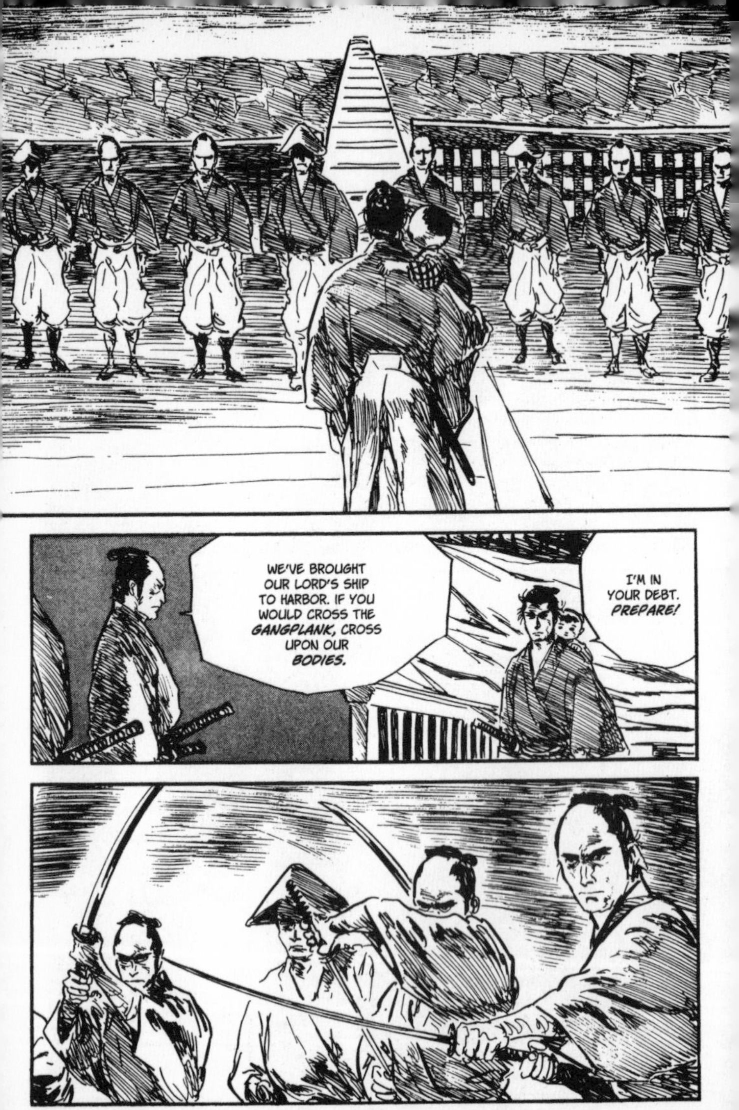
WE'VE BROUGHT OUR LORD'S SHIP TO HARBOR. IF YOU WOULD CROSS THE *GANGPLANK*, CROSS UPON OUR *BODIES*.
I'M IN YOUR DEBT. *PREPARE!*

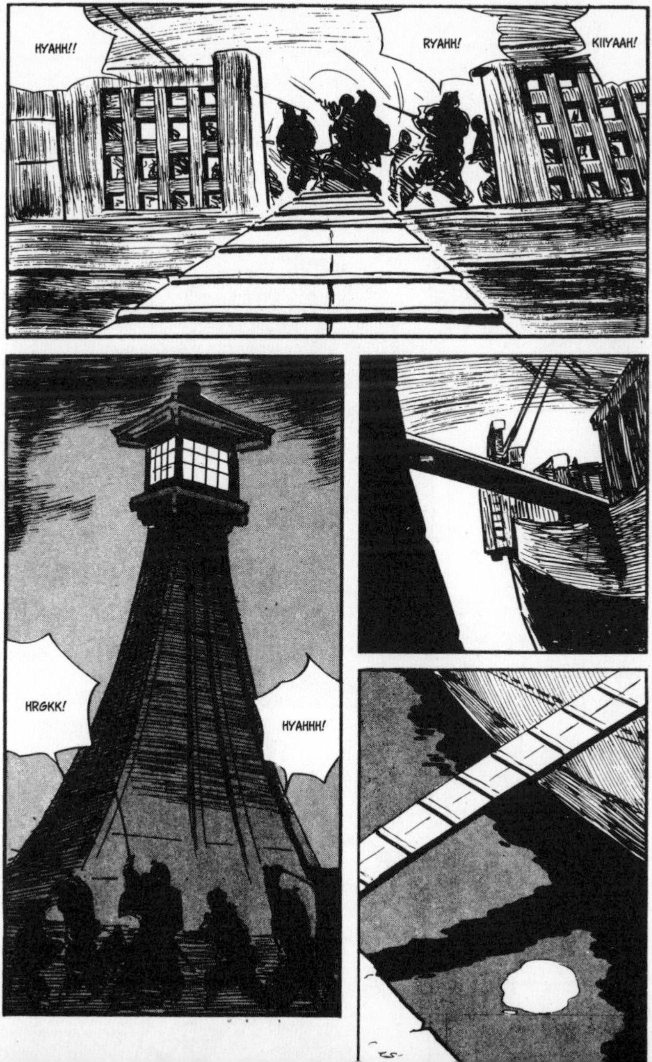
HYAHH!!
RYAHH!
KIIYAAH!
HRGKK!
HYAHHH!

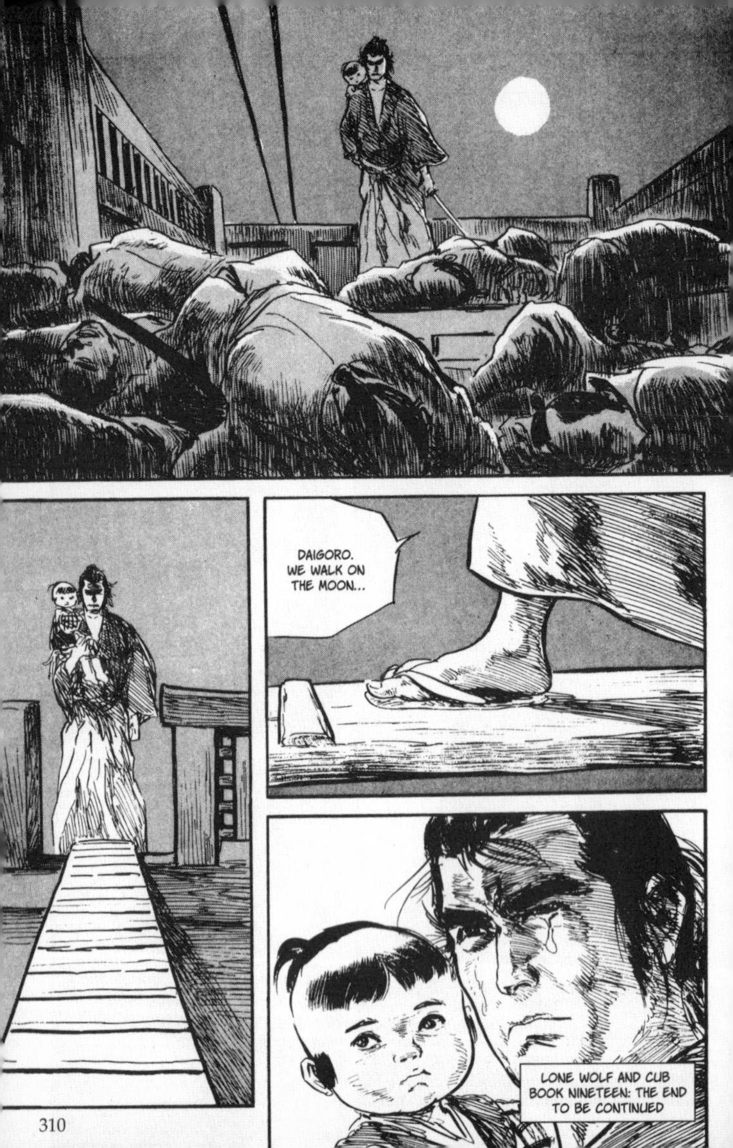
DAIGORO.
WE WALK ON
THE MOON...
LONE WOLF AND CUB
BOOK NINETEEN: THE END
TO BE CONTINUED

GLOSSARY

bodhi tree
In Japanese, *bodaiju*. The banyan (fig) tree where Buddha achieved enlightenment.

bushi
A samurai. A member of the warrior class.

bushidō
The way of the warrior. Also known as *shidō*.

Daigorō
Ittō has given Daigorō a name that, while using different Chinese characters than *daigo*, shares the same pronunciation. *Ro* is a common addition at the end of a male name.

daikan
An official who collected taxes owed to Edo and oversaw public works, agriculture, and other projects administered by the central government.

daikansho
The office of the *daikan*.

daimyō
A feudal lord.

Edo
The capital of medieval Japan and the seat of the shōgunate. The site of modern-day Tokyo.

enlightenment
In Japanese, *daigo*, one of many terms for enlightenment. There are also many versions of Shakyamuni's long night before his moment of *daigo*. In most,

Shakyamuni achieves enlightenment at the sight of the morning star.

han
A feudal domain.

honorifics
Japan is a class and status society, and proper forms of address are critical. Common markers of respect are the prefixes *o* and *go*, and a wide range of suffixes. Some of the suffixes you will encounter in *Lone Wolf and Cub*:
chan – for children, young women, and close friends
dono – archaic; used for higher-ranked or highly respected figures
san – the most common, used among equals or near-equals
sama – used for superiors
sensei – used for teachers, masters, respected entertainers, and politicians

koku
A bale of rice. The traditional measure of a *han*'s wealth, a measure of its agricultural land and productivity.

Kōmei
Famed Chinese general and tactician who lived during the warring states period. Born 181 A.D., died 234 A.D.

Mara
In Sanskrit, death, or hindrance to enlightenment. Also, the deva (god) Mara, Lord of the Sixth Heaven in the World of Desire in which humankind live, known in some forms as

The Slayer or the god of death. In Japanese, *Rokuyokuten*, abbreviated here to *Rokuten*.

meifumadō
The Buddhist Hell. The way of demons and damnation.

metsuke
Inspector. A post combining the functions of chief of police and chief intelligence officer.

mon
A copper coin.

ofunate-gashira
Commander of the shogun's warships. The admiral of Japan's fledgling navy.

oyabun
The boss of a *yakuza* gang. Literally, "father status." His underlings were known as *kobun*, or children.

rōnin
A masterless samurai. Literally, "one adrift on the waves." Members of the samurai caste who have lost their masters through the dissolution of *han*, expulsion for misbehavior, or other reasons. Prohibited from working as farmers or merchants under the strict Confucian caste system imposed by the Tokugawa shōgunate, many impoverished *rōnin* became "hired guns" for whom the code of the samurai was nothing but empty words.

ryō
A gold piece, worth 60 *monme*.

ryū
Often translated as "school." The many variations of

swordsmanship and other martial arts were passed down from generation to generation to the offspring of the originator of the technique or set of techniques, and to any *deishi* students that sought to learn from the master. The largest schools had their own *dōjō* training centers and scores of students. An effective swordsman had to study the different techniques of the various schools to know how to block them in combat. Many *ryū* also had a set of special, secret techniques that were only taught to school initiates.

sekisho
Checkpoint regulating travel from Edo to other parts of the country. All travelers had to submit papers at official checkpoints along the main highways in and out of Edo.

Shaka
Common abbreviation of Shakamuni, Japanese for the Buddha, from the Sanskrit "Shakyamuni." Siddhartha Gautama, the founder of Buddhism.

shōya
The senior peasant leader, entrusted with local administration by the local *daikan*.

yakuza
Japan's criminal syndicates. In the Edo period, *yakuza* were a common part of the landscape, running houses of gambling and prostitution. As long as they did not overstep their bounds, they were tolerated by the authorities, a tradition little changed in modern Japan.

KAZUO KOIKE

Though widely respected as a powerful writer of graphic fiction, Kazuo Koike has spent a lifetime reaching beyond the bounds of the comics medium. Aside from co-creating and writing the successful *Lone Wolf and Cub* and *Crying Freeman* manga, Koike has hosted television programs; founded a golf magazine; produced movies; written popular fiction, poetry, and screenplays; and mentored some of Japan's best manga talent.

Lone Wolf and Cub was first serialized in Japan in 1970 (under the title *Kozure Okami*) in *Manga Action* magazine and continued its hugely popular run for many years, being collected as the stories were published, and reprinted worldwide. Koike collected numerous awards for his work on the series throughout the next decade. Starting in 1972, Koike adapted the popular manga into a series of six films, the *Baby Cart Assassin* saga, garnering widespread commercial success and critical acclaim for his screenwriting.

This wasn't Koike's only foray into film and video. In 1996, *Crying Freeman*, the manga Koike created with artist Ryoichi Ikegami, was produced in Hollywood and released to commercial success in Europe and is currently awaiting release in America.

And to give something back to the medium that gave him so much, Koike started the *Gekiga Sonjuku*, a college course aimed at helping talented writers and artists — such as *Ranma 1/2* creator Rumiko Takahashi — break into the comics field.

The driving focus of Koike's narrative is character development, and his commitment to character is clear: "Comics are carried by characters. If a character is well created, the comic becomes a hit." Kazuo Koike's continued success in comics and literature has proven this philosophy true.

GOSEKI KOJIMA

Goseki Kojima was born on November 3, 1928, the very same day as the godfather of Japanese comics, Osamu Tezuka. While just out of junior high school, the self-taught Kojima began painting advertising posters for movie theaters to pay his bills.

In 1950, Kojima moved to Tokyo, where the postwar devastation had given rise to special manga forms for audiences too poor to buy the new manga magazines. Kojima created art for *kami-shibai*, or "paper-play" narrators, who would use manga story sheets to present narrated street plays. Kojima moved on to creating works for the *kashi-bon* market, bookstores that rented out books, magazines, and manga to mostly low-income readers. He soon became highly popular among *kashi-bon* readers.

In 1967, Kojima broke into the magazine market with his series *Dojinki*. As the manga magazine market grew and diversified, he turned out a steady stream of popular series.

In 1970, in collaboration with Kazuo Koike, Kojima began the work that would seal his reputation, *Kozure*

Okami (*Lone Wolf and Cub*). Before long the story had become a gigantic hit, eventually spinning off a television series, six motion pictures, and even theme song records. Koike and Kojima were soon dubbed the "golden duo" and produced success after success on their way to the pinnacle of the manga world.

When *Manga Japan* magazine was launched in 1994, Kojima was asked to serve as consultant, and he helped train the next generation of manga artists.

In his final years, Kojima turned to creating original graphic novels based on the movies of his favorite director, Akira Kurosawa. Kojima passed away on January 5, 2000 at the age of 71.

LONE WOLF AND CUB

VOLUME 1:
THE ASSASSIN'S ROAD
1-56971-502-5
$9.95 U.S., $14.95 Canada

VOLUME 2: THE GATELESS
BARRIER
1-56971-503-3
$9.95 U.S., $14.95 Canada

VOLUME 3: THE FLUTE OF
THE FALLEN TIGER
1-56971-504-1
$9.95 U.S., $14.95 Canada

**VOLUME 4:
THE BELL WARDEN**
1-56971-505-X
$9.95 U.S., $14.95 Canada

**VOLUME 5:
BLACK WIND**
1-56971-506-8
$9.95 U.S., $14.95 Canada

**VOLUME 6: LANTERNS FOR
THE DEAD**
1-56971-507-6
$9.95 U.S., $14.95 Canada

**VOLUME 7: CLOUD
DRAGON, WIND TIGER**
1-56971-508-4
$9.95 U.S., $14.95 Canada

**VOLUME 8: CHAINS
OF DEATH**
1-56971-509-2
$9.95 U.S., $14.95 Canada

**VOLUME 9: ECHO OF
THE ASSASSIN**
1-56971-510-6
$9.95 U.S., $14.95 Canada

**VOLUME 10:
HOSTAGE CHILD**
1-56971-511-4
$9.95 U.S., $14.95 Canada

**VOLUME 11:
TALISMAN OF HADES**
1-56971-512-2
$9.95 U.S., $14.95 Canada

VOLUME 12:
SHATTERED STONES
1-56971-513-0
$9.95 U.S., $14.95 Canada

VOLUME 13: THE MOON IN THE
EAST, THE SUN IN THE WEST
1-56971-585-8
$9.95 U.S., $14.95 Canada

VOLUME 14: DAY OF
THE DEMONS
1-56971-586-6
$9.95 U.S., $14.95 Canada

VOLUME 15: BROTHERS
OF THE GRASS
1-56971-587-4
$9.95 U.S., $14.95 Canada

**VOLUME 16:
GATEWAY INTO WINTER**
1-56971-588-2
$9.95 U.S., $14.95 Canada

**VOLUME 17:
THE WILL OF THE FANG**
1-56971-589-0
$9.95 U.S., $14.95 Canada

**VOLUME 18: TWILIGHT
OF THE KUROKUWA**
1-56971-590-4
$9.95 U.S., $14.95 Canada

**VOLUME 19: THE MOON
IN OUR HEARTS**
1-56971-591-2
$9.95 U.S., $14.95 Canada

MANGA! MANGA! MANGA! DARK HORSE HAS THE BEST IN MANGA COLLECTIONS!

Available from your local comics shop or bookstore!